Computer Representation and Manipulation of Chemical Information

Computer Representation and Manipulation of Chemical Information

EDITED BY

W. TODD WIPKE

Department of Chemistry
Princeton University
Princeton, New Jersey

STEPHEN R. HELLER

Division of Computer Research & Technology
National Institutes of Health
Bethesda, Maryland

RICHARD J. FELDMANN

Division of Computer Research & Technology
National Institutes of Health
Bethesda, Maryland

ERNEST HYDE

ICI Pharmaceutical Division
Cheshire, England

A WILEY-INTERSCIENCE PUBLICATION

JOHN WILEY & SONS, New York · London · Sydney · **Toronto**

Copyright © 1974, by John Wiley & Sons, Inc.

All rights reserved. Published simultaneously in Canada.

No part of this book may be reproduced by any means, nor transmitted, nor translated into a machine language without the written permission of the publisher.

Library of Congress Cataloging in Publication Data:

NATO Advanced Study Institute, Noordwijkerhout, Netherlands, 1973.
   Computer representation and manipulation of chemical information.

   "A Wiley-Interscience publication."
   Invited lectures presented at the NATO Advanced Study Institute held at Noordwijkerhout, Netherlands, June 4–15, 1973 sponsored by NATO Scientific Affairs Division and the Chemical Notation Association.

   1. Information storage and retrieval systems-Chemistry-Congresses. 2. Electronic data processing-Chemistry-Congresses. I. Wipke, W. Todd, ed. II. North Atlantic Treaty Organization. Division of Scientific Affairs. III. Chemical Notation Association. IV. Title.
[DNLM: 1. Chemistry-Congresses. 2. Computers-Congresses.   QD8.3 N864c 1973]

Z699.5.C5N15 1973   029′ .9′54   73-20036
ISBN 0-471-95595-7

Printed in the United States of America

10 9 8 7 6 5 4 3 2 1

Preface

This book deals with the fundamental issues of how chemical structural information can be represented and how this choice of representation affects the types of manipulations that can be performed. By presenting the computer approaches taken in diverse chemical information problem areas, it illustrates how the selection of problem representation is made and the ways in which proper representation results in a simplification of the problem solving process.

First, the fundamental features of information storage/retrieval systems are described in the context of some of the most advanced implemented systems. Remaining problems in representing chemical structures and reactions are described as well as the advances in the state of the art. On-line interactive systems for substructure searching and retrieval are representative of future systems but well-designed manual systems still hold an important place with today's practicing chemist.

Next, computer applications to organic synthesis are explored. Two very different systems for designing synthesis are described in detail for the first time. These chapters provide a basis for understanding the tremendous potential of this area of research.

The discussion then turns to analysis of mass spectra using an interactive system versus the DENDRAL artificial intelligence approach versus the pattern recognition approach. The French DARC system and its unique topological representation is described as well as computerized molecular modeling, an activity of increasing importance. Throughout these discussions, the dominant theme is representation and manipulation of information.

This book can be used in college courses dealing with applications of computers in chemistry and information handling. It should also serve the research chemist as an introduction into this developing area of chemistry. A comprehensive index is provided for quick reference regarding definitions of terms and concepts.

This book also represents the proceedings of the NATO Advanced Study Institute by the same name held June 4–15, 1973, at the Leeuwenhorst

Congress Center, Noordwijkerhout, The Netherlands. The organizing committee consisted of W. T. Wipke (Director), E. Hyde (Director), R. J. Feldmann, and S. R. Heller. Besides the invited lectures, which appear in this book, there were contributed papers which have not been included because of space limitations, and there were on-line demonstrations of many programs, some using computers in the United States over the trans-Atlantic cable. These demonstrations are described in the appendix.

We thank the sponsors, the Scientific Affairs Division of NATO, and the Chemical Notation Association. We also thank

Comgraph International B.V.
Digital Equipment Co., Maynard, Mass. and Rijswijk
General Electric International
Honeywell Bull (Nederland) B.V.
IBM Nederland N.V.
International Computers Ltd.
ITT Nederlandse Standard Electric Mij N.V.
K.L.M. Royal Dutch Airlines
National Science Foundation

Netherlands Organisation for Chemical Information
Netherlands Tourist Office (New York-The Hague)
Philips Nederland B.V.
Dr. M. A. T. Rogers
RCA Communications
Tektronix Datatek N.V.
Texas Instruments
Western Union International
Zeta Research Inc.
Charles Gailis, NIH (front cover)

Special thanks go to Charles Citroen of NOCI, who was the superbly patient and efficient Local Arrangements Chairman, and finally we thank the twelve speakers and seventy participants who made this Advanced Study Institute a success.

W. T. WIPKE
S. R. HELLER
R. J. FELDMANN
E. HYDE

November 1973

Contents

1. Evaluation of On-Line Techniques in a Sub-Structure Search System

   D. R. Eakin and E. Hyde ... 1

2. The Microstructure of Chemical Data-Bases and the Choice of Representation for Retrieval ... 31

   Michael F. Lynch

3. Interactive Graphic Chemical Structure Searching ... 55

   Richard J. Feldmann

4. Reaction Documentation ... 83

   J. Valls

5. Topological Search for Classes of Compounds in Large Files at Reasonable Machine Cost ... 105

   Computer Generated Peekaboo Cards for Medium Sized Files (40,000 Items) ... 123

   Ernst Meyer

6. CICLOPS—A Computer Program For the Design of Syntheses on the Basis of a Mathematical Model ... 129

   Janet Blair, Johann Gasteiger, Carol Gillespie, P. D. Gillespie, and Ivar Ugi

7. Computer-Assisted Three-Dimensional Synthetic Analysis   147

   W. Todd Wipke

8. Computer Techniques for Interpreting Mass Spectrometry Data   175

   Stephen R. Heller

9. Computer Modeling of Chemical Structures: Applications in Crystallography, Conformational Analysis, and Drug Design   203

   Garland R. Marshall, Heinz E. Bosshard, and Robert A. Ellis

10. DARC System in Chemistry   239

    Jacques-Emile Dubois

11. Chemical Data Interpretation Using Pattern Recognition Techniques   265

    Peter C. Jurs

12. Heuristic Dendral; Analysis of Molecular Structure   287
    Dennis H. Smith, Larry N. Masinter, and Natesa S. Sridharan

Appendix: Details of Graphics Equipment and Trans-Atlantic Communication Used in Demonstration at NATO ASI in Holland   317

Index   320

EVALUATION OF ON-LINE TECHNIQUES IN A SUB-STRUCTURE
SEARCH SYSTEM

D.R. Eakin and E. Hyde

Data Services Section, ICI Pharmaceuticals Division,
P.O. Box 25, Alderley Park, Macclesfield, Cheshire, SK10 4TG.

ON-LINE SYSTEMS IN A SCIENTIFIC ENVIRONMENT

On-line techniques have not been fully exploited in Great Britain. Commercial applications, including banking, have developed a number of systems, but on close scrutiny, many of these are confined to data acquisition, and many are, in fact, remote job entry systems using on-line equipment. In scientific applications, a few on-line acquisition facilities are in operation, but by far the main use is in mathematical calculations using bureau facilities, such as CALL 360.

There is evidence from information systems that scientific users are already turning away from on-line enquiry and retrieval and are prepared to allow information specialists to deal with the computer phase of their problem.

This rejection lies not in the interface provided, but mainly in the quality of the information retrieved. Most systems designers have considered the need to provide easy access and much thought has often been given to the way in which a query can be expressed, and to the validation and security aspects to safeguard both the user and the system.

These systems fail in their objectives. It is important to make available a comprehensive system designed not to retrieve facts, but to present knowledge. It is important that the system is designed to retrieve information and to put that information retrieved into context, so that the user can correctly deduce its value. Such a system must be interactive, and have the capability of accessing a number of related files by various keys. Programs available must cover both information retrieval and information analysis.

These have been the objectives behind the design of the system at ICI Pharmaceuticals Division.

MULTIDISCIPLINE FILES

Before one can evaluate on-line requirements in a scientific environment, it is essential to consider not only the files of information and the programs necessary for update, retrieval and analysis, but also the organisation which the system is to serve.

ICI Pharmaceuticals Division supports a large research department with wide-ranging objectives in the medical and veterinary field. It is a large user of chemical compounds, constantly looking for new structural types. It is interested in the organic compounds produced in every other research department within ICI and therefore maintains a "Company Compound File" which it operates as an information centre for the whole company. In addition, the Division maintains data files on biology, toxicology, clinical history and physical property, covering information generated by the Division.

The system devised, therefore, is bound to reflect the need to hold diverse data files at various levels of detail for novelty checking, retrospective search and information evaluation. Structure manipulation at total compound and substructure levels is an essential facility which must be incorporated into the system for use with experimental data files. Finally, the system should be capable of operation in batch, on-line or interactive modes.

A comprehensive system of this nature is obviously very different to limited, but highly specialised systems designed to explore specific problems. Chemists, biologists and mathematicians within a large organisation will always have the need to work independently with highly personalised files and programs, often, outside the main system.

CHEMICAL STRUCTURE FILES. When considering the research data generated within a large pharmaceutical company, it is soon evident that the chemical structure files pose problems of a different order of complexity to the problems which arise from the use of property data files. An important part of the system design was to recognise and deal with this problem.

Firstly, it was recognised that the chemical files would be used for a wide variety of purposes such as retrieving single compounds, substructure classification and for interactive systems dealing with reaction mechanisms. In addition, the chemical files were to be compatible with the various property data files where compounds were to be examined for structure/activity relationships. Furthermore, research targets change constantly and an additional requirement was that the structure files were capable of modification. This created the need for record descriptions to be kept to a minimum and for additional data to be generated by algorithm.

Essential features, therefore, of any structure system for use in this type of environment are:

A. Structure files must contain a total description of the molecule.
B. Data should be accessible through a variety of keys at a number of levels of structure description.
C. It should be simple to prepare subfiles from the total files - this could be an economic necessity where complex data analysis is involved.
D. The structure files must be suitable for use in both batch and on-line methods of file interrogation.

CHEMICAL STRUCTURE REPRESENTATION

Research on the recording of chemical data began, for use, with the choice of a method of representing a structure suitable for computer manipulation. The Wiswesser Line Notation (WLN) was the method finally chosen (ref. 1).

Although the notation is concise, unique and provides a total description of the molecule, it is not ideal for all the demands on structure manipulation in a chemical search environment. To meet these requirements, we have developed three levels of description:

(1) Fragmentation
(2) Wiswesser Line Notation
(3) Atom Connectivity Table

FRAGMENTATION. A number of programs have been written to generate chemically significant fragments from the notation record. The latest, developed on a Burroughs 4700, generates 150 fragments directly from the notation, and stores them in binary form. A generation run for the 135,000 compounds on our company file took 45 minutes of machine time and failed to generate fragments for less than 150 compounds.

This fragment code ties together information not readily obtained by direct scanning of the notation. It can be very simply and effectively interpreted by those with little or no knowledge of the WLN.

WISWESSER LINE NOTATION. The WLN represents a unique and complete description of the organic molecule and its length may vary from 1 or 2 symbols to 140 to 180 **symbols.** In our compound files, the average length of the notation is 19 characters.

ATOM CONNECTIVITY TABLE. A further program is available which converts a WLN record to a **con**nection table which explicitly defines each atom (other than hydrogen) in a molecule. This connectivity record forms the basis of the CROSSBOW technology. Unlike the fragment record, which occupies little space, the connection table representation is large. For this reason, the connection table is not stored but generated when required. A connection table description is usually required for small parts of the total file and the generation program is fast. The form of the connection table will be described when discussing the search system.

The WLN provides a structure record which is a good balance - concise enough for storage purposes, yet detailed enough for interpretation. In addition, the WLN record itself is suitable for computer scanning. This is particularly true in that portion of the molecule dealing with ring information, and this aspect will **al**so be referred to when describing the search system.

RESEARCH DEPARTMENT DATA FILES

Research information is collected from all departments within the Division and therefore reflects the interdisciplinary nature of a large scientific establishment (see Figure 1).

Figure 1 - Inter-Disciplinary System

Files Covered	Size
Chemical	130,000 compounds
Biological	1 million test results
Toxicology	167,000 details per test
Clinical data	20 running concurrently

In organising the data, it is inevitable that the system devised will reflect the essential differences between chemical and property data files. In the system set up, the chemical structure data base has been designated the main file. The subsidiary property files are linked to the main structure file by an accession number.

CHEMICAL DATA BASE. The chemical data base consists of the following data elements:

(1) WLN
(2) Molecular formula
(3) Fragments
(4) Accession numbers to the various property files.

These are organised as shown in Figure 2.

Figure 2 - Chemical Data Base

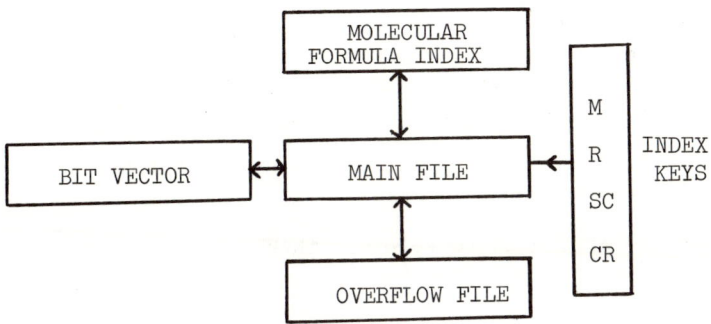

To aid file organisation, the WLN record was designated a fixed length. 99% of the molecules have a unique description at the 24th character, although only 85% are complete. The remaining characters of the notation, above the 24th character, are stored in the overflow file. Any interrogation of the file interprets all the notation records and the user is unaware of the separation.

The molecular formula provides an additional structure record. It is also concise and is held as a fixed length record of 18 characters. There is an average of 2.5 molecules under each molecular formula entry and the maximum number is 64 compounds. Hence, the molecular formula provides an easy access to the system for those without knowledge of WLN.

It has not been the policy to restrict access to the data base to those chemists with a knowledge of the notation. Molecular formula with additional fragment information can be used successfully to recover data on a single compound.

The company chemical data file is held on disks and consists of 20 million bytes of information. This includes all linking data to the subsidiary data files. The file is edited daily, with a validation and WLN/molecular formula check prior to update. Retrieval of specific compounds and their associated data present no problem. Entry point may be any of the data elements or any combination of them.

EXTERNAL DATA FILES. The WLN provides a link between compound files generated within the company and those available from external sources.

The information includes:

(A) Literature data from the Index Chemicus Registry System tapes. Access is possible to the past 12 months data.
(B) Physical data from the Hansch data base from Pomona College.
(C) Compound availability and price from Aldrich Chemical Company files.

Programs are available to reformat these files into forms compatible with the internal data banks.

SUBSTRUCTURE SEARCH

Retrieval of compounds by substructure classification presents problems of a different magnitude to the problem of the storage and retrieval of single compounds.

The complexity and variety of substructure search questions posed to the system at ICI have led to the development of a multi-level search facility.

MULTI-LEVEL SEARCH FACILITY. No one search technique could be economically used to answer every type of search question met in practise. The best method depends upon the exact nature of the question, the size of the file being searched and the expected number of results. Often a sequence of search methods may be required: a quick and cheap preliminary screen to reduce large volumes (say to 5,000 or less) followed by a more accurate technique to select the final answers.

Figure 3 - Three-Level Structural Search System

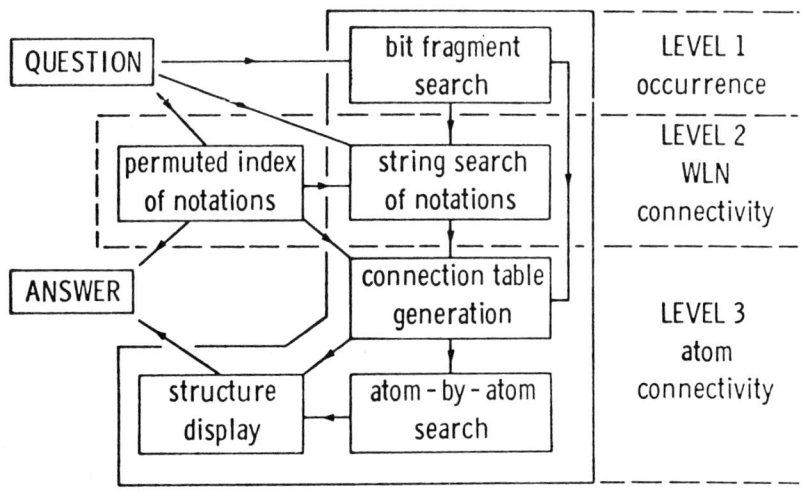

The multi-level search system devised for use on the WLN file is split into three levels of increasing definition.

The first level depends upon a search for the occurrence of

specific chemical fragments without regard to their inter-connectivity.

The second level depends upon a search of the Wiswesser Line Notation for connected sequences of fragments. It will only detect that connectivity which is explicitly stated in the notation and which can be found from direct scanning.

The third level depends upon an atom network match. It requires an atom connectivity table, which may be derived from the notation, but which covers the full topology of the molecule.

Let us examine each level in turn.

Level 1 - Bit Fragment Screen

The first level depends on searching for the occurrence of specific chemical fragments. Fast and efficient searching is possible using the fixed field fragment code. Each of the 150 predetermined fragments is assigned a specific bit location in the compound record, and its presence or absence is recorded as 1 or 0.

The search provides the facilities shown in Figure 4.

Figure 4 - Bit Search Logic

(1) Boolean Logic   AND, OR, NOT
(2) Maximum   100 concepts
(3) Maximum   40 enquiries
(4) Run type:
       a) Selection
       b) Count.

Level 2 - String Search

The next level, string search, involves scanning the WLN record in a manner similar to the search of test in a natural language system. The program, like the fragment search, can handle up to 40 batched enquiries, hence optimising on machine processing time.

Search Logic

The WLN string search facilities are shown in Figure 5.

Figure 5 - String Search Logic WLN

(1) Maximum 127 characteristics per string
(2) Maximum 400 strings
(3) AND, OR, NOT and 'followed by' logic
(4) Character expression:
        a) Specific
        b) Not space
        c) Alternatives.

The molecular formula is also suitable for computer scanning and is complimentary to WLN string search. It is particularly effective when an element must occur a large number of times or when an unusual element is requested. The molecular formula contains only a maximum of 18 characters of information, hence the processing time for its interpretation is short.

The molecular formula string search facilities are shown in Figure 6.

Figure 6 - String Search Logic Molecular Formula

(1) Only one element per string
(2) Maximum 400 strings
(3) AND, OR, NOT logic
(4) Character expression:
        a) Element
        b) Minimum
        c) Maximum

Level 3 - Atom-by-atom Search of the CROSSBOW Connection Table

The third level in the multi-stage search system requires a more explicit level of description of a molecule than that provided by WLN.

The CROSSBOW connection tables are generated for those molecules which have been selected at previous search levels.

On-Line Techniques in Substructure Searching

DESCRIPTION OF CONNECTION TABLES. The CROSSBOW connection table consists of five basic records (see Figure 7).

Figure 7 - CROSSBOW Connection Table

(1) Unit section
(2) Connection transfers
(3) Ring section
(4) Ring connectors
(5) Modifier section.

An example will illustrate the use of the various sections.

Figure 8 - Example of CROSSBOW Connection Table

Units:	TQTDTTTDDDDTONLLQLL
Connection transfers:	13129919
Rings:	$0_{15}F06F07066_{146}$
Ring connectors:	$0_{1}03_{0}114_{000_{3}}$

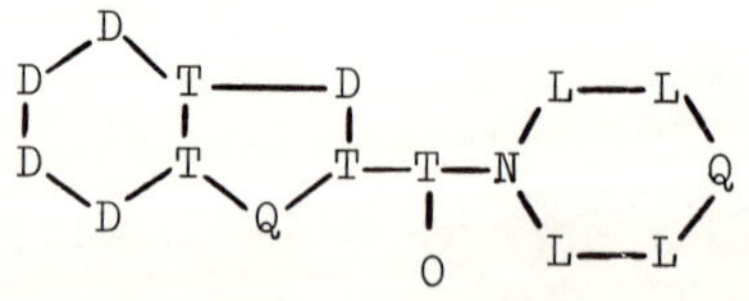

Wiswesser notation: $T_5 6$ BOJ CV- AT6N DOTJ

The diagram illustrates the structure with its atoms (or nodes) replaced by the "unit values". These values show the atom and its surrounding bonds.

L represents $-CH_2-$
D represents $-CH=$
T represents $-\underset{|}{C}=$

Altogether, there are 8 values for the states of carbon.

Following the rules of the notation, the units are numbered and defined from the face fusion of the two-ring system

Description of Connection Tables 11

and continue first around the smaller ring.

The connection transfers give the network of the acyclic portions of the molecule and indicate terminal points and the reconnecting branch points.

13 is the terminal oxygen and 12 is the reconnecting carbon atom (as defined by a T value).

The ring section and the ring connectors describe the type of ring system, the pathway through each ring, and also how the rings are linked to the acyclic network.

The modifier section, not applicable in this example, contains additional data such as radio isotopes, stereo information and unusual atom/bond conditions (ref. 2).

The connection table produced is more informative than the normal topological connectivity record. In generating an explicit atom-bond connection table from the WLN, it is possible to preserve molecular association. The WLN record is particularly useful in this respect. The arrangement of the record enables the atoms of individual rings to be grouped together by the connectivity generation program.

This additional information can be used during an atomic network search, and hence the logic available is more extensive than in a normal atom-by-atom search program. Furthermore, the element/bond combinations can be compounded into more descriptive values for the search phase.

Atom-by-atom search. The first two levels, fragment and string search, are used to screen as many records as possible from the structure file prior to attempting the third level, atom-by-atom search.

This phase is not usually employed on files greater than 6,000 molecules.

In practise, the previous search levels rarely select more than 2,000 compounds. The small file is first submitted to the generation program and the resulting connection tables are searched using the atom-by-atom program.

For each molecule, the network specified by the search question is matched against all possible atomic configurations in the connection table. The search facilities available are shown in Figure 9.

Figure 9 - Atom-by-Atom Search Logic

(1) Maximum 10 nodes

(2) One or two branch networks

(3) Maximum 4 connections per node

(4) Node expression:

        a) 10 values, present or absent
        b) Any value
        c) Ring/not ring
        d) Terminal/not terminal.

The questions are very simple to express and this is best illustrated by an example. Consider,

$$\underset{1\quad 2\quad 3\quad 5}{Cl - C - \overset{\overset{X}{\|}4}{C} - N}$$

A network is required where first node must be chloride, the second any carbon and the fifth node must be a substituted or unsubstituted nitrogen. The third and fourth nodes must be carbonyl or thiocarbonyl. The node values are therefore:

(1) G   Chlorine

(2) LTUXY   Expressing the various states of carbon

(3) TU   Indicating carbon with double bond

(4) OW   Either terminal oxygen or terminal sulphur

(5) JKMN   Various states of nitrogen.

In addition, a network parameter is necessary to indicate the breakpoint in the linear path. This is expressed as:

                        0304

and indicates the network terminates at 4 and reconnects at 3.

EXAMPLE OF A MULTI-LEVEL SEARCH. Having now examined all three levels of the search system, it is possible to take an example

Example of Multi-Level Search

question and to consider how it would be dealt with by the system.

Figure 10 - Search Example

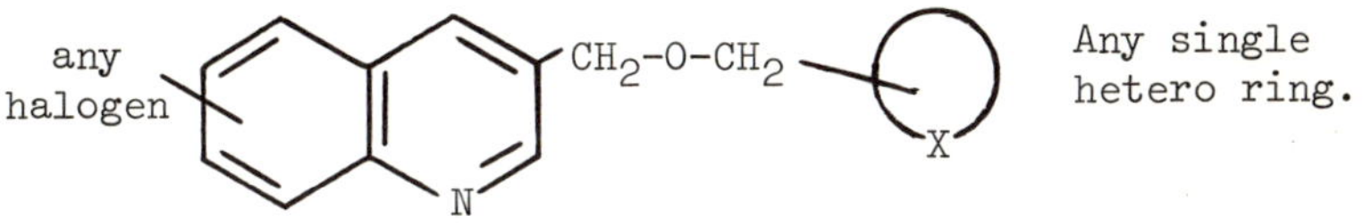

$$\text{any halogen} \quad \text{[quinoline ring]} \quad CH_2\text{-}O\text{-}CH_2 \quad \text{[ring with X]} \quad \text{Any single hetero ring.}$$

The first level fragmentation can be used effectively to locate all molecules which contain:

(1) Any halogen.
(2) Linking acyclic oxygen, i.e. oxygen not part of a ring or linked directly to a ring.
(3) Ring with one nitrogen (describes individual ring, not total ring system).
(4) One hetero/carbo fusion.

It is also possible to specify that there must be at least two ring systems present.

The second level, string search, takes advantage of the explicit ring statement which is part of the WLN record.

(1) T66 BNJ   fully defines the quinoline ring.

The position of the sidechain is fixed and in the notation could be expressed as:

(2) D101

D indicates the position of attachment on the quinoline and 101 denotes the $-CH_2OCH_2-$ side chain. This character string must be preceded by the ring system and therefore the "followed by" logic can be applied.

The atom-by-atom level can correctly locate a network commencing in the quinoline ring and proceeding through the sidechain to the ill-defined ring. This requires a linear path, and hence no network parameters indicating branch points is necessary. The node values are expressed as in Figure 11.

Figure 11 - Atom-by-Atom Search Example

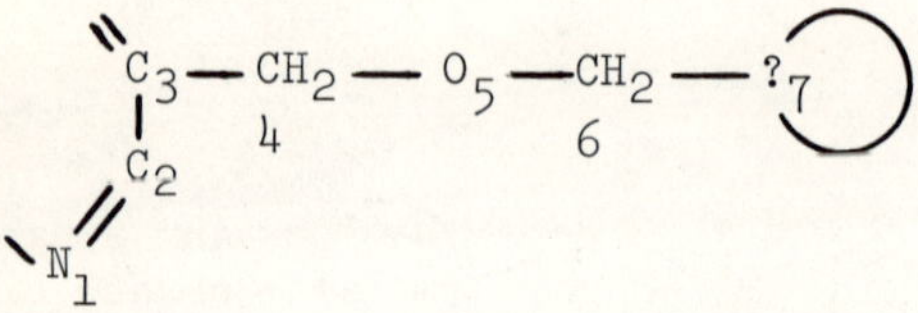

$$C_3 \!\!=\!\! N_1 \quad C_3\!-\!CH_2\!-\!O_5\!-\!CH_2\!-\!?_7 \bigcirc$$

(1) N   6 Ring
(2) D or T   6 Ring
     (may or may not
     be substituted)
(3) T   6 Ring
(4) L
(5) Q
(6) L
(7) *

where * indicates that the node may have any value.

SEARCH OUTPUT. Output has been carefully considered in the system. At various search levels, data is accumulated, and at the final chemical stage, the connection table is used to generate a two-dimensional structure diagram. This generated display is stored along with the associated data records. In batch mode, structures and data relevant to the search question are printed onto 8" by 5" index cards using a standard line printer which has had 5 characters changed. Using on-line methods, the compounds can be inspected on a visual display unit or printed on a teletype printer.

Figure 12 - Example of Structure Output

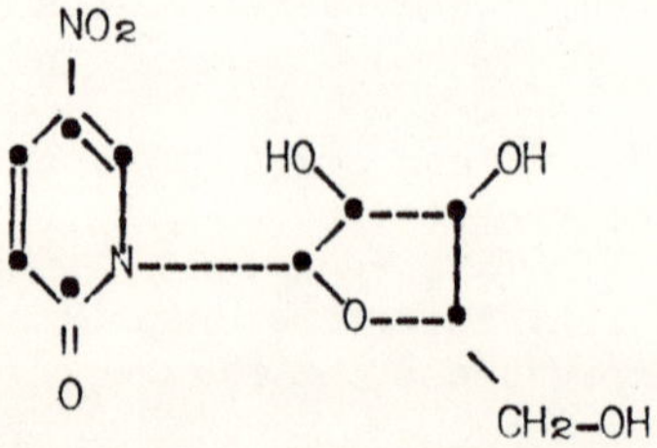

USE OF THE SEARCH SYSTEM

The three techniques available in the multi-level system are complimentary. For string search purposes, the ring portion of the notation provides a concise record which enables rapid screening for total systems.

In our company compound file, 75% of compounds contain ring systems other than benzene, and almost 90% of questions posed to the system demand a ring or part-ring structure as one parameter. In nearly all searches, all three levels of the search system are used, and the use of all three levels usually results in the easier construction of search parameters and an increased efficiency of operation.

An important aid to the formulation of a search question is the availability of an on-line count program. Using this facility, the enquirer can check the number of hits against the chemical fragment file, and interactively construct his search question to achieve the desired performance.

Experience with this aid indicates that some users ask too precise a question in the first instance, and by widening their parameters save repeated entry into a full file search. Furthermore, users asking too precise a question are liable to accept the limited output without realising that vital information has been excluded from the answer set. A bit fragment search such as this would take the user 2-5 minutes depending upon the complexity of the search and the machine load. He would be searching the fragment file for 135,000 compounds.

About 400 substructure enquiries have been dealt with so far this year. 360 have been analysed and gave the following information:

　　Questions involving rings　　　　　　　315*

　　Questions involving acyclic units　　　90
　　(not simple ring substituents)

* The 315 ring questions contained:

　　189 fully defined rings
　　135 partially defined rings.

DATA CORRELATION

The main chemical data base and search programs are used

with research data files. Data in these files is obtained from information produced in laboratory experiments. These files hold the primary data and these are supplemented by a summary statement. These summary results are subjective and liable to be affected by subsequent experimental evidence, and also by changes in research targets. Provided the primary data is recorded, subjective data files can be regenerated to meet the changes made.

Programs for data correlation are general purpose packages provided by International Computers Limited (ICL). These are very flexible and cover aspects of file manipulation, search logic, survey analysis and statistics. They are useful for the survey of large files or for the reformatting and analysis of specifically generated sub-files. Thus, it is possible to retrieve and correlate information from both structure and experimental data files using the packages either in batch or on-line mode.

Cross comparisons of both structure and data are performed routinely. As an example, recent biological tests indicated that certain simple and widely available compounds were showing activity. The system was used to build-up a sub-file, first of 800 related structures extracted from the literature. To these were added all internal information.

Further classification by activity suggested substructure relationships, and compounds recommended for testing were obtained by searching other files within the system for sample availability.

Information accumulated during processing was displayed on 8" by 5" cards, and the project team responsible for the biological test has, therefore, a manual sub-file available for browsing or for the addition of further data.

There are, therefore, comprehensive data files and programs available for a variety of users within Research Department. Files covering a number of topics have been built up without creating large integrated files. Each data bank whether chemical, biological, toxicological, medical or physical property, and whether holding primary data or summary information is held in separate, but compatible, files. Programs can operate universally across these files, and packages are included which are suitable for data base generation and realignment to meet the changing needs of research.

INTRODUCTION TO ON-LINE EVALUATION

The main objective has been to create a system where the scientist could access data in an interactive environment.

It was considered that a chemical reactants file would produce ideal testing circumstances for the techniques which have been developed so far.

THE VALUE OF INTERACTION. If, when constructing a multi-disciplinary system, it is important to consider the organisation served, then when designing an interactive system, the individual scientist must be taken into account.

Computers and scientists are complimentary. A computer is consistent, capable of associating large numbers of concepts, and able to perform tedious tasks. However, it is lacking in the creativity and insight of the scientific expert.

Consider the problem of the storage and retrieval of reaction information. Studies have shown the computer can analyse large numbers of reactions satisfactorily. The problem arises when unusual conditions are involved and the computer fails to recognise anything but the simple analysis. An experienced chemist can classify reactions very rapidly taking into account any special features. Unfortunately, he can almost as quickly forget.

The computer, on the other hand, can store vast numbers of reactions and can be used to recall relevant information which may not have been retained by the chemist.

In systems design, it is essential to identify the most efficient role the computer can play. At ICI, we have realised this and wish to optimise the interaction between man and machine.

As yet our technology and equipment have been mainly restricted to batch processing. Some on-line experience has been built up, but operations have, so far, been confined to information staff.

Now we are ready to examine "user reaction". For the purpose of this Advanced Study Institute, the programs, usually operated in batch mode, have been adapted for on-line use. The changes have been kept to a minimum because we feel the enhancements required for an interactive capability need critical evaluation.

THE REACTION DATA BASE

A chemical reaction index has been set up from some 700 literature references. There are several questions we hope to answer in the setting up and use of such a file.

THE VALUE OF RAPID ACCESS TO REACTION INFORMATION. How valuable to the chemist would be a computerised index capable of providing rapid access to relevant chemical reaction information?

METHODS FOR CODING CHEMICAL REACTIONS. Various methods of reaction classification have been tried with varying degrees of success, but what is an effective reaction coding scheme?

APPLICABILITY OF CROSSBOW TECHNOLOGY. We know CROSSBOW technology is effective in batch mode. We do not know if it is adaptable for on-line processing or if it is too specialised for the chemist himself to apply?

WHAT IS A REACTION?

What would you consider to be a single "reaction"? A compound is easy to define and hence simple to code. A reaction, however, is not so straightforward, and a number of concepts require definition.

A reaction may be represented in terms of starting materials, conditions and products. Furthermore, starting materials are usually subdivided into reagents and reactants.

A reagent will normally reproducably effect the same transformation within a series of reactants, but its definition is by no means precise.

A chemist often identifies reagents on the basis of availability, cost and frequency of use.

If a system is to distinguish between reactants and reagents, and it is an advantage, some form of consistent distinction is required.

Similarly, some definition is required for the term product. Consider the reaction of cyclohexane and N-bromo succinimide:

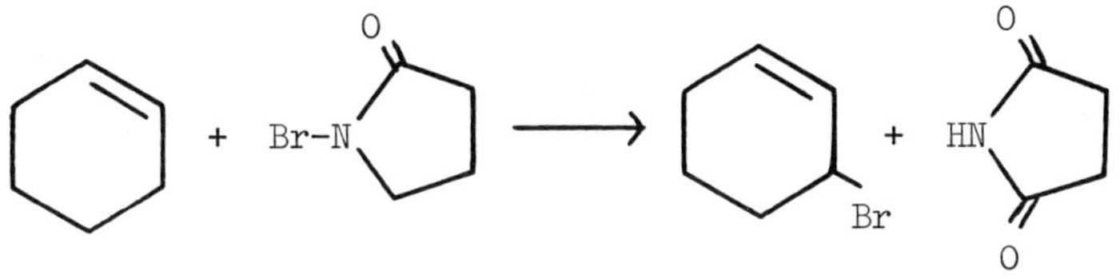

[Reaction scheme: cyclohexene + Br-N(succinimide) → 3-bromocyclohexene + HN(succinimide)]

Would you consider succinimide to be a byproduct? Should the reaction be coded as cyclohexane to 3-bromocyclohexane and represented as:

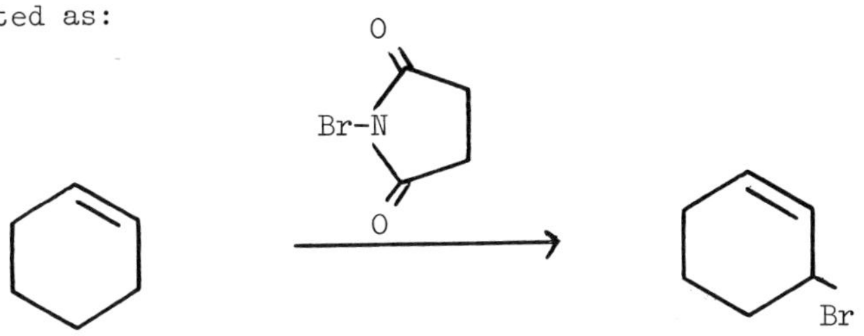

[Reaction scheme: cyclohexene → 3-bromocyclohexene, with Br-N succinimide over the arrow]

In an attempt to overcome these problems, we established two rules:

(1) A reactant or product must contain carbon, but it must not be on a list of carbon containing exceptions. These include such things as hydrogen cyanides.

(2) It must seem to react or be produced in any given reaction equation.

Although these rules are simple and should be capable of consistent application, ambiguities have still arisen. Consider and compare the next two reactions:

(A) In the first reaction, an aldehyde and an amine react in ethyl alcohol to give the imine. Ethyl alcohol is the solvent and plays no part in the reaction.

[Reaction scheme: CH₃-O-C₆H₄-CHO + NH₂-C₆H₄-CH₃ →(EtOH, reflux) CH₃-O-C₆H₄-CH=N-C₆H₄-CH₃]

(B) In the second reaction, a similar aldehyde and amine react in the presence of formic acid to give the substituted benzylamine.

[Reaction scheme: Cl-C₆H₄-CHO + NH₂-C₆H₃(Cl)(C(=O)-C₆H₅) →(HCOOH, 16 hrs) Cl-C₆H₄-CH₂-NH-C₆H₃(Cl)(C(=O)-C₆H₅)]

Close examination of all the products in this second reaction shows that the formic acid has, in fact, acted as a reducing agent and could, therefore, be said to have taken part in the reaction. However, would you record the formic acid as a reactant or a reagent? Should the reaction be coded as multi-stage, and, if so, is the role of the formic acid at each stage, and the nature of the intermediate known?

THE INFORMATION STORED

The overall objective in setting up a reaction index was to evaluate the application of modern documentation techniques to the data being amassed in the individual files of chemists.

The data requires to be readily available to aid the chemist in the decision processes involved in synthesis. It should be easy to use and complimentary to literature searching. At the same time, it should contain enough information for the chemist to evaluate any reaction in the light of his needs.

To meet these objectives, it was felt that the following data should be recorded:

(A) COMPOUND INFORMATION. A complete description of all compounds involved in the reaction was thought essential, whether they were reactants, products or intermediates in a multi-stage reaction.

For simplicity, each unique compound is coded once only - a compound number being assigned to identify the molecule within the reaction.

The compounds are coded as all other molecules within the CROSSBOW system - uncontracted Wiswesser Line Notation and Richter-ordered molecular formula. The reaction compound files are then compatible with other data bases and programs within the CROSSBOW system.

(B) CONDITION DATA. Condition data includes any modification to compound information such as the quantity; additional chemical information including reagents, catalysts and solvents; physical properties such as temperature, pressure, time; and any available data on the yield.

It is stored in a free text statement. Agreed abbreviations have been established and standard text searching packages can be used to examine the condition data.

(C) BIBLIOGRAPHIC DATA. The bibliographic data forms the link to the literature such that the user can make further investigations into the applicability of a reaction in a given situation.

(D) REACTION SITE ANALYSIS. The basis of any reaction index scheme is the classification method used. A great deal of research has been spent on the interpretation and analysis of the reaction site. This will now be considered in more detail.

REACTION CENTRE APPROACH

We were looking for a high degree of versatility together with computerisation, and of all the methods available, we were particularly attracted to the reaction centre approach.

A reaction centre is the bonds formed or broken in a reaction and the atoms attached thereto.

In a totally computerised system, reaction centre descriptions could be generated automatically. Atom pairs and the bonds between them could be generated for total molecules from a connection table record. Any pairs, not common to both reactants and products, could be retained as a reaction descriptor.

The main obstacle to the computer generation of reaction site was that structural changes alone were often not a sufficient record of the reaction. Consider the transformation of a nitro to an amine group using ammonia.

For example:

$$\text{Cl-C}_6\text{H}_3(\text{NO}_2)_2 \xrightarrow{\text{NH}_3} \text{Cl-C}_6\text{H}_3(\text{NH}_2)(\text{NO}_2)$$

Only the analysis of all starting materials and products will avoid the false conclusion that O is replaced by H.

In a fully automated approach, such reactions incorrectly analysed, would very probably be lost in the system to those looking for the transformation:

$$-\text{NO}_2 \longrightarrow -\text{NH}_2$$

Reaction Center Approach

A program could possibly be written to deal with these problems, but it could be uneconomic. Our final decision was, therefore, to adopt a manually assigned reaction descriptor based on the reaction centre approached.

REACTION SITE CLASSIFICATION. We are analysing reactions as comprehensively as possible using three levels of description.

GENERAL CLASSIFICATION SCHEME. At a summary level, a general reaction class is assigned. The classification scheme used closely followed that in operation at Roussel-Uclaf, where there is a well-established manual reaction index widely used by the chemist.

The 12 reaction classes are not mutually exclusive and a reaction may fall into more than one class. For example, the Fischer Indole Synthesis:

$$\text{C}_6\text{H}_5\text{-NH-N=C(CH}_3\text{)CH}_3 \longrightarrow \text{2-methylindoline} + NH_3$$

A new ring system is formed, hence, this is a CLASS 8 reaction. But a carbon-carbon bond is formed. No heteroatoms are attached to either of the carbons, hence, this is also a CLASS 3 reaction.

This classification scheme does not give an even distribution across the classes. In the reactions so far coded, there is a heavy bias towards functional group transformations and cyclisations.

Would you say a general reaction scheme should produce an even distribution or should it be of chemical significance, and provide an extra reaction analysis tool?

The second level of description of the reaction site is the bond and ring classification.

BOND CLASSIFICATION. An analysis is made of all bonds broken and all bonds formed. No account is taken of bonds merely modified such as a carbon-carbon double bond to a carbon-carbon triple bond.

$$\diagup C=C\diagdown \longrightarrow -C\equiv C-$$

Atom-hydrogen bonds are also ignored. Consider:

[Reaction scheme: bicyclic pyrroline + NaIO₄ → 8-membered keto lactam]

In this reaction, the carbon-carbon double bond across the ring fusion is broken. Two carbonyl bonds are formed in the product.

The bond information would be coded as shown:

$$-C=C: +2C=O$$

The bond descriptor is canonicalised. Broken bonds are coded before bonds formed. All atoms are arranged in order and singly-bonded atoms precede double-bonded ones of the same type.

RING CLASSIFICATION. An analysis is also made of the rings broken and the rings formed in a reaction. These are coded as the individual rings, not as the total ring system.

The information recorded includes ring size, the heteroatoms present and their position, and whether or not the ring is part of a larger ring system. No account is taken of ring saturation. Hence for the above reaction, the rings broken would be coded as:

$$-(-55 \text{ BM}$$

Two five-membered rings fused together, indicated by the numerals are connected to a larger ring system, indicated by the hyphen.

The heteroatom information uses Wiswesser Notation rules, but these are applied only to the rings taking part in the reaction, not to the total ring system.

Similarly, the coding for the ring formed:

$$+(-8\text{VM EV})$$

indicating the 8-membered keto lactam configuration.

Ring Classification

REACTION CENTRE ANALYSIS. The reaction centre analysis represents the most extensive description of the reaction and is complex. In a session such as this, it is only possible to give an outline of the approach used.

The system of coding which we devised allows a variable descriptor for the reaction centre. It is based on the Wiswesser Notation, with two basic additions.

<u>Carbon atom descriptors</u>. Within a ring system, the Wiswesser Notation does not detail all carbon atoms. In the reaction site analysis, ring carbon atoms are therefore expressed as connection table units. In the notation rules, all atoms are treated by Rule 2 - latest alphanumeric position first (Ref. 3).

<u>Terminal and linking descriptors</u>. A code to deal with fragmentary parts of a molecule was essential. Where ambiguous, it was necessary to specify whether an atom was terminal, linking or branched. This was simply achieved by using the symbol, hyphen, to signify linking, and the symbol, ampersand, to signify terminal. Using the previous reaction, the reaction centre would be coded as:

$$DD = \&OA/\&AO$$

The "&" indicates the oxygen atoms are terminal. "D" represents the carbon atom in an endocyclic double bond, and "A" represents the carbon atom in an exocyclic double bond.

All part-fragments are canonicalised as is each side of the equation. Once again, the standard WLN rule is used - latest alphanumeric position first.

Two part-fragments in the same molecule are separated by a slash mark and two part-fragments in different molecules would be separated by a plus sign.

To cater for those cases when the reaction centre was not considered sufficient to give the full information about the reaction, facilities are available to code a larger reaction centre. For example: see the previous reaction.

The heteroatom adjacent to the double bond may influence the reaction, hence the additional information about the fusion is coded as:

$$OO1 = MDDD$$

This facility is used at the discretion of the coder and contains any information which may affect the chemists decision to accept/reject the reaction.

In this way, three levels of description of the reaction have been set up, as well as a total description of all compounds involved in the reaction.

FILE ORGANISATION

Having successfully analysed a reaction and set up a data base, our next main function is to examine the best form of file organisation for the reaction index.

Standard textbooks and encyclopedias of reactions have failed since they usually only offer the chemist one means of entry. For example, the book <u>Reagents for Organic Synthesis</u> by Fieser and Fieser (ref. 4). Here, reactions are indexed by the reagents used in the process. Use of such an index demands a good knowledge of reagents and, therefore, takes part of the wanted information for granted.

A chemist requires access to a reaction index not for simple reactions. He needs help, for example, in those complicated by more than one reactive site in the molecule. He would be interested in two index points:

(1) The reaction site.
(2) Elements present in the starting material and remaining unchanged in the product.

The second index point requires knowledge of the total compound information.

ON-LINE SYSTEM

He needs access to standard substructure search facilities on the reactant and product information. These are readily available through the CROSSBOW package.

Three disk files have been set up:

(1) ICIFWREACTN   Fragments, WLN and molecular formula for reactants.

(2) ICIFWPROD   Fragments, WLN and molecular formula for products.

File Organization

(3) ICIFWADDT   Conditions, analysis and bibliographic data for each reaction.

    Reactant and product information is separated and each file contains fragments, notation and molecular formula for each of the compounds.

    Intermediates in a multi-stage process are coded on both files.

    The third file, the additional details file, gives information on the conditions, analysis and bibliography.

    Each of these files can be searched via an ICL terminal. The search facilities include 3 macros:

(1) BASSMACRO   Searches the fragment, WLN or molecular formula on one or the other file, and produces a hit file suitable for further searching or interpretation.

(2) ABAPMACRO   If search parameters have been input, the program will:

                                          (a) generate connection table records,
                                          (b) execute an atom-by-atom search,
                                          (c) generate structural descriptors from the connection table,
                                          (d) collect data from the other files and print the result on the terminal.

                        If no search parameters are present, the atom-by-atom step is by-passed.

The data file may be searched using:

(3) FINDMACRO   Performs text searching of the additional details file and prints the result.

    The BASSMACRO allows substructure searches to be carried out on the reactant or product file. Techniques involve fragment, WLN or molecular formula searches.

The ABAPMACRO operates on the hit file from the BASSMACRO. It will generate connected tables, perform an atom-by-atom search if required, and display the compound and any other information about the reaction onto the terminal.

The additional data file may be searched independently of the compound file using the FINDMACRO. This is the standard ICL package for text searching.

The application of these search proceedures is best seen in an example:

"A class of compounds has shown biological activity, and a chemist wishes to make compounds of the type:

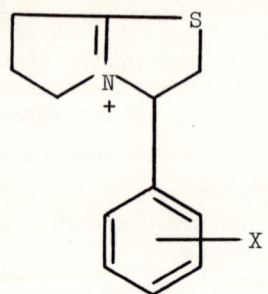

where X is any substituent and the hetero rings may be part of a larger ring system".

He is unfamiliar with the system, and knows no Wiswesser Notation. He needs to access the product file and can use two levels - the fragment level 1 and the atom-by-atom level 3.

Using a dictionary, he examines his molecule and breaks it down into the fragments shown. The fragments required would be:

        1 nitrogen in more than 1 ring.
        1 sulphur in one or more rings.
        5-membered heterocyclic ring.
        At least 1 ring system.
        At least 1 benzene ring.

He assigns the appropriate code numbers. Use of a manual shows him how to operate the BASSMACRO and to specify his search as:

        AND, @81 105@ #85 83# /1100/

The 'at' sign indicates both fragment 81 and 105 must be set and the number sign indicates at least one of the numbers must be present. The slash marks enclose the ring counts, a minimum of one ring system and one benzene ring, but any number of heterocyclic and carbocyclic rings. Knowing the hetero content of his rings, he could also have asked for a minimum of two hetero rings, but he has enough information for an effective screen.

He now analyses his question for the required atom-by-atom network. He needs to define 5 nodes:

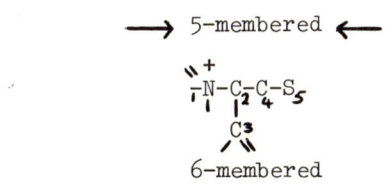

Note	Ring	Units
1	RING5	K
2	RING5	YT
3	RING5	T
4	RING5	DTLY
5	RING5	S/W
B		32
P		0001

and examination of the connection table symbol dictionary translates his node definition to the alternative unit values.

He assigns a branch parameter to indicate that the third node branches onto the second node, and a print parameter to monitor his progress every compound.

The manual informs him how to operate the ABAPMACRO and he runs his search to completion. These answers are expressed as structural diagrams with associated reaction data as free text.

REFERENCES

1. Thomson, L.H., Hyde, E. and Matthews, F.W.
    "Organic Search and Display Using a Connectivity Matrix
    Derived from Wiswesser Notation".
    J. Chem. Doc. 7, 204 (1967).

2. Hyde, E. and Ash, J.E.
    "Chemical Information Systems".
    In press.

3. Smith, E.G.
    "The Wiswesser Line-Formula Chemical Notation".
    McGraw-Hill, 1968.

4. Fieser, L.F. and Fieser, M.
    "Reagents for Organic Synthesis".
    Wiley - Interscience, 1967.

THE MICROSTRUCTURE OF CHEMICAL DATA-BASES AND THE CHOICE OF REPRESENTATION FOR RETRIEVAL

Michael F. Lynch
Postgraduate School of Librarianship and Information Science
University of Sheffield, Western Bank, Sheffield, S10 2TN

INTRODUCTION

In this presentation I wish to consider the question of characteristics of records of chemical information and their representation for purposes of retrieval. I shall deal both with structural and with textual forms of chemical information, and shall present a simple but powerful principle with implications in each case for the costs of file creation and search, as well as of storage.

The particular problem at issue - and it is equally widespread in information systems in disciplines other than chemistry - is the distribution of characteristics in the microstructure of records and the implications of these for searches for substrings. I shall argue that taking adequate account of the distributions can lead to cost reductions which may reach even order-of-magnitude dimensions. By substring searches I mean the identification of strings of symbols within records. In the case of substructure searches, the strings consist of atom and bond symbols, rings and chains, each of which may on occasion be defined in general rather than specific terms. In the case of text searches, the substrings are words, word sequences and word stems. There is an essential similarity between the two, which has hitherto been largely ignored; methods devised for substructure searching are, as I shall show, directly transferable to text searches.

The principle is simple; it considers two factors implicit in the hyperbolic distributions which are commonly encountered in bibliographic systems, variety and variant frequencies. The strategy involves the differential description of characteristics so that those which are frequent are described in detail, while those which are infrequent are described in general terms. It thus stands in contrast to certain traditional applications of information theory, in which, for economy in transmission or storage of information, symbols or groups of symbols which are frequent are described by the least number of bits, while those which are least frequent are described by greater numbers of bits.

The principal result of the differential description of characteristics is that the variety of the search representations is kept relatively low, while the problem of variant frequencies is largely overcome.

The method is not in itself new; in a qualitative sense it has been used in the design of fragmentation codes in chemical documentation as well as for certain specialised language codes such as shorthand and Braille. At a more intuitive level it is implicit in the design of indexing languages and probably in most aspects of communication. As we have articulated it, however, it has lead to an extension of coding practice, and to a more substantive basis for substring retrieval. In general, our approach represents a departure from methods of retrieval which reflect traditional human activities in the adoption of one more appropriate to computer-oriented activities. In addition, it has enabled us to devise a novel method for the organisation of search files for archival data-bases which offers considerable advantages over those previously employed. As I shall show, this method of file-organisation flows directly from the basic theoretical considerations. It allows us to contemplate a simplifying and unifying conceptual basis for the organisation of retrieval systems, in which varied data types can be accommodated with great flexibility. Furthermore, it provides systems operators with a number of parameters on the basis of which their search systems can be tuned to the level of performance appropriate to their particular needs.

Hyperbolic distributions are a natural phenomenon in information systems[1]. Natural language itself exhibits them in two respects, both in the distribution of words and of symbols in the text[2]. In bibliographies, Bradford[3] demonstrated that periodicals involving papers relevant to particular topics could be divided into groups yielding equal numbers of papers, the number of periodicals in each group forming harmonic series. Similar distributions have been noted for the use of subject headings[4].

We saw the question of data-base characteristics as being the dominant factor in providing for economic searches of large data-bases of several million structures, since the distribution of chemical elements in these collections is extreme in its variation. However, other factors taken into account include profile characteristics, the degree of statistical association between fragments (and its effect on search performance), as well as simplicity of query encoding, and simplicity and compactness of software. I would emphasise, however, that our objective has been the development and evaluation of a general methodology for the design of screening systems, which can be applied, as appropriate, to collections differing in size and composition, rather than specification of any single set of characteristics. In this respect, it seemed essential to select discrete numbers of structural characteristics, with more or less equal probabilities of being used in screen searches. This set of structural keys would be equally applicable in serial bit screens, or in direct access files.

CHEMICAL STRUCTURE DATA-BASES

Considering first the distribution of elements in a sample file of structures - we have used a random sample of almost 30,000 structures from the Chemical Abstracts Registry System - we see that for the 68 elements identified in the file, the distribution is such that it varies from the incidence of carbon atoms in 99.7% of structures in the file, to nine elements, each of which occurs once only[5]. A log-log plot of the incidence of the elements is shown in Figure 1. The variety of elements is thus 68, while the frequency of incidence ranges over four orders of magnitude for this file.

In order to characterise this distribution further, we have selected three primary foci for fragments, the atom, the bond and the ring. Fragment types centred on each of these in turn have been studied systematically, both in the sample file - Regmaster - and in the Common Data Base. Each fragment type is produced by considering a uniformly defined part of the immediate environment of each occurrence of the focus, atom, bond or ring. Thus, in the case of atom-centred fragments, we have the progression:-

Fragment type:	Atom	Coordinated atom	Bonded atom	Augmented atom
Example:	C	C4	—C—	C—C—Cl with C above and C below

In the sample file, the variety of fragment types increases from 68 for elements, to 136 for coordinated atoms, 313 for bonded atoms, and then suddenly to 2331 for augmented atoms. Of these 2331 augmented atom types, 960 each occurred in a single structure only (Figure 1). Decrease in frequency goes hand in hand with increase in variety; the most frequent coordinated

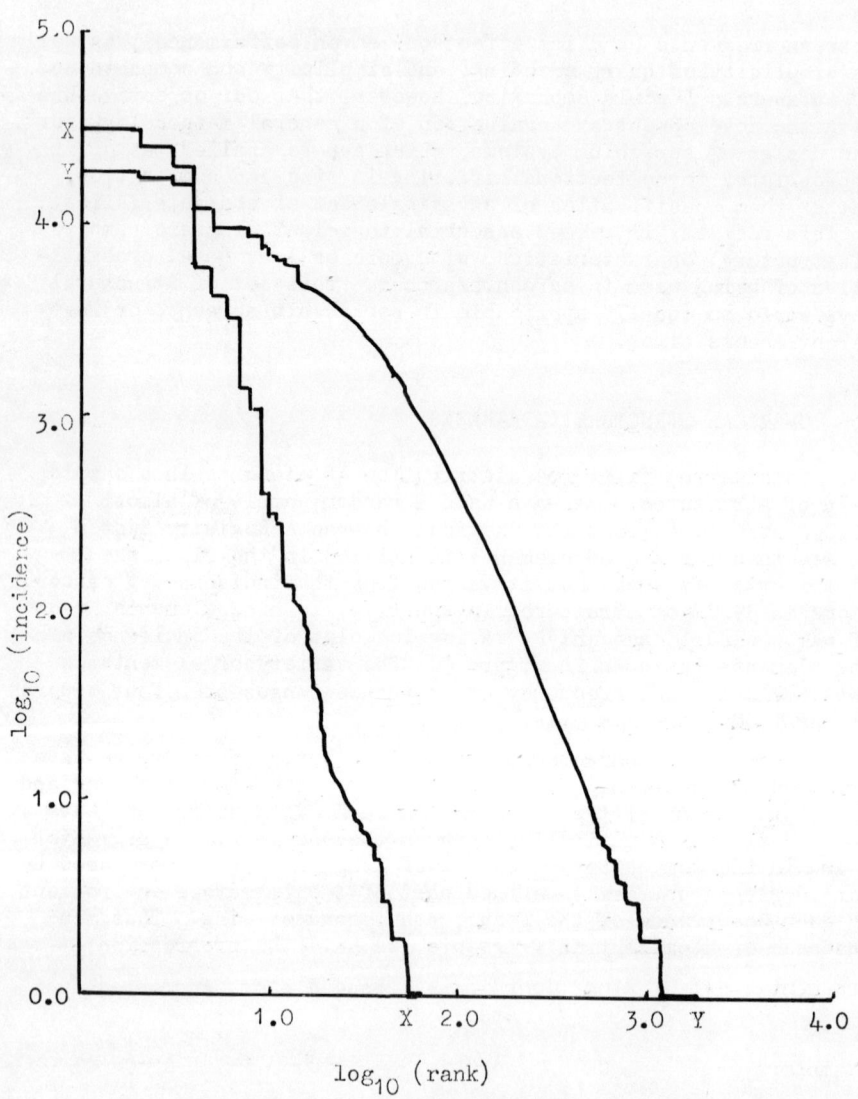

Figure 1. Graphs of $\log_{10}$ (incidence) against $\log_{10}$ (rank) for atoms (curve XX) and augmented atoms (curve YY).

atom occurs in 96% of compounds, while the figures for bonded atoms and augmented atoms are 62% and 61% respectively. In each case the fragment type derives from the doubly-connected carbon of aromatic rings[6].

In the case of the bond-centred fragment types, the progression is as follows:

Fragment type:	Bond	Simple pair	Augmented pair	Bonded pair	Octuplet
Example:	—	C—C	2C—C1	$\geq$C—C=	$\geq$C—C—C

The variety of the bond-centred fragments increases more evenly through the series; the number of simple pair types was found to be 393, that of augmented pairs 841, and bonded pairs 1731. The decrease in frequencies is greater than with the atom-centred fragments. The most frequent in each case have incidences of 63%, 62% and 57% respectively. The octuplets (so-called because atoms with coordinations of 5 or greater are treated separately) are a special case, in that the variety is reduced both by considering only carbon atoms and other elements and by neglecting bond types; the variety is small, totalling 204 in this file.

Analysis of ring-centred fragments was carried out next[7], using a simple algorithm which, although it includes only monocycles and 1:1- and 1:2-fused cyclic systems, deals with over 95% of the 42,000 ring systems identified. Of these simple rings, the great majority, or over 63%, consisted of 6-membered carbocyclic rings; the next most frequent, 6-membered rings with a simple nitrogen atom, were less than 10% of the latter. Other simple ring types, expressed in terms of their ring molecular formula, exhibited the usual frequency distribution. A more detailed analysis of 6-membered carbocyclic simple rings was carried out, treating the ring as a focus in the same manner as with augmented atoms[8]. Without going into detail, the distributions encountered at each of the subsequent levels further illustrated the basic point.

The choice of fragment types for study as screens thus lay largely between atom-centred and bond-centred fragments, with the addition in each case of ring-type screens. Atom-centred fragments were in use in the prototype substructure screening system of Chemical Abstracts Service, and are implicit in certain of the GREMAS screens. It was, therefore, at least of interest to study bond-centred fragments. However, additional arguments can be adduced in their favour, not least because they form a natural hierarchy in the even progression from the simple pair to the bonded pair, and on to the octuplet. Two substantial advantages arise, the first that they facilitate the selection of a series of levels of detail at which characteristics of differing frequency can be described, the second that they simplify the process of query encoding. Neither of these is the case with atom-centred fragments.

These factors are also related to the question of the design of simple software in which the decisions as to level of description are implemented. Thus at the simple pair level, the eighteen most common pairs of atoms, with various bond types, are accommodated. This procedure reduces the variety of simple pairs treated at this level from 393 to 60. At the augmented pair level, two-dimensional tables which are implicit in the software, operate on the carbon-carbon, carbon-oxygen and carbon-nitrogen simple pairs shown in Table 1 and produce the augmented pair screen set. These number 175 as against a total

				Bond symbols
C—C	C—O	C—N	—	single acyclic
C=C & C:C	C=O	C=N & C:N	=	double "
C*C	C•O	C*N	•	single cyclic
C≡C & C:C		C≡N & C:N	:	double cyclic
C•C		C•N	*	'aromatic'

Table 1. Augmented pair types included in bit string.

variety of 841. A yet more restricted set of carbon-carbon, carbon-oxygen and carbon-nitrogen simple pairs (shown in Table 2) is used to select the bonded pairs, reducing the variety from

C—C	C—O	C—N
C=C	C=O	
C•C	C•O	C•N
C:C		
C*C		C*N

Table 2. The pairs represented as bonded pairs.

1733 to 300. A special feature of the program is that when a fragment is identified at a high level of specificity, the appropriate bits are set at each lower level as well. This has proved to be valuable in providing for easy query coding. To provide a yardstick for efficiency, screen generation, including pair types, ring analysis, atom-counts and certain other characteristics requires a program which occupies 9.3 K 24-bit words of core storage. Screen records are produced at the rate of 14 per CPU second, and stored on magnetic tape for search.[9]

We had based the selection of the most frequent of each of these types as screens on the assumption that, in general terms, the characteristics of search requests would mirror the characteristics of the file. We have recently substantiated this by an analysis of substructure queries provided by the Oxford Experimental Information Unit. The queries were analysed in terms of each of the bond-centred fragment types - not necessarily those we chose for the screen set. Comparison of the top-ranking fragments in queries and data-base showed close correlations at each level of description[10].

Before discussing the evaluation of this screen set, it is appropriate to describe one of the factors which can affect screen fragment performance both positively and negatively. This is the degree of dependence between the incidence of fragments, which, in addition, complicates attempts at predicting the performance of screens based solely on incidences. Using the sample file, association coefficients have been calculated between the 15 most frequently occurring elements, and each of the 20 most frequent simple pairs, bonded pairs and augmented atoms, as also between the last two types[11]. Statistical associations between pairs of fragments have been determined using Kendal's coefficient V, the value of which lies between -1 and +1. Values between -0·02 and +0·02 are not significant. If the value equals -1, then no structure which contains one fragment contains the other. The reverse holds for positive associations, i.e., for a positive association equal to +1 between two fragments, all structures containing the one fragment also contain the other.

Both positive and negative associations are found, the range of values encountered increasing as the size of the fragments considered increases. The associations between atoms is small, 99% of the values lying between -0·10 to +0·10. Between simple pairs, the values ranged from -0·15 to +0·63, the latter in the case of the pairs S=O and C-S. On the basis of incidence alone, with fragment independence, these two pairs would be expected to co-occur in 258 compounds; in fact, they actually occur together in 1810 compounds.

With bonded pairs, the values are greater still; the highest positive value, 0·91, is found for the combination *Ċ*Ċ* and *C*Ċ*; the explanation for this is obvious because of the large potential and actual overlap between these fragments. Associations of similar magnitude were determined also between bonded pairs and augmented atoms, e.g., *C*C* and C*C*C, also with a value of 0.91.

The implication of these findings for the design of screening systems are that certain of the values, especially on the positive side, are large enough to have significant effects on the performance of combinations of screens. Thus in the case of the last combination above, used in a description of a query substructure containing *C*C*C, the bonded pair *C*C*, used alone, would cause 12,374 compounds out of 28,831 file structures to be screened out. The augmented atom C*C*C would eliminate 11,182 structures. The combination of the two (by intersection) would result in 12,393 being eliminated, i.e., an increase of only 19 structures, or less than 0.1%. This instance, however, is the worst possible case, and clearly, where negative associations exist between fragments, considerable enhancement of performance would occur. The findings do imply, however, that when larger fragments than those considered here are introduced, the benefits may be less than expected.

We have now carried out an evaluation of the screen-set which consists primarily of the bond-centred fragments (simple, augmented and bonded pairs) detailed already, with the addition of descriptions of monocycles and 1:1- and 1:2-fused rings, in terms both of ring-size and ring molecular formulae, as well as certain details of atom and bond requirements. The evaluation has thus far been confined to the determination of screen-out levels. Precision ratios will shortly be available.

108 substructure queries from an operational service at Oxford were used. Query encoding is simple; the system requires that the user analyse the query and decide on its minimum requirements. These are then expressed as structural fragments, but the user need not know at what level of description the system represents the fragment. The user simply chooses the level of description which best fits the demands of the query, and the program matches the fragments chosen with those available in the screen-set. In particular, the availability of the simple and augmented pairs simplifies search profile preparation by reducing the need for taking the union of many related fragments, yet without sacrificing the high screen-out obtainable with more specific fragments. The logic available is Boolean, accommodating the intersection or negation of a number of parameters, each of which may contain alternatives.

Using these 108 queries, the average value of the screen-out was determined to be 98.4%, with an average search time per

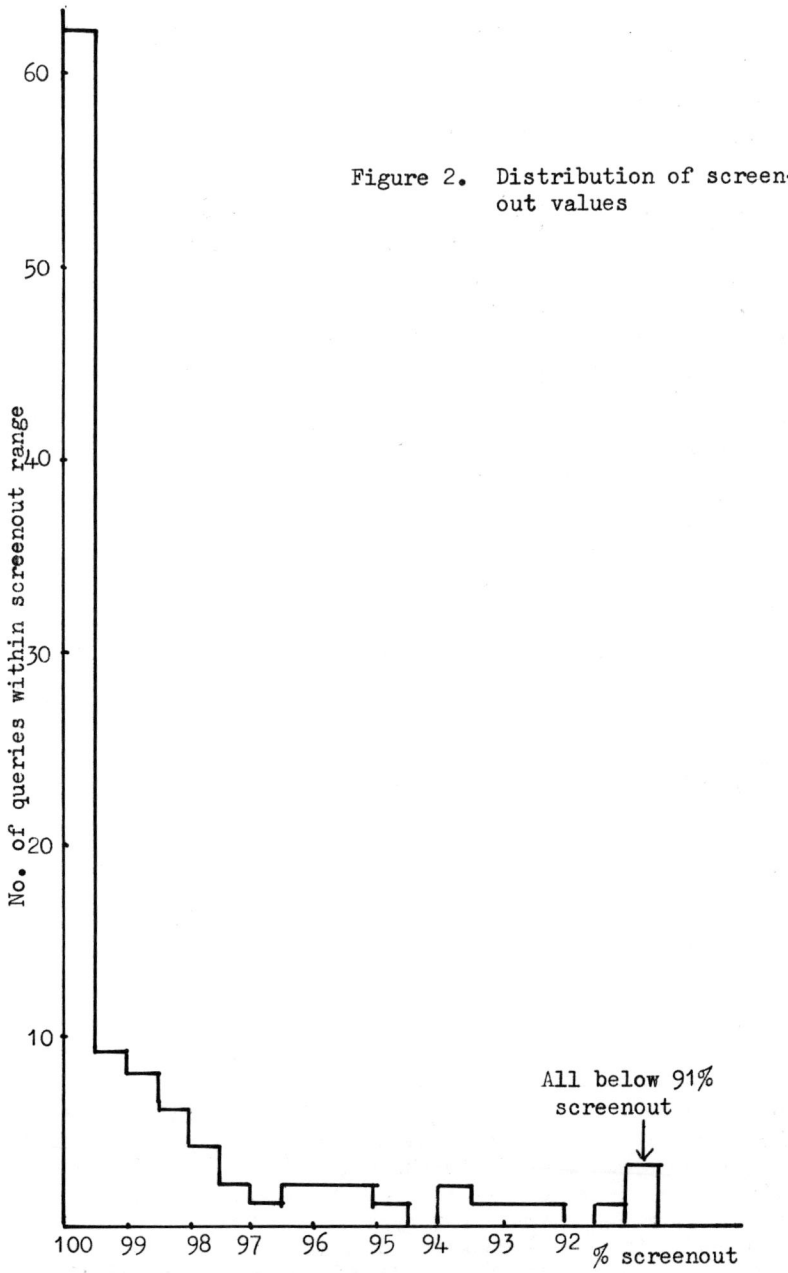

Figure 2. Distribution of screen-out values

query of 28 seconds of CPU time for the 28,963 structures. The results show a highly skewed distribution, as shown in Figure 2. Over 55% of the queries show screen-out in the range 99·5 to 100%, while only 3% of the queries showed values lower than 91%. Table 3 shows a breakdown of query types, with average screen-out values for each group.

Query Type	Number of queries	Percentage of queries	Average screen-out %
(1) Acyclic	20	18·5	98·9
(2) Cyclic	38	35·1	98·1
(3) Cyclic + acyclic	44	40·7	99·1
(4) Acyclic + unspecified component	2	1·8	95·6
(5) Cyclic + unspecified component	1	0·9	98·5
(6) Unspecified	3	2·7	90·2
(7) Cyclic + acyclic + unspecified	0	0	—
TOTAL	108	100	98·42

Table 3. Analysis of query types.

We are now engaged in an assessment of the performance of atom-centred fragments, as compared with the bond-centred fragments detailed here. In addition, we are assessing the value of adding further screen types, including the octuplets and certain linear chains of atoms, and will shortly report on these, together with precision values. Our objective, as before is to assess the relative advantages of the various options which operators of such systems may need to consider to tailor a system to particular requirements.

CHEMICAL REACTION DATA-BASE

At this point it is logical to consider the application of analogous thinking to text search procedures, but I first want to mention our work on the retrieval of chemical reactions. Our objective here has been to try to utilize available data-bases which are a by-product of the preparation of publications, and to enable searches by reaction type, reactants or products to be performed. This has proved to be a refractory area thus far, and I shall only try to highlight the problems; perhaps the most significant of these is that of great variety and variation in frequency of reaction types in the data-base.

The data-base has been compiled by scanning 10 months' issues of Current Abstracts of Chemistry - Index Chemicus and including those reactions for which Index Chemicus Registry System compound numbers are provided both for product and reactant molecules. These are recorded to enable us to identify the structures as Wiswesser notations from the ICRS files.

Our approach has been to compare the records of reactant and product molecules and to isolate those parts of the molecules which undergo change. In the first instance, we convert the WLN's to connection table records, and analyse these by generating small structural fragments; we compare the lists of these from each, and rebuild using fragments which are present on one side and absent on the other, or present in unequal numbers on each side[12]. The rebuilding process is intended to provide a summary of reaction changes. In the second instance we analyse the WLN symbols and determine changes in the symbols on each side, which, with subsequent checks, provide a representation of certain changes[13].

The second approach has proved easier to evaluate thus far, and we have shown that it provides characterisations of approximately 40% of reaction types in the data-base, with good recall and precision. The reaction types dealt with include functional group interconversions, hydrogenations and dehydrogenations, and ring-closures and ring-cleavages. However, extensions to deal with a significantly higher proportion of the data-base appears problematic at present.

The first approach, using connection table records to produce a characterisation, is still under development. One problem is the difficulty of assessing when an automatically-produced reaction scheme is a reasonable representation of the actuality; related to this is the question of determining the extent to which description of the environment of the reaction site is necessary.

Part of the overall problem, however, is the distribution of reaction types in the data-base, which is once again hyperbolic. This is demonstrated by the curve of Figure 3, which shows the distribution of functional group interconversions in a portion of the CAC-IC data-base.

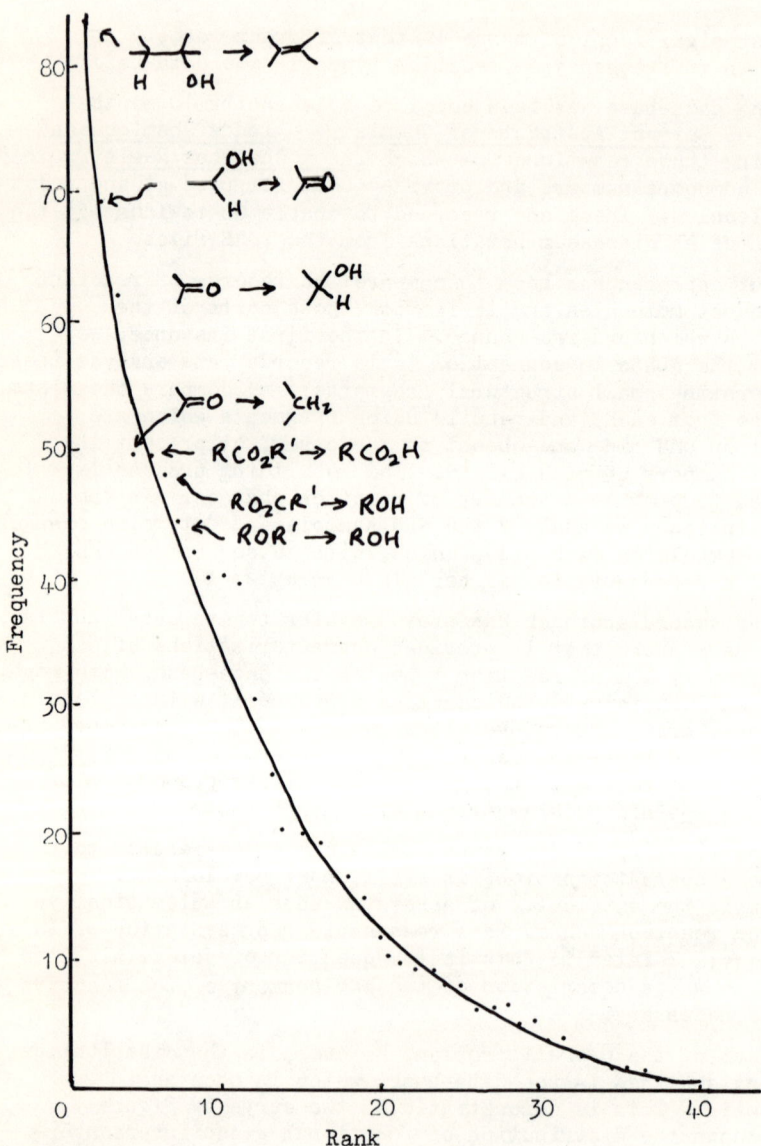

Figure 3. Rank-frequency distribution of functional interchange reactions.

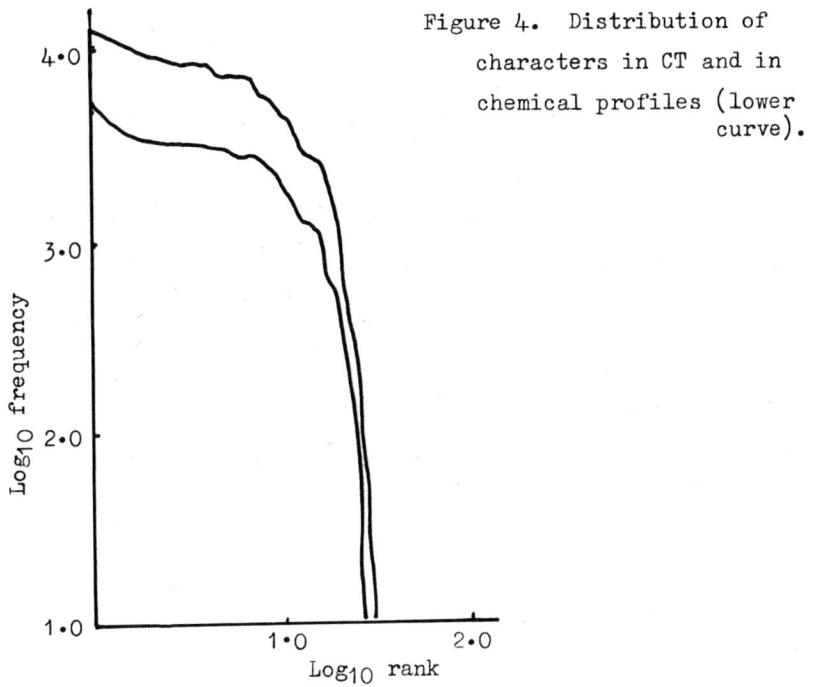

Figure 4. Distribution of characters in CT and in chemical profiles (lower curve).

TEXTUAL DATA-BASES IN CHEMISTRY

The question we posed in regard to text-search procedures was essentially similar to the approach to the selection of an optimal screen set. We assumed that here too there would be a close correlation between the micro-structure of profile terms and that of the data-base in which they were sought. Figure 4 demonstrates this point, showing the distributions of alphabetic characters in 100,000 characters from title data elements in <u>Chemical Titles</u>, and from almost 40,000 characters from profile terms used in searches of chemical data-bases at UKCIS. Table 4 shows the rankings for the same characters. Taking the

Data-base: ▽ E I O N T A R S C L D M F H U P Y G B V X W Z K Q J
Profile
   terms: ▽ E I O A R N T L C S M P D H U Y G B F X V Z K Q W J

Table 4. Ranking of characters in <u>CT</u> and in chemical profiles.

character J, for instance, which occurs 26 times in 100,000 title characters, and 10 times in the profile terms, we reckoned that if the presence of J in a title were indicated, the great majority of titles could be eliminated. This would be valuable at most in 10 profile terms, however.

We then applied the same strategy used with the structural descriptions to text. This is a much simpler case, since text is a linear string, and searches for substrings, as in currently used profiles, do not contain generalised characters. We therefore analysed the text of <u>Chemical Titles</u> and generated from it sets of more or less equifrequent character strings. These are, of necessity, variable length strings. An easy way to visualise the process is to think of taking a window <u>n</u> characters long, moving this window along the text a character at a time, and recording the pattern of characters in each window. For each length, say 1 to 10, the <u>n</u>-grams are ranked and listed with their frequencies, as shown in Table 5. The

CHEMICAL TITLES

CHAR.		DIGRAM		TRIGRAM		TETRAGR.		PENTAGR.	
␣	12,793	IN	1578	OF␣	1177	␣OF␣	1067	TION␣	593
E	7,440	E␣	1578	␣OF	1177	TION	843	ATION	497
I	6902	TI	1529	ION	910	ION␣	640	␣AND␣	446
O	6659	ON	1526	ON␣	843	ATIO	497	ION␣O	371
T	5882	N␣	1514	TIO	805	AND␣	453	N␣OF␣	369
A	5769	␣O	1496	ATI	595	␣AND	447	ON␣OF	363
N	5738	␣A	1441	␣AN	582	␣THE	421	S␣OF␣	336

etc.

Table 5. Frequency-ranked <u>n</u>-grams from <u>Chemical Titles</u>.

characters comprise the initial symbol set, with a hyperbolic distribution. We now extend the set of symbols by adding the most frequent digrams. As this process continues, the frequencies attributable to the most frequent single characters are reduced. The process is continued by considering a threshold frequency. When the frequency of the digram next in line for inclusion falls below that of the most frequent trigram, that is included, and so on.

The result of this process is a set of variable-length character strings, with more or less equivalent frequencies in text. We term these key-sets. Another way of looking at them is as <u>variety-generators</u>, in the sense that any text can be produced either from a basic symbol set, or alphabet, or from a word-dictionary. Both of these, however, have hyperbolic distributions, and the dictionary, especially, very high variety. The key-sets, however, are limited in variety and approximately equivalent in frequency. They can thus be employed to provide representations of text such that each key has an equal probability of use in search. Moreover, the size of the key-sets can be adjusted readily to any desired level[14]. I have described a manual method of generating a key-set; in fact we have developed and used several algorithms for key-set generation from suitable text samples[15]. The size of the key-set is determined by varying a frequency limit. Table 6 shows a key-set generated automatically from <u>Chemical Titles</u>, which consists of 256 keys including all the basic symbols occurring in the text, while Figure 5 shows the constitutions of four key-sets from titles in the INSPEC data-base, in terms of the numbers of each size of <u>n</u>-grams.

CT KEY-SET - 256 KEYS

n =					
9	ATION∇OF∇				
8	∇ON∇THE∇		TION∇OF∇		
7	ION∇OF∇		OF∇THE∇		
6	ATION∇	F∇THE∇	ON∇OF∇		
5	∇AND∇	∇THE∇	N∇OF∇	N∇THE	
	S∇OF∇	TION∇			
4	∇IN∇	∇OF∇	∇PRO	AND∇	INE∇
	ING∇	ION∇	S∇IN∇	THE∇	TION
3	∇AC	∇CA	∇CH	∇CO	∇DE	∇DI
	etc.	(TOTAL= 49)				
2	∇A	∇B	∇C	∇E	etc.	
	(TOTAL =136)					
1	47 characters					

Table 6. Key-set of size 256 from <u>Chemical Titles</u>.

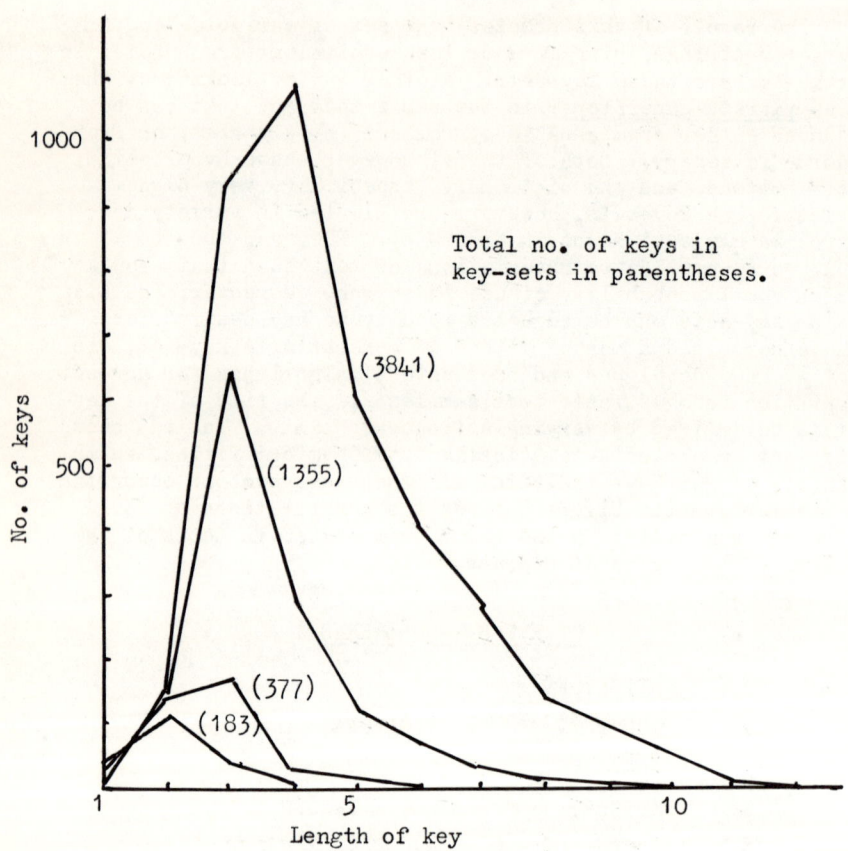

Figure 5. Distribution of <u>n</u>-grams in key-sets from INSPEC titles.

One purpose for which the key-sets can be applied is for the compression of text for storage or transmission[16]. I will not elaborate on this, but rather on their use for retrieval. In essence the key-sets characterise a body of text, and may be used to represent it in a form suitable for the identification of text substrings. Methods employed until now in inverted file systems for text employ words as keys, although substrings of words may also be required, as when left-hand or right-hand truncations are used. Word-based methods incur the same disadvantages in that the lists of document numbers are hyperbolic. The dictionaries are large, and many of the words occur once only. Schipma has cogently described the dimensions of the problem, noting that searches of a year's issues of <u>CA Condensates</u> requires a dictionary of no less than 220,000 word types17. Creation of search files necessitates major sorting procedures, and storage of large dictionaries for search purposes.

The use of key-sets or variety generators is a tempting prospect. Their use corresponds to a mapping from a hyperbolic distribution onto one which is virtually rectangular, because of the equiprobability of the strings. This feature suggested a novel form of file organisation, in which the number of keys and the mapping of document identifications is related to the basic geometry of disc storage devices.

We first represent the texts of document titles in terms of the key-set. This involves examination of the titles, and mapping the strings beginning with each character in turn onto the longest available key, as shown below:-

```
        TERPENE BIOSYNTHESIS
    ∇TE   ENE∇   IO    THE    S∇
    TER   NE∇    OS    HE
    ER    E∇     SY    ESIS
    R     ∇B     YN    SIS∇
    PE    BI     NTH   IS∇
```

We construct a binary matrix, in which the rows correspond to the keys, and the columns to document numbers. A document containing a specific key will have a 1 at the corresponding key position.

We choose the number of keys so as to equal or be a small multiple of the number of blocks on a cylinder. In this case, using a 30 megabyte disc with 296 blocks per cylinder, we chose a key-set of 592 keys, some of which are shown above. As the documents are analysed serially, the binary matrix is built up on the disc cylinders, so that search file creation is now a rapid serial process, proportional only to the number of documents to be stored.

The search procedure is immediately obvious. We analyse the profile term in exactly the same way:-

OLEFIN

OLE

LE

EF

FI

IN (union of several keys)

The binary vectors corresponding to the keys are read from the cylinder, the intersection or union of these found, and candidate hits read out. Two examples are shown below, the first correct, the second a miss, since although it contains the necessary strings, they are in the wrong relation to one another.

1). ZIEGLER POLYMERIZATION OF OLEFINS

2). CALCULATION OF COEFFICIENTS OF MOLECULAR DIFFUSION IN A MULTICOMPONENT LIQUID MIXTURE

Since the process is probabilistic, this is bound to happen. The average ratio of hits to misses, however, is entirely under the system operator's control, depending primarily on the size of the key-set employed.

In a preliminary test on Chemical Titles, creation of the search file for 3072 documents took 180 CPU seconds. Search of 200 profile terms from UKCIS profiles took 16 CPU seconds. Figure 6 shows a histogram of the profile terms and their performance, and Table 7 shows the relation between the length of terms and their performance. Clearly, the shorter the term the fewer the keys, and the greater the probability that the strings will not be present in the desired relationship. It must be noted that some of the terms (a selection of which are shown in Table 8) Have been artificially shortened to suit the characteristics of the earlier UKCIS serial search system. The overall systems precision for search terms, measured as the average of individual figures for the ratio of hits to false drops was 58.4%; the gross average, i.e., the ratio of hits to false drops, was 55%. A serial string search was used to confirm that no recall failures occurred.

The fact that as term length increases, 100% systems precision and recall are obtained, means that we can predict term performance. For those which score less than 100% systems precision, a string search in display file to confirm the presence of the desired term may be necessary, but if this is

Textual Data-bases in Chemistry

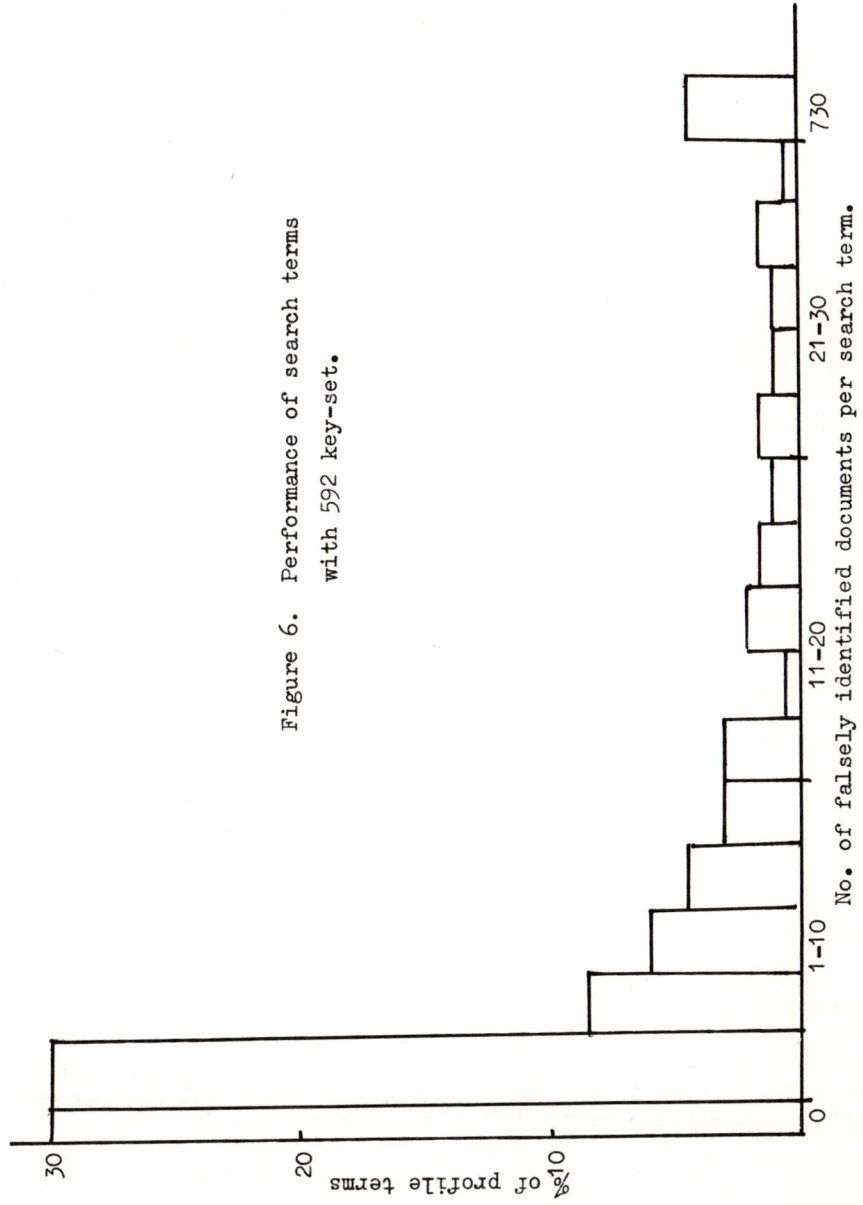

Figure 6. Performance of search terms with 592 key-set.

Length of term in characters	Number of terms	Average number of false drops
3	1	49
4	6	46·5
5	25	24·0
6	26	5·8
7	26	5·8
8	21	2·6
9	29	2·6
10	16	0·5
11	14	1·7
12	9	1·3
13	10	1·8
14	6	0·3
15	5	1·2
16	3	1·6
17	1	0
18	2	1

Table 7. Variation of the average number of false drops with term length.

ALKALI MET*	*CLEROD*	*LAR WEIGHT
ANILIN	*DEPOS*	*MELLEIN*
BIOGEN*	EP	*MYCIN*
CARBOXYLAT	*FURANO*	POTENTIAL ENERGY
CEPHAM	HELICES	*SOME*

Table 8. Examples of chemical profile terms.

applied after profile logic is used, the number of documents requiring string search may be reduced significantly.

Performance thus comes very much within the control of the system operator. By increasing key-set size, systems precision can be increased. When key-set size is increased, the size of the matrix, if stored explicitly, also increases. At the same time, the density of the matrix, i.e., the ratio of 1-bits to 0-bits, decreases, and the bit vectors become sparse. The possibility therefore exists of compressing these, for instance, by use of run-length coding, thus avoiding undue expansion of the search file.

The significance of this method, especially for on-line use, is that head-movement over the file during search is reduced to an absolute minimum, and head-movement is one of the dominant factors determining response time. In fact, a complete search of a device dedicated to a search file can be made by a single traverse of the disc cylinders.

This holds two inviting prospects. The first is that it may well prove possible to create and to search large files by mini-computer in a multi-user environment, thus scaling down the hardware requirements and costs by possibly an order of magnitude. Nor should we forget possible simple developments in hardware which would make this approach yet more attractive, including perhaps such devices as the associative processor, to which, for instance, Meyer has referred.[19]

The second prospect is that the approach provides a unifying framework for integrated structure-text searches, such as are required to make the large resources of chemical information readily and widely available. At present the approach is generally to have separate structure and text files, to search one first, using the output of the first search as parameters in the second. If, however, we think of the structures associated with a particular document as sub-documents, we can store them, using the file-organisation I have described, or one closely related to it. Access to structures is by screen keys, access to text by character-string keys, but the same simple software for file generation and search can be employed for each.

A simple extension of this would also deal with searches for reactions, in the sense that a specially designed set of screens, oriented towards reactive groups, would be used twice within a key-set, once for reactant molecules, and again for product molecules. This method would also overcome the problem mentioned earlier, that of the great variety of reaction types, and the difficulty of devising an accurate representation of each type.

The variety generator method, in summary, appears to promise substantial advantages in the representation and search of a variety of records of chemical information. Not least, it is an exciting area to be working in, and I hope that you have shared some of this excitement today.

I wish to record my indebtedness to present and past members of the Research Group, in particular to George Adamson, Ian Barton, Judy Bush, Sue Creasey, Bob Clinging, Alice McLure, Howard Petrie, Janet Radcliffe and Mike Snell for their endeavours in this work. We also gratefully acknowledge continuing support, in a number of projects, from the Office for Scientific and Technical Information, and thank Chemical Abstracts Service, UKCIS, ISI, and the Oxford E.I.U. for data-bases and queries.

References

1. R.A. Fairthorne, J. Doc., 25, 319-343 (1969).
2. C.K. Zipf, Human behaviour and the principle of least effort, Cambridge, Mass., Addison-Wesley, 1949.
3. S.C. Bradford, Documentation, London, Crosby Lockwood, 1948.
4. N. Houston and E. Wall, Am. Doc., 15, 109 (1964).
5. J.E. Crowe, M.F. Lynch and W.G. Town, J. Chem. Soc., (C), 1970, 990-6.
6. G.W. Adamson, M.F. Lynch and W.G. Town, ibid., 1971, 3702-6.
7. G.W. Adamson, J. Cowell, M.F. Lynch, W.G. Town and A.M. Yapp, J. Chem. Soc., (Perkin 1), 1973, 863-5.
8. G.W. Adamson, S.E. Creasey, J.P. Eakins and M.F. Lynch, ibid., (in press).
9. G.W. Adamson, J. Cowell, M.F. Lynch, A.H.W. McLure, W.G. Town and A.M. Yapp, Strategic considerations in the design of a screening system for substructure searches of chemical structure files, J. Chem. Doc., (in press).
10. G.W. Adamson, V.A. Clinch and M.F. Lynch, Relationship between query and data-base microstructure in general substructure search systems (in preparation).
11. G.W. Adamson, D.R. Lambourne and M.F. Lynch, J. Chem. Soc., (Perkin 1), 1972, 2428-33.
12. J.M. Harrison and M.F. Lynch, J. Chem. Soc., (C), 1970, 2082-7.
13. R. Clinging and M.F. Lynch, Production of printed indexes of chemical reactions, Part I, Analysis of functional group interconversions, J. Chem. Doc., (in press).
14. A.C. Clare, E.M. Cook and M.F. Lynch, Computer J., 15, 259-62 (1972).
15. M.F. Lynch, J.H. Petrie and M.J. Snell, Analysis of the microstructure of titles in the INSPEC data-base, Inf. Stor. Retr., (in press).
16. I.J. Barton, M.F. Lynch, J.H. Petrie and M.J. Snell, Variable-length character string analyses of three data-bases and their application in data compression, Proc. INFORMATICS-1 Conf., University of Durham, April 11-13, 1973.

17. P.B. Schipman, Term fragment analysis for inversion of large files, IIT Research Institute Report, June 4, 1971.
18. I.J. Barton, S.C. Creasey, M.F. Lynch and M.J. Snell, An information-theoretic approach to text searching (in preparation).
19. E. Meyer, Retrospektive Recherche und Informationsnetzwerke, Lecture on Course "Information und Dokumentation in der Chemie", Deidesheim, 18 Nov., 1971.

Interactive Graphic Chemical Structure Searching

by

Richard J. Feldmann

Division of Computer Research and Technology
National Institutes of Health
Bethesda, Maryland, U.S.A.

INTRODUCTION

The evolution of chemical structure representation and searching methods has followed quite closely the evolution of computer hardware and operating systems. The earliest structure search systems were either completely manual or used primitive mechanical sorting computers (1). As magnetic tape storage devices evolved search systems were implemented using these devices as the main structure storage medium (2,3). The chief characteristics of these magnetic tape based search systems are derived from the sequential accessibility of the tape on which the structures and related search screens are stored. As direct access storage devices evolved several systems were implemented so that classes of structures with the same structural features could be randomly accessed (4). Lynch (5) gives a summary of structure representation and searching methods thru 1970. Recent developments in computer operating systems and in graphic displays (6) have prompted the reformulation of chemical structure representation and earching concepts to take advantage of these computational possibilities. Computer operating systems have evolved to the point where a person working in a remote location can interact via a terminal with the computer over ordinary dial-up telephone lines. Heller (7) shows how interactive computing can be used to do mass spectrum search and retrieval. Graphic displays have evolved to the point where the communication between the person and the computer can be in completely graphical terms. The concepts for interactive graphical structure input have evolved from the work of Corey and Wipke (8). The concepts for computer generation of structure output have evolved from the work of Hyde (9) and Zimmerman (10). The graphical interaction between the user and a chemical structure search program makes it possible, all in real time, to formulate structure queries, to do structure searches, and to review structure retrievals. The chemical structure search system presented in this chapter has these interactive and graphic features (11). The structure search system has been used for over 500 hours by workers at the Stanford Research Institute in California. Communication to the DCRT PDP-10 computer in Bethesda, Maryland is over dial-up telephone lines and all structure input, search and structure reviews are conducted with the terminal and computer being separated by almost 3000 miles.

INTERACTIVE STRUCTURE INPUT

The user of the chemical structure search system interacts with the program by giving a series of commands (12). Commands are separated roughly into two classes, structure input commands and structure search and retrieval commands. Structure input can be initiated by generating either a ring or a chain. When the RING command is given the connection table for a six member ring is generated. The connection table is then spatialized in two

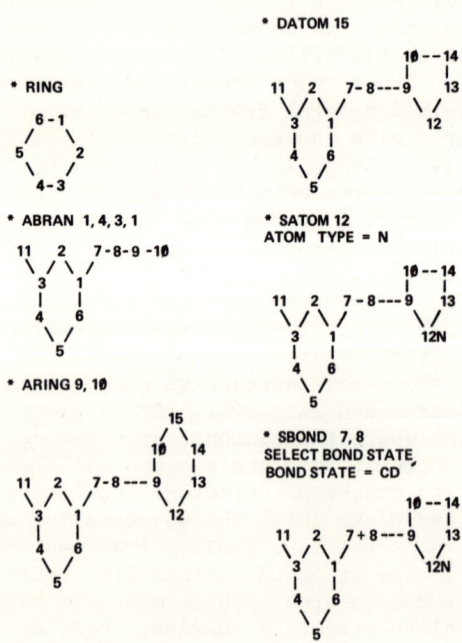

Figure 1.   Sample Interactive Structure Input

dimensions. Figure 1 shows the result of the specification of six structure input commands. Structure input commands can require several arguments. The ABRAN command requires two arguments. The first argument specifies the node number to which the branch is to be added while the second argument specifies the number of nodes to be added. The node numbers are not in the least canonical in the IUPAC sense. The node numbers are the mechanism by which the user points to a particular node. Several instances of a command can be given in the same command string. In figure 1 the ABRAN command adds a branch to node 1 as well as a branch to node 3. A ring can be added to the structure by giving the command ARING followed by two arguments which specify the nodes to which the ring is to be attached. A six member ring is generated when the RING and RING commands are given because a six member ring is the most probable ring size to be used in structure query. If the user wants a five member ring a node can be deleted by giving the command DATOM. Notice that the form of the structure is constantly changing as the structure is specified. When a node is specified it is assumed to be a carbon atom unless otherwise specified by giving the command SATOM. In the same manner the exact nature of a bond can be specified by giving the command SBOND. In the structure figures the following symbol-bond relationships hold:

                Single Bond   / % | -
                Double Bond   +
                Triple Bond   #
                Tautomer Bond   %
                Resonant Bond   .

Figure 1 presents structures as they are seen on an ordinary character terminal. If the user has a graphics terminal the structure shown in figure 2 would be seen. The user tells the system what type of terminal is being used by giving the command OMNI (13). There are many other structure input commands which can be found in the user manual (12). The NUC command is however worth special mention. Clearly the user can build up a complicated ring nucleus by giving a series of ARING commands. After each command the structure must be redrawn so that the numbers associated with the newly added nodes can be known. The structure drawing takes time since the user is normally communicating with the computer over a telephone line which transmits only 30 characters per second. The ring nucleus generation process can be compressed by giving the command NUC followed by an argument which specifies a chain of rings and direction commands.

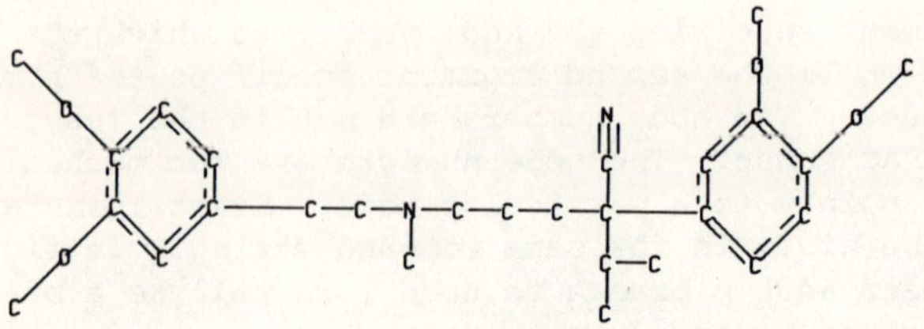

58   Interactive Graphic Substructure Searching

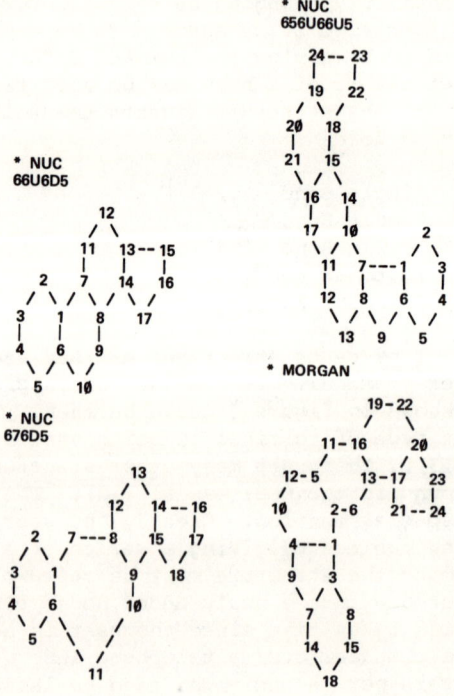

Figure 2. Structure as it Appears on a Graphics Terminal

Figure 3. Structures Generated by the NUC Command

As shown in figure 3 the NUC command 66U6D5 generates a steriod nucleus. A more complicated ring nucleus 656U66U5 can be renumbered by giving the command MORGAN which applies the Morgan algorithm (14) to the structure. This algorithm causes the structure numbering to radiate from the most central node. Note that the structure numbering affects the way that the structure is drawn. This is in a sense a "feature" of the structure spatialization routines. Figure 4 shows the manner in which the structure spatialization routines operate on a typical structure. The spatialization process starts at a ring nucleus whereupon each of the rings are positioned in turn. After the rings have been positioned, the branches are positioned.

Since there is no particular penalty attached to making mistakes users can learn the structure input commands in approximately 1/2 hour. As a part of the DCRT Chemical Information System scientists throughout the United States have in the past

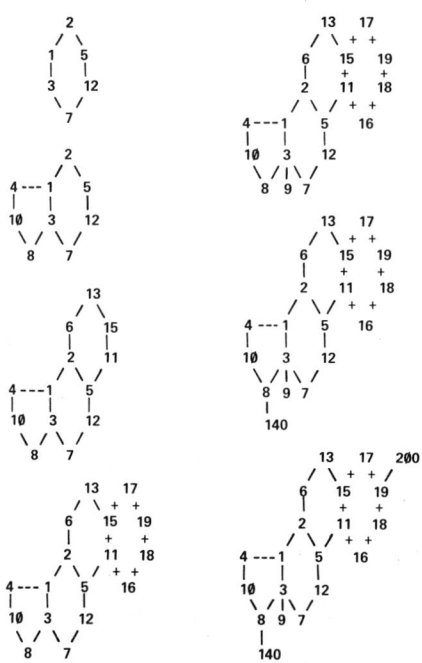

Figure 4. Spatialization of a Structure

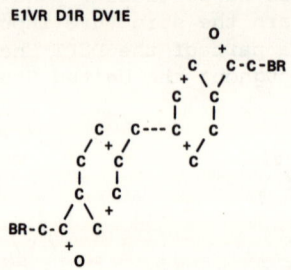

Figure 5. (a) Structure to WLN
(b) WLN to Structure

been able to experiment with the system in order to learn the commands. The structure input commands which are both interactive and graphic provide the mechanism for generating structures to be used for doing searches or other forms of structure related activity. Figure 5 illustrates how these structure commands can be harnessed to routines which do the coding and decoding of Wisswesser Line Notations (15) (16).

INTERACTIVE STRUCTURE SEARCHING

The interactive formulation of structure queries must be coupled to an interactive structure searching capability if the system is to be utilized in real time. If the structure searching takes more than a few seconds the user begins to lose interest. Rather than seeking ways to avoid wasting the users

Interactive Structure Searching   61

time, the goal is to maximize the interaction between the user
and the search process. There are several very simple ways to
maximize this interaction. The user is presented with information during a search which indicates how many structures are
being retrieved. If too many or too few structures are being
retrieved the user can give a command which terminates the search
Once a search has been made and an acceptable number of structures are retrieved the user can view several structures to see
if the retrieved structures really satisfy the query. If the
structure retrievals are not correct or there are too many or
too few retrievals the user can alter the structure used to make
the search and then make another search.

   As in the structure input, the structure search and
retrieval functions are implemented by a collection of commands.
The command REG will retrieve a particular structure. The
structure search system has developed around structure files
which are subsets of the CAS Structure Registry file (17).
There are presently about 2.2 million structures in the CAS
structure registry file. The identifier for a structure is its
universal CAS registry number. Figure 6 shows the retrieval of
CAS registry number 50033. The command REG can be used only
when the user knows the registry number. The command SSHOW
permits the user to browse through the results of a structure
search by drawing each structure in turn. In figure 7 the command SMOLF which does a Molecular Formula search is followed
by the command SSHOW. The search program waits for a user
response after each structure is drawn. If the user responds

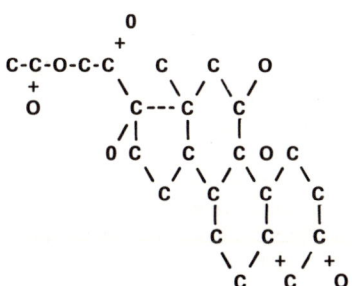

Figure 6. Registry Retrieval

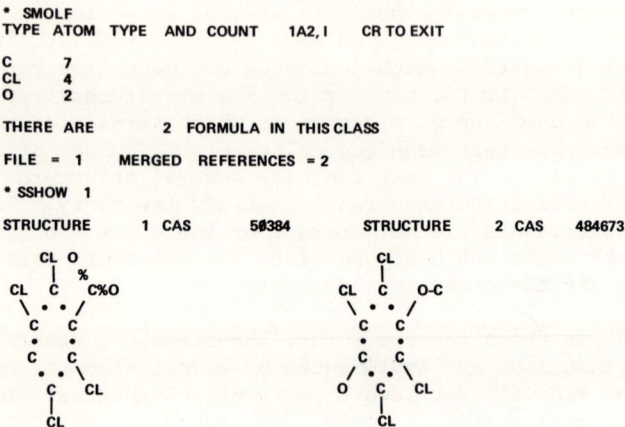

Figure 7. Molecular Formula Retrieval

with a carriage return the next structure is drawn but if the
user response is an E, then the program leaves the routine which
is sequentially drawing the search results. Figure 7 illustrates
the use of the temporary files. A temporary file is created
whenever a successful structure search occurs. The temporary
file contains a list of CAS registry numbers. The temporary
files can be manipulated by three commands. The command MERGE
will perform the logical OR on any number of temporary files.
The command INTER will perform the logical AND on any number of
teporary files. The command NOT will delete from the file named
in its first argument any registry numbers contained in the file
named in its second argument. By separating the structure search
from the logic of temporary file manipulation the user is given
the flexibility to combine search results in many different ways.

In addition to registry and molecular formula retrieval
the structure search system permits the user to retrieve structures based on the following broad structural properties:

        1 Weight Range
        2 Atom Count Range
        3 Atom Count Range by Atom Type
        4 Ring Count Range
        5 Ring Count Range by Ring Size

Interactive Structure Searching

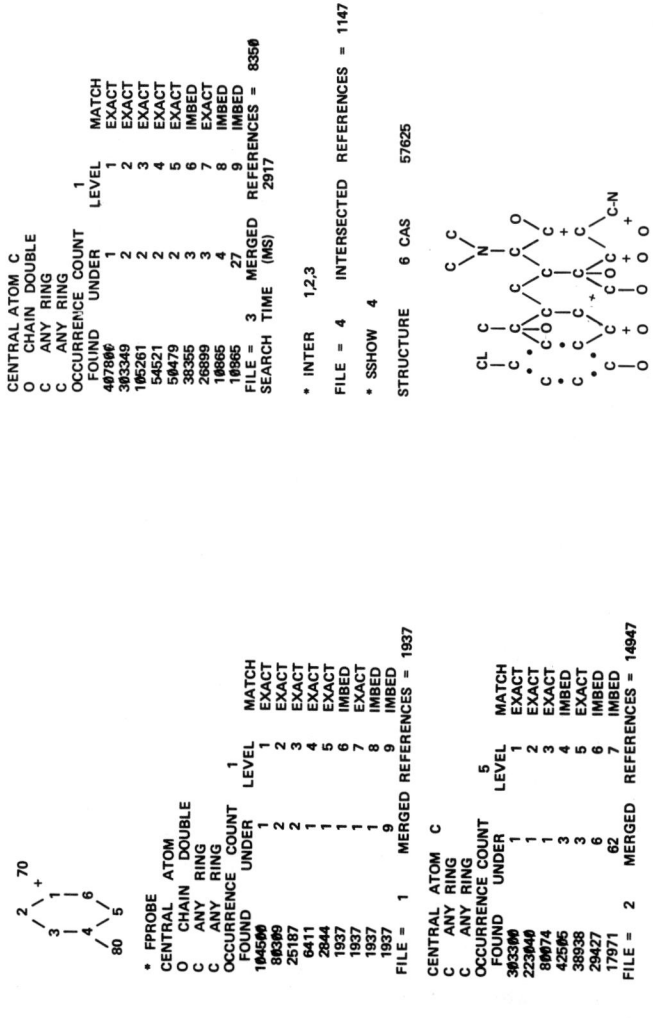

Figure 8. Nested Atom Centered Fragment Retrieval Query Structure and First Fragment Retrieval

For example, the command SMOLS can be used to retrieve all structures in the file which have between 3 and 5 six member rings.

While providing a part of the spectrum of search specificity the commands REG (retrieves a class with only one member), SMOLF (retrieves a class with normally fewer than 100 members) and SMOLS (can retrieve a class with a large portion of the entire file) do not search for structures using the input structure. The command FPROBE decomposes the input structure into atom centered fragments. The structure in figure 8 has three distinct atom centered fragments. The first fragment is a carbonyl. The information which is given to the user during the search indicates that in a file of 25,800 compounds there are 104,500 fragments such that the central atom has 3 neighbors. Of this number 80,309 fragments have a carbon as the central atom. Of this number 25,187 have an oxygen as first (least probable) neighbor. Of this number 6,411 have the oxygen atom bonded to the central carbon atom by a chain double bond. Since the bond between the central carbon atom and either of its ring carbon neighbors is not specified, the search will permit any bond type. The column headed by the word MATCH indicates whether the search will retrieve only one property (EXACT) or whether any available property (IMBED) will be retrieved. Finally all structures with at least one occurence of this structure fragment are retrieved. The result for this fragment is 1937 distinct registry numbers (temporary file 1). When a search is made for the second fragment, the two neighbor C-C-C fragment, the lack of bond specificity produces a broadening of the number of fragment nodes to be examined. At level 4 in this particular portion of the fragment tree there are three different bond types. Again at level 6 in the second fragment search, the lack of bond specificity broadens the search to six nodes. At level 7, where the minimum occurrence count is considered, the search broadens out to 62 nodes. The 17,971 fragments contain 14,947 distinct registry numbers (temporary file 2). The second fragment is a bad fragment because it produces too many results. The user can decide later not to include this fragment. The third fragment produces 8,350 structures (temporary file 3). The intersection of the three fragment results produces 1,147 structures (temporary file 4). Note that the search of the three fragments with the merger at the end of each fragment and the final intersection of the three fragment files took only 2.9 seconds of CPU time. The command SSS is then applied to the intersected file to extract only those structures which have the input structure imbedded (temporary file 5). This is the so-called sub-structure search function. Temporary file 5 which has at least 7 members is the result. CAS 57625 is one of the structures which has input structure imbedded in it. Note that the sub-structure search which was ended by the user took 21.5 seconds. The user has control over how much time is spent on this portion of the structure search. The fragment search command when used in conjunction with the INTER and SSS commands can yield a suitably small result class. The structure fragment used in this type of search is, however, quite small. The size of the structure fragment in relation to the size of an average CAS structure (an average structure has between 20 and 30 atoms) means that an average structure will produce a large number of atom centered fragments.

The trade-off between the size of a structure fragment and the number of occurrences of that fragment has been examined in a number of different ways. The Wisswesser Line Notation (WLN) (18) and the IUPAC notation (19) in some way reflect this trade-off. The WLN decomposes a structure into ring nucleus, the pattern and type of the hetero atoms in the ring nucleus, the pattern of the substituents with respect to the nucleus and the structure of the substituents. The structure search system tries to capture the spirit of the WLN decomposition by providing a command to search a tree which has four levels:

1 Ring Nucleus.
2 Pattern of Hetero Atoms with respect to the Ring Nucleus.
3 Sequence of Hetero Atoms with respect to the Pattern.
4 Pattern of Substituents with respect to the Ring Nucleus.

Figure 9 shows the retrieval using the command RPROBE. As the ring search starts the search routine generates an internal canonical ordering for the nucleus as shown in the upper right structure in figure 9. The search information indicates that in a file of 25,800 compounds there are 1791 fused 5-6 nuclei. Of this number only 64 have no hetero atoms. When a nucleus has no hetero atoms the second and third levels of the tree retrieve the same number of structures. Only 21 structures have substituents in the 2,3,4 positions with respect to the renumbered nucleus. CAS structure 82666 satisfies the input structure as far as the imbedment of the ring nucleus is concerned. The command EXIM can be given to broaden the search

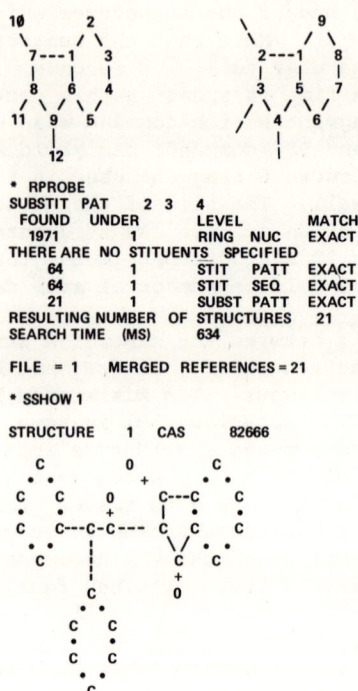

Figure 9. Nested Ring Retrieval

of the ring tree. If, as in figure 10, level four of the ring tree is changed from EXACT search to IMBEDment search, two additional nodes are examined. The result is that six additional structures are retrieved. CAS structure 485472 has two substituents in the 3 position with respect to the renumbered nucleus (see figure 9). When a hetero atom is specified as in figure 11 the search of the ring tree produces 413 structures which have one hetero atom in the 2 position, 277 structures which have a nitrogen as that hetero atom and 6 structures which have the exact substituent pattern. CAS structure 607056 satisfies this structure query. Note that the retrieval times for the ring tree are all less than one second.

The structure search system aims at providing a spectrum of search capabilities. Only by providing a spectrum of

```
        * EXIM
        TYPE NEST LEVELS TO BE CHANGED
        LEVEL = 4

        * RPROBE
        SUBSTIT PAT    2  3   4
          FOUND   UNDER      LEVEL         MATCH
          1971       1       RING NUC      EXACT
        THERE ARE NO STITUENTS SPECIFIED
            64       1       STIT PATT     EXACT
            64       1       STIT SEQ      EXACT
            27       3       SUBST PATT    IMBED
        MERGE    NUMBER OF REFERENCES       27
        RESULTING  NUMBER   STRUCTURES      27
        SEARCH  TIME  (MS)     733

        STRUCTURE      10 CAS    485472

             O        C
             +       • •
             C---C    C
             |      • •
             C   C    C
            /|\ /   • •
           O O C    C
               +
               O
```

Figure 10: Use of the EXIM Command to Broaden Nested Ring Retrieval

capabilities can both the interactiveness and the quality of the search be maintained. The five search capabilities can now be ranked according to the search specificity:

1. Registry Retrieval
2. Molecular Formula Retrieval
3. Ring Retrieval
4. Fragment Retrieval
5. Molecular Property Retrieval

Clearly the registry retrieval is the most specific as a registry number retrieves only one structure. The molecular formula retrieval which requires the exact atomic composition of the structure retrieves normally a rather small class. The ring retrieval requires a ring nucleus to be specified in the structure input. The ring retrieval is a very powerful search tool, if the ring nucleus is known and is in itself not imbedded. The fragment retrieval is less specific than the ring retrieval since

68   Interactive Graphic Substructure Searching

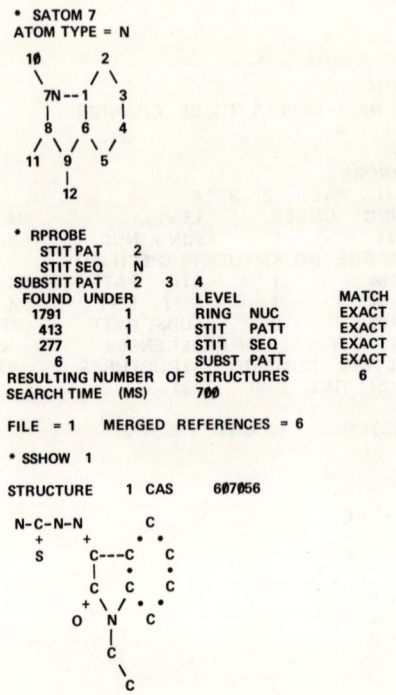

Figure 11. Specification of Ring Hetero Atom
and Nested Ring Retrieval

retrieval since the atom centered fragment is smaller than the
ring fragment. The molecular property retrieval is the least
specific of all the retrieval modes since only the general structural properties are used. In any case the user can choose the
most appropriate search mode for the particular query. Because
the search and retrieval are virtually instantaneous the user
can make experiments quickly and easily (this is why the structure search commands are called probe). The interactive structure input, search and structure retrieval review result in the
enhancement of the users rate of hypothesis formulation.

FILE ORGANIZATION FOR INTERACTIVE STRUCTURE SEARCH

The interactiveness of the structure search system is in
equal part determined by the organization of the structure input
and output functions and by the organization of the structure
search and retrieval functions. The structure input functions

are implemented by a collection of routines each corresponding
to a command. The structure output function is implemented as a
collection of routines which spatialize a connection table in
two dimensions and draw the structure on the terminal in the appropriate graphic mode. The structure retrieval function is implemented by a collection of routines which access structure data
stored on the disk (direct access storage device). The five
structure search functions are each implemented as a collection
of routines which access data stored on the disk. The molecular
formula search and the molecular property search are relatively
straight forward since the user specifies the data to be used in
the search. The fragment retrieval and the ring retrieval are
more complicated in that the input structure must be decomposed
into the appropriate fragments. In the ring search for example
the input structure is decomposed into ring nuclei, each ring
nucleus is canonically renumbered, the hetero atom pattern and
sequence are found, and the substituent pattern is found. As
each piece of data is abstracted from the input structure it is
applied in the search of the ring tree. Figure 12 shows a portion of a hypothetical ring tree. The ring tree has four search
levels. Each level corresponds to an aspect of the ring decomposition of the input structure. The first level of the tree is
the ring nucleus. Each node represents a distinct configuration
of rings which were recognized as the tree was generated. The
nodes of level one are all linked together to form a list. The

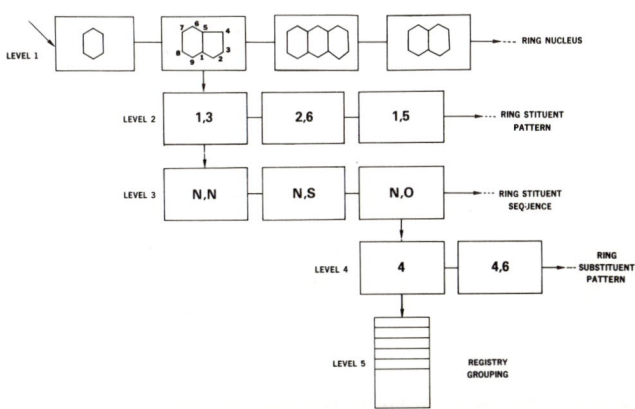

Figure 12. Nested Ring Tree

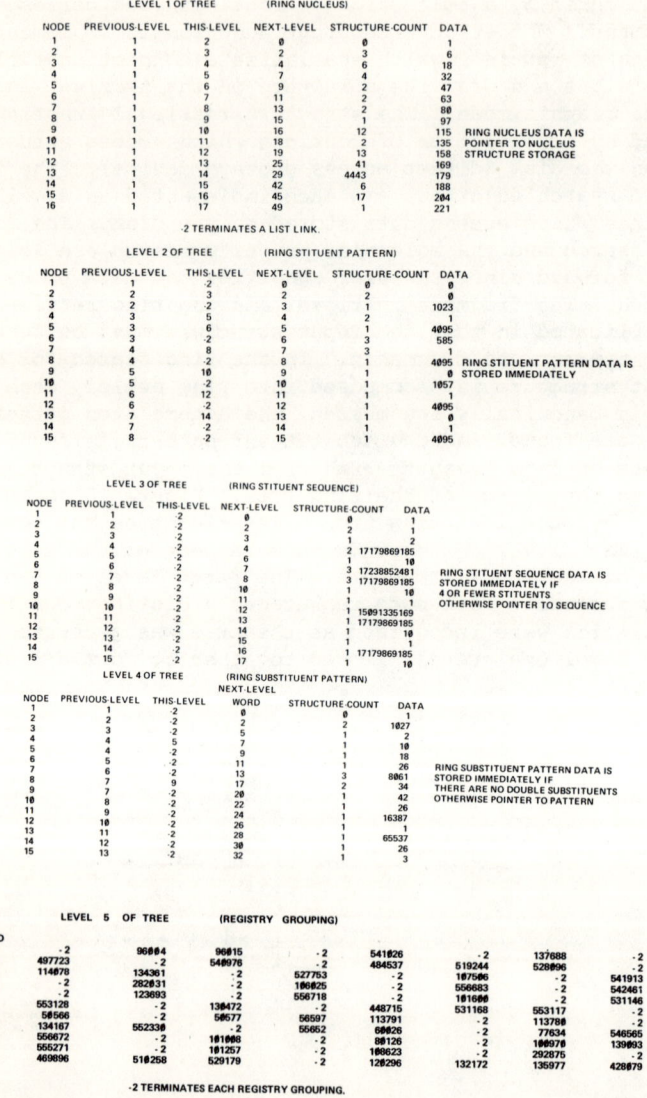

Figure 13. Data Structure for Nested Ring Tree
(a) Levels 1 and 2
(b) Levels 3 and 4
(c) Level 5

File Organization

search for a ring nucleus starts at the beginning of the level one list and a scan is made along the list until either the nucleus is found or the list ends. Each nucleus has associated with it on level two a list of nodes which represent all the patterns of hetero atom placement with respect to that nucleus. If in the search of level one the nucleus is found, the associated list of level two nodes will be the beginning point for the search of level two. The pattern of hetero atom placement abstracted from the input structure is then used to search the list of level two nodes. If the hetero atom pattern is found the search proceeds to level three and subsequently to level four. Each node at level four in the ring tree points to a list on level five of all the registry numbers of the structures which have a particular ring decomposition. Each node in the ring tree is composed of five words.

Word	Use
1	Pointer to Previous Level
2	Pointer to Next Node on This Level
3	Pointer to Next Level
4	Structure Count
5	Data

Figure 13 shows a portion of a typical ring tree. A -2 in figure 13 is used to indicate the end of a list. The structure count at a node is the sum of the lengths of the registry number lists of the portion of the tree under the node. This is the structure retrieval information which is given to the user during the structure search. The structure search command IMBED broadens the search at a given level in the tree by retrieving nodes which have at least the specified property. In contrast to the ring tree which has only four searchable levels the fragment tree has eleven searchable levels. A fragment in which the central atom is connected to four neighbors will use all eleven levels whereas a two neighbor fragment will use only seven search levels. The structure search in both the ring and fragment modes is instantaneous because in the search only a small portion of the total tree is examined and nothing is done with the retrieved registry numbers until the user gives a command which will do some logical operation, a sub structure search, or a structure retrieval review. At each level in a ring or fragment tree structures with the same properties are brought together. Because the two schemes of structure decomposition proceed in a hierarchical fashion from least specific at the top of the tree

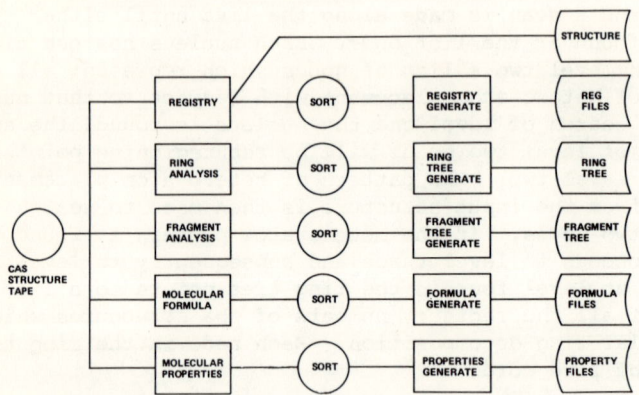

Figure 14. File Generation Flow Diagram

to most specific at the bottom, the trees generate a nest of structural properties.

The organization of the structure search centers on the tree structures for the five search and retrieval functions. The tree structures are generated as the result of processing a CAS structure tape. The processing flow is shown in figure 14. There are five autonomous passes through the structure tape. The ring analysis program, for example, decomposes each structure on the tape into ring nuclei with the appropriate hetero atom pattern, hetero atom sequence and substituent pattern. Figure 15 shows part of a ring analysis. The ring analysis data is then sorted as in figure 16. The sorting brings together first struc-

REGISTRY NUMBER	RING COUNT SIZE 3-8 3 4 5 6 7 8	NUCLEUS HASH	RING STITUENT PATTERN	RING STITUENT SEQUENCE	RING SUBSTITUENT PATTERN
50022	1 3	2735142768	1		4 5 5 6 8 91013
50033	1 3	2735142768	1		5 5 6 81013
50044	1 3	2735142768	1		5 5 6 81013
50066	1	585051634	1 1 3	N N	2 4 5 5 6
50066	1	585051634	2		1
50077	1 2 1	1062251424	1 3 6	N N	1 8 9101113
50099	1	585051634	1 1 3	N N	1 2 4 5 5 6
50099	1	585051634	2		1
50102	1	585051634	1		1
50102	1	585051634	2		1
50113	1	585051634	1 1 3	N N	1 2 4 5 5 6
50124	1	381626754	1 1 3	N N	1 2 4 4 5
50124	1	585051634	2		1
50135	1	585051634	1 1	N	1 4 4
50135	1	585051634	2		1
50146	1	909504362	1		1 2 6
50146	1	585051634	2		1 4 5
50180	1	585051634	1 1 2 6	P N O	1 1
50191	1	585051634	1		1
50226	1 3	2735142768	1		5 6 81013

Figure 15. Unsorted Nested Ring Analysis Output

File Organization

REGISTRY NUMBER	RING COUNT SIZE 3-8 3 4 5 6 7 8	NUCLEUS HASH	RING STITUENT PATTERN	RING STITUENT SEQUENCE	RING SUBSTITUENT PATTERN
50124	1	381626754	1 1 3	N N	1 2 4 4 5
50066	1	585651634	2		1
50099	1	585651634	2		1
50102	1	585651634	1		1
50102	1	585651634	2		1
50124	1	585651634	2		1
50135	1	585651634	2		1
50191	1	585651634	1		1
50146	1	585651634	2	1	N	1 4 5
50135	1	585651634	1 1	N	1 4 4
50180	1	585651634	1 1 2 6	P N O	1 1
50099	?	585651634	1 1 3	N N	1 2 4 5 5 6
50113	1	585651634	1 1 3	N N	1 2 4 5 5 6
50066	1	585651634	1 1 3	N N	2 4 5 5 6
50146	1	909504362	1		1 2 6
50077	1 2 1	1032251424	1 3 6	N N	1 8 9101113
50022	13	2735142768	1		4 5 5 6 8 91013
50033	13	2735142768	1		5 5 6 81013
50044	13	2735142768	1		5 5 6 81013
50226	13	2735142768	1		5 6 81013

Figure 16. Sorted Nested Ring Analysis Output

tures with the same nucleus, then structures with the same hetero atom pattern, then structures with the same hetero atom sequence, and finally structures with the same substituent pattern. The ring tree generation program then transforms the sorted ring analysis data into a tree. The ring tree is generated as five separate files (one for each level in the tree and one for the registry groupings).

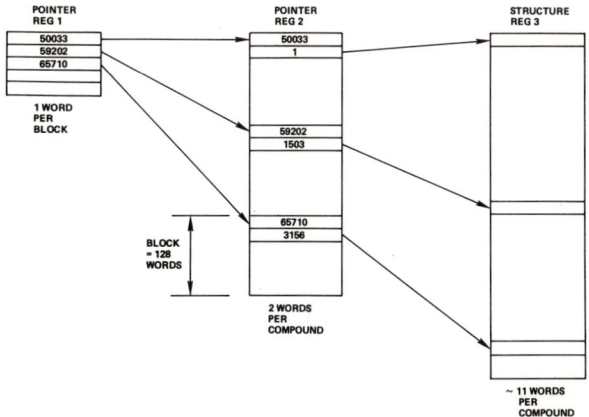

Figure 17. Registry File Structure

The fragment tree is organized along the same lines as the ring tree. Registry and molecular formula trees however have a somewhat different organization. The registry tree shown in figure 17 has three levels. The first level has one word for each block of 128 words in level two. For a given registry number a scan is made through level one until a higher registry number is found. If the given registry number is in the tree it must be in the previous block of level two of the registry tree. A scan is then made through the appropriate block of the second level of the tree. If the registry number is present the following word is a pointer to the position in the third level of the tree where the data for the connection table of the structure is stored. Like the registry tree the molecular formula tree has three levels as shown in figure 18. The first level acts as a quick index to the second level which in turn contains a pointer to a list of registry numbers in level three. The data stored in levels one and two of the molecular formula tree is a compressed representation of the molecular formula. The compression technique known as Hashing (see reference 20 for a discussion of programming methods) reduces a string of arbitrary length (in this case the molecular formula of a compound) to one computer word in a statistically unique mapping. Hashing is used extensively in the name file of the CAS registry system. The molecular formula tree permits a class of molecula formula to be rapidly accessed.

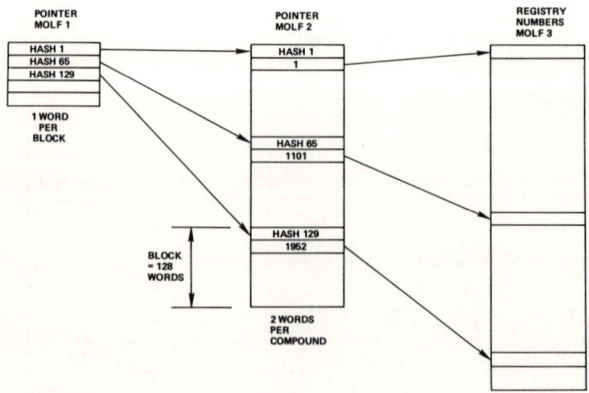

Figure 18. Molecular Formula File Structure

LIMITATIONS TO INTERACTIVE STRUCTURE SEARCHING

This chapter began with a discussion of how structure search systems derive their chief characterisitics from the state of hardware and operating system development at the time of implementation. It is easy to say of earlier systems that the chief characteristics were in fact the chief limitation. What is true of the past is true of the present. The direct access storage device on which the structure search data is maintained is the source of the ability to perform structure searches instantaneously. Direct access storage devices have quite finite storage capacities. The limitation on storage capacity effectively limits the size of the structure file which can be interactively searched. In an effort to make a structure search interactive a trade-off is made between search time and storage size. During the evolution of the interactive structure search system presented in this chapter consideration was given to the various trade-off possibilities. The largest sink of storage capacity is the fragment tree. A typical CAS structure yields about 30 atom centered fragments. The ring tree which embodies an inherently larger structure fragment yields only two nuclei per structure. Milne et al. (21) have proposed several fragment categories which range in size from the atom centered fragment to a fragment somewhat smaller than a typical ring fragment. A spectrum of search fragment sizes would broaden the spectrum of search capabilities. Because each larger fragment has fewer occurrences the total spectrum of fragments may indeed require less storage capacity than the ring and fragment tree implemented in the structure search system just presented.

The file generation process shown in figure 14 indicates that each structure property file must be sorted. As the size of the file increases the sorting time rises at best as the log of the number of structures regardless of whether the sorting is done on tape or disk. A certain amount of presorting can be done in each of the analysis programs. The ring analysis separates the ubiquitous six member ring from the other less probable nuclei. The fragment analysis separates each size of atom fragment into an individual file. In this way the two neighbor atom centered fragments which constitute the bulk of the fragment analysis, sort only against themselves. Similarly the format of a particular unsorted analysis file can be minimized. In the ring analysis the presorted six member nuclei file need have places for only six hetero atoms (pattern and sequence). By taking advantage of constraints on a particular analysis file which are generated by presorting, the size of the unsorted and sorted analysis files can be reduced by as much as half. There are any number of other strategies for reducing the size of the unsorted analysis files (not the number of entries). One possible strategy is to keep a dictionary of fragments in the analysis program. If a fragment is in the dictionary the name (number) of the fragment can be substituted for the fragment descriptor string. If the fragment is not in the dictionary which means in effect that it is not very probable, the fragment descriptor string can be put into the analysis file.

The presorting of analysis data is an attempt to reduce the sorting time by breaking the items to be sorted down into smaller files. There is a machine dependent limit to the number of files which can be concurrently generated. On the PDP-10 (the machine on which the interactive structure search is implemented) this limit is 16. To carry presorting to the ultimate limit is in effect to incrementally generate the ring and fragment trees. The latency characterisitics of direct access storage devices impose a serious limitation on the size of structure files which can be incrementally generated. A drum is a fixed head rotating storage device which has a latency. Rotation latency is the average time required to rotate a particular piece of data under the head of the drum for reading or writing. A disk is a moveable head rotating storage device which in addition to rotation latency has a latency caused by movement of the heads. A typical disk transfers data at the rate of one word in each $14.8 * 10^{-6}$ seconds. For the same disk the rotational latency is $13.1 * 10^{-3}$ seconds. The head motion latency is $20.0 * 10^{-3}$ seconds. In a ring or fragment tree the access of any node in the tree requires a disk read which normally requires a head motion in addition to the rotational latency. In the retrieval function of the structure search system only six data items on the average must be examined in each search. In the incremental generation of a ring or fragment file the analysis program must read and then write the same average of six data items in order to place the registry reference in the approriate place in the tree. The disk latency increases the real time required for incremental file generation to the limit of hardware reliability.

Developments in computer technology indicate that the two chief limitations to direct access storage devices (storage capacity and latency) will be removed in the next five years. Most disks currently in use store approximately $2 * 10^8$ bits. Newer disks double the bit storage capacity. The rotating magnetic storage technology however has reached maturity and no further dramatic increases in storage capacity are expected. Rather new storage technologies are developing around the laser (22) and around semiconductor materials (23). Laser memories with a bit capacity of 10^{12} bits are currently under development. The laser memories have a constraint which can be used to advantage in chemical structure storage. The laser memories can only change a bit from 0 to 1 once. The mnemonic description is WORT (Write One Read Thereafter). The incremental tree generation process can be adapted to work in a laser WORT memory. The main feature of the laser memory is the dramatic increase in storage capacity. Presently available laser memories however have rotational and head access latency which is roughly equivalent to magnetic storage devices. Developments in laser beam steering may lead to the removal of this mechanical latency. The memory technology developing around semiconductor materials involves the storage of data in magnetic and charge domains. Devices which arise from this type of technology are not different in principle from the delay lines which were used in the earliest computers. A magnetic domain memory can be thought of as a motionless drum. A rotation latency will be associated with these devices. This latency could be used to advantage in structure search. Since all the data passes by the read mechanism during a cycle (twice the latency) a small processor associated with the read mechanism could make comparisons and matches. This would be in effect the associative memory which would eliminate the necessity of sorting data during file construction and updating. As the technology of the domain memory devices matures a broad range of memory capacity and data access rates should result.

FUTURE USE OF THE INTERACTIVE STRUCTURE SEARCHING SYSTEM

The CAS structure registry file provides a very large source of structure data. The structures for a sub file can be extracted from the registry file when the registry numbers for the sub file are known. The CAS registry number provides a valuable link between structure files and other data files. The cumulative indices generated by CAS and available on magnetic tape can be made interactively searchable. The CAS journal CBAC which is a prototype of all future CAS journals contains the CAS registry numbers imbedded in the abstract text. Bibliographic references to authors, terms and journals can be extracted from the abstracts and generated into interactively searchable files. The CAS nomenclature file can be used to link chemical names to registry numbers. The problem is not so much whether an index or an abstract file can be made searchable but rather given the present limitation on disk storage capacity what file subset should be made searchable. The nomenclature file is being used to find registry numbers for the names of the compounds in a mass spectrum file. The registry numbers will be used to extract the structures from the registry file in order to add structure searching as an option to the mass spectrum search system described by Heller in chapter 9.

The CAS structure registry file contains only the connection table data for a compound. The Cambridge crystal file (24) however contains in addition to connection table data, crystal coordinates and bibliographic data. The crystal file is particularly useful in that it is a natural subset. All crystallographic papers published after 1960 are represented in the file in whatever detail is available. The size of the crystal file (9000 bibliographic references, 5000 crystal data entries and 3000 crystal cordinates) makes it completely amenable to implementation in the interactive search mode. The structure search has been augmented with a collection of commands which provide for bibliographic search functions. The three dimensional crystal coordinates can be viewed and manipulated by another program in the DRCT Chemical Information System (25).

CONCLUSION

The interactive structure search system presented in this chapter makes it possible for a chemist to rapidly learn to input structure queries, to do structures searches virtually instantaneously, and to interactively review structure search results. The implementation of the system makes extensive use of an interactive time shared computer, of direct access storage devices, and new graphic display terminals. The structure search system has been designed to maximize the interaction between the user and the system. The user communicates with the system in graphical terms and has complete control over the structure search.

References

(1) Survey of Chemical Notation Systems. Report of the National Academy of Sciences/ National Research Council Committee on Modern Methods of Handling of Chemical Information. NAS/NRC Publication 150 Washington, D.C. (1964).

(2) Jacobus, D.P., Davidson, D.E., Feldman, A.P., and Schafer, J.A., "Experience with the Mechanized Chemical and Biological Information Retrieval System," J. Chem Doc. 10,135-40 (1970).

(3) Meyer, E., "The IDC System for Chemical Documentation," J. Chem. Doc. 9,109-13 (1969).

(4) Milne, M., Lefkovitz, D., Hill, H., and Power, R., "Search of CA Registry (1.25 million Compounds) with the Topological Screens System," J. Chem. Doc. 12,183-9 (1972).

(5) Lynch, M.F., Harrison, J.M., Town, W.G., and Ash, J.E., "Computer Handling of Chemical Structure Information," MacDonald, London (1971).

(6) Newman, W.M., and Sproull, R.F., "Principles of Interactive Computer Graphics," McGraw-Hill, New York (1973).

(7) Heller, S.R., Chapter 9, "Computer Techniques for Interpreting Mass Spectrometry Data," in the proceedings of the NATO/CNA ASI on Computer Representation and Manipulation of Chemical Information, edited by Wipke, W.T., Heller, S.R., Feldmann, R.J., and Hyde, E., John Wiley, New York (1973).

(8) Corey, E.J., and Wipke, W.T., "Computer-Assisted Design of Complex Organic Synthesis," Science 166,179-92 (1969).

(9) Hyde, E. et al., "Conversion of Wiswesser Notation to a Connectivity Matrix for Organic Compounds," J. Chem. Doc., 9, 200-4 (1967).

(10) Zimmerman, B.L., "Computer-Generated Chemical Structural Formulas with Standard Ring Orientations," Ph.D dissertation, University of Pennsylvania, Philadelphia, Penna. (1971).

(11) Feldmann, R.J., and Heller, S.R., "An Application of Interactive Graphics- The Nested Retrieval of Chemical Structures," J. Chem. Doc. 12,48-54 (1972).

(12) Feldmann, R.J., "DRCT/CIS Structure Search User Manual," Division of Computer Research and Technology, Bethesda, Md. February 1972.

(13) Sproull, R.F., "PDP-10 Display Systems," Division of Computer Research and Technology, Bethesda, Md. October 1972.

(14) Morgan, H.L., "The Generation of Unique Machine Description for Chemical Structures-A Technique Developed at Chemical Abstracts Service," J.Chem. Doc. 5,107-13 (1965).

(15) Farrell, C.D., Chauvenet, A.R., and Koniver, D. A., "Computer Generation of Wiswesser Line Notation," J. Chem. Doc. 11,52-9 (1971).

(16) Miller, G.A., "Encoding and Decoding WLN," J.Chem. Doc. 12,60-7 (1972).

(17) Rowlett, R.J., and Tate, F.A., "A Computer-Based System for Handling Chemical Nomenclature and Structure Representations," J.Chem. Doc. 12, 125:28 (1972).

(18) Smith, E.J., "W.J. Wiswesser's Line Formula Chemical Notation," McGraw-Hill, New York (1968).

(19) International Union for Pure and Applied Chemistry, "Rules for IUPAC Notation for Organic Compounds," Longmans, London (1961).

(20) Feldmann, R.J., "Interactive Structure Searching-Program Examples," unpublished results.

References

(21) Milne, M., Plotkin, M., Powers, R.V., Hill, H., Lefkovitz, D., and Hazard G.S. "Design of Screens and Indexes for an On-Line Sub Structure Search System," A.C.S. 164th National Meeting, New York (1972).

(22) "System 290 - A Trillion Bit Memory System," Precision Instrument Co., Palo Alto, Cal., (1973).

(23) Bobeck, A.H., and Scovil, H.E.D., "Magnetic Bubbles," Scientific American 224,78-90 (1971).

(24) Kennard, O., Watson, D.G., and Town, W.G., "Cambridge Crystallographic Data Centre. I. Bibliographic File," J.Chem. Doc. 12,14-9 (1972).

(25) Feldmann, R.J., Heller, S.R., and Bacon, C.R.T., "An Interactive, Versatile, Three-Dimensional Display, Manipulation and Plotting System for Biomedical Research," J.Chem. Doc, 12,234-6 (1972).

REACTION DOCUMENTATION

by J. VALLS (Roussel-Uclaf, France)

The first question we may ask ourselves is :
Do Chemists need an efficient Chemical Reactions Documentation ?
My personal answer to this question is backed by a twenty years' experience in that field. In 1950, we decided in our Research Center to create a Reaction file, which has now about 300 000 cards. I do not intend to describe it here because it is a manual file not at the sophisticated computerized level of this Institute, but what I wish to underline is the fact that this Reaction file has become the most popular and used file of our Documentation department. Our Chemists are using it constantly and just cannot imagine doing without a Reaction file. So my answer is very clear-cut : I am convinced Chemists badly need a Reaction Documentation and when such a tool is put at their disposal they use it intensively.
That really ought not to be found surprising. After all Organic Chemistry is made up of two things : Compounds and Reactions. What are the good of Compounds to the Chemist if he does not know how to transform them into other compounds, that is to say if he cannot perform reactions with them. Reactions are an aspect of Organic Chemistry at least as important as compounds are.
This seems obvious ! But if you bring that obvious fact at the level of Information science it means that retrieving information on Reactions is of major - I would say of vital importance and at least as necessary as retrieving information on chemical compounds.
Convinced of these facts I must say I have often been amazed to realise the minor importance given to Reaction Documentation in the field of Information Science !
Whereas Chemical structures' indexing has developped considerably in the past years - giving rise to a large number of fragmentation codes, linear notations and topological coding systems [12,13,14] - reactions' indexing has been disregarded by most information scientists. And strangely enough Chemists have done nothing to call attention on the serious lack of good

retrieval means for chemical reactions. The Chemists seemed rather fatalistically to accept the idea that retrieving information on reactions was very limited and just considered they had to do without it !

Another rather astonishing fact worth mentionning is that in most of the very few efforts made to find means of retrieving reaction information, scientists have been to a large extent blinded by Compounds' coding and retrieval methods. I am sorry to underline once more a very obvious thing : a Compound is not a Reaction ! Even a starting and an end products are not a reaction : they are merely the initial and final states of a transformation but they do not characterize necesseraly the true nature of the dynamic reaction process and this ought to figure in a really efficient and specific indexing method for chemical reactions.

Of course, another reason for the slow development of Reaction Documentation is that the problem as you are all aware and as we shall see later on is a far more difficult one than that of Compound Documentation.

In stating that Reaction Documentation has been overlooked, I do not mean that no efforts whatever have been made in that field. Were it so there would be no point in having several lectures of our Institute bearing on that topic and we might just as well break up now and go for a walk !

I hope this Institute will enable us to have a clear idea of the present status of Reaction Documentation and of its possible developments in the coming years.

In my lecture, I shall give special emphasis to the user's requirements and to the conditions to be fulfilled by Reaction indexing to meet these requirements. Then I shall give a brief survey of the existing Reaction codes, not developping the important achievements which shall be described here by other lecturers but describing in a more detailled way a Reaction code to the creation of which I contributed.

I. REQUIREMENTS OF THE CHEMIST

Let us first of all analyse the requirements of the Chemist as far as chemical reactions are concerned. What type of questions will the Chemist put to a Reaction Documentation file ?

From my experience, I can say these questions are of many widely different types, because the Chemist's interest may be focused primeraly on one or on several of the following topics : on the final product, on the starting product, on both the starting and the final products, on the reaction's experi-

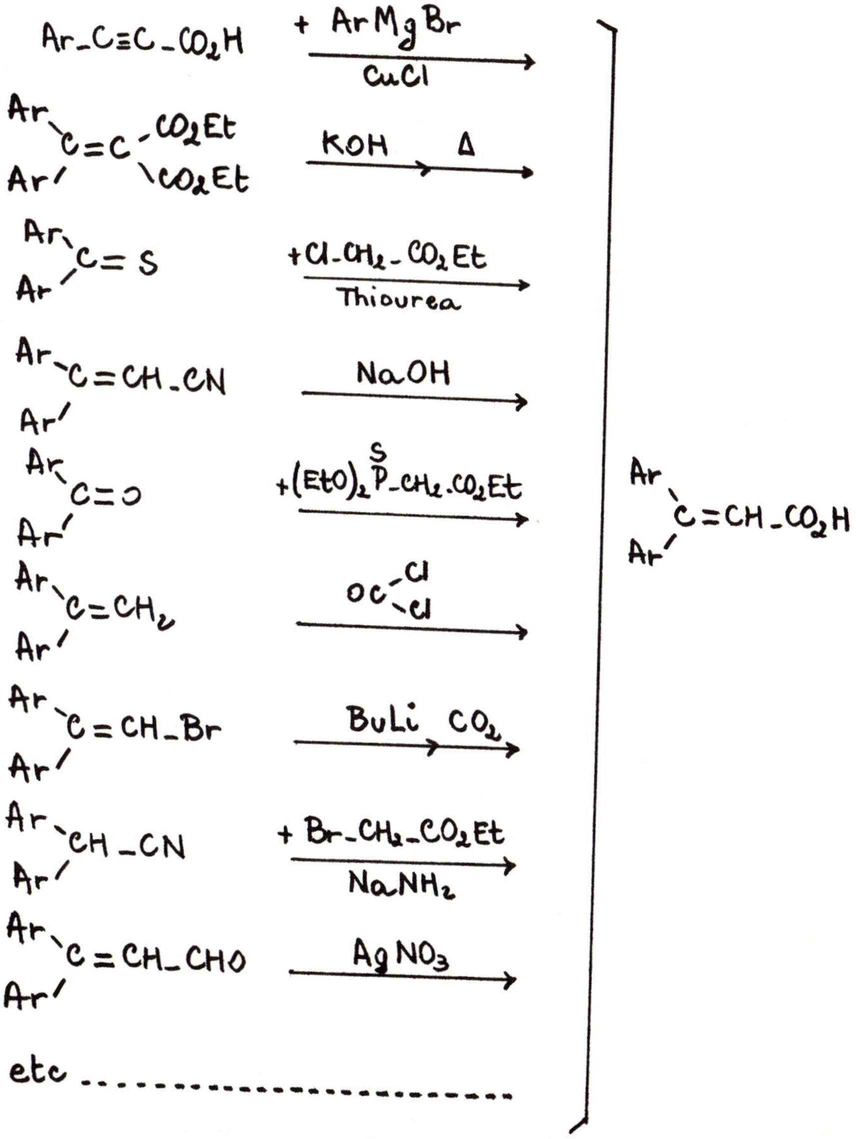

$$Ar\text{-}C\equiv C\text{-}CO_2H \quad \xrightarrow{+ ArMgBr,\ CuCl}$$

$$\begin{array}{c}Ar\\ \diagdown\\ \end{array}C=C\begin{array}{c}\text{-}CO_2Et\\ \diagdown CO_2Et\end{array} \quad \xrightarrow{KOH,\ \Delta}$$

$$\begin{array}{c}Ar\\Ar\end{array}\!\!\!\!>\!C=S \quad \xrightarrow{+Cl\text{-}CH_2\text{-}CO_2Et,\ \text{Thiourea}}$$

$$\begin{array}{c}Ar\\Ar'\end{array}\!\!\!\!>\!C=CH\text{-}CN \quad \xrightarrow{NaOH}$$

$$\begin{array}{c}Ar\\Ar'\end{array}\!\!\!\!>\!C=O \quad \xrightarrow{+(EtO)_2\overset{S}{P}\text{-}CH_2\text{-}CO_2Et}$$

$$\begin{array}{c}Ar\\Ar'\end{array}\!\!\!\!>\!C=CH_2 \quad \xrightarrow{OC\begin{smallmatrix}Cl\\Cl\end{smallmatrix}}$$

$$\begin{array}{c}Ar\\Ar'\end{array}\!\!\!\!>\!C=CH\text{-}Br \quad \xrightarrow{BuLi,\ CO_2}$$

$$\begin{array}{c}Ar\\Ar'\end{array}\!\!\!\!>\!CH\text{-}CN \quad \xrightarrow{+Br\text{-}CH_2\text{-}CO_2Et,\ NaNH_2}$$

$$\begin{array}{c}Ar\\Ar'\end{array}\!\!\!\!>\!C=CH\text{-}CHO \quad \xrightarrow{AgNO_3}$$

etc ......

$$\Biggr\} \quad \begin{array}{c}Ar\\Ar'\end{array}\!\!\!\!>\!C=CH\text{-}CO_2H$$

Fig. 1

mental conditions, on the type of reaction, on indirect methods, on selectivity, on the reaction's mechanism and particularly on its stereochemical course, etc...

FINAL PRODUCT. That is an obviously frequent question of the Chemist who having to prepare a well defined product wants to know if that product or similar derivatives have been already prepared and by what reactions.

That type of question can be illustrated by a simple example : the Chemist wanting to prepare a 2,2-diphenylacrylic acid derivative will be interested to know that the following reactions giving access to that type of product have been described in the literature (figure 1).

STARTING PRODUCT. The Chemist having a certain product may need information on the type of reaction which have been performed on this product or on similar derivatives. It is the same type of question as the previous one but with interest being focused on the starting compound instead of the end product.

STARTING AND END PRODUCTS. A very classical type of question of the Chemist implies both the starting and the end products. Wanting to make a certain product starting from another given structure, he needs to know the reactions which have been used to perform that transformation.

For instance, if a Chemist wishes to prepare quinolines starting from anilines ortho substituted by a C=Z containing group (eq. 3.1), he will be interested to know that reactions such as (3.2) (3.3) and (3.4) have been described [1, 2, 3] (figure 2):

3.1

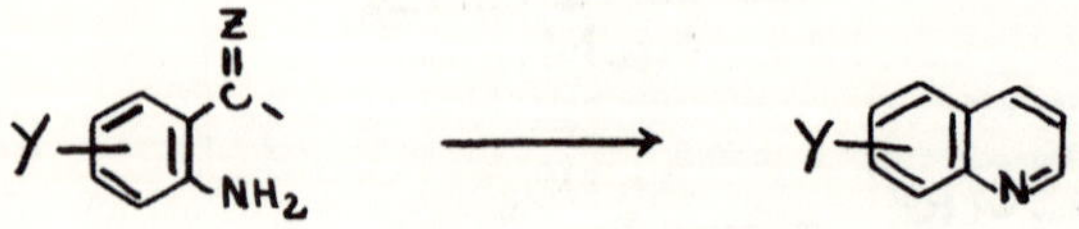

3.2

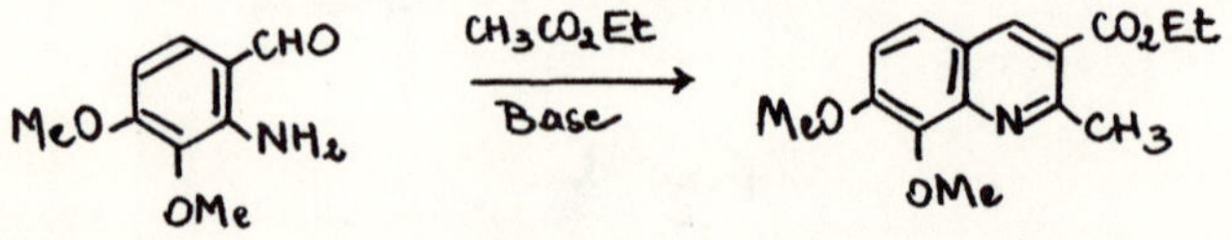

3.3 [reaction scheme: o-aminobenzaldimine (CH=N-C₆H₄CH₃, NH₂) + dimedone-type ketone →(Base) fused quinoline product]

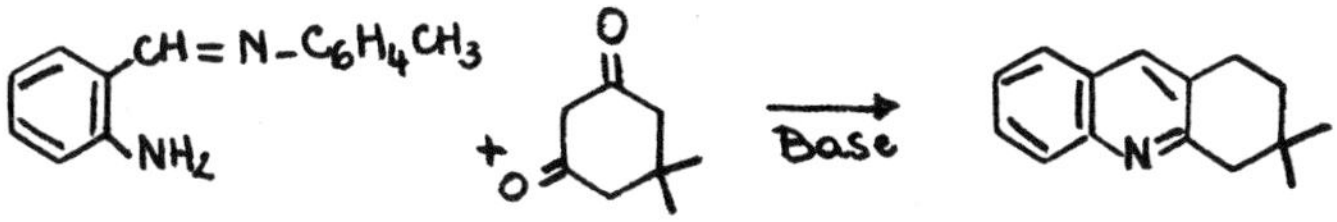

3.4 [reaction scheme: Cl-substituted methyl anthranilate (CO₂Me, NH₂) + H₂C(CO₂Et)₂ →(Na, EtOH) Cl-substituted 4-hydroxyquinoline-3-carboxylate]

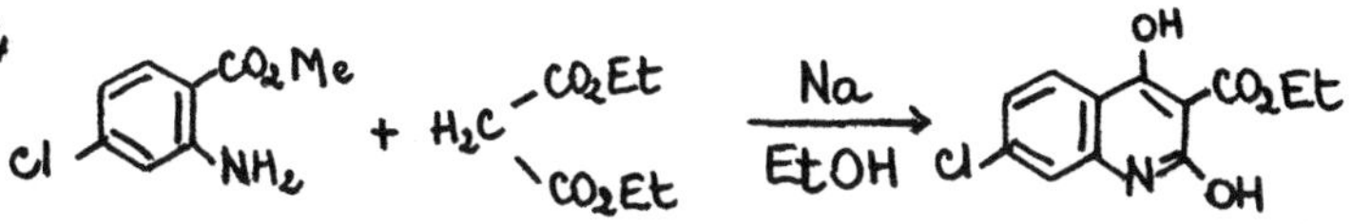

Fig. 2

REACTIONS' EXPERIMENTAL CONDITIONS. The Chemist may wish to put special emphasis on reaction conditions. He may want to have examples of one specific reaction type using different experimental conditions or he may wish to avoid certain conditions (for instance acidic medium) or he may ask only for examples of a given reaction using very special conditions (for instance only by irradiation), etc...

As an example, let us suppose the Chemist is looking for a cleavage method of a ketalic blocking group in <u>non acidic conditions</u>, he will want to find the following reaction (4.1)

4.1 $C_{11}H_{23}-CH(O-CH(CH_2Br)-O-CH_2)$ →(Zn, MeOH) $C_{11}H_{23}-CHO$

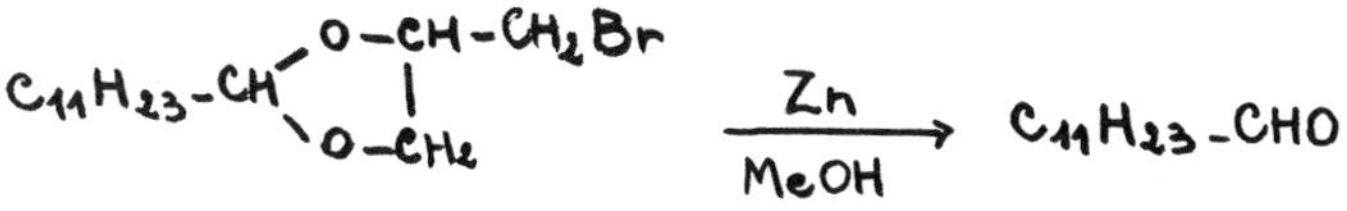

REACTION TYPE. The Chemist wants sometimes to have examples of a certain type of reaction more or less regardess of the compounds involved. For instance, he may need to have examples of the Dieckman's ring closure reaction (5.1) :

5.1

$$\begin{matrix} -CH-CO_2R \\ -CO_2R \end{matrix} \longrightarrow \begin{matrix} -C-CO_2R \\ | \\ C=O \end{matrix}$$

INDIRECT METHODS. In many of his questions the Chemist wants to have information not only on direct (one step) reactions but also on indirect, multistep ways of performing the transformation he is aiming at. The importance of these indirect methods has considerably increased in the last years and many total synthesis have made use of such indirect, often very clever and far from obvious, synthetic pathways.

The following simple examples (6.1) and (6.2) illustrate this type of question (for another example see [6]).

6.1. In planning to substitute an allylic chlorine atom by a cyano group the Chemist having realised that direct substitution gives only poor yields will need to know he can achieve the transformation by a three step indirect method [5]

$$\underset{R}{\overset{R}{>}}C=C-CH_2-Cl \xrightarrow{\quad\times\quad} \underset{R}{\overset{R}{>}}C=C-CH_2-CN$$

$$C_6H_{11}-\underset{CH_3}{\overset{|}{C}}=CH-CH_2-Cl \xrightarrow{+ H_2C(CO_2Et)_2} C_6H_{11}-\underset{CH_3}{\overset{|}{C}}=CH-CH_2-CH(CO_2Et)_2$$

$$\xrightarrow{NH_2OH} C_6H_{11}-\underset{CH_3}{\overset{|}{C}}=CH-\underset{H_2}{\overset{NOH}{\underset{||}{C}}}-CO_2Et \longrightarrow C_6H_{11}-\underset{CH_3}{\overset{|}{C}}=CH-CH_2-CN$$

6.2 To prepare a carboxylic acid from a ketone it can be interesting to know it can be performed according to the following two step sequence [7] : (figure 4)

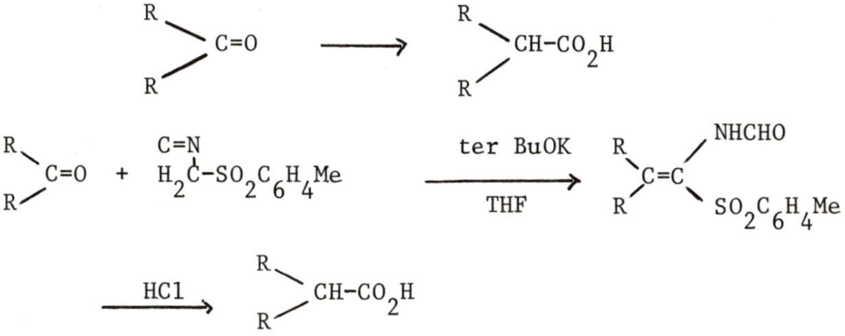

$$\begin{array}{c} R_2C=O \longrightarrow R_2CH\text{-}CO_2H \end{array}$$

$$R_2C=O + H_2\underset{C=N}{C}\text{-}SO_2C_6H_4Me \xrightarrow[\text{THF}]{\text{ter BuOK}} \underset{R_2C=C}{\overset{NHCHO}{\diagup}}_{SO_2C_6H_4Me}$$

$$\xrightarrow{HCl} R_2CH\text{-}CO_2H$$

figure 4

SELECTIVITY. Specially when involved in delicate synthesis, the Chemist is often faced with problems of selective reactions - only one functional group in a molecule having several similar groups must be transformed. To achieve this, he needs either an appropriate selective reagent or has to make use of blocking groups or indirect methods.

The following reactions (7.1) [8] and (7.2) [9] are examples of selective transformations : (figure 5)

7.2

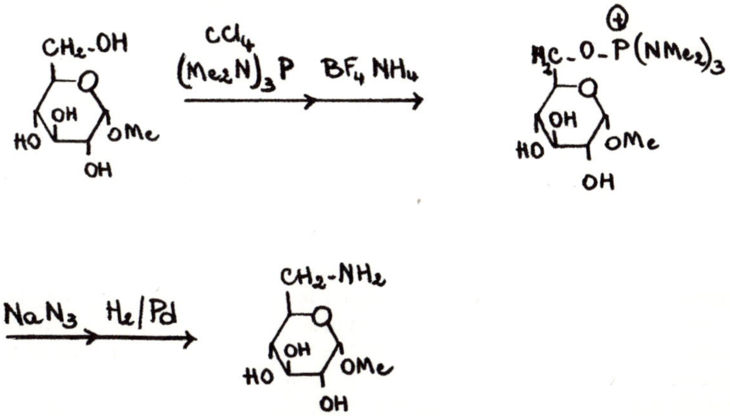

$$\text{sugar-CH}_2\text{-OH} \xrightarrow[(Me_2N)_3P \; BF_4 \; NH_4]{CCl_4} \text{sugar-CH}_2\text{-O-}\overset{\oplus}{P}(NMe_2)_3$$

$$\xrightarrow{NaN_3} \xrightarrow{H_2/Pd} \text{sugar-CH}_2\text{-NH}_2$$

7.1 [reaction scheme: steroid diketone + NaBH₃CN / THF → hydroxy ketone]

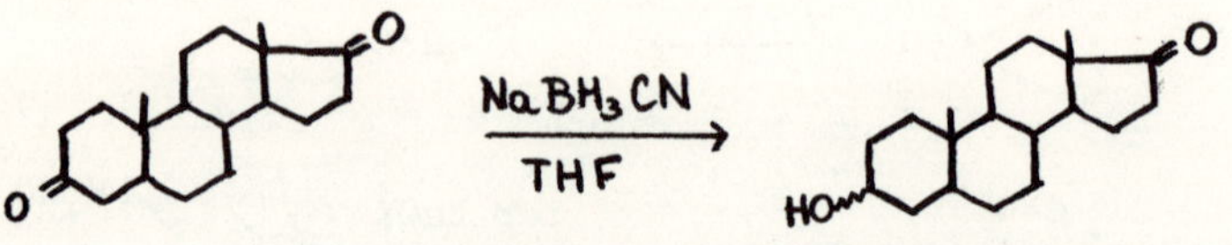

Fig. 5

REACTIONS'MECHANISMS. Many synthetic steps often force the Chemist to have deeper insight in the mechanisms of the reactions being considered. For instance, in multistep synthesis of natural products a vital problem is that of forming the right asymetric carbon atoms. This means to have some information on the stereochemical course of the reactions which will be used [10, 11] . Classical examples are Cram's rule for reactions on Carbonyl groups and Woodward-Hoffmann's rules based on orbital symetry for sigmatropic and electrocyclic reactions.

II. CHARACTERISTICS OF AN EFFICIENT REACTION INDEXING SYSTEM

After having analyzed the Chemist's requirements, let us consider what they imply from the Documentalist point of view for creating an efficient Reaction Indexing system.
The problems are mainly of two types : structure indexing and reaction indexing.

FOR STRUCTURE INDEXING. It is necessary to have a good chemical code for encoding the starting and end products. Such a code must enable retrieval not only of well defined products but also of substructures or fragments. The substructure searching capacity of the system is here of major importance.

THE REACTION INDEXING must be descriptive of the transformation itself and to a rather large extent independant of the reacting or formed compounds. Otherwise, all questions focused on the reaction type rather than on the reacting products will not be retrieved efficiently and much information on reactions will be completely lost.
As seen previously, the Reaction Code must include possibilities for encoding experimental conditions (reagents, solvents, media, physical conditions, etc...) and ought also to provide means of indexing information on the reactions' mechanisms.

In addition to retrieve indirect methods, the system must enable linking compounds separated from one another by several successive reactions.

All these conditions a Reaction indexing system ought to fulfil make the problem a difficult one to solve completely in a satisfying way.

For encoding structures, there are many codes available and the main difficulty here is choosing the right one.

The real fundamental difficulty lies in point 2 : finding an efficient and simple indexing of the reaction itself. All efforts made in the Reaction Documentation field have stumbled on that obstacle.

In many of these efforts, the basic principle considered is to describe the reaction through the structures of starting and end products. These I shall call "Compound orientated indexing methods".

In other attempts, the idea was to describe the transformation itself, what happened in the process regardless of the compounds involved. These I shall call "Transformation orientated indexing methods".

"The Compound orientated reaction indexing methods" are based on the simple idea that comparison of the starting and end products reveals structural differences which are considered as describing the corresponding reaction. The tendancy to consider this type of reaction indexing was probably encouraged by the large development and availability of structural codes.

Such systems provide means of answering satisfactorily questions mainly focused on compounds : for instance, how to prepare a certain type of product whatever the methods used. But they have very serious shortcomings for questions in which the reaction itself is the main target.

As already underlined starting and end products are only the initial and final states of the reaction and do not necessarily describe its true nature. A few examples will easily illustrate what I mean.

Let us consider the two following reactions [15, 16] (figure 6)

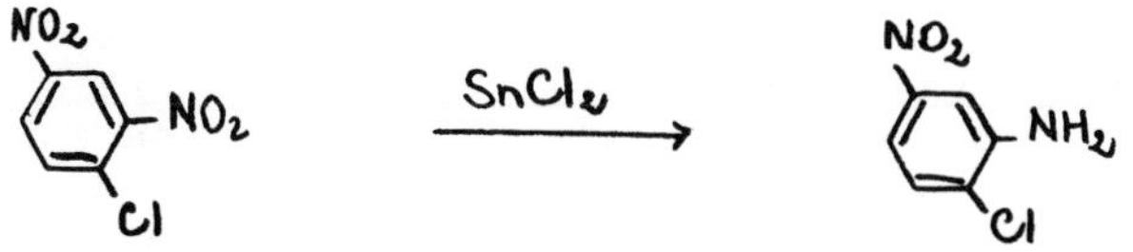

Fig. 6

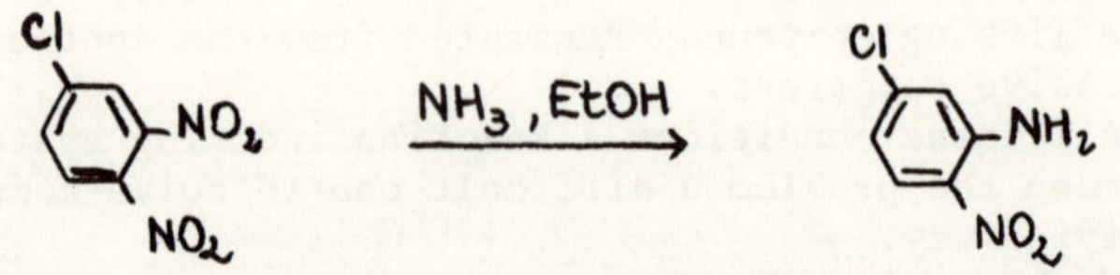

[Reaction scheme: 1-chloro-2,3-dinitrobenzene + NH₃, EtOH → 2-amino-3-nitro-1-chlorobenzene]

Looking only at starting and end products, these two reactions would be classified in the same reaction type; forming of an amine from a nitro derivative :

$$Ar-NO_2 \longrightarrow Ar-NH_2$$

but as chemical transformations, they belong to two widely different classes. The first one is a reduction of a nitro group (with splitting of N,O bonds and forming of N,H bonds). The second one is a nucleophilic substitution of a nitro group by an amino group (with splitting of C,N bond and forming of C,N bond).

The following transacetalization reaction provides a further example [17] (figure 7)

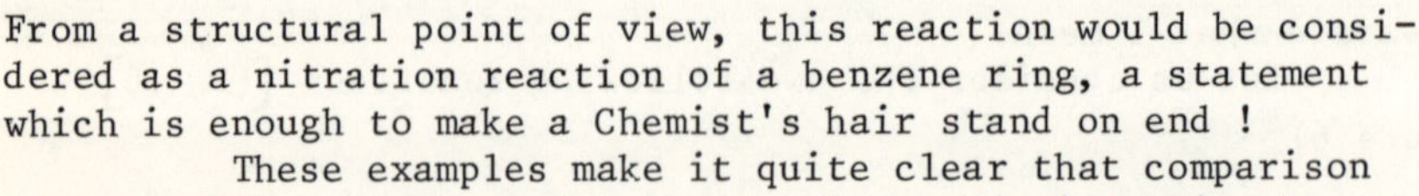

[Fig. 7: transacetalization reaction scheme]

Fig. 7

From a structural point of view, this reaction would be considered as a nitration reaction of a benzene ring, a statement which is enough to make a Chemist's hair stand on end !

These examples make it quite clear that comparison of compounds, though useful in certain cases, is obviously not enough to give a precise, specific description of a reaction.

To achieve this, we must get deeper insight in the real chemical process involved that is to say in the reaction's mechanism. And here unfortunately we stumble on many difficulties.

First of all, we must admit that though reactions' mechanisms knowledge has considerably developped, there are still much to be learnt in that field.

Secondly, even for well known reaction mechanisms, these can vary according to the structural type of reagents. For instance, in the very simple esterification reaction, we know that the mechanism and consequently the bonds cleaved or formed depend on the type of alcohol. If it is a primary alcohol, there is an electrophilic attack on the alcoholic oxygen (a), if the alcohol is tertiary, the electrophilic attack is on the carboxylic acid's oxygen (b)

(a) $R-\overset{O}{\overset{\|}{C}}\dagger O-H \;+\; H\dagger O-CH_2R' \longrightarrow R-\overset{O}{\overset{\|}{C}}-O-CH_2R'$

(b) $R-\overset{O}{\overset{\|}{C}}-O-H \;+\; H-O\dagger\overset{R'}{\underset{R'''}{C}}-R'' \longrightarrow R-\overset{O}{\overset{\|}{C}}-O-\overset{R'}{\underset{R'''}{C}}-R''$

A third difficulty is in fact a consequence of the two previous ones. Such reaction indexings will need for encoding and for retrieval, very learned Chemists, highly skilled in the field of reaction mechanisms. Unfortunately, I believe that average Chemists, even if good at experimental work in their labs, have not the high level of knowledge in mechanisms needed for making or using reaction files based on such indexing principles.

To summarize, we are faced by a difficult dilemma !

Either index reactions by comparison of compounds : it is rather easy, but an incomplete, partly unsatisfactory description of reactions,

Or index reactions by considering their mechanism, a truer description of reactions but a very difficult, and partly impossible, task at the present time.

III. EXISTING REACTION INDEXING SYSTEMS

After having reviewed the user's requirements, the conditions to be fulfilled by a reaction code and after having discussed the problems and difficulties of the general approaches which can be envisaged to solve this question, let us see now what are the existing reaction indexing systems.

I shall not dwell on various classifications of reactions which though useful in certain cases are of very limited efficiency, as for instance the classifications by author's names of reactions, or the 3 letter terms description of reactions created by Chemical Abstracts [18] for its subject indexes.

THE "COMPOUND ORIENTATED REACTION INDEXING METHODS" can be divided into two groups depending on whether the comparison between starting and end products involve the complete structures or only certain fragments of these compounds.

1. The most sophisticated example of direct comparison of starting and end products is the remarkable work done by Professor Lynch and his Sheffield team [19, 20, 13]. Chemical reactions are registered by computer analysis of structural changes. I shall not dwell on these achievements as Pr Lynch will describe them himself in his lecture.

The use of the Wiswesser Line Notation for coding the starting and end products in a reactant index described by Gelberg in 1966 [21] can also be mentionned here.

2. The comparison of fragments of starting and of end products has been used in many reaction indexing methods. The basic idea is to select in the products the reactive sites or functional groups and to describe the reaction as a transformation of certain functional groups into other functional groups.

a) In Ziegler's "Reactiones Organicae" system [22], first described in 1965, a reaction is described by the so-called "reaction centers" in both starting and end products. For instance, the following reaction :

$$H_2C=CH-C\equiv CH \xrightarrow[HgO]{H_2SO_4} H_2C=CH-\overset{O}{\underset{\|}{C}}-CH_3$$

is considered as the transformation of the "reaction centers" :

$$\boxed{-C\equiv C-} \longrightarrow \boxed{-\overset{O}{\underset{\|}{C}}-CH_2^-}$$

b) In an analogous but more sophisticated way, the GREMAS' reaction indexing method [23, 24] considers the functional carbon atoms, coded with three letters, which change in the reaction. (figure 9)

Example :

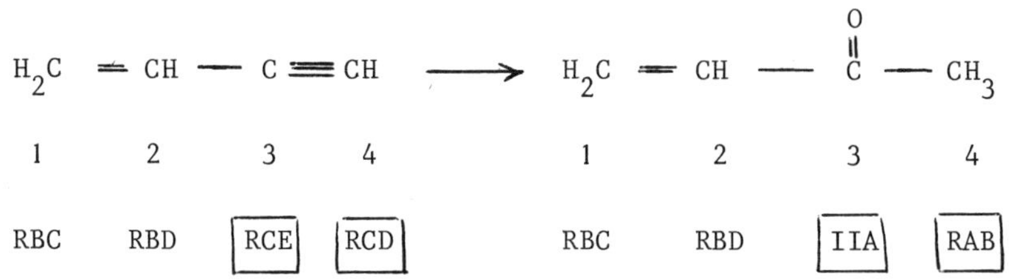

$H_2C = CH — C \equiv CH \longrightarrow H_2C = CH — \overset{\overset{O}{\|}}{C} — CH_3$

  1   2   3   4   1   2   3   4

RBC   RBD |RCE| |RCD| RBC   RBD |IIA| |RAB|

Reaction coding :

    ⓐ   DR   RCE   IIA   3

        DR   RCD   RAB   4

figure 9

I shall not develop further the description of this important GREMAS method as it will certainly be described later on during our Institute.

    c) A very similar reaction indexing by means of modified functional groups is used in my firm's manual file I was mentionning at the start of my lecture and gave rise to a book on Organic Synthesis called "Cahiers de Synthèse Organique [25].

In addition to the indication of the modified fragments all these indexing devices include a coding by numerals or letters giving a more or less rough idea of the general type of reaction: cyclization, chain-lenthening, rearrangement, etc...

Though that type of indexing method is still "compound orientated", it is certainly more accurate in describing a reaction than the systematic comparison of the entire starting and end structures. The difference lies in the fact that the coder using his knowledge of chemistry has to select small fragments which are true reactive sites. Even if he does not know exactly the reaction's mechanism and which bonds are cleaved or formed, he can as a Chemist determine the functional groups really involved in the reaction.

For instance, in the transacetalization reaction, we discussed previously (cf. page   ) the Chemist coder knows it is a transacetalization and   not a nitration. Consequently he will select the right reactive sites : the aldehyde and acetalic groups :

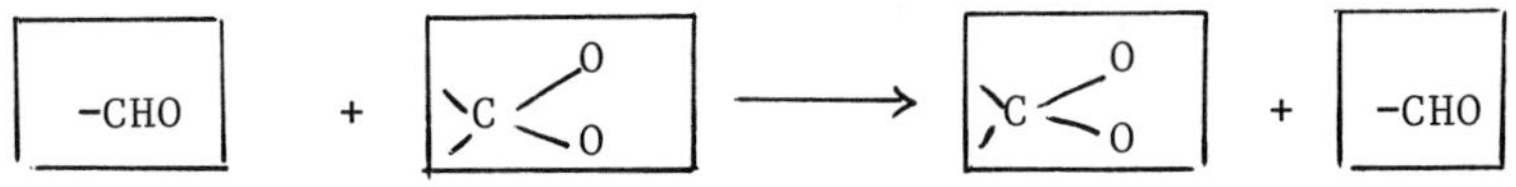

| -CHO | + | $\rangle C \langle_O^O$ | $\longrightarrow$ | $\rangle C \langle_O^O$ | + | -CHO |

and the reaction will be indexed in the proper way as a transacetalization.

That is an important improvement but does not enable still to differentiate many reactions such as the two examples given previously. (cf. page   ) of amino forming reactions from nitro derivatives which would both be indexed here the same way :

$$Ar-NO_2 \longrightarrow Ar-NH_2$$

though they are two very different chemical reactions.

THE "TRANSFORMATION ORIENTATED INDEXING METHODS" are fewer, probably on account of the difficulties involved.

In most of the indexing methods of this type, the basic idea is to describe a reaction by the bonds broken and by the bonds formed in the process.

This approach was first developped by Weygand in his book "Organisch-Chemische Experimentierkunst" [26] and later on in a modified form by Theilheimer in his series "Synthetic Methods of Organic Chemistry" [27] . In 1964 - 1966, Vleduts and al. described also a reaction code giving the reacting and formed bonds [28, 29, 30, 31] .

That basic idea was chosen and much developped in the Reaction Code created as from 1967 by the Pharma-Dokumentationsring e.V. [32, 33, 34] of which I shall now give a detailed description.

The making of this Reaction Code and file is a joint venture of 12 European Chemical and Pharmaceutical Firms [35] already well known for the development of a fragmentation coding system called "Ring codes" which won world wide recognition and distribution as part of Derwent's Ringdoc documentation service designed for Pharmaceutical industries.

The system uses IBM 80 columns punch cards and can be searched with card-sorters or by computer. Figure 10 gives an idea of the general lay-out of the card.

- The starting material and the reaction product are coded respectively in columns 1-27 and 28-54, according to the Ring fragmentation codes [36] .

- The reaction code is in columns 55 to 74 in two parts : modified bonds and reaction descriptors are coded in columns 55 to 62 ; reagents, solvents, and other reaction modifiers are coded in columns 64 to 73 ; physical data are to be found in columns 74.

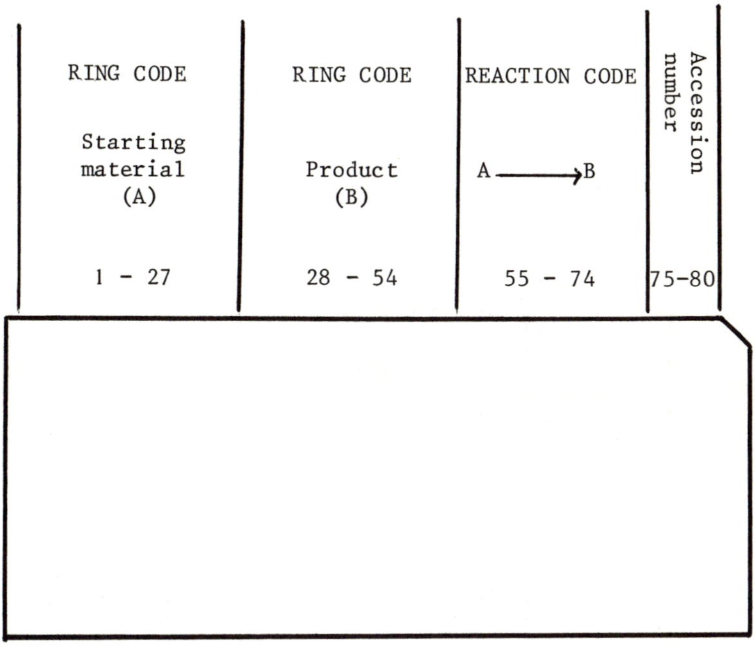

Existing Reaction Indexing Systems   97

RING CODE Starting material (A) 1 - 27	RING CODE Product (B) 28 - 54	REACTION CODE A ⟶ B 55 - 74	Accession number 75-80

figure 10

I shall not describe the Ring codes, familiar to users of the Ringdoc service. It is a good fragmentation code with the advantages and the limitations usually found for that type of code. One of its most useful advantages is to provide easy substructure searching, an important condition for a Reaction file.

Let us look closer at the Reaction code (cf. figure 11). The description by modified bonds uses most of 8 columns. Some of these bonds have been subdivided according to their importance. For instance, forming of Carbon-Nitrogen bond is subdivided in 5 possibilities :

$$-\overset{O}{\underset{}{C}}\!\!\not|N\!\!<\ ,\ -\overset{N-}{\underset{}{C}}\!\!\not|N\!\!<\ ,\ \rangle C\!\!\not|N-\ ,\ -C\!\!\not\equiv\!\!N\ ,\ C\!\!\not|N\ \text{(other)}$$

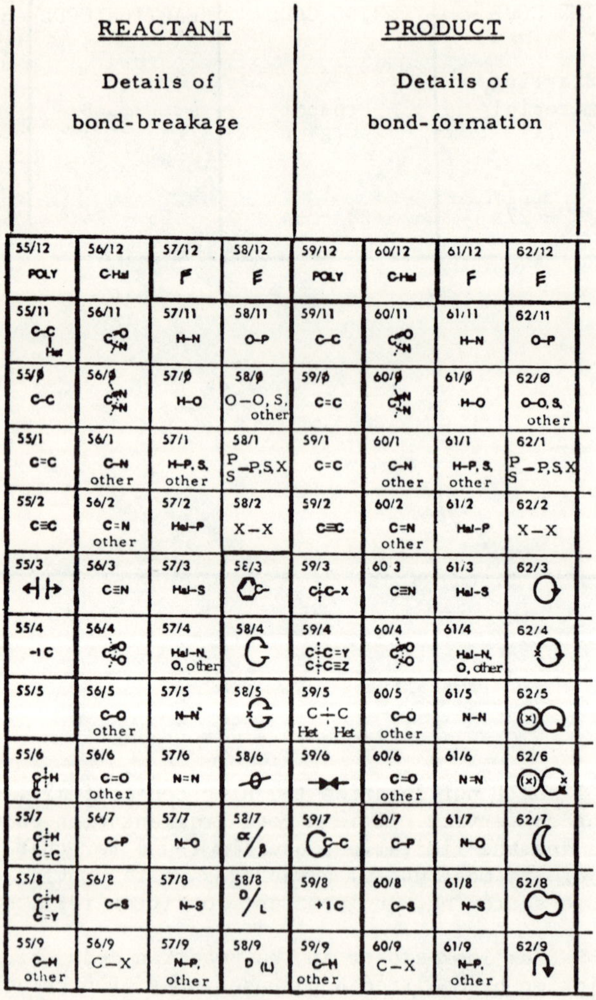

Reaction Documentation

	REACTANT Details of bond-breakage				PRODUCT Details of bond-formation		
55/12 POLY	56/12 C-Hal	57/12 F	58/12 E	59/12 POLY	60/12 C-Hal	61/12 F	62/12 E
55/11 C-C	56/11 C=O / C-N	57/11 H-N	58/11 O-P	59/11 C-C	60/11 C=O / C-N	61/11 H-N	62/11 O-P
55/∅ C-C	56/∅ C=O / C-N	57/∅ H-O	58/∅ O-O, S, other	59/∅ C=C	60/∅ C=O / C-N	61/∅ H-O	62/∅ O-O, S, other
55/1 C=C	56/1 C-N other	57/1 H-P, S, other	58/1 P-P,S,X / S	59/1 C=C	60/1 C-N other	61/1 H-P, S, other	62/1 P-P,S,X / S
55/2 C≡C	56/2 C=N other	57/2 Hal-P	58/2 X-X	59/2 C≡C	60/2 C=N other	61/2 Hal-P	62/2 X-X
55/3 ←|→	56/3 C≡N	57/3 Hal-S	58/3	59/3 C⁺C-X	60 3 C≡N	61/3 Hal-S	62/3
55/4 -IC	56/4 C=O / =O	57/4 Hal-N, O, other	58/4	59/4 C⁺C=Y / C⁺C≡Z	60/4 C=O / =O	61/4 Hal-N, O, other	62/4
55/5	56/5 C-O other	57/5 N-N	58/5	59/5 C÷C Het Het	60/5 C-O other	61/5 N-N	62/5
55/6 C⁺H / C	56/6 C=O other	57/6 N=N	58/6	59/6	60/6 C=O other	61/6 N=N	62/6
55/7 C⁺H / C=C	56/7 C-P	57/7 N-O	58/7 α/β	59/7 C-C	60/7 C-P	61/7 N-O	62/7
55/8 C⁺H / C=Y	56/8 C-S	57/8 N-S	58/8 D/L	59/8 +IC	60/8 C-S	61/8 N-S	62/8
55/9 C-H other	56/9 C-X	57/9 N-P, other	58/9 D (L)	59/9 C-H other	60/9 C-X	61/9 N-P, other	62/9

Fig. 11

Some bond modifications have been chosen on account of their special interest in synthesis. For instance, C,C bond formation is divided in 9 categories (which can occur simultaneously) :

    C-C (alkylations)

    C=C (without condensation)

    C=C (with C,C condensation)

    C≡C

    C-C (hydroxyalkylations)
     |
    Het.

    C-C (acylations)
    ‖
    Het.

     C-C (i.e. acyloin formation)
    / \
   Het. Het.

   (C-C (C,C bond on a ring)

   + 1C (1C atom added only)

    In addition to the coding of modified bonds, 16 reaction descriptors enable a further description of the general type of reaction : chain shortening, chain lengthening, carbocycle ring opening, carbocycle ring closure, rearrangement, etc...
    Only 1 starting and 1 end products are coded on earch card. For a one step reaction of the type :

$$A + B \longrightarrow C$$

two cards are made $A \longrightarrow C$ and $B \longrightarrow C$.
    The system provides for retrieving indirect, multistep methods. If for instance, we have the following reactions sequence :

$$A \longrightarrow B \longrightarrow C \longrightarrow D$$

six cards will be made :

    $A \longrightarrow B$ $A \longrightarrow C$
    $B \longrightarrow C$ $A \longrightarrow D$
    $C \longrightarrow D$ $B \longrightarrow D$

thus enabling for instance to find the indirect method of making D from A in 3 steps.
    The following example will illustrate coding according to this Reaction Code.

$H_2C=CH-C\equiv CH \xrightarrow[HgO, 50°]{H_2SO_4} H_2C=CH-\overset{\overset{O}{\|}}{C}-CH \begin{matrix} H \\ H \end{matrix}$

Bond modifications :

$C\equiv C$ split (55/2)

C=O   formed (60/6)

C-H   formed (59/9)

+ "poly" (59/12)

Reagents :   acidic medium (64/0)
H_2SO_4 (72/1)

HgO   (72/11 + 73/1)

Temperature above 30°   (74/1)

This reaction code of the Pharma-Dokumentationsring fulfils many of the conditions required by an efficient Reaction file; it has also the merit to be simple and easy to use but it has of course various limitations.
Some of these are obvious : they are the usual limitations of any chemical fragmentation code. Other difficulties are of the type we discussed previously. This system implies the coder and the retriever know which bonds are broken or formed in the reaction, that is to say it means they have a fair knowledge of the reaction's mechanism. In most case, there is no problem but sometimes difficulties may arise. We find here once more the antagonism between a mechanistic or a formal structure - dependant ways of looking at things.
In the Ring's reaction file, it was decided that when widely different codings arise from looking at the bonds' modifications in a formal or in a mechanistic way, these would both be coded, on two different cards.
Still as it stands, with its limitations, this Reaction code which is the result of many years of work and improvements through experience can be considered as a useful tool for retrieving information on Reactions. The backbone of the Reaction file is formed by about 22 000 reactions taken from the 25 Theilheimer volumes. Though at the present time its use is restricted to members of the Pharma-Dokumentationsring, this Association will probably hand it over to Derwent Publications which is planning to start a new service "Chemical Reaction

Documentation Service" on January 1st, 1974. Derwent intends to code about 4 000 Reactions per year (2 000 from the literature + 2 000 from patents), offering also as an option Wiswesser Line Notation Coding of the products. The subscription price is expected to be about 250 pounds (750 $) per annum. The cost of the backlog file would be 750 £ (2 250 $).

The computer retrieval fo this Reaction file can be made using one of the already numerous existing programs for retrieving the Ringdoc Documentation [37]. Some of them, like the Derwent Robins program or the very efficient Merck (Darmstadt) program are written for sequential files, others like the Marabou program ([37] p. B6) use inverted files providing teleprocessing, time-sharing and dialoguing facilities.

Now what are the prospects for the future of Reaction Documentation. I may have sounded too pessimistic specially when underlining the difficulties of describing a reaction according to its mechanism. To be fair I must say there are gleams of hope that things might change in the future. The best reason for optimism comes from the remarkable achievements of Corey and Wipke [38, 39], you all know and we hope to hear more about during this Institute. Though their aim was not Reaction Documentation the intensive and successfull use of reactions' mechanisms in devicing synthetic pathways shows that our knowledge in that field, if far from complete, is already of a sufficient level to help solving efficiently reaction problems. It would be very interesting to see whether some of the ideas Corey and Wipke developped so successufully in a certain direction could not be applied to solve the different problem of Reaction Indexing for Documentation purposes.

CONCLUSION

To summarize briefly this lecture, I would like to say that although a few very valuable efforts have been made to meet the Chemists' requirements in Reaction Documentation, the problem of Reaction indexing is a very difficult one and no completely satisfying solution has been found so far.

My main hope in giving this lecture is to have made more Chemists and Information Scientists "reaction conscious" and spur on further efforts to find better solutions to the vital problem of Reaction Documentation.

References

1. W.Borsche, W.Ried, Chem.Ber., 76, 1011 (1943)
2. W.Borsche and al., Annalen, 550, 160 (1942)
3. R.E. Lutz and al., J.Amer.Chem.Soc., 68, 1285 (1946)
4. E.J. Corey, J.Org.Chem., 38, 834 (1973)
5. D.Barnard, L.Bateman, J.Chem.Soc., 1950, 926
6. Mühlstädt M., Tetrahedron, 28, 4389 (1972)
7. Schöllkopf and al., Annalen, 766, 130 (1972)
8. M.H. Boutique and R. Jacquesy, Comptes Rendus (C), 276, 437 (1973)
9. B. Castro and al., Tetrahedron Letters, 1972, 5001
10. L. Velluz, J.Valls and G.Nominé, Angew.Chem.Int.ed., 4, 181 (1965)
11. L. Velluz, J.Valls and J.Mathieu, Angew.Chem.Int.ed., 6, 778 (1967)
12. "Chemical Structure Information Handling", National Academy of Sciences, Washington DC, 1969
13. "Computer Handling of Chemical Structure Information", M.F.Lynch, J.M. Harrison, W.G. Town, J.E. Ash, ed. Macdonald and American Elsevier, 1971
14. "Chemical Information Systems", ed. van Nostrand (in print)
15. A. Claus and A. Stiehel, Chem. Ber., 20, 1379 (1887)
16. A. Laubenheimer, Chem. Ber., 9, 1826 (1876)
17. E. Bograchov, J.Am.Chem.Soc., 72, 2268 (1950)
18. G.M. Dyson and E.F. Riley, J.Chem.Documentation, 2, 19 (1962)
19. J.E. Armitage, J.E. Growe, P.N. Evans, M.F. Lynch and Mc Guirk J.A., J.Chem. Documentation, 7, 209 (1967)
20. J.M. Harrison and M.F. Lynch, J.Chem.Soc. (C), 1970, 2082
21. A.J. Gelberg, J.Chem.Documentation, 6, 60 (1966)
22. H.J. Ziegler, J.Chem.Documentation, 6, 81 (1966)
23. M.A. Lobeck, Angew.Chem.Int.ed., 9, 576 (1970)
24. S. Rössler and A. Kolb, J.Chem.Documentation, 10, 128 (1970)
25. "Cahiers de Synthèse Organique", J. Mathieu, A.Allais and J.Valls, ed. Masson (Paris), (1957-1966)
26. "Organisch-chemische Experimentierkunst", C. Weygand, 1st ed. Barth, Leipzig (1939) ; 4th ed. Barth, Leipzig (1970)
27. "Synthetic Methods of Organic Chemistry", W. Theilheimer, 26 vols., Karger, Basel, New-York (1946-1972)
28. G.E. Vleduts and G.L. Mishchenko, Zavodsk Lab, 30, 329 (1964) ; C.A. 60, 14 341 b
29. G.E. Vleduts and G.L. Mishchenko, Inform.Systemy, Moskow Sb, 1964, 88 ; C.A. 64, 11 832 a
30. G.E. Vleduts and al., Tr. Vses Konf.Inform. Poiskovym Sist. Avtomat.Obrab.Nauch., Tekh.Inform., 3d - 1966, 37 (1967) ; C.A. 70, 25 535 m

31. G.E. Vleduts and G.L.Mishchenko, ibid., 1966, 54 (1967) ;
    C.A. 70, 43 991 m
32. O.Schier, W.Nübling, W.Steidle and J.Valls, Angew.Chem.Ind.
    ed., 9, 599 (1970)
33. K.H. Bork, Chemiker Zeitung, 96, 330 (1972)
34. "Chemical Reactions Documentation Service", Part.I, April 1973
    Derwent Publications (London)
35. W. Nübling and W. Steidle, Angew.Chem.Int.ed., 9, 596 (1970)
36. Ringdoc Instruction Bulletins n°5, 6 and 7, issued by
    Derwent Publications, London (1964-1972)
37. Computer Meeting Frankfurt/Washington, December 1971 -
    Derwent Publications, London
38. E.J.Corey and W.T. Wipke, Science, 166, 178 (1969)
39. E.J.Corey, Quaterly Rev., 25, 455 (1971)

Topological Search for Classes of Compounds
in Large Files - even of Markush Formulas -
at Reasonable Machine Cost.

By Ernst Meyer

BASF AG., D-67 Ludwigshafen, C 6

Survey:

Cheap and decentralized off-line input of structural
formulas with alternative substituents is described.
Topological search in connection tables representing
Markush formulas and asking for arbitrary substructures or even more general classes of compounds is
outlined. Machine cost is decreased by using a two-step preselection system which takes account of the
usual questions as well as of the special features of
computers.

Substructure Search:

Both organic chemistry and chemical industry have
a vital interest in a good documentation because their
work is based in a large extent on experimental facts
and previously worked-out procedures. Therefore chemical industry recognized very early the necessity of
using computers in documentation, and this was the reason why I was charged already 15 years ago with the
development of computer methods. Structural formulae
seemed to be an especially suitable subject matter,
and here the papers of Opler and Norton (1) as well as
that of Ray and Kirsch (2) - which were based on a proposal of C.N. Mooers (3) - led us to the topological
encoding. The idea not to be forced to fix already at
input time the fragments to be used for precise searches in the future was fascinating. But we had to fulfil
some additional requirements for a successful industrial documentation.

We had to take care not only for the possibility of asking for chemical individuals and classes of compounds characterized by well defined partial structures, but also for searches directed to types of reactions and classes with unambiguously but not completely described substituents (e.g. alkyl, aryl etc.). Corresponding questions have to give hits also in formulas which represent complete structures. Such questions occur frequently in industry, e.g. for patent reasons; and from the patents arose still another difficulty: The Markush-formulae, i.e. formulae representing a group of compounds, e.g. having a common constant structure part with one or several "alternative" centers to which given varieties of substituents can be assigned to. To resolve these formulas into single individuals would have blown up the information files far too much. On the contrary it is advisable to contract similar formulas of the same document into Markush formulas. In the IDC file (4) which includes almost equal parts of journals and patents literature and contains more than 1.5 million formulas, every third of them is a Markush formula. So we had to take care for topological encoding also of these formulas right from the beginning as well as for searcheability even in those cases where the partial structure asked-for covers partially the constant part and one of the alternative substituents. This was provided therefore already by our first topological test searches in 1959.

These test searches and the corresponding preparation of about 1,000 formulas led us to the knowledge that encoding had to be made more economical and error-proof by mechanization, and that the machine cost of the search could be kept within a reasonable limit only by drastic reduction of the number of formulas to be checked topologically, i.e. by suitable and cheap preselection methods.

For encoding purposes we developed a machine (5) which scans by photocells the structures of formulas drawn on a grid sheet and records this information on magnetic or paper tape (Fig. 1). In the meantime several other devices for the same purpose have been published: The chemical typewriters of A. Feldman (6) and J.M. Mullen (7) as well as several on-line input tools. A profound comparison of the economy of these methods would be desirable; the optimum will depend presumably

Fig. 1: Formula reader. The structure is scanned with 12 photocells and recorded on magnetic or punched tape which is evaluated by the computer later on.

on the different working conditions. The tape typewriter e.g. is preferable where printed formulae are required for other reasons, and encoding is wanted as a byproduct. An economical advantage of our formulae reading machine is the possibility to have drawn the formulas machine-ready by chemists at different locations and to write them off-line onto magnetic tape using one machine. We perform such a procedure already for several years with our collaboration of German firms in dyestuff documentation.

The structures are drawn with lead pencil or black ink onto the grid (Fig. 2); hetero atoms, double bonds and other additional information is drawn with red ink (eosine) which does not influence the scanning photocells. Previously we recorded this "red information" via a keyboard, but recently we constructed an array of photothyristors onto which the grid sheet is placed; by using a light pen, non-carbon atoms and additional information can be recorded now still more conveniently.

By this method our input problem was solved for us satisfactory and economically. But industry has still two other important requirements to the documentation of structural formulas: The search has to be precise and cheap, and it has to allow for extremely flexible formulations of questions for classes of compounds.

As mentioned above, the cost of topological search in large files can be reduced sufficiently only by a good preselection system, and mainly fragmentation codes should be considered for this purpose in order to keep questioning flexible. The GREMAS system worked out by R. Fugmann et al. at Farbwerke Hoechst (8) seemed us to be particularly useful because it took special care for handling Markush formulas. An additional manual GREMAS coding, however, would have been too expensive and error-prone. Fortunately it should be possible in principle to generate any other code by machine from topological representations since these preserve the full information of the structure formula. So we wrote sophisticated programs for computer generation of GREMAS.

The GREMAS system allows for very multiform questions. It is adapted more to the requirements of the chemist than to those of the machine. Therefore the GREMAS search caused yet rather high computer expenses.

For further reduction of these, we additionally developed a second, more machine-oriented preselection step, the so-called "superimposed bit screen" (9). This screen is generated automatically during formula storage as well as with the automatic analysis of the GREMAS question, and both screens are compared at search time by very few machine operations. So we remove more than 99.5 % of the formulas (in the average) very fast as sure non-hits; less than .5 % have then to be examined by the sophisticated GREMAS search program, and still a much smaller part remains for topological comparison (if this is worthwhile at all), rarely more than a few hundred formulae. Therefore usually the cost of topological post-selection does not play any remarkable part; and running batches of very few queries in a file of more than 1.5 million formulas, the GREMAS search with bit screen costs not more than 20 $ per question on the average, machine operation included.

Obviously, like every search system, also GREMAS has some weak points at extraordinary fields and questions. In order to have an effective preselection system even in such rare cases, we additionally developed a "topological superimposed bit screen" generated immediately from the topological representation. This screen has its strength just at the weak points of GREMAS. Furthermore, for the dyestuff field with its special requirements which are served not so well by GREMAS, we developed, in cooperation with Bayer, Hoechst and Cassella, a separate efficient preselection code which is machine-generated from the topological representation as well. By this variety of codes the economy and efficiency of preselection was granted also for difficult queries occuring in industry and in preparative chemistry.

There remained the requirement of high flexibility also of topological questioning which had to be effective in Markush formulas too. This search is performed in redundant connection tables which are designed according to following principles:

A reference number is attached to every atom (except of hydrogen) of the structural formula (fig.3); the order in which these numbers are assigned does not matter. Each atom is then coded (on a separate line), the code consisting of the symbol for the element and the numbers of its "ligands" (neighboring atoms). Each

Speicherstruktur:

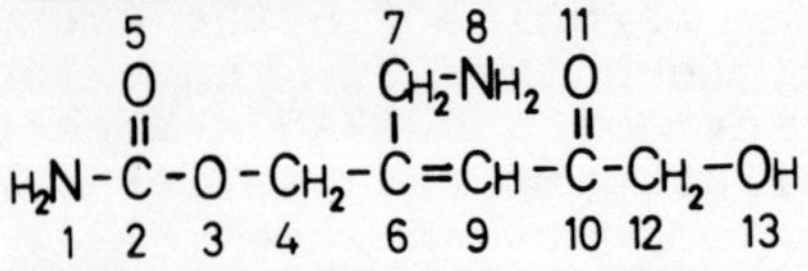

$$\underset{1}{H_2N}-\underset{2}{\overset{\overset{5}{O}}{\underset{\|}{C}}}-\underset{3}{O}-\underset{4}{CH_2}-\underset{6}{\overset{\overset{7}{CH_2}\overset{8}{NH_2}}{\underset{|}{C}}}=\underset{9}{CH}-\underset{10}{\overset{\overset{11}{O}}{\underset{\|}{C}}}-\underset{12}{CH_2}-\underset{13}{OH}$$

1	N	1–2.
2	C	1–1, 1–3, 2–5.
3	O	1–2, 1–4.
4	C	1–3, 1–6.
5	O	2–2.
6	C	1–4, 1–7, 2–9.
7	C	1–6, 1–8.
8	N	1–7.
9	C	2–6, 1–10.
10	C	1–9, 2–11, 1–12.
11	O	2–10.
12	C	1–10, 1–13.
13	O	1–12.

Bindungstypen:
1 = Einfachbindung
2 = Doppelbindung

Fragestruktur:

$$\underset{1}{H_2N}-\underset{2}{CH_2}-\underset{3}{C}=\underset{4}{CH}-\underset{5}{\overset{\overset{7}{O}}{\underset{\|}{C}}}-\underset{6}{C}\cdots$$

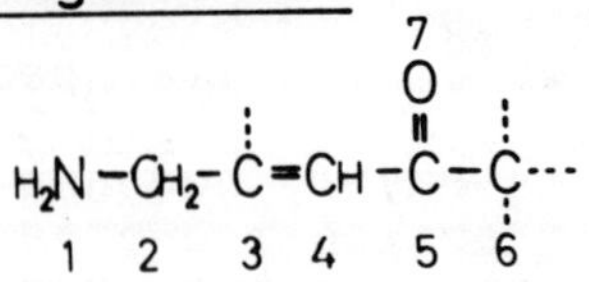

1	N	1–2.
2	C	1–1, 1–3.
3	C	1–2, 2–4, ...
4	C	2–3, 1–5.
5	C	1–4, 1–6, 2–7.
6	C	1–5, ...
7	O	2–5.

Übereinstimmung:
Frage   : 1 2 3 4 5 6 7
Speicher : 8 7 6 9 10 12 11

Fig. 3: Topological structural formula coding (simplified example). Above is a stored formula, and below is shown the required substructure both as fragment and code.

ligand number is prefixed by a code number for the type of bond with which the ligand is connected to the coded atom. In this way we derive a connectivity matrix that may appear at first glance to be heavily influenced by the chance sequence in which the atoms were numbered, but which nevertheless can be used to reconstruct unambiguously the original structural formula.

The structure for which a search is being run can be encoded in similar fashion. It is highly unlikely that the numbers assigned to the atoms in the search structure will coincide with those in the corresponding stored structure which answers the question, but the computer can "recognize" equivalent structures. In fig. 3, this is done as follows: Atom No. 1 in the search structure is nitrogen, and the first nitrogen atom in the file structure is also numbered 1. Both have only one ligand, attached by a single bond, and in both cases this is carbon. If we continue the comparison, however, a difference appears: Atom No. 2 of the search structure should have only two single bonded ligands, but No. 2 of the file structure has three. No. 2 (and consequently also No. 1) thus does not meet the requirements of the question. The computer therefore supposes that the next nitrogen atom of the stored structure (No. 8) might correspond to No. 1 of the search structure. For this to be so its ligand (No. 7) must correspond to No. 2 of the search structure. Both are carbon atoms with two singlybonded ligands. The next atom of the search structure (No. 3) would then have to correspond to the (still unchecked) ligand of atom No. 7 of the file structure, i.e. No. 6. Both are carbons, and the atom of the file structure - as required - has at least one singly and one doubly-bonded ligand. The latter, No. 9, would then have to correspond to atom No. 4 of the search structure (see the comparison in Fig. 3). This process is continued to give a list of possibly matching assigned atom numbers. At branching points it is possible that several atoms of the file structure will have to be considered as possible matches for one atom of the search structure, and these are carefully noted. If the further search shows discrepancies, the computer program jumps back to the last branching point and follows an alternative path. This is repeated until the required structure (or structural fragment) has been found, or until all possible paths have been exhausted.

Parameter-Nr. (Adresse)	Elementsymbol	Bindungswert	Ringwert	Zahl d. H-Atome	Zahl d. Liganden	offene Bindungen (Ladung)	Heteroorientierung	Komplex-Bindungen	Flags	1. Ligand Bindgs.-Typ	1. Ligand Nr.	2. Ligand Bindgs.-Typ	2. Ligand Nr.	3. Ligand Bindgs.-Typ	3. Ligand Nr.	4. Ligand Bindgs.-Typ	4. Ligand Nr.	5. Ligand Bindgs.-Typ	5. Ligand Nr.	6. Ligand Bindgs.-Typ	6. Ligand Nr.	Ringzugehörigkeiten Nr.	Ringzugehörigkeiten Nr.	Ringzugehörigkeiten Nr.	Ringzugehörigkeiten Nr.
	a	b	c	d	e	f	g	h	i	k	l	m	n	o	p	q	r	s	t	u	v	w	x	y	z
HAUPTMATRIX MAT MAT	1	2	3	4	5	6	7	8	9	10	11	12	13	14	15	16	17	18	19	20	21	22	23	24	25
1	5	1	5	1	2	0	0	C	29	3	2	3	3	0	0	0	0	0	0	0	C	19	0	0	0
2	5	1	5	1	2	0	0	0	40	3	1	3	4	0	0	0	0	0	0	0	0	19	0	0	0
3	5	1	5	1	2	0	0	0	42	3	1	3	5	0	0	0	0	0	0	0	0	19	0	0	0
4	5	1	5	1	2	0	0	0	52	3	2	3	6	0	0	0	0	0	0	0	0	19	0	0	0
5	5	1	5	1	2	0	0	0	54	3	3	3	6	0	0	0	0	0	0	0	0	19	0	0	0
6	5	1	5	0	3	0	1	0	65	3	5	3	4	0	7	0	0	0	0	0	0	19	0	0	0
7	7	0	0	1	2	0	0	0	77	0	6	0	8	0	0	0	0	0	0	0	0	0	0	0	0
8	7	1	0	0	2	0	0	0	89	0	7	4	9	0	0	0	0	0	0	0	0	0	0	0	0
9	5	1	0	1	2	0	2	0	101	4	8	0	10	0	0	0	0	0	0	0	0	0	0	0	0
10	5	1	5	0	3	0	0	0	113	0	9	3	11	3	12	0	0	0	0	0	0	20	0	0	0
11	5	1	5	1	2	0	0	0	124	3	10	3	13	0	0	0	0	0	0	0	0	20	0	0	0
12	5	1	5	1	2	0	0	0	126	3	10	3	14	0	0	0	0	0	0	0	0	20	0	0	0
13	5	1	5	1	2	0	0	0	136	3	11	3	15	0	0	0	0	0	0	0	0	20	0	0	0
14	5	1	5	1	2	0	0	0	138	3	12	3	15	0	0	0	0	0	0	0	0	20	0	0	0
15	5	1	5	0	3	0	1	0	149	3	14	3	13	0	16	0	0	0	0	0	0	20	0	0	0
16	7	2	0	0	3	0	0	0	161	4	17	0	15	4	18	0	0	0	0	0	0	0	0	0	0
17	6	1	0	0	1	0	0	0	162	4	16	0	0	0	0	0	0	0	0	0	0	0	0	0	0
18	6	1	0	0	1	0	0	0	160	4	16	0	0	0	0	0	0	0	0	0	0	0	0	0	0
19	4	3	5	0	0	0	6	0	41	0	0	0	0	0	0	0	0	0	0	0	21	0	0	0	0
20	4	3	5	0	0	0	6	0	125	0	0	0	0	0	0	0	0	0	0	0	22	0	0	0	0
21	160	19	1	2	4	6	5	3	0	0	0	0	0	0	0	0	0	0	0	0	0	0	0	0	0
22	160	20	10	11	13	15	14	12	0	0	0	0	0	0	0	0	0	0	0	0	0	0	0	0	0

Fig. 4: Topoligical connectivity matrix with redundant data ("Main matrix"), as used in core storage for the production of the GREMAS code and for searching. "Flags" denote the previous dot numbers on the grid sheet, inter alia for easier reconstruction and display of the formulas.

We call this search strategy "iterative path finding". There is still another strategy which was introduced by Salton and Sussenguth (10): The set reduction method. It is more elegant because in contrast to the path search it requires the greatest search effort only in the rare cases of probable hits. But the path finding better simulates the thoughts of the structure comparing chemist, and this might be the reason why additional search requirements like handling of Markush formulas could be fulfilled without great difficulties.

For easier search and generation of other codes, we supplemented our connection table - the so-called "main matrix" - by further redundant data which were accounted by the computer during the storage process (fig. 4). We added special lines which represent a ring rather than an atom (from now on we shall refer to both these concepts by the more generalized term "parameter") (11). The introduction of ring parameters enables general questions to be put concerning ring structures, such as the number of the members, number and type of multiple bonds, number of substituents and/ or condensed rings, etc.

We retain a number of characteristic redundant data in our main matrix for each parameter. For this we made use of concepts like "ring value", "bond value", "degree of hetero orientation", and we record also explicitly the numbers of ring members, of the attached hydrogen atoms or other ligands, the charges, etc.; we entered all these data into the main matrix, thus making them rapidly accessible for searching.

For example, the ring value indicates the type of ring to which an atom belongs (heterocyclic,⌠or other carbocyclic). The bond value shows the number of double and/or triple bonds in which the atom is involved, irrespective of the neighboring atoms to which they lead; this information is particularly valuable in cases of tautomerism. The degree of hetero orientation, on which GREMAS coding is based,indicates the number of bonds that are not part of a ring and lead to hetero atoms. Special columns are used to record the numbers of the rings to which the atom concerned belongs or with which the ring concerned is condensed. In addition to this, in ring parameters a reference address leads to special matrix lines with a counting up of the ring members. Furthermore, we may distinguish eight types of bonds: single, sesqui, double, and triple bonds, either in chains or rings. ⌠aromatic

114　Topological Search for Classes of Compounds

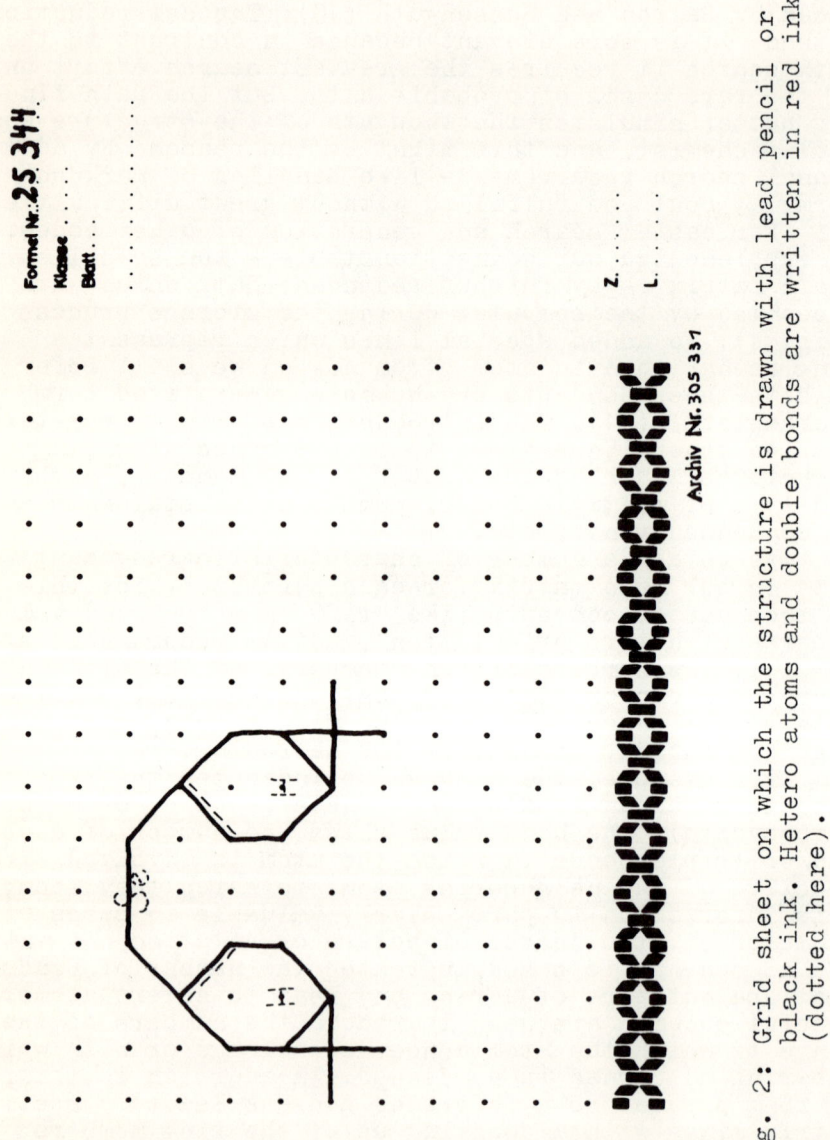

Fig. 2: Grid sheet on which the structure is drawn with lead pencil or black ink. Hetero atoms and double bonds are written in red ink (dotted here).

For encoding of Markush formulas we introduced dummy atoms (R_1, R_2, etc.) attached to the constant part instead of the alternative substituents whose points of attachment, on the other hand, are marked on the grid sheet by other dummies (X_1, X_2, etc.). The reference numbers (i.e. line addresses) of the substituent atoms attached to all X_1 (i.e. to the first alternative center) are recorded in a special main matrix line corresponding to the dummy R_1; those of the second substituent class X_2 are written in the R_2 line, etc.

Every time the machine encounters during search an R-dummy instead of the element asked-for, it moves to the first recorded address and continues there the comparison; if the search conditions are not fulfilled in this substituent, it moves to the second address, etc.. In our jargon we call this "jumping across the creek".

This "jumping" is necessary only if the path-finding came from the constant part of the Markush formula. If the search started in an alternative substituent, the machine does not notice the crossing because the reference number of the R-dummy-bearing atom is recorded as a ligand immediately instead of the X-dummy so that path-finding is not interrupted.

For the query coding we introduced a variety of pseudo-element symbols (fig. 5) in order to make questioning still more flexible. Their effect in searching is to call up appropriate subroutines which test for definite requirements laid down in the program. For example, the subroutine for "alkenyl" will search in the direction given, and will check whether the structure stored there has only carbon (and hydrogen) atoms and at least one double bond, and has chain bonds exclusively. By building in further such subroutines we can, if required, introduce any other search concept that is well-defined but not explicitly describable by a substructure.

Formulation of search questions:

A high flexibility in asking questions inevitably complicates the coding of the enquiry. We have used a set schedule in an attempt to keep the question input as simple as possible, reducing the risk of error and simplifying checking; apart from this, the computer

Topological Search for Classes of Compounds

Code	Significance
$A	Anything, not H
$B	Hetero atom
$C	Nonmetallic hetero atom
$D	Metallic hetero atom
$I	Nonaromatic ring ⎫ in store "Position undetermined"
$J	Aromatic ring ⎭
$K	Hydrocarbon residue, general
$L	Alkyl ⎫
$M	Cycloalkyl ⎪
$N	Aryl residue ⎬ unsubstituted
$O	Isocyclic residue ⎭
$P	Alkenyl (position of double bond unimportant)
$Q	Alkynyl (position of triple bond unimportant)
$R	Unsaturated hydrocarbon chain (position unimportant)
$S	Hetero- or ring-substituted alkyl
$Z	Ring closure
HL	Any halogen

Bond values (completely additive)

0	Only single bonds
1	One (possibly delocalized) double bond
2	Two double bonds (etc. additive)
6	One triple bond

Fig. 4. List of pseudo-element symbols and bond values used in topological searches. The computer follows this direction and checks whether any fragments other than those given occupy this position.

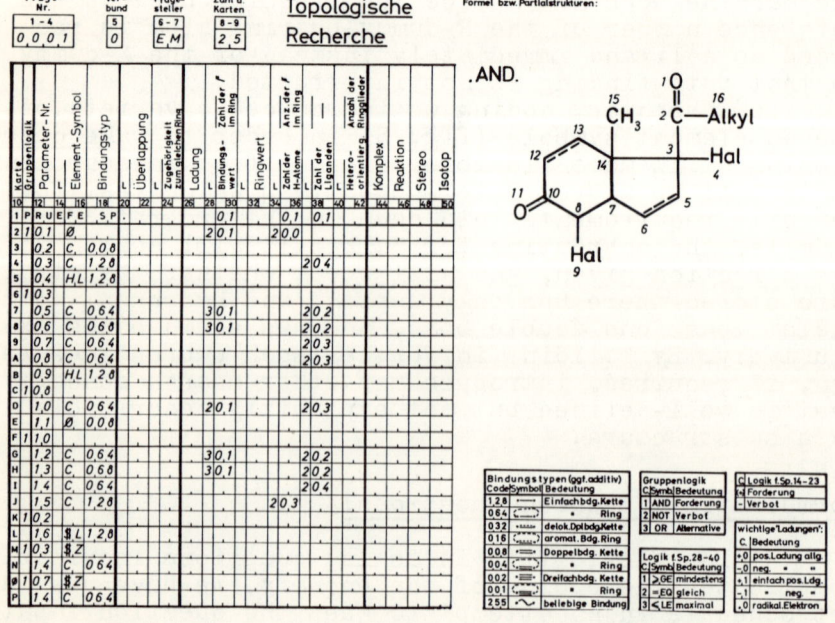

Fig. 6: Sample question: the type of compound required is shown in the formula.

checks the question for formal errors and internal inconsistencies. In order to demonstrate just how many ways there are of putting a question to the system, we are going to describe the process of encoding the question in more detail. It begins, as in the case of formula input, with the drawing of the structural fragments required to be present (or absent) and a numbering of the atoms (except for hydrogen) and rings (Fig. 6).

The sequence of numbering is quite arbitrary, but it is possible to save much computer time by following certain rules; for example, it is preferable to start with the least common hetero atom and then to number in the direction of some other uncommon characteristic. As has already been indicated, it is possible to put a number of partial structure requirements linked by the logical operators AND, OR, and NOT to the same formula on the same question form (Fig. 6); for this it is possible to ask for the identity (overlapping) or nonidentity of individual atoms in different subquestions (col. 20-22) and also to require or prohibit that individual atoms should belong to given ring parameters or to the same ring as a certain other atom does (col. 23-25).

The question form is filled in by first placing a "1" in column 11 (logic operator) of the second line; further subquestions start in this column with a number corresponding to their logic. In columns 12 and 13 is entered the number of the atom or ring to be described, in this case "01", and in columns 15-16 the symbol for the element or pseudoelement. Further characteristics for this parameter are entered into the appropriate columns of the same line.

Most of the columns describing properties of the parameter have a logic (L) column prefixed to them; this indicates whether the property in question is required or prohibited, or whether it is to be greater than, less than, or equal to a given value.

In the case of the following atoms it is assumed - provided that there is no entry in column 11 - that they are bonded to the atom immediately preceding them, and the type of bond is indicated in columns 17-19. If more than one type of bond is permitted, then their code numbers are added together and the sum is entered into the coding schedule. (The fact that the code numbers are all in powers of two will make it at once obvious to the expert that we are working with bit strings and masks, and thus the use of alternatives does not require any additional machine time.) If a continuous chain of atoms has been coded in this way and we then want to jump back to a branching point from which a side chain is next to be encoded, then we must first of all enter a "1" in column 11 of a new line and then repeat the number of the branching point in columns 12 -13; the rest of this line is empty. Ring closures are coded in a similar way, but here the symbol "$Z" is entered in the element symbol column, and in the following line are given the atom number of the ring closure partner, its element symbol, and the type of bond required for ring closure.

The "overlap" column (21-22) is used when a parameter of a given partial structure is to be identical (or nonidentical) with a parameter from a previous partial structure; the number of the earlier one is entered here (in the second partial structure the atom or ring would be given a new number). In the same way, the number of a previously quoted ring or ring atom is entered into columns 24-25 if the atom which is being encoded is to belong (or not to belong) to the same ring. Some of the columns have different significances when ring parameters and not atom parameters are involved; if required, it is possible to enter the number of double bonds in the "bonding value" column, the number of triple bonds in the ring in place of the number of hydrogen atoms, and the number of ring members in place of the hetero orientation. This permits question formulations of the type "Heterocycle with a least seven members and not more than two double bonds". (The maximal ring that can be stored as a ring parameter is a nine-membered one; larger rings can only be searched for as chains with ring closure.)

As already mentioned, alternative formulations can be coded as partial structures in their own right with the appropriate logic operators. If the only alternative requirements are individual atoms or pseudoelements the coding is even simpler; they are given the same atom number, and are thus entered in successive lines of the question form (Fig. 7, rows 8 and 9).

Redundant data, i.e. those that can be derived from the rest of the question coding, do not need to be entered. Nevertheless, it is often expedient to do so, since then under certain circumstances the computer will discover more quickly that it is on a false track; this can save computer time but it should be remembered that an increase in the number of redundant

Search Questions

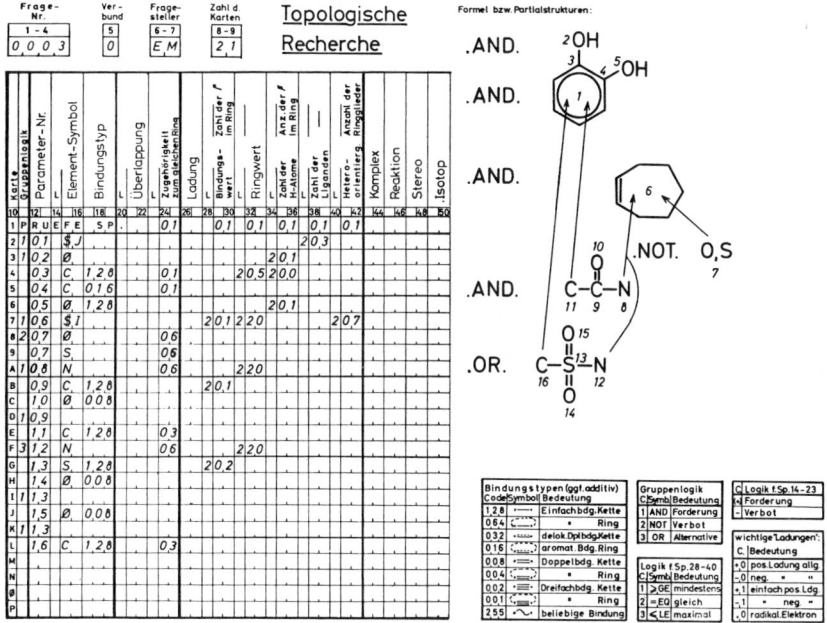

Fig. 7. Sample question: a search for all compounds having the formula

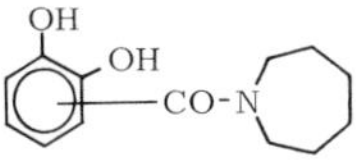

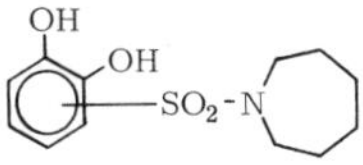

in which the pyrocatechol ring has no other substituents or rings condensed with it, and the seven-membered heterocycle has one double bond but does not contain either oxygen or sulfur.

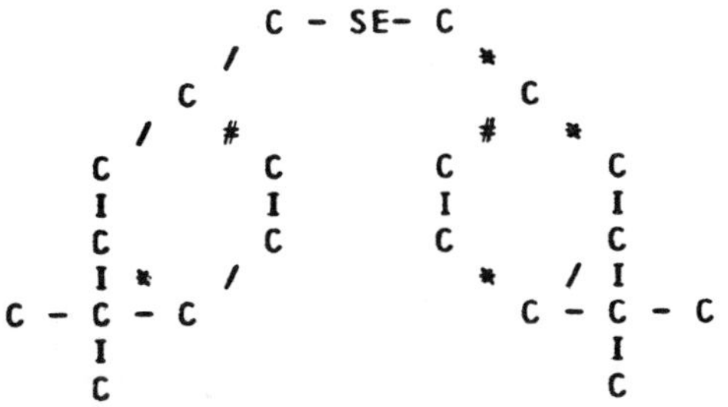

```
          C - SE- C
         /         *                    FORMELNR.000004
        C           C
       /  #       #  *                  VERBINDUNG D
      C    C     C    C
      I    I     I    I                 C12H30SE
      C    C     C    C
      I  *         /  I
   C - C - C      C - C - C
      I               I
      C               C
```

Fig. 8: Formula printed by an usual line printer (IBM 1403)

data also leads to an increase in the danger of erroneous question coding.

For the simpler type of enquiry there is no need for all the columns of the question form to be used. In order to exclude these requirements from the question and thus to save computer time, we have introduced a "column vector". In the first line of the form an "01" is entered into each column to be used; the others are not checked. If one form is not sufficient for a question, others can be attached to it; in each continuation sheet the first line is struck out. Figures 6 and 7 show the coding for two sample questions, which illustrates some important search requirements and the way in which they are encoded. There is no space here to describe further possibilities or details.

Once the form has been filled out and checked, the information it contains is transferred to punched cards, each line of the form being punched on a separate card. These cards, together with a list (on tape or disk) of the formula numbers that have passed the preselection steps, are fed into the computer with the search program and are then compared by the machine with the tape of topological data. In oder to save reading time, the latter tape contains the main matrices in a greatly abbreviated form. The redundant data are still explicitly given, but the overwhelming number of zero elements of the matrices are suppressed by simple routines; it does not require a great deal of computing time to blow them up again in the core storage. The computer prints out the answers either in the form of literature references or as abstract numbers; in most cases we copy the abstracts and send them to the inquirer. If required, the structural formula can also be reconstructed from the main matrix by computer, and can be printed out. This may be done even during input for checking purposes; however, the commercial high-speed printers currently used are not very good at printing out formulas (fig. 8).

In order to help the machine in finding easily the suitable places on the paper for printing the atom symbols, we preserve the topography of our grid sheet by storing the numbers of the grid dots corresponding to the atoms in column 8 of our main matrix (fig. 4). Obviously the output of the picture on the video screen is possible, too. Using a more comfortable video display and corresponding computer programs, it might be possible to get better pictures, taking perhaps into account also the approximate atom distances and bond angles, and considering in suitable cases the most stable hydrogen bonds or the conformation of the lowest energy level. Using such programs the hits of a topological search could be further reduced according to the topography (and possible topochemistry) of the compounds.

Once a very large number of chemical compounds has been encoded topologically and can be searched at low cost for almost any substructure and compound class, the organic chemical literature can be surveyed more easily, and the knowledge of chemistry can be evaluated much better than before. We are going to reach this point now.

Acknowledgement:

The generation and search programs for the main matrix and for the superimposed GREMAS screen were written by Mr. Peter Schilling; the generation of the GREMAS code, as well as of the dyestuff code and of the topological superimposed screen were programmed by Mr. Ehrhard Sens. The work was partially financed by IDC, Bayer and Hoechst.

Literature:

(1) A. Opler and T.R. Norton, Chem. & Eng. News 34 (1956), pp. 2812 - 2816
(2) L.C. Ray and R.A. Kirsch, Science 126 (1957), pp. 814 - 819.
(3) C.N. Mooers, Zator Technical Bulletin 59 (1951).
(4) IDC International Documentation in Chemistry; see E. Meyer, J. Chem. Doc. 9 (1969), pp. 109 - 113.
(5) E. Meyer, Nachrichten für Dokumentation 13 (1962), S. 144 - 146.
(6) A. Feldman, D.B. Holland and D.P. Jacobus, J. Chem. Doc. 3 (1963), pp. 187 ff.
(7) J.M. Mullen, J. Chem.Doc. 7 (1967), pp. 88 - 93.
(8) R. Fugmann, W. Braun und W. Vaupel, Angew. Chemie 73 (1961), S. 745 - 751.
(9) E. Meyer in "Mechanized Information Storage, Retrieval, and Dissemination - Proceedings of the FID/IFIP Joint Conference, Rome, 1967" (Editor K. Samuelson), North Holland Publishing Company, Amsterdam 1968, pp. 280 - 288.

(10) G. Salton and E.W. Sussenguth jr., ADI Annual Meeting 1963, Short Papers, Part 2, p. 143; Scientific Report No. ISR 6 to the NSF (1964).
(11) E. Meyer, Angewandte Chemie internat. Edit. 4 (1965), pp. 347 - 352.

Computer-generated Peekaboo Cards for Medium-sized Files (up to 40 000 Items)

By Ernst Meyer

D-67 Ludwigshafen, BASF AG., C6

Summary:

A special type of punched card has been developed which can be punched immediately by the computer and used for fast and simple off-line peephole searches. Document numbers can be read out without mental arithmetic. All card decks can be mixed and sorted by descriptors since change by mistake (i.e. combination of wrong sets) is not possible.

Computers have been assisting us successfully to cope with the literature in Chemistry. But we must not ignore that the card files used previously in industry had certain advantages, too. Retrospective dialog searches in large files are not practicable until now, for cost and other reasons, and batch searches require a precise formulation of the question; this means that the user of computerized documentation services, before directing his query to the machine, has to decide exactly what he actually wants. The feedback and reformulation of the question, based on the number of hits and on the contents of the first answers, is delayed and rendered more difficult. In other words: For browsing in order to get inspirations, computer batch searches are less useful than the old card files.

This might be the reason why many of our users are running SDI profiles in our tape files not only for current awareness purposes. We experienced that in many laboratories the abstracts from our SDI services were pasted onto cards and collected in browsing files.

Obiously these card files were sorted in a special way, and as they grew, more and more time was needed by the subscriber to classify the incoming abstracts and to put them in order. Nevertheless it seemed worthwhile for many teams to spend a lot of time and effort in order to get browsing files for their special fields of interest.

    Being aware of these needs of our scientists, we reflected on how to save much of this effort by using computer assistance for the encoding of such medium-sized card files. The codes need not to be as efficient as those of the tape services; e.g. for formulas a fragment code will be sufficient. The handling of the file should be so simple that it could be done without any difficulties by all bench chemists. For this purpose the peekaboo card file method offered itself. In these files each descriptor is represented by a special card on which a particular hole position is assigned to each file item (e.g. to each document number). These document numbers are unbroken ascending, and for all descriptors of a given document the position of its number is punched in the corresponding peekaboo cards. If the number of documents in the file exceeds that of the hole positions of the cards, two or perhaps more decks of peekaboo descriptor cards must be installed. The documents themselves or the corresponding abstracts are arranged by their sequential numbers and kept besides the peekaboo file which is arranged by notations or descriptors in numerical or alphabetical order, respectively. During search the descriptor cards asked-for are drawn from the file and combined. AND conditions are handled by superimposing of the cards and peeping through the holes, OR conditions by exchanging the corresponding cards. In doing so, the numbers of the peepholes are noted. NOT conditions are regarded by subsequent superimposing of the corresponding cards and cancelling of the numbers of the remaining peepholes.

    Normal computers can punch Hollerith (IBM) cards only. Using these cards as peekaboo cards, not more than 700 to 800 hole positions can be used for document numbers. This means that for every 700 or 800 documents a new deck of descriptor cards has to be installed. Searching in a file of 10,000 documents, more than 10 cards would have to be drawn for each descriptor asked-for; therefore changing by mistake and combination of

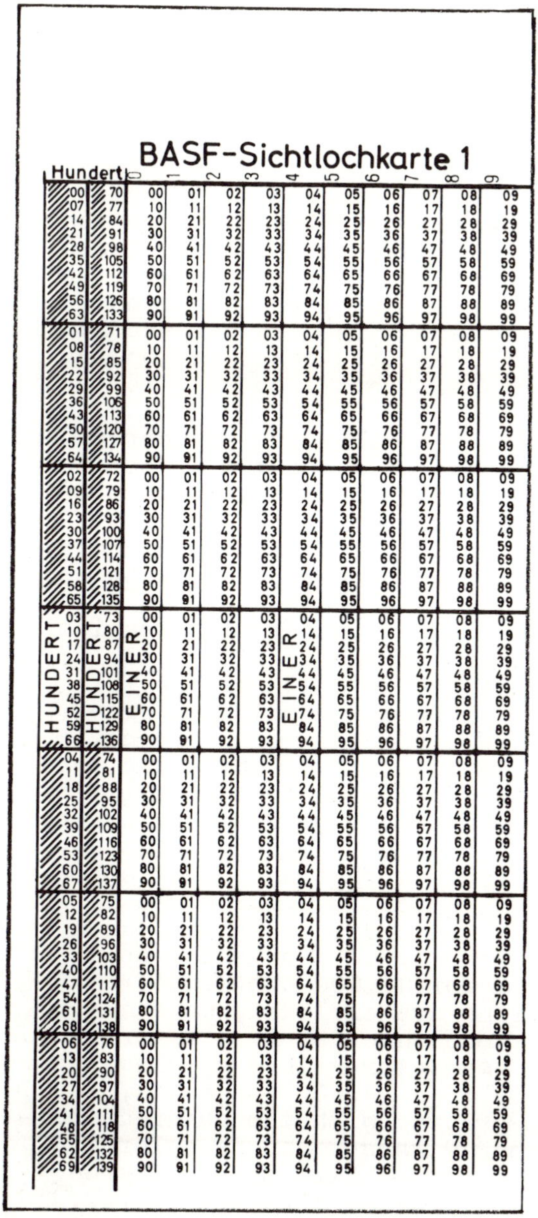

Search Logic

Fig. 1: BASF-peekaboo card. Two numbers have to be read out besides the holes for each hit: the hundreds in the coloured zone (shady here) and the tens and units in the white field. Therefore the document numbers can be read immediately although the same card type is used for 20 different decks.

wrong cards could happen very easily. Furthermore, as far as the same type of cards with hole numbers from 1 through 700 are used, one has to add by mental arithmetic a certain number (700, 1400, etc.) for each deck except of the first one. In order to avoid these drawbacks, we developed a new type of cards (fig. 1).

In these Hollerith cards the area of columns 1 through 70 is subdivided into fields of 10 columns each, in which the numeric positions are numbered from 00 through 99. The "zone" positions besides these fields are numbered in steps of 7, starting with 00 in the 12-line of column 70 up to 63 in column 61, and from 70 to 133 in the 11-line. In the second field (i.e. in columns 60 through 51) the corresponding numbers run from 01 to 64 and from 71 to 134, respectively, and so on.

The hundreds which are valid for the corresponding field are then punched in these two lines: for the first deck of descriptor cards the numbers 00, 01, 02, ... 06; for the second deck 07, 08, ... 13; for the third one 14, 15, ... 20, and so on. For reading out document numbers the ciphers besides two holes have to be read: the hundreds in the 12- and 11-zone (which is coloured yellow for easier differentiation), and the tens and units in the white field itself.

Since in the first twenty decks of the file the zone holes are put at different positions, wrong combinations of cards from different decks are noticed immediately because the hundreds do not shine through. But in searching a file of 14,000 documents, it is very tedious to combine cards from 20 decks. Therefore we constructed a machine which helps us to stick together the cards precisely with transparent adhesive tape. So for every descriptor we combine the cards from respective 5 decks in order to get one deck only of handy larger cards for 3,500 documents. Doing so we get four decks only for 14,000 documents, and since wrong combinations are excluded, we can mix these four decks into one in order to draw or restore all four cards for a descriptor with a single grasp.

For files of more than 14,000 documents, we additionally had cards printed with the hundreds running from 140 through 279 whose zone is colored blue instead of yellow; and for a third type of cards (with hundreds from 280 to 419) the zone is red. So we can mix the peekaboo cards of 42,000 documents into a single deck, and we can draw or restore all

the 12 cards for a descriptor with one grip. For
searches in files of this size we have to repeat the
card combination twelve times, but probably this is
yet done faster than the corresponding LOGON and
dialog procedures via terminal, and in any case it is
much cheaper since almost no maintenance cost will
occur, no computer nor terminal rent, no line cost
etc. You have to pay only for the preparation of the
cards, for the numbering and filing (and sometimes
copying) of the documents or abstracts.

So we concluded that it is not worthwhile to use
computers for searches in files of less than 42,000
documents, provided that a simple Boolean combination
of descriptors (AND, OR, and NOT) is sufficient. If
the file should grow beyond this size, we can change
easily to computer searches since we generate the
cards from magnetic tapes which are preserved carefully.

By corresponding machine programs we can excerpt
and transcode doughter card files from existing tape
services. Files for special areas for which sufficient tape services are not available can be generated
as well. In the BASF group we did this for the field
of coatings, for instance, in the following manner.
We printed a descriptor list of this field in a lucid
form on both sides of a paper sheet, each of the 550
descriptors being prefixed by a four-digit notation
and a check digit. The indexer cancels the assigned
descriptors of a document on the corresponding sheet
using a red crayon. Then the assigned notations and
check digits are recorded on punched cards or magnetic
tape. All that we need furthermore is a suitable program, our cards, perhaps a device for sticking them together, and a little bit of computer time. The computer must be equipped with a punch for binary cards;
but if our own machine is not, we can prepare at
least a suitable tape and have the cards punched at
a service station. If more than one copy of the card
file is desired, duplication can be made off-line.
So we supply e.g. our coatings file to seven different
teams in our company.

Updating is done in small batches, i.e. for every
350 documents, by supply of a deck of small descriptor
cards which is punched half or completely. After
filing of 3,500 documents, the users send us the 5
decks, and we stick them together and send them back.

The notations are punched into some of the last

columns (71 through 80) of the descriptor cards, and printed onto the edge of the cards. After preparation of the large cards we can record them in enlarged form via self-adhesive labels or felt pen at the free space of the cards. In order to avoid trouble by cards which were restored at wrong places, we notch te cards at the upper edge corresponding to their notations which are used for the file order. So we can find a stray card easily.

By a simple trick we can also perform generic searches in two hierarchical levels. The narrower terms of the lower level are given notations with an alphabetic character in the fourth position instead of a cipher. The corresponding broader term gets the same numeric notation with a zero in fourth position, and the document numbers from the corresponding narrower term cards are collected automatically and punched into the card of the broader term. Asking for metals e.g. we also get documents in which iron or lead or copper etc. is indexed only.

These card files became rather favorite soon with our research teams. Therefore I wanted to report here this approach although it is not a sophisticated computer method. Let me summarize briefly the advantages over computer search and conventional peekaboo card files:
1) Much lower search cost, compared with dialog browsing.
2) Lower card-file preparation effort, compared with conventional peekaboo files.
3) Reading off-the document numbers without mental arthmetic.
4) Exact position of the holes, therefore faster handling.
5) Wrong combination of cards from different decks is almost impossible.
6) Easy duplication of the peekaboo card file.
7) Preparation via computer, therefore good possibility to change to computer searches as soon as the file becomes too large for peephole searches.
8) Updating cheap and in small portions.

Computer input does not also mean computer search in all cases; sometimes we ought to remember of the old latin proverb: Simplex sigillum veri.

CICLOPS

A COMPUTER PROGRAM FOR THE DESIGN OF SYNTHESES ON THE BASIS OF A MATHEMATICAL MODEL

Janet Blair, Johann Gasteiger, Carol Gillespie, P.D. Gillespie, and Ivar Ugi
Laboratorium für Organische Chemie der Technischen Universität München

1. INTRODUCTION
1.1 Synthetic Pathways

The synthesis of a given target molecule Z involves the conversion of an ensemble of starting material molecules EM_A into an isomeric EM containing Z, by a chemical reaction, or sequences of such reactions. The initial compounds are previously prepared chemicals belonging to a starting material list $\pounds$, which could be taken from various chemical supply house catalogs.

The detailed characterization of an individual synthesis comprises all initial, intermediate and final compounds in terms of their constitutional and stereochemical features, as well as reactions with their conditions. Such detailed synthesis procedures can not be reasonably included in today's synthesis planning program. Instead one must disregard certain details and single out the most important aspects for which an effective use of computers can be insured. Thus, one chooses representation of the target and its precursors in sequence as the most important feature of a synthesis. In this context we introduce the term <u>constitutional synthetic pathway</u>. If stereochemical features are included it is a <u>stereochemical synthetic pathway</u>.

1.2 Chemical Reactions and Synthetic Pathways as Interconversions of EM within an FIEM

In the initial phase of synthesis design the constitutional and steric features of the target Z are known. The starting material list contains further pertinent information, and if synthetic planning is confined to the use of known reactions and their analogs, additional empirical data is required.

As a rule, neither the particular starting materials, nor byproducts of the target Z, nor any of the reactions to be used are immediately obvious or predetermined. However, most by-products of the potentially useful reactions belong to a small list of relatively simple compounds. It includes H_2O, $NaCl$, CO_2, $(C_6H_5)_3PO$, etc., or their formal equivalents which differ from the latter merely by replacing some atoms by others in the same Periodic Group or by chemically similar groups. It should be noted that any single synthesis may not require all members of a standard by-product list $C_{(Z)}$. Therefore, the set $\{Z, C_{(Z)}\} = \overline{EM}_Z$ is a superset of the EM_Z for almost all reasonable syntheses of Z.

The syntheses of Z lead from the various $EM_A \subset \pounds$ to $EM_Z \subset \overline{EM}_Z$ and are representable in terms of sequences of intermediate EM belonging to the FIEM (Family of Isomeric Ensembles of Mole-

Introduction

cules, i. e., all possible EM derived from the atoms of EM_Z) of that set of atoms $A = \{A_1, \ldots, A_n\}$ which EM_Z contains.

1.3 The BE-Matrices and R-Matrices of an FIEM

The chemical constitution of an EM with n atoms can be represented by a symmetric nxn BE-matrix E. Its off-diagonal entries $e_{ij} = e_{ji} = 0, 1, 2, 3$ ($i \neq j$) are the formal covalent bond orders between atom pairs (A_i, A_j), and its diagonal entries $e_{ii} = 0, 1, 2, \ldots$ are the numbers of free valence electrons of the atoms A_i.

The following example, using α-hydroxy acetonitrile, illustrates a BE-matrix.

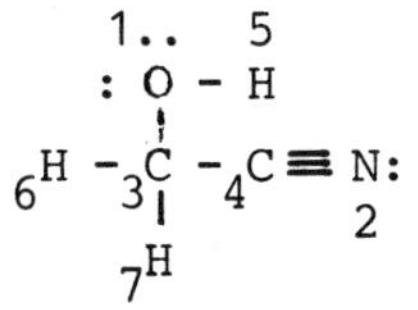

```
        1..  5
        :O - H
     H    |
    6  -3C -4C≡N:
         |     2
        7H
```

Fig. 1
α-hydroxy acetonitrile

$$E \equiv \begin{array}{c} \\ 1 \\ 2 \\ 3 \\ 4 \\ 5 \\ 6 \\ 7 \end{array} \begin{array}{c} 1\;2\;3\;4\;5\;6\;7 \\ \begin{bmatrix} 4 & 0 & 1 & 0 & 1 & 0 & 0 \\ 0 & 2 & 0 & 3 & 0 & 0 & 0 \\ 1 & 0 & 0 & 1 & 0 & 1 & 1 \\ 0 & 3 & 1 & 0 & 0 & 0 & 0 \\ 1 & 0 & 0 & 0 & 0 & 0 & 0 \\ 0 & 0 & 1 & 0 & 0 & 0 & 0 \\ 0 & 0 & 1 & 0 & 0 & 0 & 0 \end{bmatrix} \end{array} \equiv \text{BE-matrix}$$

The row/column sums $e_i = \sum_j e_{ij} = \sum_j e_{ji}$ indicate how many valence electrons belong to the A_i, and can be used to compute the formal electronic charges on atoms, whereas the "cross-sums" $\hat{e}_i = 2e_i - e_{ii}$ refer to total numbers of valence electrons in the orbitals of the A_i (see CHEMLIM).

The row/column indices of an nxn BE-matrix are the indices of an indexed set of atoms $A = A_1, \ldots, A_n$. There are n! different ways to assign n indices to n distinguishable atoms. Accordingly, a molecule or EM of n distinguishable atoms is representable by n equivalent BE-matrices which differ by row/column permutations. BE-matrices are invariant against permutations of row/columns belonging to constitutionally equivalent atoms (see below), such as the H-atoms in CH_4.

The BE-matrices of EM with more than one molecule can be represented in block form where each block refers to a molecule. If it is necessary to identify the molecules of an EM, BE-matrices in block form have obvious advantage. It is further desirable to assign unique canonical indices to all atoms of a molecule yielding an unambiguous selection of one from the n! BE-matrices[2].

Since our standardized indexing of these atoms depends upon the chemical constitution of the molecules, the indices are not necessarily retained during a chemical reaction. Therefore the transformation of a canonical BE-matrix by an R-matrix (see below) yields a BE-matrix whose canonical form must be restored by a suitable row/column permutation.

This indexing of atoms is needed not only for the identification of molecules, but can also be used for the representation of their stereochemical features[2].

Chemical reactions are interconversions of isomeric EM and can be represented as a transformation E→E' of BE-matrices by addition of R-matrices.

$$E + R = E' \qquad \text{eq. (1)}$$

The off-diagonal entries $r_{ij} = r_{ji} = 0, \pm 1, \pm 2, \pm 3$ indicate which covalent bonds are made ($r_{ij} > 0$), or broken ($r_{ij} < 0$) by the reaction, and the diagonal entries $r_{ii} = 0, \pm 1, \pm 2, \ldots$ refer to changes in the distribution of free valence electrons. An R-matrix may be considered as an "electron pushing" instruction.

Any sum of R-matrices is also an R-matrix. The conversion of α-hydroxy acetonitrile (eq. (2)) into its components is represented by the following matrix transformation (eq. (3)):

$$\overset{1}{:}\!\overset{..}{O} - H^5 \quad | \quad {}^6H - \overset{3}{C} - \overset{4}{C} \equiv \overset{2}{N}: \quad \longrightarrow \quad {}^6H - \overset{3}{C} = \overset{..}{\overset{1}{O}}{}_{..} \;+\; {}^5H - \overset{4}{C} \equiv \overset{2}{N}: \qquad \text{eq. (2)}$$

with H on position 7.

$$\begin{bmatrix} & 1 & 2 & 3 & 4 & 5 & 6 & 7 \\ 1 & 4 & & 1 & & 1 & & \\ 2 & & 2 & & 3 & & & \\ 3 & 1 & & & 1 & & 1 & 1 \\ 4 & & 3 & 1 & & & & \\ 5 & 1 & & & & & & \\ 6 & & & 1 & & & & \\ 7 & & & 1 & & & & \end{bmatrix} + \begin{bmatrix} & 1 & 2 & 3 & 4 & 5 & 6 & 7 \\ 1 & & & +1 & -1 & & & \\ 2 & & & & & & & \\ 3 & +1 & & & -1 & & & \\ 4 & & & -1 & +1 & & & \\ 5 & -1 & & & +1 & & & \\ 6 & & & & & & & \\ 7 & & & & & & & \end{bmatrix} = \begin{bmatrix} & 1 & 2 & 3 & 4 & 5 & 6 & 7 \\ 1 & 4 & & 2 & & & & \\ 2 & & 2 & & 3 & & & \\ 3 & 2 & & & & & 1 & 1 \\ 4 & & 3 & & & 1 & & \\ 5 & & & & & 1 & & \\ 6 & & & 1 & & & & \\ 7 & & & 1 & & & & \end{bmatrix}$$

eq. (3)

Introduction

It follows that $\sum_{ij} r_{ij} = 0$, because the number of valence electrons stays constant during chemical reactions. The sum of the absolute values of the entries of an R-matrix $D = \sum_{ij} |r_{ij}|$ is twice the number of valence electrons participating in the reaction. An R-matrix does not represent an individual chemical reaction, but may be characteristic of a number of chemical reactions.

1.4 Fitting Requirements of R-Matrices

The addition of an R-matrix to a BE-matrix E corresponds to a transformation $E \rightarrow E'$, if R fits E. Accordingly, R may have entries $r_{ij} < 0$ only where E has non-zero entries $e_{ij} \geq |r_{ij}|$. Thus, non-zero entries of an E can be used to manufacture fitting R-matrices. Addition of the fitting R-matrix R_Z to E_Z results in the BE-matrix E_Y of a potential synthetic precursor.

The reverse process, $EM_Y \rightarrow EM_Z$, representing the synthetic step of interest, is accomplished with $R_Y = -R_Z$ fitted to EM_Y.

Not every R-matrix fitting a BE-matrix corresponds to a single step chemical reaction, but can also refer to a sequence of reactions whose R-matrix is the sum of the R-matrices of individual reactive steps. This feature generates a representation leading to an analysis of single step mechanistic alternatives[1].

1.5 The Search for Synthetic Pathways by Matrix Fitting and Some General Features of CICLOPS

Transformation of a BE-matrix E_Z by all fitting R-matrices generates the complete family of BE-matrices of the FIEM containing EM_Z. This could be used for synthetic design by first scanning the FIEM for those EM containing starting materials listed in £, and then establishing pathways via sequences of intermediates. An approach of this type is not feasible because the FIEM involved are generally too large to be generated and analyzed within reasonable time limits.

The CICLOPS program corresponds to a practical approximation for an idealized synthetic design based upon the previously discussed mathematical model and promises effectiveness without serious neglect of interesting intermediates, or pathways.

CICLOPS is confined to <u>closed shell Chemistry</u>, i. e., to chemical systems whose valence orbitals contain pairs of electrons with opposite spin. The diagonal entries of the BE-matrices of closed shell Chemistry are zero or even integers. Although this does eliminate radical chemistry, no pathways of synthetic interest are lost[1c].

CICLOPS is being developed in PL/1 on an IBM 360/91. PL/1 was selected because of algebraic as well as list handling capabilities.

2. DATA STRUCTURES
2.1 BE-Matrices

The BE-matrix of a molecule containing n atoms is n×n, sparsely filled, and symmetric. Storage of the entire matrix and corresponding atomic numbers would require n(n+1) entries, consisting mainly of zeros. Internally, the BE-matrix is represented by an upper triangular packed bond matrix (a weighted connectivity matrix), a vector of unshared valence electron pairs (diagonal entries of BE), and a vector of atomic numbers, requiring in the neighborhood of 3n entries. This is illustrated in Fig.2 using $C_2H_4O_2$ as an example.

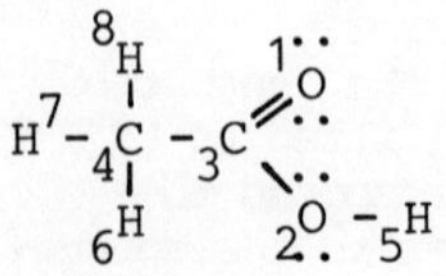

	1	2	3	4	5	6	7	8
1	4	0	2	0	0	0	0	0
2	0	4	1	0	1	0	0	0
3	2	1	0	1	0	0	0	0
4	0	0	1	0	0	1	1	1
5	0	1	0	0	0	0	0	0
6	0	0	0	1	0	0	0	0
7	0	0	0	1	0	0	0	0
8	0	0	0	1	0	0	0	0

BE-Matrix

1	O
2	O
3	C
4	C
5	H
6	H
7	H
8	H

Atomic Symbols

Fig. 2

Internal Representation:

Packed BE bond matrix, upper triangular:
```
1 2 2 3 4 4 4
3 3 5 4 6 7 8
2 1 1 1 1 1 1
```

Diagonal entry vector:
```
1 2 3 4 5 6 7 8
4 4 0 0 0 0 0 0
```

Atomic symbol vector:
```
1 2 3 4 5 6 7 8
O O C C H H H H
```

When used by the R-matrix generation program, the upper triangular BE-matrix is expanded to a complete packed matrix enabling fast access to row sums and connectivities.

2.2 R-Matrices

R-matrices are not represented internally in matrix form. Rather, the negative off-diagonal entries are added to the BE-matrix, the diagonal entries are added to the diagonal vector and the positive off-diagonal entries are contained in an 8x3 matrix of made bonds. The resulting BE-matrix is separated into molecular fragments which are sequentially ordered and further evaluated.

2.3 Atomic Sequential Indexing of a BE-Matrix

To enable library lookup of molecules it is necessary to uniquely order the atoms within the BE-matrix. A system has been implemented which provides such a set of sequential indices as well as other useful information. During this ordering process constitutionally equivalent atom groups are discovered and this information is used later in the selection of breakable bonds. Further, all resonance structures have the same sequential indices although the entries in the BE-matrix will differ[2].

In this ordering scheme atoms with the higher atomic numbers receive the lower atomic sequence indices (ASI). Equivalence classes of atoms with like atomic numbers are formed. These classes are arranged in order of descending atomic number. Each member of an equivalence class receives the same tentative ASI $k = n+1$ where n = number of atoms with higher atomic number.

Beginning with equivalence class 1 the atoms within the class are given their final indices as follows. When atomic numbers alone do not permit an unambiguous index assignment, the ASI's of the first sphere neighbors of the atom are considered. A neighbor weight vector (NWV) consisting of the ASI's of neighbors arranged in ascending order is formed. The atoms with the lower NWV's are then assigned lower ASI's. This process is repeated with the 2nd, 3rd, etc. sphere neighbor until all atoms within the equivalence class are assigned unique ASI's or all neighbors are considered. When all NWV's have been compared and atoms are still ambiguously assigned their bonds are examined. Atoms with triple bonds are given lower ASI's than atoms with double or single bonds and likewise atoms with double bonds receive lower ASI's than atoms with single bonds. Atoms not differentiated at this point are constitutionally equivalent and can be arbitrarily assigned the remaining ASI's within the range of their equivalence class.

When all atoms of equivalence class K are assigned final atomic sequence indices the above process is repeated with equivalence class K+1.

An example of this indexing is given in Fig. 3.

Sequential Ordering Process   Fig. 3

$$\begin{array}{c} {}_1^1H \\ {}_2H - {}_1^1C - {}_2C \diagup\!\!\!\diagdown {}_1^{\cdot\cdot}O{}^{\cdot\cdot} \\ {}_3H \quad\quad {}_2O^{\cdot\cdot} - {}_4H \end{array}$$

Equivalence Classes   Minimum ASI

1) O_1, O_2 1
2) C_1, C_2 3
3) H_1, H_2, H_3, H_4 5

Assign ASI's to Equivalence Class 1

Atom	NWV	ASI
O_1	30	1
O_2	35	2

Assign ASI's to Equivalence Class 2

Atom	NWV	ASI
C_1	3555	4
C_2	1230	3

Assign ASI's to Equivalence Class 3

Atom	NWV	ASI
H_1	4	6
H_2	4	6
H_3	4	6
H_4	2	5

	NWV 2nd sphere	
H_1	3	6
H_2	3	6
H_3	3	6

H_1, H_2, H_3 are constitutionally equivalent and are arbitrarily assigned ASI's 6-8.

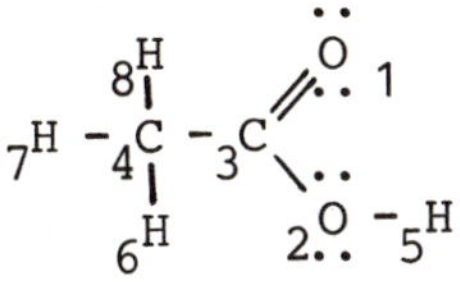

$$\begin{array}{c} {}_{8}H \\ {}_{7}H - {}_{4}C - {}_{3}C \overset{\displaystyle \overset{..}{O}}{\underset{\displaystyle \underset{..}{O}-{}_{5}H}{\diagdown}} {}^{1} \\ {}_{6}H \quad {}_{2} \end{array}$$ Sequentially Ordered Molecule

3. REACTION MATRIX GENERATION

For any BE-matrix there exists a finite number of mathematically fitting reaction matrices (R-matrices). Analysis of the latter based upon their definitions (see section 1) and limited to the breaking of one, two or three bonds shows that they may be classified into 38 general R-matrix types. As an illustration, the reaction type

$$\begin{array}{c} I-J \\ K-L \end{array} \longrightarrow \begin{array}{c} I-K \\ J-L \end{array}$$

includes, among others, such reactions as additions to multiple bonds e. g.,

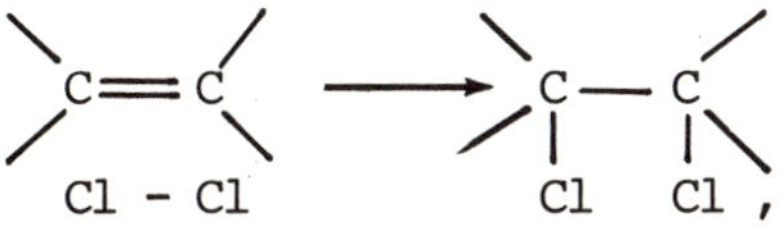

$$\underset{Cl - Cl}{\diagup C = C \diagdown} \longrightarrow \underset{Cl \quad Cl}{\diagup C - C \diagdown}$$ Fig. 4

and the Wagner-Meerwein Rearrangement of Pinene Hydrochloride to Bornylchloride.

Fig. 5

Each type is generated with the assignment of non-zero values to an R-matrix element identified by its row/column indices. All the possibilities for each R-matrix type acting upon a single BE-matrix are achieved by permutations on the indices.

In order to eliminate generation of meaningless, redundant or uninteresting reactions, a sub-set of R-matrices is chosen on the basis of some selection rules. First, certain bonds in the BE-matrix are flagged as breakable. These include all multiple bonds, carbon and hydrogen bonds to heteroatoms, and bonds one and two neighbors distant. Before considering reactions, the

atoms of the target molecule are scanned and evaluated against
the chemical limits table. This valence bond analysis sets up 10
bit vectors which enable elimination of many R-matrices which,
though fitting, would generate unacceptable BE-matrices. For
example, if atom A_i has its maximum permissable number of bonds
and free electrons, those R-matrices increasing the number of
surrounding electrons are ignored. Reactions having a single
atom exchange are similarly skipped. Other, more specific rules,
avoiding certain multiple bonds, etc. are included.

The 38 R-matrix types are arranged into 3 separate groups:
1.) those breaking one bond (5), 2.) those breaking two bonds
(12), 3.) and those breaking three bonds (21). It has been shown[1b]
that all R-matrices breaking 4 bonds are sums of 2 R-matrices
which break 2 bonds. The R-matrix types breaking 1 bond are as
follows:

$$I-J \longrightarrow I+J:$$
$$I-J+Y \longrightarrow I+J-Y$$
$$I-J+:X \longrightarrow I:+J-X$$
$$I-J+:X \longrightarrow J-X-I$$
$$I-J+:X+Y \longrightarrow I-X+J-Y$$

In the following discussion outlining the generation of R-
matrices (R-GEN), A_i, A_j represent atoms bonded together in the
target molecule, $A_y \in EM_z$, ($y \neq i, j$), A_y can take
one additional bond, and $A_x \in EM_z$ ($x \neq i, j, y$) can give up two
electrons and take 1 bond. Note that i, j, y, x are the BE- and
R-matrix row/column indices for those atoms and all non-zero
entries in the R-matrix are in these rows. For example, breaking
bond A_i-A_j corresponds to an R-matrix with $r_{ij} = r_{ji} = -1$.
The three programs R-GEN 1, 2, and 3 are cycled through on
atom indices x, (i, j), (k, l), (m, n), y as loop variables.

R-GEN 1 matrices break one bond A_i-A_j and make 0, 1 or 2
bonds. Bond A_i-A_j is pre-selected as breakable. When bonds
(A_i-A_j) are constitutionally equivalent, only one bond A_i-A_j
from the set is broken. The loop nesting order is x, (i, j), y
with y varying most rapidly.

R-GEN 2 matrices break two bonds (A_i-A_j),(A_k-A_l). Bond A_i-A_j
is breakable and A_k-A_l is either breakable and within 6 bonds of
A_i-A_j or it belongs to the by-products and is breakable. Non-
zero indices of R are i, j, k, l, x, y. R-GEN 2 is looped on x,
(i, j), (k, l), y, y being the innermost loop.

R-GEN 3 matrices break three bonds (A_i-A_j),(A_k-A_l), and
(A_m-A_n). Bonds (A_i-A_j), and (A_k-A_l) are chosen if they are less
than 7 bonds apart. Bond (A_m-A_n) is any bond in the EM. The non-
zero rows of R are i, j, k, l, m, n, x and y. R-GEN 3 is cycled

through on loop variables x, (i, j), (k, l), (m, n) and y with y varying most rapidly.

4. BASIC DESIGN

CICLOPS takes a target molecule as input, sequentially orders it and applies pre-selected R-matrices generating first level precursors. Based upon several evaluation procedures, a selected group of precursors is output on a file. This file is then used as input and the next level precursors are generated, evaluated, and saved on the corresponding level file. This process is repeated, using the most recently generated file as input, creating a tree structure of syntheses. A synthesis is complete when each component is found in the starting material library. Fig. 6 contains an outline of the basic design.

5. FILES

CICLOPS uses two types of structurally organized files. The first is an indexed sequential file allowing variable length blocked records and random access. This sort of file is used for data, which, although primarily sequentially processed, requires random access. When processed sequentially, it can be as fast as a consecutive file[3]. The second file type is a direct sequential one with fixed length records. This file provides a more rapid access time and is used for data that is often written and read, and does not need random access.

Each reaction at a tree level is stored on an indexed sequential file. The latter is usually written and read in a sequential mode and processed in a random access mode only when it is necessary to trace a synthesis pathway. Each file block contains a header and one reaction. This header contains information concerning component molecules in the reaction. The starting material library file consists of 5,000 molecules stored in upper triangular sequentially ordered BE-matrices. This library is a keyed indexed sequential file. To facilitate rapid library lookup, a nine character alpha-numeric key is used. This key contains the total number of atoms in the molecule and numbers of carbon, hydrogen, oxygen and nitrogen atoms. Using this particular choice, most keys will point to single library entries, maximum 10, minimizing library search time.

The save file is a direct access sequential one used as a scratch file while the tree level file is being generated. Reactions from one level are written on this file and re-read for a comparison with other reactions of the same level in order to select the best reactions which are then saved on the level file. The latter is repeatedly being sorted.

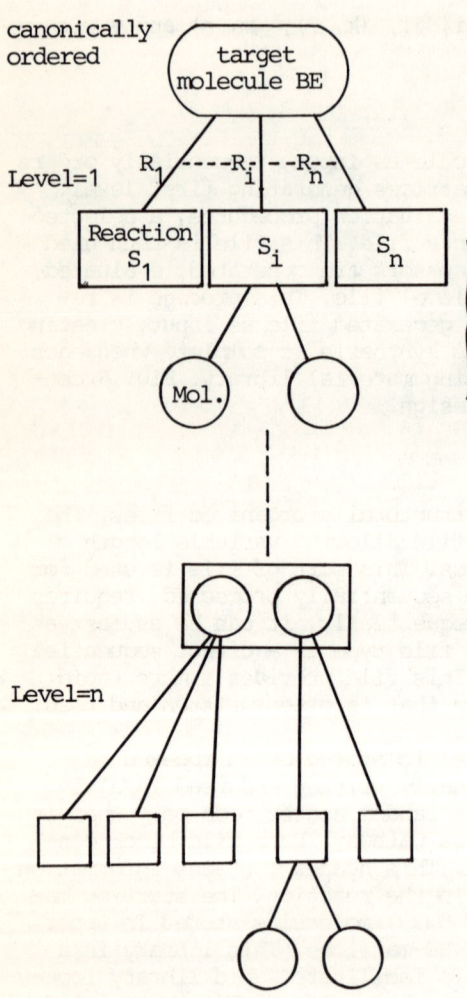

Fig. 6

Add selected R-matrices, generating synthetic precursors

Each reaction at this level is broken into its molecular parts, ordered and evaluated.

Selected reactions are saved on file Level 1.

The next level is processed; each molecule being the target molecule, and a synthesis TREE is generated.

A complete synthesis is found when all parts of the precursors are in the starting material library, and the pathway is traced up the TREE.

6. EVALUATION OF BE-MATRICES AND SYNTHETIC PATHWAYS

Evaluation serves three functions in synthesis planning programs. It provides a criterion for eliminating improbable, unprofitable or redundant molecules. Secondly, individual, single step syntheses for the same molecule can be compared and finally, complete synthetic pathways from starting materials to the target may be judged.

Evaluation begins with the fitting of R-matrices where chemical limits considerations are used to eliminate reactions leading to electronically impossible molecules. Next, energies for those bonds broken and made are calculated, allowing reactions to be rejected when energy differences are too great. Kinetic and steric parameters are also evaluated, producing further yes/no decisions for retaining reactions (EVAL 1 PROCEDURES).

After the reaction has been blocked and the molecules sequentially indexed, they are compared with the starting material library and, if not identified therein, further evaluated on the basis of other chemical parameters. This leads to the assignment of weights to each molecule and then to the reaction as a whole. These weights are inversely proportional to the value of the molecule, i. e., they are "badness" indicators. Naturally, molecules found in the starting material list receive low values while the rest have larger numbers. The farther one proceeds down the tree, the higher the weight values become, accounting for the fact that more reaction steps are involved, synthetically less attractive than shorter pathways.

Assignment of weights to a reaction starts with the calculation of a "badness" value for each of its molecular components. This value, P, is formed from the product of many terms, Q_1, representing various chemical parameters as shown in eq. (3).

$$P = \Pi\, C_1 Q_1 \qquad \text{eq. (3)}$$

The coefficients C_1 are varied in an effort to fit P to chemical reality.

Reaction weights at a particular level L, WT_L, are then calculated as the sum of P's from its molecules plus the reaction weight, WT_{L-1}, from the precursor reaction at level L-1, where N = number of molecules in reaction as given by eq. (4).

$$WT_L = \frac{1}{N}\sum P_N + WT_{L-1} \qquad \text{eq. (4)}$$

Finally, WT values for all those reactions required for one complete synthesis of the target are summed, yielding WTS, an evaluation of the total synthetic pathway. eq. (5).

$$WTS = \sum WT \qquad \text{eq. (5)}$$

7. TREE STRUCTURE AND TREE GENERATION

Tree book-keeping information is kept as a doubly linked list in central memory, each node representing a reaction and its components. Pertinent information such as the number of molecules in a reaction, various evaluations on the latter, the file address of molecules or their starting material library entries is contained in the node entry.

Actual chemical information, represented as upper triangular BE-matrices is kept on files, one file for each tree level.

Beginning at Level 0, where the root node is the target molecule, 15 reactions are selected as promising on the basis of evaluation (EVAL 1). Ten of these reactions are saved for possible later consideration, the best 5 selected for expansion as the first level of the tree. The tree is then expanded in a staged breadth first method, the number of reactions selected per level being a function of the tree depth. Selection is based upon the various evaluation procedures and present tree construction as required. CICLOPS terminates when a predetermined number of complete (all fragments found in starting material library) syntheses are found and they are traced to the root with each reaction step being output. If a maximum tree depth is reached before the required number of syntheses is generated, complete reactions are output as above. Then, from storage, CICLOPS takes the 5 next best initial reactions on the root as Level 1 and repeats as above.

8. FUNCTION FLOW

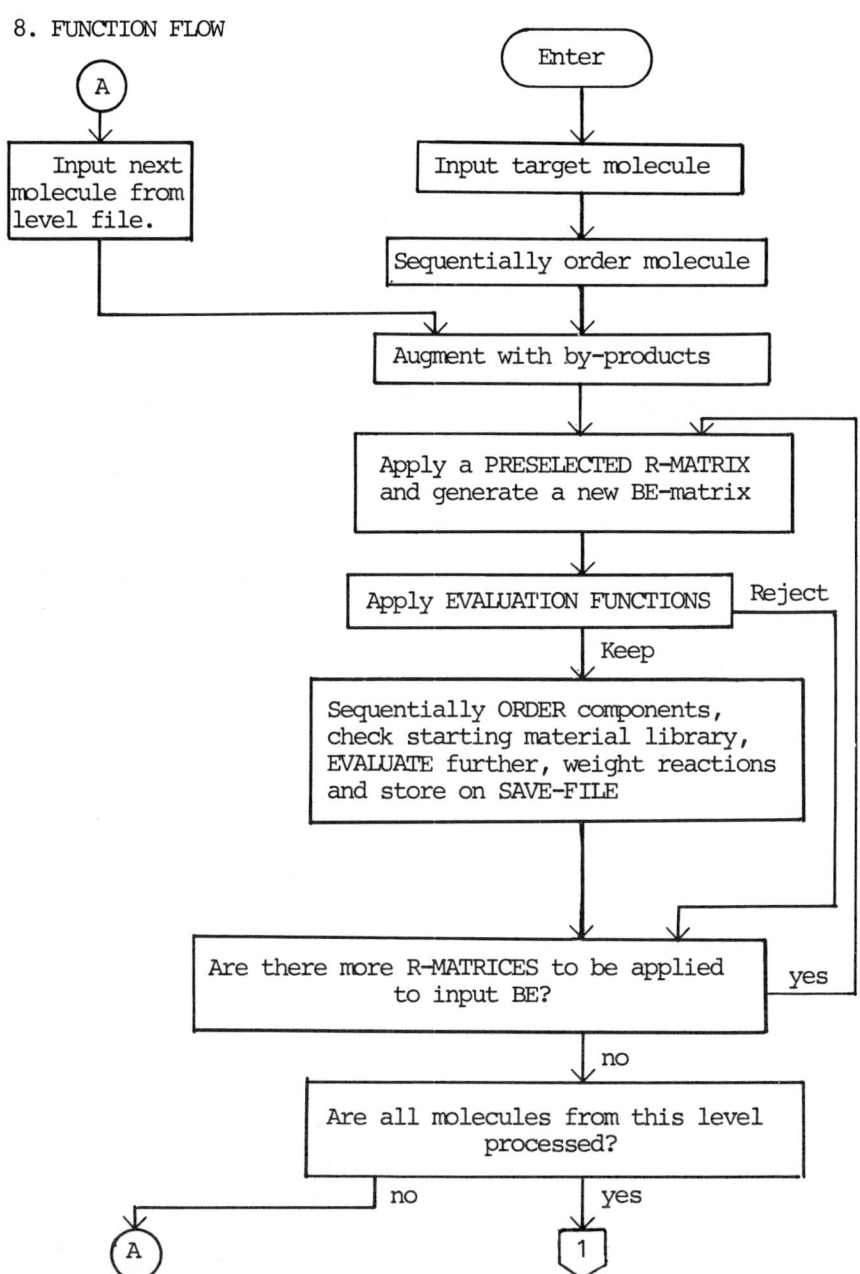

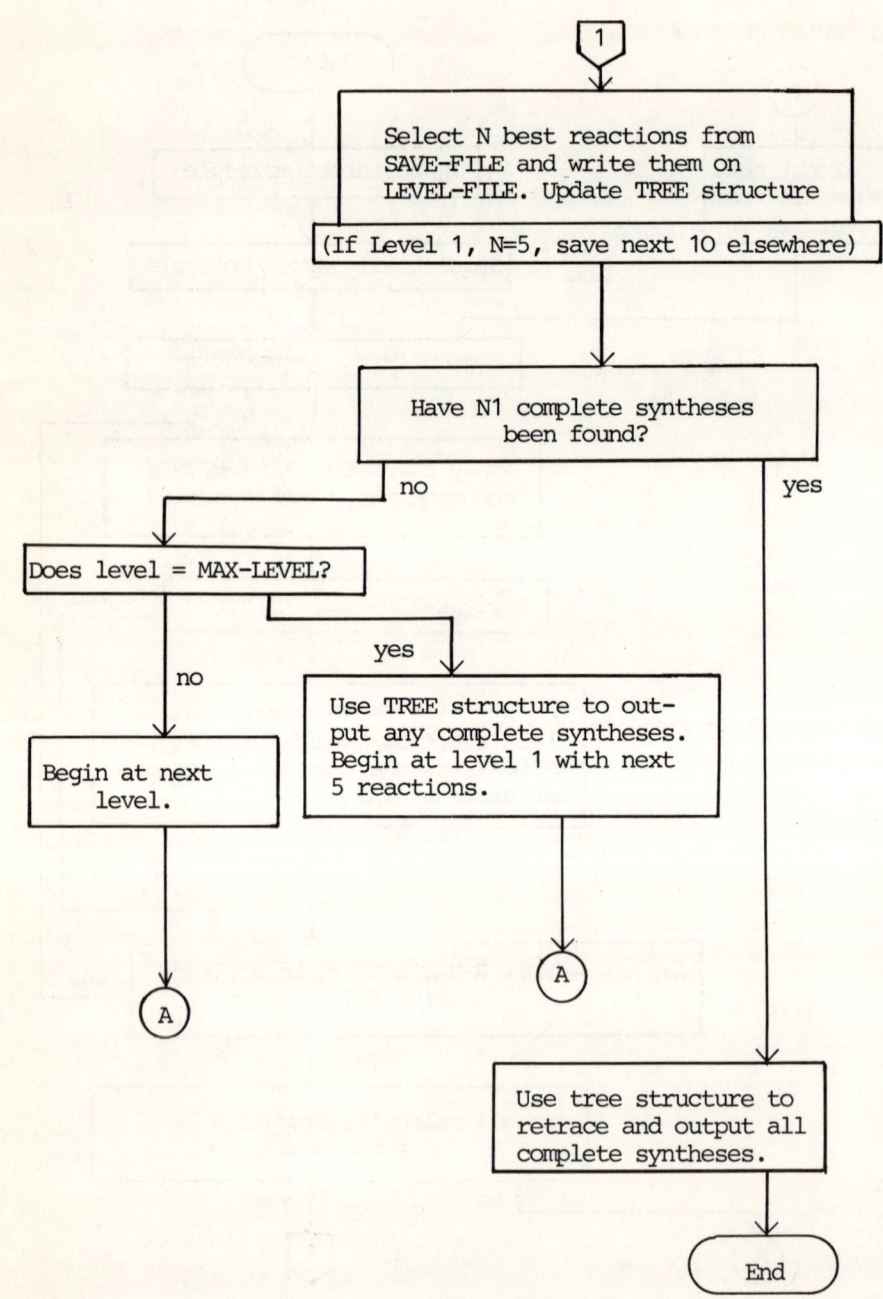

Acknowledgements

Hereby we gratefully acknowledge the partial support of this work by The National Science Foundation, USA, (Grant No. 28927X), Deutsche Forschungsgemeinschaft and Volkswagen-Stiftung e. V. We also thank Ms. Sharon Cutri and Ms. Helga Hofmann for their aid in preparing the manuscript.

References

1. a) I. Ugi and P. Gillespie, Angew. Chem., 83, 980 (1971); Angew. Chem. Intern. Edit., 10, 914 (1971)
   b) I. Ugi and P. Gillespie, Angew. Chem., 83, 982 (1971); Angew. Chem. Intern. Edit., 10, 915 (1971)
   c) I. Ugi, P. Gillespie, and C. Gillespie, Trans. New York Acad. of Sci., 34, 416 (1972)
   d) J. Dugundji and I. Ugi, Topics in Current Chemistry, Springer Verlag, Heidelberg, (in press)
2. J. Blair, J. Dugundji, J. Gasteiger, C. Gillespie, P. P. Gillespie, and I. Ugi, Angew. Chem. (in preparation)
3. I. Weinberg, PL/1 Programming: A Manual of Style, McGraw-Hill, New York, (1971)

Abbreviations

ASI:	Atomic Sequence Index
BE-MATRIX:	Bond and Electron Matrix
CHEMLIM:	Chemical Limitations
CICLOPS:	Chemical Implementation of Computers in the Logic Oriented Planning of Syntheses
EM:	Ensemble of Molecules
FIEM:	Family of Isomeric Ensembles of Molecules
NWV:	Neighbor Weight Vector
R-MATRIX:	Reaction Matrix

COMPUTER-ASSISTED THREE-DIMENSIONAL SYNTHETIC ANALYSIS

W. Todd Wipke
Department of Chemistry
Princeton University, Princeton, N. J.

1. INTRODUCTION

Problems in chemical synthesis may be divided into several classes on the basis of what is given and what is required in the problem. In a class I problem, we are given starting material A and asked what can be made in a few steps using a limited range

$$\begin{array}{ll} \text{I} & A \longrightarrow ? \\ \text{II} & A \longrightarrow T \\ \text{III} & ? \longrightarrow T \end{array}$$

of reagents (a common industrial problem). This problem requires working forward. Many drug syntheses fall into class II; a complex target T is given and a similar complex molecule A is chosen as the starting material, the problem being to find interconnecting paths between them. One can work both forward and backward on this problem. Class III is the mirror image of class I and characterizes the most innovative syntheses. The target T is specified, but the reactions and starting materials to be used are left unspecified. This problem requires working backward from T, attempting to deduce the potential precursors of T, recursively. This discussion centers on solving problems of class III, but the techniques and representations mentioned here should also be applicable to problems of class I and II.

The potential of the computer in synthetic planning was recognized ten years ago by Sarett: "Automated planning of synthetic routes could enhance progress by five-fold and develop the state of the art to the same high level achieved in the elucidation of structure. It seems quite reasonable to anticipate that computer automation will eventually come to synthetic chemistry just as new instrumentation has come to structural problems."[1]

Five years later the first computer program (OCSS) for the design of constitutional syntheses was reported.[2] This program (and a later version, LHASA[3]) demonstrated a simple yet powerful technique for the design of organic syntheses termed the "logic-centered" approach. In its "pure" form this approach utilizes features of the synthetic objective as clues in determining what transformations might be used to obtain this structure and consequently deduces the structure of the possible precursors.[4] Although the diagrams produced by OCSS-LHASA appeared to carry stereochemical information, molecules were treated only in a constitutional sense and stereochemistry was totally ignored.

In most complex targets of interest stereochemistry is a valuable clue to be utilized. In some targets, the major obstacle is stereochemistry. Success in synthesizing complex polyfunctional compounds depends on utilizing differences in functional group reactivities, but functional group reactivities are quite sensitive to steric environment. How then can one rationally ignore stereochemistry and yet hope to develop a good synthetic plan?—He can't.

For these reasons, we began in 1969 to build a new program (SECS) to concentrate on both aspects of stereochemistry: the conformation independent part (recognizable by symbol manipulation, cis-trans), and the conformation dependent part (spatial relationships, proximity, steric effects).

The partial sequence below, taken from the synthesis of aromadendrene, 1, by Buchi,[5] illustrates the use of stereochemistry in synthetic analysis. Inferring 2 from 1 requires specific changes in configuration resulting from the pinacol rearrangement. ($\Rightarrow$ indicates logical implication in the analytical or antithetic direction.) The cis relationship of the two hydroxyl groups in 2 infers 3 as a possible precursor, if attack by the oxidizing agent on the double bond in 3 occurs from the top.

NEED FOR INTERACTIVE SYSTEM. In theory the computer could solve the entire synthesis problem without human intervention, but in practice the problem space is too extensive to enumerate completely, and we have insufficient knowledge of chemical reactivity and of proper evaluation criteria to permit a closed solution. To close the solution, we use the chemist to evaluate results and guide further search. By saving some of our human chemical input for execution time, we gain flexibility and power to meet situations unanticipated by the programmer. Thus, we delegate to the computer those tasks that the computer can do best and retain for the chemist, guidance, evaluation, and termination prerogatives. The chemist-computer combination seems more flexible and for now seems to be the most powerful arrangement.

2. USER'S VIEW OF THE SIMULATION AND EVALUATION OF CHEMICAL SYNTHESIS (SECS) PROGRAM

The SECS program, in contrast to other synthesis programs (e.g., Chap. 6), does treat stereochemistry in deriving synthetic routes. SECS was first demonstrated publically via teletype at a Gordon Conference July 1972, and then via GT40 graphics terminal and trans-Atlantic cable at the NATO Advanced Study Institute in Holland, June 1973 (see Chap. 13). The operation of the program will now be described as a chemist would use it on a DEC GT40 graphics terminal over the telephone. Use of SECS with the Evans and Sutherland LDS-1 graphics system locally at the Princeton Computer Graphics Laboratory is essentially the same, except a three-dimensional acoustic tablet is used for drawing rather than a light pen.

Typically the user comes to the computer with a specific synthetic target in mind. He dials the Princeton Computer Graphics Laboratory on the phone and logs onto a terminal such as shown in Figure 1. He types RUN DSK SECS; the program asks for RESTART FILENAME. If he is continuing an old problem, he types the problem name, otherwise a carriage return. SECS responds with a ":" and he types GO to begin execution. The user then picks up the pen and positions it over the word DRAW on the screen which acts as a "button" to enter drawing mode. (See Figure 2.) To draw a bond, he positions the tracking cross at the beginning of the bond, depresses the space bar on the key board, moves the cross to the end of the bond, and depresses the space bar again. Multiple bonds are made by drawing over the same bond again. DELETE is used to delete atoms or bonds. ERASE clears the entire structure. Hetero-atoms are specified by selecting the desired atom type on the right side of the screen and touching the atom with the cross, and depressing

150   Three-Dimensional Synthetic Analysis

Figure 1. The SECS synthesis program on a Digital Equipment Corporation GT40 graphics terminal with light pen. The GT40 has 8K 16-bit words of memory and a PDP-11/05 processor.

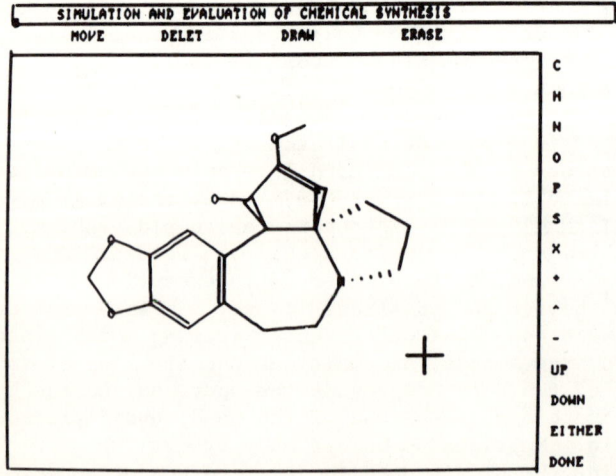

Figure 2. Input phase of SECS. The cross is for light pen tracking. The structure is cephalotaxine.

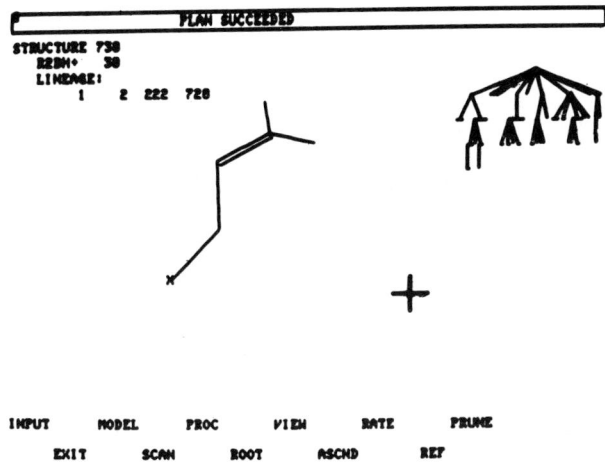

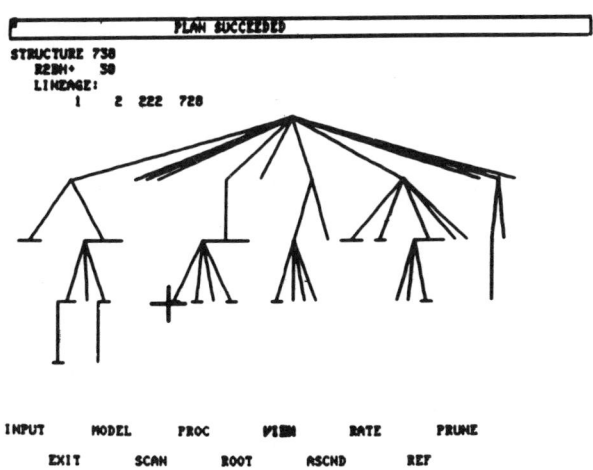

Figure 3. SECS processing mode. Top, a precursor is displayed. Bottom, VIEW mode expands the tree for selection of a precursor for viewing and further processing.

the space bar. To specify stereochemistry, he selects UP, DOWN or EITHER, hits the bond to be specified, and finally hits the atom with respect to which the bond is up or down. MOVE allows repositioning atoms on the screen.

When the structure is complete, the chemist points to the DONE button, transferring control to the display shown in Figure 3. He then may point to MODEL to generate a three-dimensional model of the target molecule. From the teletype he may obtain bond angles, bond lengths, dihedral angles, etc., if he requests them. To begin analysis, the chemist points to the PROCESS button, causing SECS to scan its chemistry library of transforms and to generate one level of synthetic precursors which are flashed on the screen as SECS evaluates them. The chemist may then evaluate one level of precursors; he points to SCAN and then to the member of the tree from which to begin the scan. The buttons GOOD, BAD, and INDIF allow the chemist to keep, delete, or shelve the precursors. He VIEWs the structure in which he is most interested by pointing to the node in the tree which represents that structure. He may then PROCESS that one further to generate another subtree. REF produces a literature reference for the transform currently on the screen. In order to see the entire synthetic sequence (see Figure 14), the chemist either types SEQ or sets one of the console switches.

INPUT returns one to the input phase (Figure 2). RATE allows evaluation of the current structure on the screen, while PRUNE automatically prunes away all structures not specified as GOOD. For very large synthetic trees, the chemist may reROOT the tree at a lower node so that fewer nodes need be displayed. ASCND then reroots the tree at the parent of the current root to return to a higher level of display. In this way, the chemist may find his way through trees too large to display in their entirety.

Other options allow display of atom types, atom numbers, translation and rotation in 3-D, rocking the molecule back and forth, display in time-separated stereo or stereo pairs, plotting of the screen, changing strategies, and saving the state of analysis. At no time in an analysis does the chemist divert his attention from chemistry, because the program understands and communicates in *his* language--the structural diagram. With this overview, we turn to details.

3. ORGANIZATION OF SECS

SECS is a modular program written in FORTRAN IV and operates on a Digital Equipment Corporation PDP-10 computer with 48 K of user memory and a disk as auxiliary storage. The relationships between the modules and hardware are shown in Figure 4. SECS can be run with the Evans and Sutherland LDS-1 display system with a three-dimensional acoustic tablet[6] or alternatively with a DEC GT40 Graphics terminal with light pen. The former has the advantage of smooth rotation and perspective hardware,

Organization of SECS

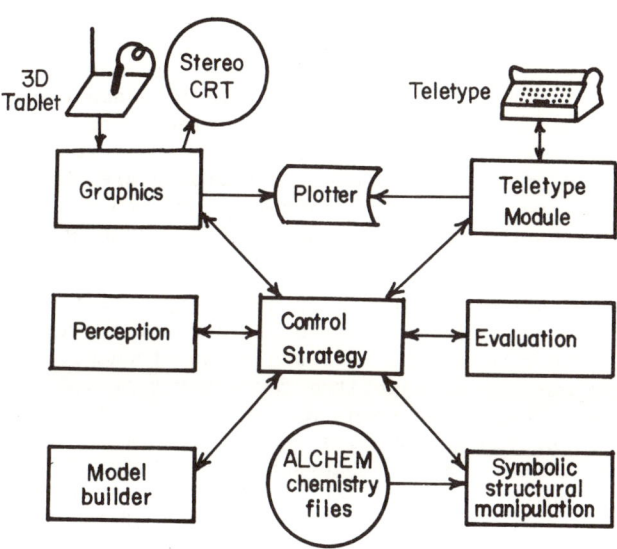

Figure 4. Block diagram of SECS program.

but the latter has the advantage of being portable, inexpensive, and the capability for operation remote from the computer using a telephone, even from Holland to Princeton. Remote access to SECS is also possible via a 22 pound thermal printing teletype, in which case structural diagrams are output as in Figure 5, and structural input is via connection table, or from a disk file. The structure may be entered with 2- or 3-D coordinates or with no coordinates. Normally structures are drawn as a two-dimensional structural diagram, but one may also trace a three-dimensional molecular model, or draw freehand in three dimensions.[6]

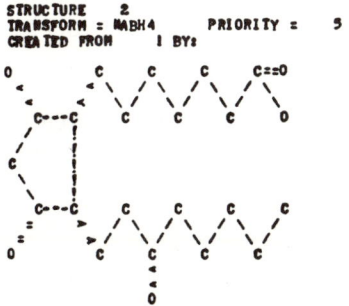

Figure 5. Structural output from teletype. Dotted bonds appear as < and wedged bonds as >.

SECS derives the necessary stereochemical information from any of the various input representations along with perception of other synthetically significant features. It may then use the model building module to rapidly obtain a reasonable 3-D model of the input structure. SECS then selects appropriate chemical transforms and generates precursor structures which are evaluated by the evaluation module. Structures are shown to the chemist as they are evaluated. Control returns to the chemist who then evaluates the precursors and processes the ones of his choosing.

INFORMATION NEEDS. First it is necessary to represent the molecular structure including stereochemistry of the target molecule; second, there must be a representation of chemical transforms or there must be an algorithm for generating valid chemical transforms. Third, one needs an applicator which selects appropriate transforms and applies each transform to the structure, generating one or more precursors. Additionally, it has been found convenient and efficient to develop a heirarchy of data structures and concepts covering features of the molecule, relationships between features of the molecule, and relationships between precursors.

4. REPRESENTATION OF STRUCTURE

Internally the structure is represented as a redundant connection table (CT)--actually two tables, an ATOM TABLE and a BOND TABLE,

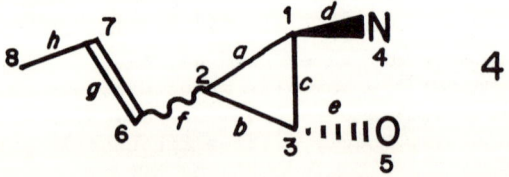

Table I. ATOM TABLE for $\underset{\sim}{4}$ before PERCEPTION

Atom Input Number	ATYPE	ASTEREO	NBDS	NATCH	ATBD	BD
1	1	1	3	3	2 3 4	a c d
2	1	2	3	3	1 3 6	a b f
3	1	1	3	3	2 1 5	b c e
4	3	0	1	1	1	d
5	4	0	1	1	3	e
6	1	1	3	2	2 7	f g
7	1	1	3	2	6 8	g h
8	1	0	1	1	7	h

Three-Dimensional Synthetic Analysis 155

Table II. BOND TABLE for 4

Bond Input Number	BTYPE	BSTEREO	AT1	AT2
a	1	0	1	2
b	1	0	2	3
c	1	0	3	1
d	1	1	1	4
e	1	6	3	5
f	1	4	2	6
g	2	0	6	7
h	1	0	7	8

where atoms are numbered in the order they were drawn; ATYPE C = 1, H = 2, N = 3, O = 4; charge and the x,y,z coordinates for each atom are also represented but not shown here; ASTEREO 0 = not stereocenter, 1 = stereocenter, 2 = unspecified stereocenter; NBDS = number of valences used; ATBD = the number of attached atoms; and BD = bond numbers of attached bonds in some order as in ATBD. BTYPE 1 = single, 2 = double, 3 = triple; BSTEREO, 0 = none, 1 = AT2 up with respect to AT1, 6 = AT2 down wrt. to AT1, 4 = AT2 either up or down wrt. to AT1; AT1 and AT2 are atom numbers of atoms involved in this bond.

During PERCEPTION of the initial input structure, the ASTEREO, BSTEREO representation of stereochemistry is converted to the systematic ordered list notation.[7,8,9] The list of attachments is ordered so that viewing down the bond from the first attachment to the central atom, the other attachments are arranged in a clockwise manner. Implicit hydrogens are permuted to the end to prevent "holes" in the list by an even number of pairwise interchanges of attachments.

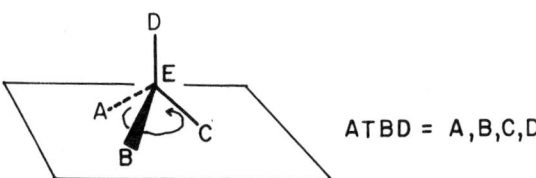

ATBD = A,B,C,D

Similarly the attachments to double bond stereocenters are ordered such that when viewed from the same side of the plane of the double bond they appear in clockwise order. Again implicit hydrogens are permuted to the end. Table III shows relevant parts of the atom table for 4 after PERCEPTION. From this point on, the ATOM TABLE is always presumed to be correct and the structural diagram is made to agree with the table!

Table III. Relevant parts of ATOM TABLE for **4** after PERCEPTION

Atom #	ASTEREO	ATBD	BD
1	1	2 4 3	a d c
2	2	1 3 6	a b f
3	1	1 2 5	c b e
4	0	1	d
5	0	3	e
6	1	7 2	g f
7	1	6 8	g h
8	0	7	h

Machine Perception of Configuration. The algorithm for perception of double bond configuration is based on the fact that <u>cis</u> attachments are closer to each other than <u>trans</u> attachments. The CT is then ordered with the doubly-bonded atoms first on the list, followed, in corresponding positions, by the <u>trans</u> attachments.[9]

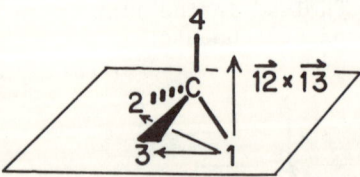

1: 2 6 8

2: 1 4 5

The most general algorithm for perception of asymmetric carbon atoms first assigns positive Z coordinates to wedged attachments and negative Z coordinates to hashed attachments, other attachments remaining Z = 0. The attachment list in the CT is initially in the arbitrary order of input. If the vector cross product 12 x 13 lies on the same side of the 123 plane as

attachment 4 then the order correctly represents the configuration, otherwise the symbolic configuration in the CT is inverted by interchanging two of the attachments. Then the coordinates are restored to Z = 0. This algorithm correctly interprets <u>any</u> unambiguous wedged/hashed representation:

but not the ambiguous formulas A or B below. If a stereobond about a center is found <u>up</u> or <u>down</u> with respect to the attachment rather than the stereocenter, the sense of the bond is reversed for use with respect to the center in question. Thus, partial diagrams C and D are considered to be equivalent. Details of these algorithms are given elsewhere.[9]

A   B   C   D

5. REPRESENTATION OF SUPPLEMENTARY INFORMATION

For efficiency and convenience in later operations the PERCEPTION module sifts through the CT and creates new data structures. These structures are utilized to form yet higher level structures recursively.

<u>Sets</u>. A "set" organization of data consists of a bit string referenced by the name of a property; the <u>i</u>th bit is a 1 if the <u>i</u>th thing has the named property. Some of the sets defined during PERCEPTION are:

'ATOM' SETS

SOCUPA	Atoms in current structure
SBND1SET	Atoms bearing a single bond
SBND2SET	Atoms bearing a double bond
SBND3SET	Atoms bearing a triple bond
SCARBON	Carbon atoms
SHYDROGEN	Hydrogen atoms
SNITROGEN	Nitrogen atoms
SOXYGEN	Oxygen atoms
SPHOSPHORUS	Phosphorus atoms
SSULFUR	Sulfur atoms
SHALIDE	Halide atoms
SPRIMARY	Atoms bearing one non-H atoms
SSECONDARY	Atoms bearing two non-H atoms
STERTIARY	Atoms bearing three non-H atoms
SQUATERNARY	Atoms bearing four non-H atoms
SNEUTRAL	Atoms bearing no charge
SCATION	Atoms bearing a positive charge
SRADICAL	Atoms bearing unpaired electron
SANION	Atoms bearing a negative charge
SALLYLIC	Allylic atoms not in SBND2SET or SBND3SET
SHETERO	Nitrogen, oxygen, sulfur, or phosphorus atoms

SHSET	Atoms bearing an H atom, implicit or explicit
SXSET	Atoms bearing an explicit H atom
STERMINAL	Atoms at end of conjugated system
SRINGA	Atoms in rings
SBRGHDA	Bridgehead atoms
SSTEREO	Stereocenters
SGORIG	Functional group origin atoms
SARMAT	Atoms in aromatic rings
SRAT(i)	Atoms in ring i
SAAA(ATOM)	Atoms adjacent to atom
SAAB(BOND)	Atoms adjacent to bond
SADA(ATOM,N)	Atoms degree N away from atom
SAASA(SETA)	Atoms adjacent to set of atoms
SAASB(SETB)	Atoms adjacent to set of bonds

'BOND' SETS

SOCUPB	Bonds in current structure
SBOND1	Single bonds
SBOND2	Double bonds
SBOND3	Triple bonds
SHETBD	Bonds to an atom in SHETERO
SHBD	Bonds to a hydrogen
SCONJBD	Conjugated multiple bonds
SRINGB	Bonds in a ring
SCTDB	Double bond stereo centers
SARMBD	Bonds in an aromatic ring
SRBD(i)	Bonds in ring i
SBAA(ATOM)	Bonds adjacent to atom
SBAB(BOND)	Bonds adjacent to bond
SBDB(BOND,N)	Bonds degree N away from bond
SBASB(SETB)	Bonds adjacent to set of bonds
SBASA(SETA)	Bonds adjacent to set of atoms

'RING' SETS

SARMRG	Aromatic rings
SAARMRG	Antiaromatic rings
SRING3	3-membered rings
SRING4	4-membered rings
SRING5	5-membered rings
SRING6	6-membered rings
SRINGL	Rings larger than 6 members

Various set functions are available to allow efficient manipulation of these sets.

SET FUNCTIONS

General:
    OR(SET1,SET2)   Inclusive or of two sets; union of sets
    AND(SET1,SET2)   Intersection of two sets
    XOR(SET1,SET2)   Exclusive or of two sets
    NOT(SET1)   Complement of a set

Logical functions:
    EQV(SET1,SET2)   T if two sets are equivalent, F otherwise
    ISM(SET1,N)   T if N is member of set SET1, else F.
    ON(SET1,N)   T if N was member of set SET1, else F.
                         Side effect: makes N a member of set SET1.
    OFF(SET1,N)   T if N was not member of set SET1, else F.
                         Side effect: removes N from set SET1.
    SUB(SET1,SET2)   T if SET1 is subset of SET2.(proper subset)

Integer functions:
    CNT(SET1)   Value is number of members in SET1.
    NXM(SET1,N)   Value is next member of set after N.
                         Value is zero if no more members.

SOXYGEN   = {8,10,12}
SCARBON   = {1,2,4,5,6,7,9}
SBOND2SET = {2,8,9,10}
SSTEREO   = {1,4,6}

Set operations are simple and easily expressed. For example, to find all stereocenters adjacent to a carbon bearing a doubly-bonded oxygen we write the expression below. Evaluating this, SET = {1}.

SET=AND(SSTEREO,SAASA(AND(SCARBON,SAASA(AND(SOXYGEN,SBOND2SET)))))

    Lists. Information which is more complex than just simple class membership is stored in linked lists, e.g., information about the chemically interesting rings which have been perceived are represented in the form:

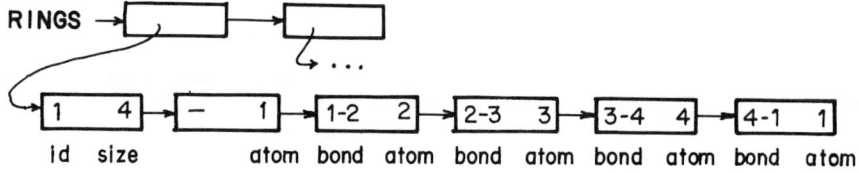

160   Three-Dimensional Synthetic Analysis

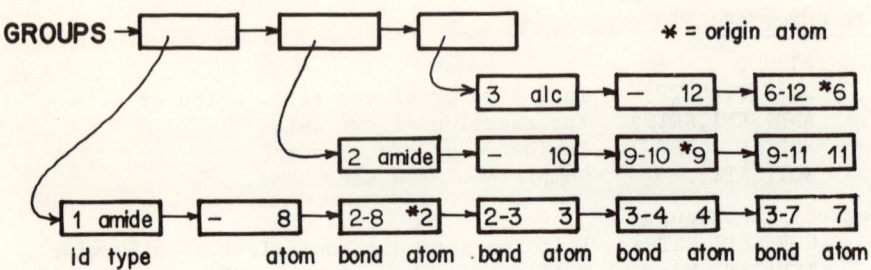

Figure 6a. List structure of functional groups.

Functional groups, being of variable size and complexity, are also most conveniently stored as lists of atoms and bonds in the format shown above. Each group has a unique identifier to distinguish between groups of the same type. Groups are recognized by a table driven recognizer similar to that already described.[2,3] Atoms and bonds are stored in the list in the order traversed by the recognizer. For reference purposes each type of group has an <u>origin</u> marked by an (*) and a predefined numbering scheme as shown for a few common groups in Figure 6b. A tertiary amine would have three origins of the same type, but an ester has two origins of different type. The part of the molecular framework attached to the carbonyl carbon sees an ester as an electron withdrawing group (WGROUP), while the part attached to the other origin of the ester sees it as an electron donating (DGROUP) and a good leaving group (XGROUP).

NAME		CLASS
ALCOHOL	−*C−O− (2 b1 1)	DGROUP, XGROUP
ACID	−*C=O, b2−O³ (2 b1 1)	OXO
OLEFIN	−*C=C− (2 b1 1)	
ESTER	−*C=O, b2−O−b3−C⁴ (2 b1 1)	WGROUP, OXO
ESTERX	O=C², −*C−O (4 3)	DGROUP, XGROUP

Figure 6b. Numbering conventions for common groups.

6. STEREOCHEMICALLY UNIQUE NAMING ALGORITHM

The next step in PERCEPTION is to uniquely identify the molecule in order that SECS may recognize duplicate precursors, and non-productive redundant synthetic sequences. Many systems[10,11] have been developed to generate a constitutionally canonical name, but no automated system existed for generating a stereochemically canonical name from the CT. The Morgan name[12]

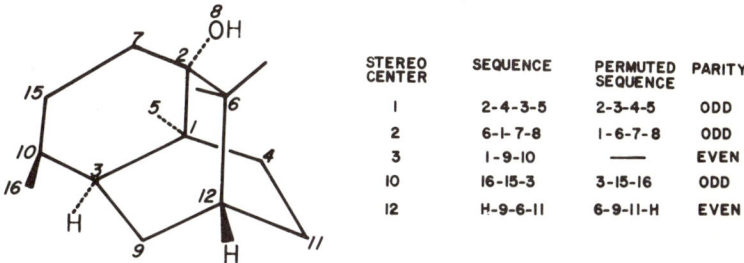

STEREO CENTER	SEQUENCE	PERMUTED SEQUENCE	PARITY
1	2-4-3-5	2-3-4-5	ODD
2	6-1-7-8	1-6-7-8	ODD
3	1-9-10	—	EVEN
10	16-15-3	3-15-16	ODD
12	H-9-6-11	6-9-11-H	EVEN

Figure 7. SEMA numbering of patchouli alcohol and resulting configuration descriptors.

is excellent for computer applications, because it is readily converted into a standard CT and is easily derived from a standard CT. Unfortunately the Morgan algorithm does not include stereochemistry. However, based on this earlier work, a Stereochemically Extended Morgan Algorithm (SEMA) has been developed which uniquely names stereoisomers and also provides for uniquely naming conformational isomers as well.[13]

First the structure is numbered as usual by the Morgan algorithm[12] as shown in Figure 7. The descriptor for a stereocenter is a 1 or 2 as the number of pairwise interchanges necessary to permute the attachments to that center into ascending order by their Morgan numbers is odd or even. The descriptor for a double bond is the sum of the parities of the two ends. A list of the parities of all double bonds, in the order in which they are referenced in the BOND TYPE list is appended to the Morgan name. Another list containing the parities of all atoms, in order of their Morgan number (i.e., their order in the FROM LIST),[13] is also appended to the name. The possible values in each list are:

        0   for non-stereocenter
        1   for stereocenter of odd parity
        2   for stereocenter of even parity
        3   for stereocenter of unknown parity

The value "3" allows naming structures whose configuration is not completely defined.

<u>Detection of stereocenters</u>. The stereochemically extended Morgan algorithm (SEMA)[13] differentiates stereocenters (inversion of which leads to a different structure) from non-stereocenters. Initially, all tri- and tetra-substituted saturated carbons and all carbon-carbon double bonds with at least one non-hydrogen substituent at each end are designated as potential stereo-

centers. If during the naming, because of a choice point, two names are generated that are identical except for the parity of one potential stereocenter; then the two attachments are identical and the center is removed from the set of stereocenters.

Note that the bridgehead atoms in the bicyclo[2.2.2]octane are stereocenters. Further note that the in, out isomer has a different set of stereo descriptors from the out, out isomer as it should. The in, in isomer has a SEMA name identical to the out, out isomer and consequently is not a different stereochemical isomer but is a conformational isomer.[14]

out, out (O,E)   in, out (O,O)   in, in (O,E)

By generating and comparing the SEMA names for two structures (see Figure 8), the machine can now determine the relationship between the two structures. Identical structures have identical names; non-isomeric structures differ by number or type of atoms; and constitutional isomers have names differing in the first part of the name. Stereoisomers differ only in the configuration descriptors. It is shown elsewhere[13] that diasteriomeric and enantiomeric relationships can also be distinguished. As a by product of SEMA, we obtain valuable information about molecular symmetry which is used later in strategic bond assignment.[13] The reader should time how long is required to relate the structures in Figure 8. This illustrates how the chemist is prejudiced by the way he views a structure; six-membered rings are less obvious in the structure at right, thus the chemist's analysis of this structure for synthesis might be different. SECS is free from this bias, and generates the same synthesis regardless how the structure is drawn.[15]

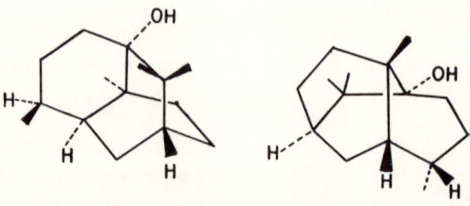

Figure 8.   IDENTICAL ?

7. AUTOMATIC CONSTRUCTION OF THREE-DIMENSIONAL MODEL

The symbolic stereochemical representation previously described is useful for synthetic analysis in <u>conformation-independent</u> areas, but for many problems, the <u>conformation dependent</u> analysis is equally important. In the example below:[16]

the clue for this inference is the Euclidian distance between the two functional groups and not the graph theoretic distance or symbolic stereochemistry. As a further example, the validity of inferring the following reaction depends upon the relative

steric hindrance of attack on both faces of the ketone. In order to evaluate this, the chemist turns to building a three-dimensional model--this behavior is simulated in SECS.

The model building module constructs a fairly accurate three-dimensional model directly from a two-dimensional diagram or even a CT without any coordinates.[17] The algorithm incorporates a heuristic classical-mechanical "energy minimization" to derive a reasonable conformation of the structure. The chemist can easily change the conformation of the final structure using the acoustic tablet in 3-D.[6] Agreement of the model builder structures with x-ray is good as is shown in Figure 9.

Figure 9. Comparison of computed model (dotted) with xray structure (solid lines) of morphine.

164   Three-Dimensional Synthetic Analysis

Using the 3-D model, proximity relationships can be simply calculated. Axial, equatorial, pseudo-axial, pseudo-equatorial, and trans-periplanar relationships can be determined by SECS from first principles by examining its own model. On the basis of the 3-D model, a function has been defined which permits SECS to quantify <u>steric congestion</u> in the ground state molecule with regard to <u>a particular reactive site</u>.[18] This rather crude function does allow SECS to anticipate the major isomer resulting from reduction of ketones which are significantly congested.[18] Work is underway to extend this capability to other types of reactions, e.g. additions to olefins. Thus, for the first time, a computer synthesis program is able to essentially make a model of the "real world molecule" and base conclusions on this model.

We may conclude then that the information needed for synthetic analysis is quite varied, requiring several types of data structure. Set operations play a dominant role in the required information processing as we shall see in the next section. Finally, we note that the hierarchal levels of information perceived from the CT and the three-dimensional model provide a rich environment to facilitate the work of the next module to be discussed--the chemistry module.

8. REPRESENTATION OF CHEMICAL TRANSFORMS

WHAT IS A CHEMICAL TRANSFORM? A chemical transform is a chemical structural change, or redistribution of electrons, generally described in the analytical direction (the inverse of the synthetic direction). A transform may represent an electron-pushing step or sequence (equation 1) which might be called the "ab initio" level. On a higher level, a transform may represent a known mechanistic step or known reaction (equation 2). At a still higher level is the transform representing a known <u>sequence</u> of reactions (equation 3). The "ab initio" level is useful for discovering new reactions, while the higher levels are useful in discovering new syntheses. As shown in Figure 4,

$R-CO_2H \implies R-CH_2-CO_2H$ (3)

the representation of chemistry is separate from the SECS program, consequently the user may choose the level of representation appropriate to his goals, and may in fact mix levels. The actual transforms are written by the chemist in a new language called ALCHEM.

ALCHEM--Associative Language for Chemistry. ALCHEM is both a language, a data structure and a system.[19] Since it is of prime importance for non-computer-programmer chemists to be able to add, modify, or even replace the transform library easily, the transforms are entirely data to SECS, rather than being completely or partially subprograms. Other advantages of this approach are that the size of the program does not increase with addition of new transforms, and each user may have his own library of special transforms.

ALCHEM is an English-like language with a particular grammar and chemical vocabulary to make it readily understandable to chemists. The process of creating a chemistry library is shown in Figure 10. The chemist describes a chemical transform in

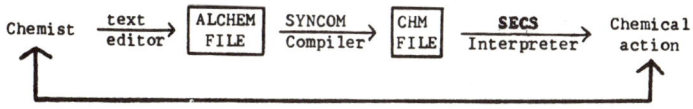

Figure 10. Information flow in SECS

ALCHEM and types this into a file with the system text editor. A FORTRAN program called SYNCOM[20] compiles this file into a very compact binary CHM file (CHM file is 10 times smaller than ALC file), creating various directories, listings if desired, and error diagnostics. The CHM files are then interpreted by SECS to produce precursors. The chemist gets feedback by observing the chemistry resulting from his transform.

Each transform description contains the following information:

1. A name, references, details about reagents
2. A minimum substructure, functional groups, etc., required in target
3. An initial PRIORITY value, a general estimate of the transform's utility
4. Questions concerning the target or precursor, and corresponding adjustments to the PRIORITY value
5. Reaction conditions
6. A description of how to accomplish the transformation (which bonds to break, etc.).

As an example, the transform above might be described in ALCHEM

```
1)  ; HO-C-C-C-W  =>      C-C  +  C-W
                           \O/
2)  ; OPENING OF EPOXIDE BY STABILIZED ANION
3)  OP-EPOX
4)  ALCOHOL WGROUP PATH 4 PRIORITY 50
5)     IF BOND 1 IS A RING BOND THEN
6)        BEGIN IF BOND 2 AND GROUP 1 ARE CIS THEN
7)        KILL ELSE ADD 20 DONE
8)     IF BOND 2 IS INRING OF SIZE 5-6 THEN ADD 20
9)     IF AN XGROUP IS ANYWHERE THEN SUBT 50 FOR EACH
10)    CONDITIONS BASIC
11)    BREAK BOND 2
12)    MAKE BOND FROM ATOM 1 IN GROUP 1 TO ATOM 2
13)    INVERT ATOM 2
14)    IF STERIC HINDRANCE AT ATOM 1 IS BETTER THAN AT ATOM 2
    &     THEN SUBT 30
15)    IF ANION AT ATOMS ALPHA TO ATOM 4 OFFPATH IS BETTER
    &     THAN AT ATOM 3 THEN SUBT 30
16)    END.
```

Figure 11. Sample transform in ALCHEM

Several processes are performed by the transform interpreter:

1. Selects transforms whose required substructure is present in the target structure.
2. Maps transform numbering onto target numbering.
3. Evaluates plausibility of transform in environment of specific target.
4. Generates the precursor(s) formed by the transform acting on the target

In the example, lines 1-2 are comments; line 3 is the code name and line 4 is the substructure required, an ALCOHOL group in a 1,4 relationship to an electron withdrawing group (WGROUP, C=O, N=O, CO_2R) and the base priority of 50. Selection of useful transforms can be done in either of two ways. Features or combinations of features occurring in the target can be used as keys into the transform library (structure driven) causing the program to select transforms which create those features, or the pattern required for each transform may be searched for in the target structure (transform driven). Both methods are used in

Representation of Chemical Transforms   167

SECS, depending upon which appears to be most efficient. Since the member of functional groups is usually small, (less than 10), while the transform library is large (> 100), the number of searches of the transform directory for the structure driven method is proportional to f^2-f when f is the number of functional groups in the target. The transform driven search requires $\underline{T}$ searches of the molecule where $\underline{T}$ is the number of transforms.

The interpreter maps the substructure, in this case HO—C—C—C—W, onto the target so that group 1 is the first group (OH) and group 2 is the second (WGROUP) and the path atoms are numbered 1-4 from the origin of group 1 to the origin of group 2. Bonds are numbered so that bond 1 is the bond from atom 1 to atom 2. Additionally, each functional group has its own numbering scheme (see Figure 6a). Line 5 prohibits application of the transform if the OH and C_2-C_3 bond are cis which only has meaning if both are attached to a ring, i.e., bond 1 is a ring bond. Line 8 increments the priority by 20 if bond 2 is in a 5-6 membered ring, i.e., that a ring is formed in the synthetic direction. Line 9 lowers the priority 50 for each leaving group (XGROUP) elsewhere in the molecule. Line 10 automatically lowers the priority 25 for each functional group that is unstable to basic conditions (the OH and WGROUP are excluded). Line 11 is a manipulative statement that decreases the bond order of bond 2 in the target structure. Line 12 makes a bond from the oxygen to C_2 and line 13 inverts C_2 since this is an S_N2 displacement. Lines 14-15 pertain to the precursor rather than the target since they follow the manipulation commands. Line 14 decreases the priority if sterically preferred attack[18] on the epoxide is not at C_2. If the chemist has prohibited the building of a model then steric hindrance is approximated by counting alkyl groups. Line 15 examines the WGROUP to see that the desired anion is in fact the most favorable one. The ampersand sign is a continuation symbol. Finally END designates the end of this transform.

For heterocyclic chemistry where there is not the clear concept of functional group that there is in carbocyclic chemistry, the simple concept of groups and distance between them becomes ineffective. In this case, the chemist may define a minimum substructure necessary for the transform. The interpreter then maps this substructure onto the target molecule.[19]

In evaluating many of the statements in a transform, the interpreter simply combines appropriate sets and examines the intersection. Thus, the complicated statement

    IF SECONDARY ATOM BETA TO STEREOCENTER ONRING OF SIZE
& OTHERTHAN 5-6 OFFPATH IS ALPHA TO BRIDGEHEAD ATOM THEN . . .

involves evaluating the following expression, and if the result is not null, the statement is true. Evaluation of qualifiers

SSECONDARY ∩ $\bigcup_{i \in \text{SSTEREO}}$ SADA(i,2) ∩ SRINGA ∩ $\sim\bigcup_{i \in (\text{SRING5} \cup \text{SRING6})}$ SRAT(i) ∩ ~SPATHA

∩ SAASA(SBRGHDA)

is very fast. A transform can have any number of qualifiers, thus it is certainly possible to express in useable form the sum total of known and extrapolated scope and limitations of a transform. So far ALCHEM has been able to describe all reactions encountered. The degree of generalization is left to the option of the chemist and depends to some extent on how he wishes to use SECS.

After interpretation of a transform, the interpreter creates a structure block (SB) to represent the precursor (see Figure 12). Prior to this, fragments are split out into their own SB. Fragments are tied together in the tree (Figure 13) by a horizontal "AND" relationship, i.e., a successful synthesis for all fragments must be found to be successful. The structures are then evaluated by EVAL for any undesirable properties which are specified by the chemist (e.g., small rings, cumulenes, double bonds to bridgeheads in small ring systems). Additional checks on valence are made to insure it is a valid structure.

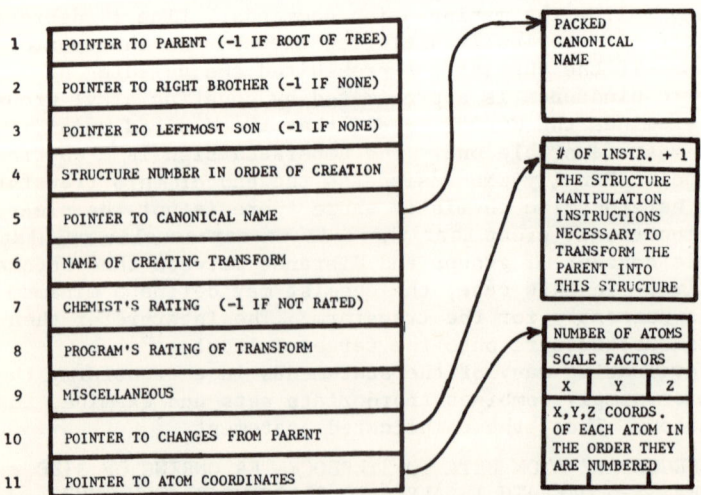

Figure 12. Format of a structure block. Each precursor is represented by such a data block.

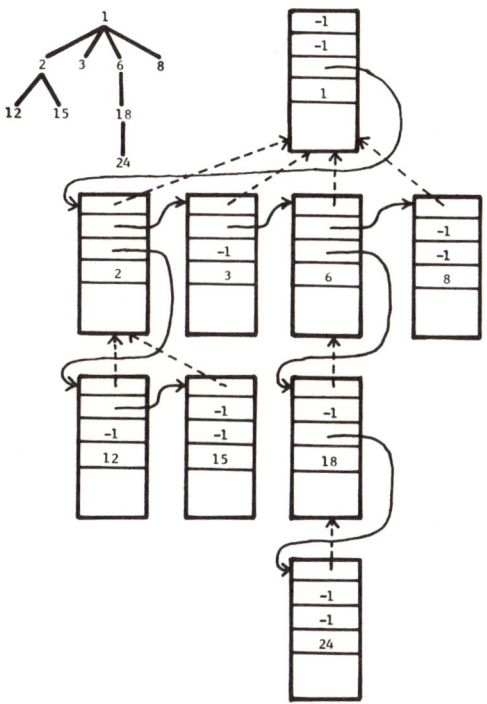

Figure 13. Synthesis tree data structure. Each block is a structure block of a precursor. See figure 3 for a more complex tree.

9. GENERATION OF STEREOCHEMICALLY CORRECT PRECURSORS

MANIPULATION OF STEREOCHEMICAL REPRESENTATION. The usefulness of the ordered list representation of configuration lies in the facility with which it can be manipulated for chemical reactions. On a molecular model, inversion is performed by physically interchanging two substituents; on the ordered list representation, inversion is performed symbolically by interchanging any two list entries.

Interconversion of the two types of stereocenters, e.g., cis addition to a double bond, involves adding each of the two new substituents to the beginning of the attachment list for the center to which the substituent is to be bonded. For addition from the opposite face, the substituents are simply added to the end of the lists. Trans addition is symbolically a cis addition followed by symbolic inversion of one stereocenter. The manipulation instructions in SECS have the presumed suprafacial course, i.e., displacements occur with retention and additions occurs in a cis manner. The INVERT command was used in Figure 11 to override this assumed course.

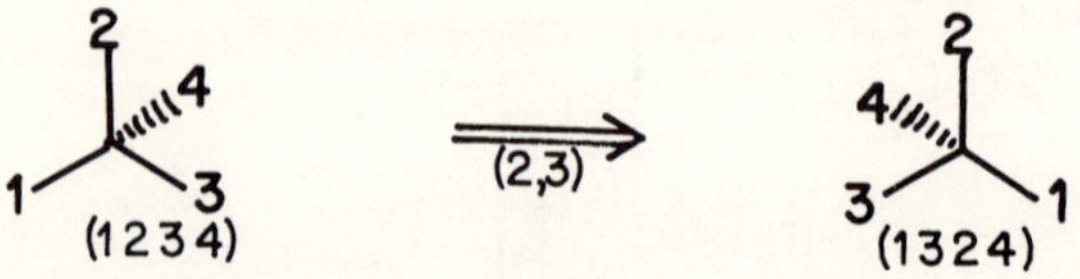

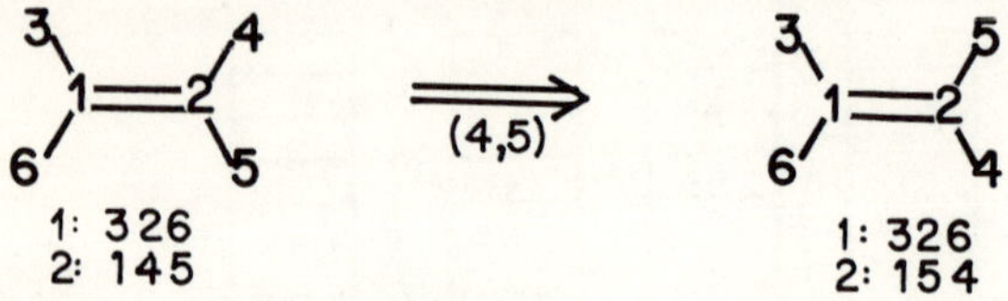

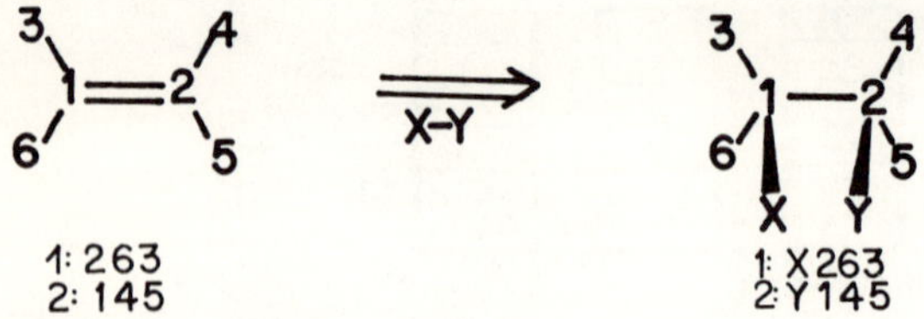

STEREOCHEMICAL MULTIPLICITIES. Many transforms imply more than one possible precursor as shown below:

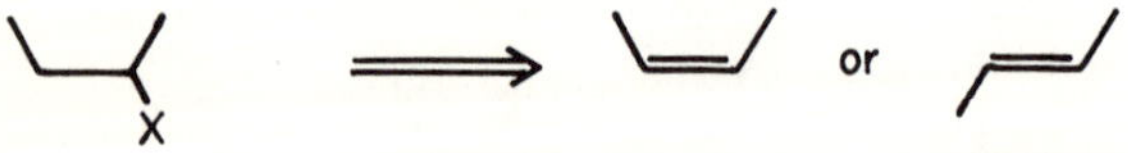

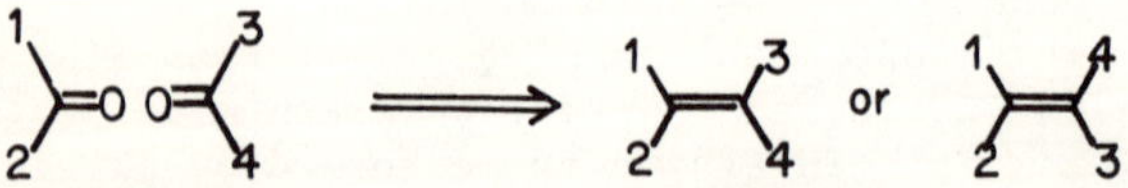

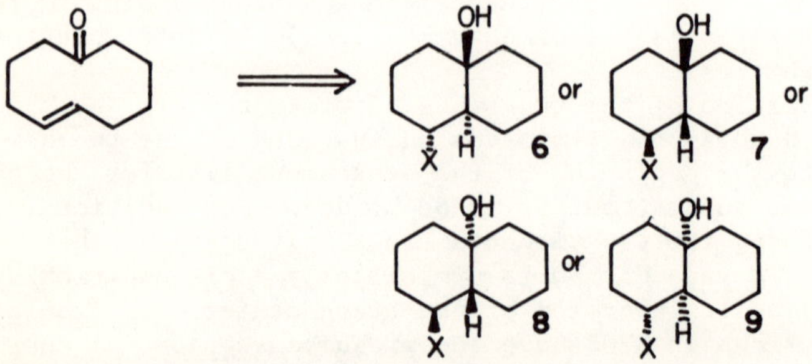

As the structure block is created, these multiplicities are detected and all valid precursors are generated automatically. Equation 10 shows the complexity that can arise. In this case, $\underline{8}$ and $\underline{9}$ happen to be enantiomers of $\underline{6}$ and $\underline{7}$, respectively, and consequently $\underline{8}$ and $\underline{9}$ would be deleted. Both structure $\underline{6}$ and $\underline{7}$ would stereospecifically produce the <u>trans</u> olefin, but $\underline{6}$ and $\underline{7}$ would not necessarily be equally hard to synthesize, thus it is important to consider them both. An important point here is that the chemist writing transforms need not worry about this complexity--it is detected and treated automatically, assuring the chemist that all valid precursors will be generated.

COMPUTER GENERATION OF STEREOCHEMICALLY VALID STRUCTURAL DIAGRAMS. After one or more transforms, we have a CT which correctly represents the chemical precursor to the target, but how do we draw the structural diagram to indicate the correct stereochemistry? The coordinates of the target may be used for the precursor, but since the connectivity is not the same, the precursor may be very distorted. Even if the model builder builds a model of the precursor, to draw an unambiguous 2-D structural diagram, appropriate bonds must be selected for hashing and wedging. Since some stereocenters have been modified and others created, we can not rely on using the wedging and hashing as it was in the target.

A simple algorithm which works well selects two bonds from a stereocenter (c: 1 2 3 4) (ring bonds preferred) to represent a reference plane (C12). If the Z component of the vector $\vec{C1}$ x $\vec{C2}$ is on the viewers side of the C12 plane, the C-4 bond should be wedged and the C-3 bond hashed, else <u>vice versa</u>. This algorithm works equally well for 2-D or 3-D structures. If a bond has already been hashed or wedged from some other atom, then the algorithm can either use the existing designations in the inverse sense and designate other bonds to be consistent or it can select the existing hashed or wedged bonds as the reference plane (C12) and proceed as normal.

If the x,y projection of a double bond, as viewed by the user, is in agreement with the CT, the bond is displayed normally, otherwise it is crossed, indicating the true configuration is opposite that shown. If the atoms are later moved by the chemist,

the program dynamically updates the stereochemical designation to maintain the correct representation. In this way the precision of the CT is maintained in the diagram. The model builder also uses the CT as the stereochemical authority and builds the model of the precursor to conform to the CT.

10. FILE STRUCTURES

Chemical transforms are currently represented in direct access files, divided arbitrarily by the type of substructures or patterns required in the target. Each file has its own directory of the transforms in that file. The ALCHEM binary files, which are the highly compacted format, currently occupy about 15 K 32-bit words, but are expected to continue to expand.

The Structure Blocks are stored in <u>virtual</u> <u>memory</u> which resides on the disk. This is a software implemented paging system, enabling dynamic allocation and recovery of storage blocks of varying length from one to several thousand words. The virtual memory is further partitioned so that allocations of a particular type can be grouped in close physical proximity, leading to more efficient access. Pages are buffered into memory on demand, replacing first those pages referenced in the least recent past. This unique system allows complex inter-twining of pointers in a very large file, yet allows very simple access by the programmer.

11. ILLUSTRATION OF RESULTS

Everything mentioned in this chapter has been implemented and tested for over a year. To illustrate performance, Figure 14 shows in the synthetic direction the unretouched output, produced by SECS on a CalComp plotter, of one of the many synthetic pathways generated for $PGF_{1\alpha}$ (structure 1). Over the arrows are the code names of the transforms, and beneath is the final priority of the transform.

Cyclopentadiene is epoxidized (<u>cis</u> addition) to give 125, followed by <u>trans</u> opening by HX to form the halohydrin 101. The side chain is attached by displacement of the allylic halide (inversion) followed by elaboration to 27. Epoxidation of 27 is guided by the proximity of the adjacent hydroxyl group, giving <u>syn-cis</u> attack. Finally the vinyl organometallic of 7 (retention) attacks 11 with inversion of the epoxide carbon atom, giving the target, 1. Of course, SECS solved the problem starting from 1 working backward and it is shown forward for convenience of the chemist. Of course protecting groups are needed at certain points and there are potential allylic rearrangements, but parts of this strategy have actually recently been achieved.[21] The alternative scheme of removing the acid side chain first in analysis is not generated, because that chain is <u>cis</u> to the OH group rather than <u>trans</u>. Thus, stereochemistry is a powerful "selection rule" for synthesis, deriving from fundamental mechanistic theory. More examples and applications to other types of problems will be reported in later publications.

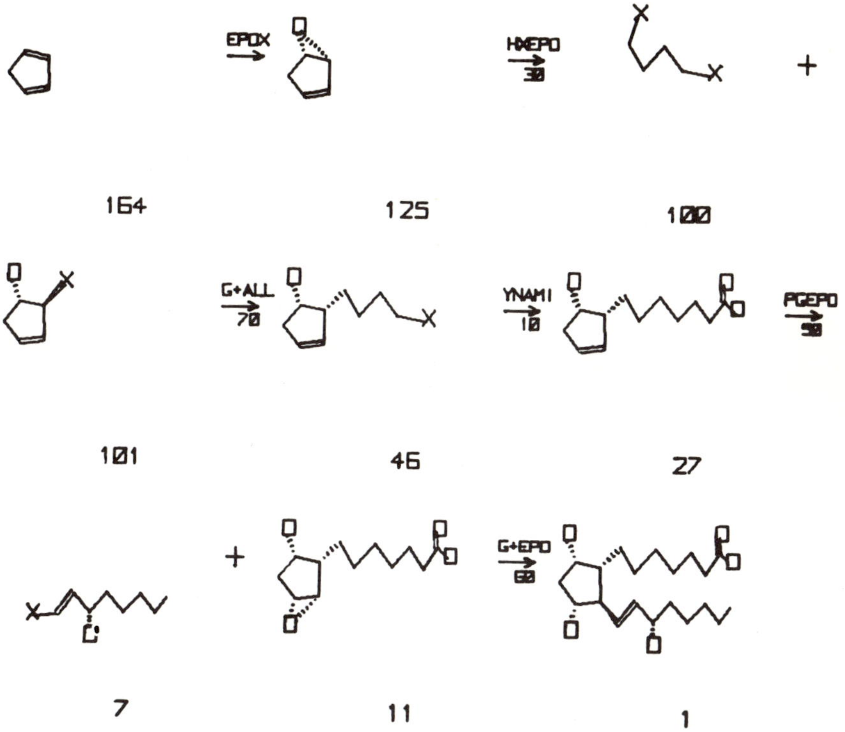

Illustration of Results 173

Figure 14. Synthetic pathway to PGF$_{1\alpha}$ produced by SECS and output directly on a CalComp plotter. This is one route of many produced.

12. ACKNOWLEDGEMENT

The author wishes to thank his collaborators whose efforts and interaction have made this research successful: Dr. Thomas M. Dyott, Mr. Joseph Verbalis, Dr. Peter H. Gund, Mr. Peter E. Friedland, Dr. Helmut Bruns, Dr. Clark Still, Dr. Thomas Brownscombe and Dr. Guenter Grethe. This work was supported by National Institutes of Health Research Resource grant RR-00578 and in part by the Merck Foundation Career Development grant; Hoffmann LaRoche, Nutley N.J., E. Merck Darmstadt, and an IBM postdoctoral fellowship to Dr. Still.

13. REFERENCES

1. Lewis H. Sarett, "Synthetic Organic Chemistry: New Techniques and Targets," presented before Synthetic Manufacturers Association, June 9, 1964.
2. E.J. Corey and W. Todd Wipke, Science, 166, 178 (1969).
3. E.J. Corey, W.T. Wipke, R.D. Cramer III, and W.J. Howe, J. Amer. Chem. Soc., 94, 421, 431 (1972).
4. W.T. Wipke, Computer Decisions, 1 (4) 39 (1970).
5. G. Büchi, et al, J. Amer. Chem. Soc., 88, 4113 (1966).
6. W.T. Wipke and A. Whetstone, Computer Graphics, 5 (4) 10 (1971).
7. A.E. Petrarca and J.E. Rush, J. Chem. Doc., 9, 32 (1969).
8. W.T. Wipke, Proc NEREM, 12, 186 (1970).
9. W.T. Wipke and T.M. Dyott, submitted.
10. E.G. Smith, "The Wiswesser Line-Formula Chemical Notation," McGraw Hill, New York, 1968.
11. J. Lederberg, G.L. Sutherland, B.G. Buchanan, E.A. Feigenbaum, A.U. Robertson, A.M. Duffield, and C. Djerassi, J. Amer. Chem. Soc., 91, 2973 (1969).
12. H.L. Morgan, J. Chem. Doc., 5, 43 (1965).
13. W.T. Wipke and T.M. Dyott, submitted.
14. C.H. Park and H.E. Simmons, J. Amer. Chem. Soc., 94, 7184 (1972).
15. They are identical.
16. R. Breslow and S.W. Baldwin, J. Amer. Chem. Soc., 92, 732 (1970).
17. W.T. Wipke, P. Gund, T. Dyott, and J. Verbalis, submitted.
18. W.T. Wipke and P. Gund, submitted.
19. W.T. Wipke, T.M. Dyott, C. Still, and P. Friedland, in preparation.
20. W.T. Wipke and P. Friedland, in preparation.
21. J. Fried and J.C. Sih, Tetrahedron Lett., 3899 (1973).

Computer Techniques for Interpreting Mass Spectometry Data
Stephen R. Heller
Division of Computer Research and Technology
National Institues of Health
Bethesda, Maryland 20014   USA

INTRODUCTION

In a previous chapter, Feldmann (1) has discussed and described the structure search component of the Chemical Information System (CIS) being developed at the National Institues of Health (NIH) in the Division of Computer Research and Technology (DCRT). This chapter will concern itself with the details of another component of CIS, the mass spectrometry search (MSS) system. The philosophy behind this work is similar in many respects to Feldmann's structure search. The techniques, methods, and facilities used in the CIS attempt to show the current use and future potential of computers in chemical information handling and processing. As the CIS develops it is hoped that it will provide a useful function to scientists interested in a particular aspect of chemistry and will generate ideas for the solution of more complex problems.

There has been a great deal of research devoted to the computer handling of mass spectral data for the purpose of structure identification. Mass spectra, which can be obtained on as little as 10 grams of material and in quantities of hundreds of spectra hour from a typical gas chromatography-mass spectrometry (GC/MS) computer system, have provided a very large and fertile field for exploring methods for the computer handling of data. Mass spectra can be obtained from a number of different types of instruments. While some variations in intensity may be expected for this reason, the general features of the spectra are independent of the spectrometer. The spectra that have found their way into the computer readable files that will be discussed in the chapters at this Advanced Study Institute (ASI) are virtually all electron ionization (EI) spectra. The spectra are all "low resolution," that is, they are measured to unit mass value rather than to the exact mass of the atom combination. Measuring the exact mass, often erroneously called "high resolution" mass spectrometry because it is usually carried out at high resolution, can distinguish between molecules having N_2, CO, and C_2H_4 groupings whose exact mass increments are 28.0061, 27.994 and 28.031 respectively. A typical EI mass spectrum is shown in Figure 1. The spectrum consists of the intensities of the various ions (isotopes, fragments, rearrangements, molecular ions, etc.) against ion m/e values. The data are usually represented as an x-y bar plot, since the peaks are constant in width.

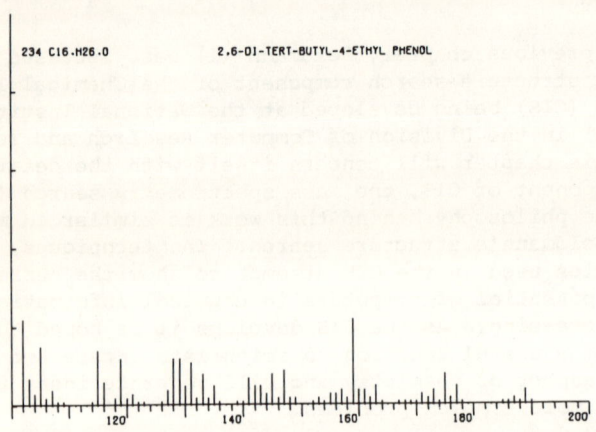

Figure 1. A Typical EI Mass Spectrum

Four approaches to the interpretation of mass spectra will be presented at this ASI:

1. Library or File Searching
2. Cluster Analysis
3. Pattern Recognition/Learning Machine
4. Artificial Intelligence

The application of all these techniques has been described previously, except for cluster analysis. This chapter will be devoted to discussing the first two techniques, and the following chapters by Jurs (2) and Smith (3) will discuss the latter two methods.

The problem of computer file searching of spectral data has been recognized for some time, in infared (IR) (4) and in mass spectrometry (5). The first attempts to handle mass spectra data by modern computers were done in Sweden by Abrahamsson

Introduction

and Stenhagen in the mid 1960's (6). They developed search techniques based on the five strongest or largest peaks in a spectrum and they further had a provision for using the molecular weight as a key for restricting the number of possible answers from the search. They also developed the first of the so-called "matching" or "similarity" indexes that would rate or rank the similarity of possible answers relative to the unknown. Later workers, pointing out that the strongest or largest peaks in a spectrum were not necessarily the most important for identification, developed a variety of other measures, such as increasing the number of strongest peaks (7). Finally Biemann and coworkers (8) developed the "abbreviated spectrum". This approach selects the n (where n=2, although others use 1 or 3) largest peaks in every 14 atomic mass unit (amu) interval starting at mass 6 since this retains most of the structurally significant peaks in a spectrum because the basic organic building block unit is the CH_2, i.e., a methylene group. An additional reason they chose this approach was to reduce the storage room required for the spectra. In the case in which n=2, the file is reduced to about 24% of its original size.

With the typical double-density disks now available (and laser memories expected shortly), this need for storage limitation becomes much less important. On the other hand their approach did illustrate that an "abbreviated spectrum" could be used for identification. More recently, McLafferty and coworkers (9) have extended the notion of preprocessing mass spectra for library searching using a variety of techniques that the chemist/mass spectroscopist brings to bear upon the problem. In addition to using a simple abbreviated file as Biemann, their Self Training Interpretative and Retrieval (STIRS) system also uses ion series, low and high mass characterisitic ions (most abundant odd and even mass ions), small and large neutral losses and secondary neutral losses. One significant problem with this system is that it is a sequential search system and thus inherently slow (in real time) and non-interactive. The fixation for storage compression has led to some very interesting studies by Grotch (10) and Isenhour (11) regarding the intensities of the peaks in a mass spectrum. In a series of papers Grotch describes the compression of intensity information into as few as two bits. Grotch also has worked on compression codes for peaks; such compression undoubtedly does speed up search times.

DCRT/CIS MASS SPECTRAL SEARCH (MSS)

The results of these studies, as well as some others, have been well reviewed by Ridley (12). Since these systems have been developed on local computers for local investigators, the main factor that they have lacked has been exposure to a wide base of users, such as organic chemists and analytical chemists, in addition to other mass spectroscopists. The non-accessibility or unavailability of these systems has been the main point to which the NIH system has addressed itself. The various techniques in the literature were assessed, and then we attempted to make the most obviously useful features of existing systems directly available to all scientists with provisions for altering or modifying searches and using other general chemical information that might be at their disposal. In other words, a flexible, interactive conversational mass spectral search and retrieval system was constructed. Table 1 lists the options provided in the system. As expected, the peak and intensity search is used predominately. However, if one knows the molecular weights or partial/complete formulae, these may also be used as keys for more efficient searching although useful homologues will be missed. With all these search options the scientist is able to test ideas quickly and to receive virtually immediate responses, which hope-

DCRT/CIS
MASS SPECTRAL SEARCH SYSTEM

1. PEAK AND INTENSITY SEARCH
2. MOLECULAR WEIGHT SEARCH
3. MOLECULAR FORMULA SEARCH
    a. Complete
    b. Imbedded
4. MOLECULAR WEIGHT AND PEAK SEARCH
5. MOLECULAR FORMULA AND PEAK SEARCH
6. MOLECULAR WEIGHT AND MOLECULAR FORMULA SEARCH
7. DISSIMILARITY COMPARISON
8. SPECTRUM PRINTOUT
9. MICROFICHE DISPLAY OF SPECTRUM
10. DISPLAY OF SPECTRUM
11. PLOTTING OF SPECTRUM
12. CRAB — COMMENTS and COMPLAINTS
13. HARVEST — ENTERING NEW DATA
14. NEWS — NEWS OF THE SYSTEM
15. MSDC CLASSIFICATION CODE LIST

Table 1. Mass Spectral Search System Options

fully prod him in to the answers. As opposed to most of the previous systems which arrive at a set of possible answers and stop, the NIH system has provided a variety of options, including a spectrum printout directly from on-line disk storage of the data or microfiche and/or graphics display of spectra for the very important (psychologically and experimentally) ultimate comparison of unknown and possible solutions.

Before describing the file structure, the various search options will be outlined. Further details are available elsewhere (13). The backbone of the search system is the peak and intensity search option, which accounts, at present, for over 95% of the searches performed with the system. The file that is being searched in this option is an abbreviated file and consists of the two largest peaks in every 14 m/e intervals, starting at m/e of 6. Quite often this is forgotten by the user, and, for example, peaks at 29, 30 and 31 are entered. The result, of course, is that no spectra in the file are matched, since there are no spectra in the abbreviated file being searched with 3 peaks in that 14 amu interval. On the other hand, m/e 33, 34 and 35 would be quite acceptable. Using the three largest peaks in the 14 amu interval would increase the file size somewhat, but might help those that have a tendency to make the above error. Owing to variations in instruments (e.g. magnetic, electric, quadrupole), it is necessary to have an intensity range factor in the peak search. By allowing the factor to be varied by the user, he can "get a feeling" for the file and how intensities do or do not affect a search for his particular class of compounds. This is especially necessary because of our group of users. It has been found that very effective searching can be done with a very few (two to four) well-chosen peaks, almost independent of the intensity range decided upon. Figure 2 is a typical peak and intensity search. The opportunity for a chemist to interact with the system (and see how a search is proceeding) is, we feel, fundamental in the success of this system, Feldmann's structure search and the synthesis programs of Corey (14) and Wipke (15).

The search option used next most often is the molecular weight (MW) search which simply provides a list of names, molecular formulae, and identification numbers (ID#'s used for other options within the system) for those compounds in the file with the specified MW. This option is particularly useful in Chemical Ionization (CI), Field Ionization (FI) and Field Desorption (FD) spectrometry where the molecular weight is

```
PROGRAM: MASS SPEC PEAK AND INTENSITY SEARCH
USER: INTENSITY RANGE FACTOR FOR THIS SEARCH IS: 2
TYPE PEAK, INT
CR TO EXIT, 1 FOR ID #/NAMES

USER: 85,100

PROGRAM: FOUND 1365 SPECTRA WITH M/E PEAK: 85

  # REFS    M/E PEAKS
    187        85

TYPE PEAK, INT
CR TO EXIT, 1 FOR ID =/NAMES

USER: 128,20

PROGRAM: FOUND 857 SPECTRA WITH M/E PEAK: 128

  # REFS    M/E PEAKS
     8       85   128

TYPE PEAK, INT
CR TO EXIT, 1 FDR ID =/NAMES

USER: 3

  ID=    MW     MF              NAME
  1722   314    C19.H38.O3      METHYL 4-HYDROXYOCTADECANDATE
  2085   198    C13.H26.O       DIHEXYL KETONE
  2543   170    C10.H18.O2      GAMMA-DECALACTONE
  2560   254    C16.H30.O2      GAMMA-PALMITOLACTONE
  2561   282    C18.H34.O2      GAMMA-STEAROLACTONE
  6505   128    C7.H12.S        6-TRIABICYCLO (3.2.1)OCTANE
  8060   246    C15.H18.O3      6-EPI-ALPHA-SANTONIN
  8470   309    C21.H27.N.O     6-DIMETHYLAMINO-4,4-DIPHENYL-3-
                                HEPTANONE (METHADONE)
```

Figure 2. Example of a Peak Search

easily deduced. Figure 3 shows an example of a MW search for a molecular weight of 103. Another search option used almost as often as the MW search is the molecular formula (MF) search option, consisting of two parts. The complete MF part allows one to search for a complete molecular formula and provides the same information output as the MW search. Figure 4 shows a typical complete MF search. The imbedded MF search allows one to search for spectra in the file using only part of the molecular formula. This option uses the individual atom type and its magnitude in that molecule. Thus, one can search for Br_2 or C_6, but not (as yet) for any Br compounds up to and including Br_2 or any number of carbon atoms up to or including C_6. Figure 5 shows a search for the same formula as shown in Figure 4,

**TYPE MOLECULAR WEIGHT
CR TO EXIT**

USER: 103

PROGRAM: FOUND 8 SPECTRA WITH MW: 103

PROGRAM: PRODUCE REFERENCES YES OR NO?

USER: YES

809	103 C4.H6.N.CL	BUTYRONITRILE, CHLORO
2315	103 C3.H9.O3.B	TRIMETHYL BORATE
2665	103 C4.H9.N.O2	TERT-NITROBUTANE
5224	103 C7.H5.N	BENZONITRILE (CYANOBENZENE)
5510	103 C4.H9.N.O2	NOR-BUTYL NITRITE
7400	103 C4.H13.N3	DIETHYLENETRIAMINE
7613	103 C6.H13.D.O.	3-D-4-METHYL-2-PENTANOL
7614	103 C6.H13.D.O.	4-D-2-METHYL-3-PENTANOL

Figure 3. Example of a Molecular Weight Search

PROGRAM: MOLECULAR FORMULA SEARCH

TO SEARCH FOR A COMPLETE MF, TYPE ALL
TO SEARCH FOR A PARTIAL MF, TYPE IMBED
CR TO EXIT

USER: ALL

PROGRAM: TYPE IN MOLECULAR FORMULA
(ORDER OF ATOMS: C,H,N,O,S)
USER: C6.H6.O2

PROGRAM: FOUND 11 REFERENCES TO MOLECULAR FORMULA C6.H6.O2

PROGRAM: PRODUCE REFERENCES YES OR NO?

USER: YES

ID#	MW	MF	NAME
625	110	C6.H6.O2	METHYLFURYL KETONE
759	110	C6.H6.O2	5-METHYL-2-FURFURAL
1025	110	C6.H6.O2	CATECHOL
1026	110	C6.H6.O2	RESORCINOL
1027	110	C6.H6.O2	HYDROQUINONE
1539	110	C6.H6.O2	PYROCATECHOL
3084	110	C6.H6.O2	PYROQUINONE
3086	110	C6.H6.O2	PYROCATECHOL
3088	110	C6.H6.O2	RESORCINOL
3089	110	C6.H6.O2	FURYL METHYL KETONE
3093	110	C6.H6.O2	2-FURYL METHYL KETONE

Figure 4. Example of a Complete Molecular Formula Search

except by allowing the formula to be part of a larger molecule, more answers are found. These three searches (peak/intensity, MW and MF) have also been combined to allow for a molecular formula and molecular weight search, a peak and molecular formula search and a peak and molecular weight search. These combined searches are extremely effective in taking a minimal amount of information and reducing the possibilities in the file to usually less than a half dozen with just a MW or MF and a peak. Figures 6 and 7 are examples of two of these combined search options. In the future, when the data is available, it is planned to add to the system Feldmann's nested structure searching, the Mass Spectrometry Data Centre's Classification Code scheme, and the references to the spectra (eg. type of instrument, conditions, literature references).

```
PROGRAM: MOLECULAR FORMULA SEARCH

TO SEARCH FOR A COMPLETE MF, TYPE ALL
TO SEARCH FOR A PARTIAL MF, TYPE IMBED
CR TO EXIT

USER: IMBED

PROGRAM: MOLECULAR FORMULA IMBEDMENT SEARCH
FIRST GIVE THE NUMBER OF ATOM TYPES YOU WANT TO SEARCH
THEN GIVE THE ACTUAL GROUPS AS THE PROGRAM REQUESTS

USER: THE NUMBER OF GROUPS WILL BE: 3

USER: GROUP 1 IS: C6

USER: GROUP 2 IS: O2

USER: GROUP 3 IS: H6

PROGRAM: FOUND 15 REFERENCES TO THAT COMBINATION OF ATOMS

PROGRAM: PRODUCE REFERENCES YES OR NO?

USER: YES
```

ID#	MW	MF	NAME
625	110	C6.H6.O2	METHYLDURYL KETONE
759	110	C6.H6.O2	5-METHYL-2-FURFURAL
874	138	C6.H6.N2.O2	1,1-DICYANOETHYL ACETATE
1025	110	C6.H6.O2	CATECHOL
1026	110	C6.H6.O2	RESORCINOL
1027	110	C6.H6.O2	HYDROQUINONE
1539	110	C6.H6.O2	PYROCATECHOL
3084	110	C6.H6.O2	HYDROQUINONE
3086	110	C6.H6.O2	PYROCATECHOL
3088	110	C6.H6.O2	RESORCINOL
3089	110	C6.H6.O2	FURYL METHYL KETONE
3093	110	C6.H6.O2	2-FURYL METHYL KETONE
4042	180	C6.H6.O2.CL2	X-METHYL-X,X-DICHLOROCYCLOPENTADIONE-1,2
7286	138	C6.H6.N2.O2	O-NITROANILINE
7295	138	C6.H6.N2.O2	P-NITROANILINE

Figure 5. Example of an Imbedded Molecular Formula Search

PROGRAM: PEAK AND PARTIAL FORMULA SEARCH

USER: INTENSITY RANGE FACTOR FOR THIS SEARCH IS: 3

TYPE PEAK, INT
CR TO EXIT

USER: 95,30

PROGRAM: FOUND 1270 SPECTRA WITH M/E PEAK: 95

PROGRAM: THE NUMBER OF GROUPS PLEASE
USER: THE NUMBER OF GROUPS WILL BE: 2

USER: GROUP 1 IS: N

USER: GROUP 2 IS: O

PROGRAM: FOUND 3 REFERENCES TO THAT COMBINATION OF PEAK AND MF

PROGRAM: PRODUCE REFERENCES YES OR NO?

USER: YES

ID#	MW	MF	NAME
542	123	C7.H9.N.O	2-ETHOXYPYRIDINE
7664	183	C11.H21.N.O	1-MORPHOLINO-3-METHYLCYCLOHEXANE
7669	181	C11.H19.N.O	1-MORPHOLINO-4-METHYLCYCLOHEXENE

Figure 6. Example of a Peak and Formula Search

PROGRAM: MOLECULAR WEIGHT AND PEAK SEARCH
CR TO EXIT

PLEASE GIVE MOLECULAR WEIGHT FIRST, THEN PEAKS

USER: THE MW IS: 156

PROGRAM: PEAK SEARCH

USER: INTENSITY RANGE FACTOR FOR THIS SEARCH IS: 5

TYPE PEAK, INT
CR TO EXIT
1 FOR ID/NAMES

USER: 100,50

PROGRAM: FOUND 3 REFERENCES TO THAT COMBINATION OF MW AND PEAKS

TYPE PEAK, INT
CR TO EXIT
1 FOR ID/NAMES

USER: 1

ID#	NAME
216	2,5-DIMETHYL-3-NORM-PROPYL-PIPERAZINE
1275	CAPROATE, ALLYL
6630	TRANS-2-THIABICYCLO(4.4.0)DECANE (TRANS-1-THIADECAHYDRONAP)

Figure 7. Example of a Peak and Molecular Weight Search

Once the user has a possible answer, he has the option of quantitatively comparing it with his unknown using the dissimilarity index (DI) option. This option takes the intensity of a file compound and the unknown at each m/e value from 12-500 (or any smaller user-specified range) and makes a comparison derived from a Euclidean geometry distance measurement. The DI in the NIH system also allows for comparison of two file spectra, which is very useful in checking for duplicates in the file. While this is an objective measure for comparison, mass spectrometry structure identification is still, we feel, basically subjective. Thus, we have provided a number of options that allow the user to judge for himself the quality of his answer. The first and simplest is the spectrum printout option, which simply types out all (or just a portion, if so specified) of the peaks and intensities in a spectrum. Figure 8 shows a typical spectrum printout. Alternatively, with a graphics terminal,

```
PROGRAM: TYPE ID# FOR PEAKS/INTENSITIES
CR TO EXIT

USER: 8167

ID#     MW      MF              NAME

8167    277     C20.H23.N       AMITRIPTYLINE

PROGRAM: THERE ARE 30 PEAKS IN SPECTRUM # 8167

PROGRAM: PRODUCE PEAKS/INTENSITIES   YES OR NO?

USER: YES

PROGRAM: PLEASE GIVE RANGE FOR PEAKS AND
INTENSITY LEVEL

USER: THE MIN PEAK IS: 0

USER: THE MAX PEAK IS: 300

USER: TYPE ALL PEAKS WITH INTENSITY > 2

M/E     INT
 58     100
 59       5
 91       2
178       2
202       3
203       2
204       2
215       2
217       2
218       2
219       2
```

<u>Figure 8</u>. Example of a Spectrum Printout

such as the GT-40 or Tektronix 4010 being demonstrated at this
ASI, the display option plots the data in a standard x-y bar
plot. Lastly, the plot option allows the same data that has
been on the display to be plotted on either a Caclomp or Zeta
Plotter. The mass spectrum plot in Figure 1 was obtained using
this option. The data base has also processed by a COM (Computer Output Microfiche) device and it is available on microfiche,
either using a manual or an automatic (and computer driven) viewer. Figure 9 shows the computer driven microfiche viewer next
to the terminal user to drive the viewer. The image on the
screen is one of 192 spectra on each fiche. The carousel in
which the fiche reside inside the viewer requires a four second
maximum access time for viewing. In addition to these options,
there are miscellaneous options for entering data, commenting
about the system and receiving news of the system. Lastly, a
fragment loss search option is currently being added, which will
allow for the searching of neutral loss from -1 (i.e. the parent
ion (P) +1 peak) to P-100. Preliminary work in using this feature as an additional tool for structure elucidation has been
very promising.

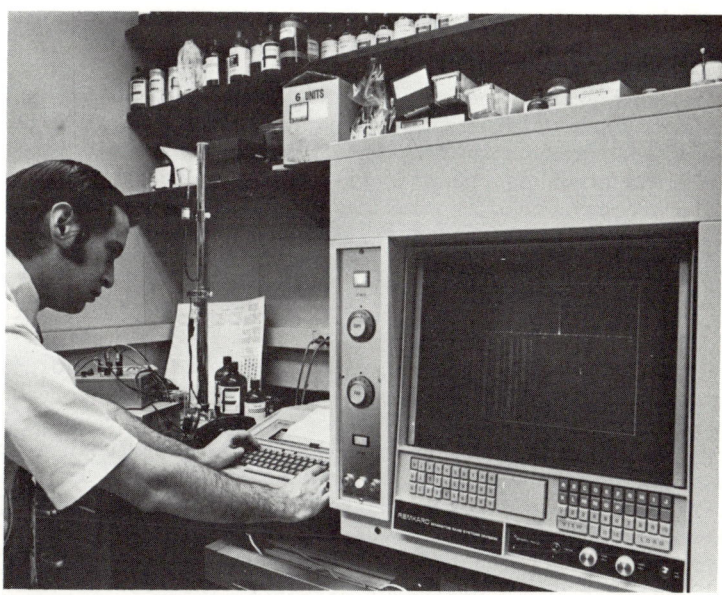

Figure 9. Computer Driven Microfiche Viewer

FILE STRUCTURE

Now that the system has been outlined, some description of the file structure is in order so that one may understand how and why the system operates. The specific examples are for a DEC PDP-10 computer, but the principles are applicable to any modern timesharing computer system. In fact, the system has recently been transferred to the GE-635 computer with a minor number of problems. Previous workers have considered that the search and retrieval system involved two problem areas--the representation of the data and the search algorithm. Actually, there is only one problem; the data representation and search algorithm are virtually indistinguishable and inseparable--if they are to be good. The file structure used in the mass spectral search is similar to Feldmann's file structure in that the method of searching is dictated by the file structure and is the reason for the interactive capability.

All the files in the mass spectral search system can be viewed as one of two types--one containing numeric search data (peaks, molecular weights, etc.) and one containing character search data (molecular formulae). If the data is binary or ASCII, packed or unpacked, these formats are just minor modifications of the basic file structure.

The abbreviated peak file consists of the identification number (ID#), peak, intensity, and molecular weight (MW), sorted by peak and ID# respectively. The file generation program takes this file and creates a pointer file which indicates whether or not there are any peaks at that mass and if so, where in the reference file the ID#, intensity, and MW are stored. The ID#, intensity and MW are all packed into one 36-bit word, 18 bits for the ID# (allowing for 2^{18} -1 or 262,143 spectra in the file), 7 bits for the intensity (allowing for the usual 0-100% intensity range), and 11 bits for the molecular weight (allowing for a MW up to 2048). When a search is performed, the value of peak is used to go to that word or cell in one of the 128-word blocks of the pointer disk file and if a non -1 number is found (-1 indicating no references for that molecular weight), that number is the starting point for the ID#, intensity, and MW in the reference file. (The 128-word size for the block is for the PDP-10 computer disk block size. The GE-635 computer uses a 315 work block and so the file on the GE system contains the same information, but located in different blocks). The program then simply looks up this starting point (subtracting it from the starting point of the next mass will give the number of references for this mass), unpacks the intensity, and checks to see if it is in the allowable range. If it is, then the ID# is written out onto a scratch disk file to be used later for further search comparisons or to look up the name associated with the ID#. The molecular weight could readily be made a search parameter by allowing for a MW range and unpacking here and checking it in addition to the intensity. Now, when there is a second, third (and so on) search, the same basic look-up is done and a Boolean AND logic operation is performed between two lists of ID#'s. Figure 3 shows a typical MW search for a MW of 103. Tables 2 and 3 are the pointer and reference files respectively for this MW search. These files were used since they are ASCII, rather than binary (which is the case for the peak reference, molecular formula pointer, and name reference files). The MW of 103 is used as a pointer to the 103rd word or cell in the 128-word block, which contains the pointer number 1563. Substracting this from the 104th word -1, gives 1572-1563-1=8, which is the answer given in Figure 3. One then goes to block 1563/128 + 1=13 (with a remainder of 27) in the reference file and the 27th word/cell is, indeed, 809. The module function was used to calculate this value. The following seven numbers are the ID numbers shown in Figure 3. These ID#'s are then used in the identical name disk file look-up to go to the name pointer and reference files. One first uses the ID# to locate the starting point and length (by subtraction from the starting point of the next sequential ID#) of the name. The name, stored as five 7-bit binary characters per 36-bit word, is then printed out. The spectrum printout option works in the same manner, but in this case, the peak and intensity are stored in binary form, 18 bits each in one 36-bit word.

In the case of molecular formulae (MF), a different approach is necessary. Molecular formulae are character strings and do not have any particular numerical value associated with them. Thus, to be handled in the computer, it is necessary to convert the molecular formula string into a number or location in the disk pointer file. One method to use in "converting" a molecular formula to numeric key pointer value is called hash coding (16). In this procedure one processes the molecular formula character string through a function which produces a number. Clearly the function must be reasonably well chosen so that two different strings will rarely produce the same number and when such a "collision" occurs it can be handled with a minimum of difficulty. Now that one has converted the molecular formula string into a numeric key-value, this number is used to address the appropriate pointer file block. In this case, the

Interpreting Mass Spectrometry Data

FILE NAME = MS	EXTENSION = MW1	BLOCK NUMBER		1
−1	1	−1	5	−1
−1	−1	−1	−1	−1
−1	−1	−1	−1	−1
7	12	15	18	20
−1	−1	−1	−1	−1
24	28	31	41	43
54	57	−1	78	75
78	87	−1	−1	89
94	97	106	108	126
135	−1	153	−1	158
−1	165	171	174	184
187	214	218	254	269
302	312	−1	326	336
338	354	365	393	398
440	449	503	528	572
581	617	620	655	662
687	696	737	742	812
819	897	911	993	1004
1059	1063	1096	1120	1153
1161	1218	1233	1333	1353
1438	1456	1563	1572	1643
1657	1714	1742	1810	1818
1896	1910	2003	2020	2098
2106	2227	2243	2338	2350
2419	2439	2521	2526	2572
2578	2673	2680		

Table 2. Molecular Weight Pointer File

FILE NAME = MS	EXTENSION = MW2	BLOCK NUMBER		13
5767	5768	5769	5770	5863
5935	5940	6100	6339	6340
6364	6646	7604	7615	7616
7617	7618	7619	7620	7621
7630	7736	7845	7864	8120
−1	809	2315	2665	5224
5510	7400	7613	7614	−1
156	647	648	826	868
888	953	1072	1074	1075
1278	1317	1319	1823	1844
2376	2470	2651	3032	3033
3034	3035	3036	3037	3038
3039	3040	3041	3042	3043
3044	3045	3046	3047	3048
3049	3050	3051	3052	3053
5074	5187	5232	5271	5305
5405	5439	5526	5633	5635
5636	5658	5660	5682	5806
5829	5830	6097	6103	6104
6128	6431	6433	6679	7099
7401	7835	7854	7855	7872
−1	157	158	159	911
912	1062	1117	2634	6004
6005	6006	6647	7000	−1
160	161	162	163	753
803	834	835		

Table 3. Molecular Weight Reference File

block is divided into two-word cells as opposed to one-word cells for the previous file structure. This is necessary because one cannot use the hashed coded numeric key valued as both an indicator to the pointer file and an indicator to the reference file. The second word in each cell of the pointer file is used as the pointer to the starting position of the ID#'s in the molecular formula reference files. Tables 4 and 5 are examples of the molecular formula pointer and reference files. If one takes the first molecular formula in the file, Ar (for the inert gas Argon) and processes it through the hash function, the result is 4682565. The number, 4682565 is found in block 14 of the pointer file, cell #7 (word #13). In the second part of that cell is the starting address position of the references and the number of references to Argon are contained in the first word of the reference file. Indeed, the second word is 1, which is where the first reference would be expected to be and Table 4 shows that the first word of Block 1 is 5, the number of Argon references plus 1. The next four words are the ID#'s for the Argon spectra. The reason for the number 5, instead of 4 is to take into account the space (i.e. one extra word) for the number of references. This then, is how the complete and partial molecular formula searches are performed.

In summary, the file structure attempts to maximize the use of the direct access disk and the 36-bit word length of the PDP-10. If one had to use a computer with a different word size, the system would, of course, still work, but would require some minor changes in the sizes of the cells to pack the peak, intensity and molecular weight.

This question of using smaller machines (that is, the so-called "mini-computer") is worth looking at from the standpoints of ease of use, value, or utility and its probable role in the future. At present, mini's are used for lab automation and often to perform numerous other tasks, but the direction in which technology is heading is towards mini-processors, which are cheaper and better to use. While search systems utilizing mini-computers have been well designed and might be viewed at first glance as a very effective alternative to the central search system described, here a few points are worth noting. First, the great variety of mini-computers with incompatible software makes use of available programs difficult. Second, assuming one did have such a mini-computer available in his laboratory, it could be used at one time either for data acquisition or data analysis - not for both. As more instrumentation is computerized, there will probably be

FILE NAME = MS	EXTENSION = MF1	BLOCK NUMBER	14	
− 1	− 1	77845312	6761	− 1
− 1	− 1	− 1	− 1	− 1
− 1	− 1	4682565	1	356279109
9699	− 1	− 1	180839240	8390
− 1	− 1	− 1	− 1	− 1
− 1	179475276	4324	353596237	11659
467411790	5875	180253518	8382	− 1
− 1	− 1	− 1	32731986	5132
− 1	− 1	− 1	− 1	180437845
3572	256496470	1482	230	− 1
250532696	2042	124023641	249492316	76264281
3627	− 1	− 1	101	1373
175604573	13190	262062942	178131804	1290527583
4071	177922911	10520	6111	13302
− 1	− 1	605926243	177378147	249013092
6475	260670307	9295	10696	13624
175747943	5278	80225128	470401898	− 1
− 1	1015227242	1260	− 1	10055
343208811	10144	− 1	179811184	− 1
− 1	− 1	− 1	8882	365
− 1	− 1	83628914	48563059	247001971
3377	123757428	7360	7406	11359
176808819	11467	250966903	186008442	122614645
12580	181003129	7546	13335	174
48128891	11159	48661365		466678653
1350	465576829	1501		

Table 4. Molecular Formula Pointer File

FILE NAME = MS	EXTENSION = MF2	BLOCK NUMBER	1	
5	2768	6296	6301	6309
− 1	2	1377	− 1	2
7121	− 1	2	1361	− 1
2	5408	− 1	2	1017
− 1	2	5410	− 1	3
953	7099	− 1	2	6357
− 1	2	4211	− 1	2
6356	− 1	3	3644	5318
− 1	2	5407	− 1	2
2766	− 1	2	5170	− 1
2	4627	− 1	2	4054
− 1	3	1105	3409	− 1
2	4344	− 1	2	3830
− 1	3	1096	3195	− 1
2	3561	− 1	2	3033
− 1	2	5412	− 1	3
2905	5116	− 1	3	1588
1970	− 1	3	1608	1974
− 1	2	5409	− 1	2
1356	− 1	2	5258	− 1
2	4320	− 1	4	948
6586	7110	3	3	1358
3800	− 1	3162	1565	1943
− 1	4	5171	5319	5406
− 1	2	2	− 1	2
2762	− 1			

Table 5. Molecular Formula Reference File

less time on a mini in the lab available for analysis/retrieval. In addition to the problem of getting time on the lab computer, there is the initial expense of the data base, the time/cost for processing it for the search program. Then there is the time/cost for correcting errors in the data and then reprocessing the data base. Along with this, there is the time/cost of obtaining new data and processing it for the file.

Let us now assume that the potential routine users of such a system have been satisfied that a central system is the right direction in which to go, considering the time, costs, and lack of manpower expertise to perform the task. What of the researcher, the scientist who would like to experiment with the data base, either for alternative retrieval methods or other types of data analysis (e.g., cluster analysis or pattern recognition)? At no cost to him, he has a very large data base available on-line and one that someone else will maintain, correct, and augment. With a versatile search system or a program of his own, he may extract those parts of the data base of interest to his research and work with only that portion. Having a large and powerful computer system at his disposal, it is much easier to write in a higher level programming language and easier to perform experiments. Thus, the central search facility approach appears to offer a valuable service to the researcher also.

LIBRARY SEARCH SYSTEM SUMMARY

As Grotch (10), Isenhour (11), and others have stated, the most desirable attributes of a search system are generally thought to be:

1. Ease of use
2. Effectiveness
3. Availability
4. Low cost

The MSS system fits these four criteria very well. Its ease of use and availability are evident from its use (25 sessions per day) and the size of the user community (over 200 users). Its effectiveness or efficiency is good and is essentially the same as most other systems'. Lastly, its overall low cost is also quite obvious. These attributes led to the system's being transferred to the GE network. A demonstration of the search system described here will be available to ASI participants from the GE node on the network here in The Hague,

The Netherlands. The management of and responsibility for the system is now being handled by the Mass Spec Data Centre (MSDC) in Aldermaston, England. In this way the value and use of the system to the world-wide mass spectrometry community can be tested and evaluated and the data base made available to research workers in the field.

Undoubtedly these concepts will take time to develop and evolve. Time-sharing systems are still in their infancy (17). At present, there is only one large international network (the GE/Honeywell network), and it goes only from Tokyo to Rome, leaving a large segment of the world outside the system. A few other companies are just starting to provide international networks, while most are regional (i.e., - serve a dozen large states and few dozen large cities in the U.S. or perhaps a few cities in England). One major goal of this presentation is to show that research efforts devoted to developing systems (programs, data bases, etc.) that can readily and easily be made available over telephone lines to computer networks are of value to the scientific community. Using such a facility will enable more research time and effort to be devoted to the actual research rather than the preparations, program rewriting, data base reformatting, etc., that are so prevalent today.

CLUSTER ANALYSIS

An example of how this large file of mass spectral data being stored continuously on-line can be used for research will now be illustrated using a technique called cluster analysis which is usually considered a part of pattern recognition. Cluster analysis is concerned with finding homogeneous sets of data points within a larger set of data. Within cluster analysis there are a number of approaches. Only one will be used here. Further details are available in a number of books and articles (18). Cluster analysis is a method that classifies, associates or clusters a set of data into a number of natural sets containing similar data. It differs, generally speaking, from the pattern recognition techniques to be described later by Jurs, in that cluster analysis is usually non-supervised learning and not limited (i.e., the number of clusters are not known). Pattern recognition methods require pre-classification or pre-labeling of the data and a predetermined number of classes into which the data can fall. However, cluster analysis allows the data to fall into whatever classes the particular clustering techniques generate; i.e., the chips fall where they may. It should be pointed out that there are, however, situations in which the cluster analysis is unsupervised but limited. By this it is meant that while the data points are un-labeled, the number of classes into which they may fall is limited. This area will not be dealt with here, but rather an example of using the unlimited and non-supervised mode will be presented since it has a great deal of potential value in chemistry in that it may enable the scientist to gain insight into the nature of the data he is analyzing. Such approaches have found value in analysing data for taxomomy classification, economics, geography, and automatic generation of the thesouri (19). Clustering opens up the possibility of discovering new facts about old data or puzzling data.

There are a number of clustering techniques available. Kowalski and Bender have discussed the Q-mode clustering method and non-linear mapping (NLM) as two techniques for separating data where there are only a few clusters (20). This latter technique reduces the n-dimensional data to 2 dimensions so that it may be visualized as x,y points and was used to perform the recognition of the classes defined by the Q-mode method. The NLM method necessarily introduces some distortion into the final picture/display in two dimensions, but the guiding principle behind the mapping dictates that the close distances are preserved, and this in turn preserves the clustering of the data. NLM suffers from the disadvantage that the mapping produced can often be too dense for a good display. Another type of cluster analysis procedure is the use of graph theory methods and Zahn (21), in a comprehensive review of this subject, describes a number of algorithms for clustering based on the so-called "minimal spanning tree" (MST) techniques.

Data point sets come in a variety of patterns. Figure 10-12 show three sample problem data sets that cluster analysis has been used to solve. Figure 10 is the trivial case of two distinct clusters which can be readily separated. However, if one looks closely, one of the two sets of ten points can probably be separated into two smaller sets of five points. Figure 11 shows a more complicated case of a set of points attached via a short "neck" and is more difficult to separate. Lastly, Figure 12 shows a possible mass spectral data problem. In Figure 12 one can readily find anywhere from five to eleven (or more) clusters, depending on what criteria one uses for "similarity." Ball (18) has discussed a number of measures of similarity. They include the dot product, similarity ratio, weighted and unweighted

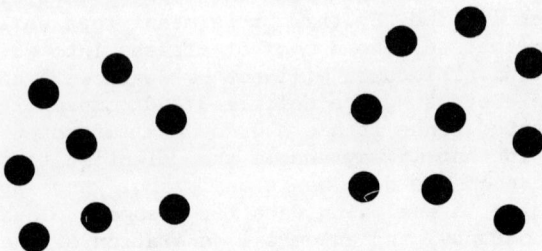

Figure 10. Two Separate Clusters

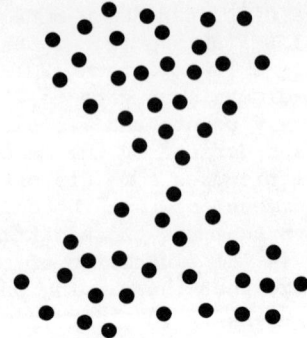

Figure 11. Two Clusters Joined at a Neck

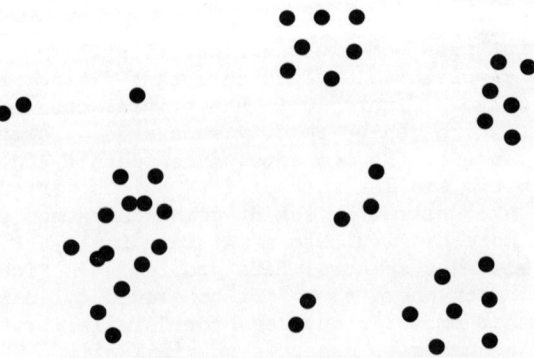

Figure 12. Multi-Cluster Pattern

Euclidean distances and weighted and unweighted Boolean "AND" normalized correlation methods.

Figure 13 illustrates one of the graph-theory methods, the shortest spanning path (SSP) cluster procedure (22). A simple distance measurement to find the two clusters in the data set (steps A-D). In part A, one has the starting point set. One then connects all pairs of points as shown in part B. In step C one obtains the SSP. In part D, the "inconsistant" edge J-K has been deleted since it has a larger distance weight than any other neighboring edges and hence the data points are clustered. If one now considers the total weight of edges in a graph as the sum of all the constituent edges, the minimum or shortest spanning path (SSP) in this graph is a spanning path whose weight is a minimum among all the spanning paths of this graph.

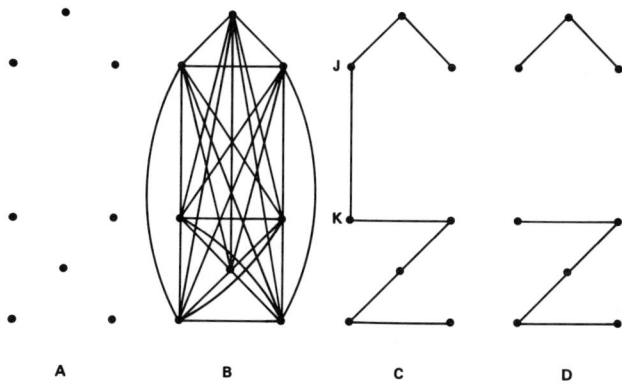

Figure 13. SSP (Shortest Spanning Path) Cluster Procedure

The SSP method can also be used in data reorganization, that is, the data can be rearranged according to the "shortest spanning path" for the data. We have used the SSP method to rearrange parts of the mass spectrometry data base (23). It has been used because it is available, is able to handle large amounts of data, and allows for a convenient presentation of the clusteral data. No comparisons with other clustering techniques have been made using this mass spectral data, so that the relative efficiency of the SSP method cannot be indicated. Since finding an absolute minimum path with a large number of data points is time consuming, the SSP method uses an approximation technique which finds a relative minimum path. This procedure is a far less time consuming process and is able to handle large amounts of data. One very serious limitation to most previous clustering methods has been their inability to handle realistic amounts of real experimental data. While the SSP does have a favorable side to it, one obvious potential problem with the SSP method is shown in Figure 14, which is very similar to the data point samples in Figure 11. Anyone looking at this data will readily conclude there are two clusters, but the closeness of the sum of the points near the neck of the two clusters and the SSP technique of finding the closest neighbors from any given pairs of points would lead to the path shown in the diagram. If one labels one cluster A and the other B, then the resulting reorganized data will not be A and B, but rather BAB. Thus, one must be cautious in using the results directly and automatically.

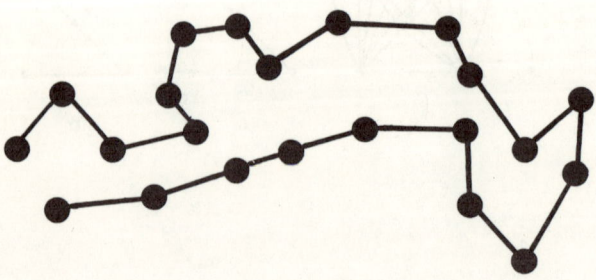

Figure 14. The SSP Through a Set of Clusters

Cluster Analysis 197

The compounds used in the sample clustering experiment were molecules containing one sulfur atom and any other element (in any combination and/or amounts) taken from the MSS data base. Using the imbedded molecular formula search for compounds with one sulfur atom, 525 answers were found. Because some of spectra do not have peaks starting at mass 26, these were discarded and 323 remained. Duplicates were not removed. The data was first used as is, without any weighting of the intensities. The peaks from m/e=14 to 140 and losses from 0 to -99 (i.e. Parent to Parent -99 amu) were considered as features for a total of 227 features. The losses were calculated from the known molecular weights of the compounds. The data was later weighted since it was found to produce better clustering. The weighting scale assigned a value of 1 to all peaks and losses with an intensity less than 10%, 2 to all peaks greater than 10%, and 4 to all losses greater than 10%. The matrix output consists of the sorted list of 323 rows of sulfur compounds (sorted according to the order of the SSP) and the 227 columns of features used to classify them. The computer program used has the ability to "sort" the 227 features as well as the compounds, but this feature analysis was discarded owing to the computer time necessary to perform this clustering and the relative lack of information that it seems to impart at this early stage of analysis. Without the sort feature, the SSP program required 86K words and about 30 minutes of cpu time (on a PDP-10) to cluster the 323 sulfur compounds. Work is underway to reduce both these factors.

We have analyzed the resulting matrix output, defining clusters partly based on the results of the SSP sorted list and partly on chemical intuition. This was done because the potential problem in Figure 14 appeared to occur in this case. Table 6 contains part of the sorted list of a sample run showing part of the sulfur cluster. It is fairly clear that some groups exist, such as: sulfur-halogen, sulfur-phosphorus, small compounds, C_2 sulfur compounds, etc. Table 7 contains a partial list of the clusters that have been tentatively identified from this method. These identifications were made with relatively little difficulty because of the matrix output representation that the SSP method produces. This output, which indicates which features (peaks, losses) are used for the clustering, distinguishes the SSP method from most other clustering techniques and is a value asset in the analysis. The true test of this technique will come as more data is made available and tested based on the results found from this small class of sulfur data.

ID	MW	MF	NAME
3417	136	C.S.F3.CL	TRIFLUOROMETHANESULFENYL CHLORIDE
2662	118	O.CL2.S	THIONYLCHLORIDE
3025	102	O2.S.F2	SULFURYL FLUORIDE
1564	102	C.H.F3.S	TRIFLUOROMETHANETHIOL
1603	182	C3.F6.S	HEXAFLUORO-2-PROPANETHIONE
1588	158	C.F6.S	TRIFLUOROMETHYLSULFUR TRIFLUORIDE
1608	196	C.F8.S	TRIFLUOROMETHYLSULFUR PENTAFLUORIDE
1598	170	C2.F6.S	BIS(TRIFLUOROMETHYL)SULFIDE
1969	153	C.N.F5.S	TRIFLUOROMETHYLIMINOSULPHURDIFLURIDE
3556	146	S.F6	SULFUR HEXAFLUORIDE
1963	108	F4.S	SULFUR TETRAFLUORIDE
1956	86	O.F2.S	THIONYL FLUORIDE
3173	118	O2.S.F.CL	SULFURYL-CHLORO-FLUORIDE
1965	118	O2.CL.F.S	SULFURYL CHLORIDE FLUORIDE
1960	102	O2.F2.S	SULFURYL FLUORIDE
1959	102	CL2.S	SULPHUR DICHLORIDE
8630	301	C10.H12.N3.O4.P.S	OXYGEN ANALOG OF GUTHION
7340	286	C14.H10.N2.O3.S	4,6-DIPHENYL-1,2,3,5-OXATHIADIAZINE-2,2-DIOXIDE
8624	277	C9.H12.N.O5.P.S	SUMITHION
8623	263	C8.H10.N.O5.P.S	METHYL PARATHION
8625	320	C8.H8.CL3.O3.P.S	RONNEL
8631	314	C10.H19.O7.P.S	OXYGEN ANALOG OF MALATHION
8629	213	C5.H12.N.O4.P.S	OXYGEN ANALOG OF DIMETHOATE
8564	225	C11.H15.N.O2.S	4-(METHYLTHIO)-3,5-DIMETHYLPHENYL N-METHYLCARBAMATE
8535	207	C10.H9.N.O2.S	4-BENZOYL THIENYL N-METHYLCARBAMATE
7358	99	C.H3.N.S.F2	METHYLIMINOSULPHUR DIFLUORIDE
4889	60	C.O.S	CARBON OXYSULFIDE
4812	64	O2.S	SULFUR DIOXIDE
5169	34	H2.S	HYDROGEN SULFIDE
4793	48	C.H4.S	METHANETHIOL (METHYL MERCAPTAN)
5185	62	C2.H6.S	ETHANETHIOL (ETHYL MERCAPTAN)
5624	62	C2.H6.S	2-THIAPROPANE (DIMETHYL SULFIDE)
1562	94	C2.H6.O2.S	DIMETHYLSULPHONE
231	78	C2.H6.O.S	2-MERCAPTO ETHANOL
1129	78	C2.H6.O.S	SULFOXIDE, DIMETHYL
5211	76	C3.H8.S	2-THIABUTANE (METHYL ETHYL SULFIDE)
6095	76	C3.H8.S	1-PROPANETHIOL (NOR-PROPYL MERCAPTAN)
5230	76	C3.H8.S	2-PROPANETHIOL (ISOPROPYL MERCAPTAN)
4876	88	C4.H8.S	THIACYCLOPENTANE (TETRAHYDROTHIOPHENE)
5231	88	C4.H8.S	THIACYCLOPENTANE (TETRAHYDROTHIOPHENE)
6127	88	C4.H8.S	3-METHYLTHIACYCLOBUTANE

Table 6. Part of the Reorganized List of Sulfur Compounds

CLUSTER ANALYSIS CLASSIFICATIONS

1. SULFONES
2. THIAZOLES, BENZOTHIAZOLES
3. AROMATIC SULFUR
4. SULFUR-HALOGEN
5. SULFUR-PHOSPHORUS
6. SULFITES AND SULFATES
7. BICYCLIC SULFUR
8. THIOL ESTERS
9. ISOTHIOCYANATES, THIOCYANATES
10. C_6-C_8 THIOLS, SULFIDES
11. C_5-C_6 CYCLIC SATURATED THIOLS, SULFIDES

Table 7. Partial List of Clustered Groups

However, even now, the peaks and losses that the SSP clustering technique has shown to be characterisitc for a group such as the monofunctional straight-chain alkyl thiol esters (RCOSR) have shown that this approach offers a great deal of potential for interpretating mass spectral data. This approach of recognition and classification of (functional) groups may lead to new empirical rules for structural elucidation.

Acknowledgements

I wish to express my deep appreciation to Dr. Henry M. Fales for his kindness and help with this work and his support of the search system. I also wish to thank Dr. Arnold W. Pratt, Director, Division of Computer Research and Technology for his foresight, continued support and interest in the computer applications work presented here.

REFERENCES

1. R.J. Feldmann, Chapter 3, "Proceedings of the NATO/CNA ASI on Computer Representation and Manuplation of Chemical Information" edited by W.T. Wipke, S.R. Heller, R.J. Feldmann, and E. Hyde, John Wiley, New York (1973).

2. P.C. Jurs, Ibid, Chapter 11

3. D. Smith, Ibid, Chapter 12

4. (a) D.H. Anderson and G.L. Covert, Anal. Chem., 39, 39 1288 (1967).
   (b) D.S. Erley, Ibid, 40, 894 (1968).
   (c,d) F.E. Lytle, Ibid, 42, 355, 1532 (1970).
   (e) P.C. Jurs, Ibid, 43, 364, (1971).
   (f) D.S. Erley, Appl. Spec., 25, 200 (1971).

5. P.D. Zemany, Anal. Chem., 22, 950 (1950).

6. (a) S. Abrahamsson, S. Stenhagen and E. Stenhagen, Biochem. J., 92, (1964).
   (b) S. Abrahamsson, Science Tools, 14, 129 (1967).

7. (a,b) V.L. Talrose, V.V. Baznikow and G.D. Tantsyrev, Dokl. Akad. Nauk SSR, 159, 182 (1964); 170, 379 (1966).
    (c) Pettersson and R. Rayhage, Arkly. Kemi, 26, 293 (1967).
    (d) B.A. Knock, I.C. Smith, D.E. Wright and R. G. Ridley, Ibid, 42, 1516 (1970).
    (e) L.R. Crawford and J.D. Morrison, Anal. Chem., 40, 1464 (1968).

8. H.S. Herz, R.A. Hites, and K. Biemann, Anal. Chem., 43, 681 (1971).

9. (a) F.W. McLafferty, Pure Appl. Chem., 7, 61 (1971).
    (b) K. Kwok, R. Venkataraghavan and F.W. McLafferty, J. Amer. Chem. Soc., 95, 4185 (1973).

10. (a) S.L. Grotch, Anal. Chem., 42, (1970).
    (b) S.L. Grotch, Ibid, 43, 1362 (1971).
    (c) S.L. Grotch, Ibid, 45, 2 (1973).

11. L.E. Wangen, W.S. Woodward, and T.L. Isenhour, Ibid, 43, 1605 (1971).

12. R.G. Ridley, Chapter 6, "Compound Identification by Computer Matching Mass Spectrometry," in "Biochemical Applications of Mass Spectrometry," edited by G.R. Waller, John Wiley, (1971), and references therein.

13. (a) S.R. Heller, Anal. Chem., 44, 1951 (1972).
    (b) S.R. Heller, H.M. Fales, and G.W.A. Milne, J. Chem. ed., 49, 725 (1972).
    (c) S.R. Heller, H.M. Fales, and G.W.A. Milne, Org. Mass Spec., 7, 107 (1973).
    (d) S.R. Heller, D.A. Koniver, H.M. Fales, and G.W.A. Milne, Anal. Chem., in press.
    (e) S.R. Heller, R.J. Feldmann, H.M. Fales, and G.W.A. Milne, J. Chem. Doc., in press.

14. (a) E.J. Corey and W.T. Wipke, Science, 166, 178 (1969).
    (b) E.J. Corey, Quarterly Rev. 25, 455 (1971).
    (c,d) E.J. Corey, W.T. Wipke, R.D. Cramer, and W.J. Howe, J. Amer. Chem. Soc., 94, 421, 431 (1972).
    (e) E.J. Corey, R.D. Cramer and W.J. Howe, Ibid, 94, 440, (1972).
    (f) E.J. Corey and G.A. Petterson, Ibid, 94, 460 (1972).

15. W.T. Wipke, Chapter 7, "Proceedings of the NATO/CNA ASI on Computer Representation and Manuplation of Chemical Information" edited by W.T. Wipke, S.R. Heller, R.J. Feldmann, and E. Hyde, John Wiley, New York (1973).

16. R. Morris, Comm. ACM., 11, 34 (1968).

17. Barrons, "Time Sharing Marches On," Barrons, January 15, 1973, p. 3.

18. (a) R.C. Tryson, "Cluster Analysis," Edwards Bros. Inc. Ann Arbor, Michigan (1939).
    (b) R.R. Sokal and P.H.A. Sneath, "Principles of Numerical Taxonomy," Freeman, San Francisco (1963).
    (c) N.J. Nilsson, "Learning Machines," McGraw-Hill, New York (1965).
    (d) G.H. Ball, Proc. AFIPS 1965 Fall Joint Comp. Conf., 27, Part 1, 533 (1965).
    (e) G. Nagy, Proc. IEEE, 56, 836 (1968).
    (f) R.F. Ling, Ph.D. Thesis, Yale University (1971).
    (g) N. Jardin and R. Gibson, "Mathematical Taxonomy," John Wiley (1971).
    (h) R. Duda and P. Hart, "Pattern Classification and Scene Analysis," John Wiley (1972).
    (i) W.S. Meisel, "Computer-Oriented Approaches to Pattern Recognition," Chapter 8, Academic Press New York (1972).

19. J.G. Auguston and J. Minker, J. Assoc. Comp. Mach., 17, 571 (1970).

20. B.R. Kowalski and C.F. Bender, J. Amer. Chem. Soc., 94, 5632 (1972) and 95. 686 (1973).

21. C.T. Zahn, IEEE, Trans. on Computers, C-20, G8 (1971).

22. J.R. Slagle, C.L. Chang, and S.R. Heller, submitted for publication.

23. S.R. Heller, C.L. Chang, K.C. Chu, Anal. Chem., in press.

COMPUTER MODELING OF CHEMICAL STRUCTURES:
APPLICATIONS IN CRYSTALLOGRAPHY, CONFORMATIONAL
ANALYSIS, AND DRUG DESIGN

Garland R. Marshall, Heinz E. Bosshard
and Robert A. Ellis
Department of Physiology and Biophysics and Computer Systems
Laboratory, Washington University, St. Louis, Mo. 63110, USA

1. INTRODUCTION

The application of computer technology to modeling of molecular structures has reached a threshold level where the useful applications begin to compensate for the effort expended to nurture this approach. We would like to review the developments in this area of overlap between computer science and chemistry since its inception in 1965 and survey applications of this technique in the areas of crystallography, conformational analysis, and drug design. While other areas such as the design of organic synthesis (1) and a priori molecular orbital calculations share somewhat both in objectives and in methodology, a lack both of space and of expertise in these areas precludes a critical review.

In order to develop a basis for comparison of the various systems for computer modeling of molecular structures which have been developed since 1965, we propose to summarize the two systems developed at Washington University as they are representative of two extremes in technological development which have been utilized in this endeavor. Comparison with various other systems both in terms of software and hardware capability will emphasize the options available in the design of such a system. As applications have proven scientifically fruitful in recent years, a representative summary of results drawing primarily from the experience at Washington University will conclude this review. While the systems development and applications have included a large number of imaginative, talented, and hard-working individuals, the invidious comparisons[*] included in this review are those of the authors alone.

---

[*] The lack of published details has not curtailed the inclusion of molecular modeling systems for comparison as most have been outlined only in brief communications, if at all. Unfortunately, this situation encourages subjective evaluation.

2. CHEMAST-A SYNOPSIS

CHEMAST (<u>CHEM</u>istry <u>AS</u>sistan<u>T</u>) permits the construction, manipulation and display of molecular structures on a small laboratory-oriented computer (LINC, PDP-12) making such a system readily available to the chemist in his laboratory. The basic computer (Spear LINC or Digital PDP-12) has a 12-bit word length, inexpensive tape mass-storage units, a cycle time of less than 1.6 microseconds, and integral keyboard, point display scope, analog-to-digital channels and other subsystems conducive to man-machine interaction. Recent commercial availability of an inexpensive hardware floating point processor has added greatly to the computational muscle of such a small machine. These machines are available in approximate price range of $30,000 to $70,000 depending primarily on the amount of core memory (4K to 32K) required. The present version of CHEMAST assumes 8K of memory although prior, less sophisticated systems have existed in development stages on 4,3 or even 2K.

The CHEMAST system (2-4) consists of two logical subsystems, CHEMGEN (<u>CHEM</u>ical <u>GEN</u>erator), and MOLGRAPH (<u>MOL</u>ecular GRAPHics). CHEMGEN is the major input to CHEMAST although an alternate program, TRICS, is available to input crystallographic data in combination with CHEMGEN. The input is oriented around a set of chemical fragments or groups which compose a directory. While it would be possible to make a special directory which would accept Wiswesser line-notation, WLN, many chemists are not as comfortable with this notation as a computer and we feel a more chemical orientation as illustrated in Fig. 1 is

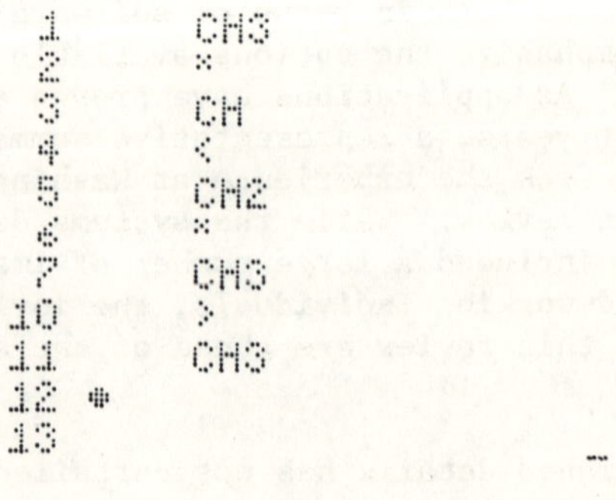

```
 1      CH3
 2      *
 3      CH
 4      <
 5      CH2
 6      *
 7      CH3
10      >
11      CH3
12      #
13
```

Fig. 1. Input description of isopentane.

generally more acceptable. The mnemonic associated with a given chemical group, e.g. CH3 for methyl group, is entered by typing on the keyboard. The topology of the molecule is denoted by the use of a few simple operands as follows:

    * linear continuation of the molecule
    < branch of the molecule
    > completion of the branch
    , termination of one but not all branches following an operator
    # termination of the molecule description

In addition, any group may be tagged with a symbol which is compiled into an attribute list of atoms tagged by a given symbol. This allows for ring closure bonds to be accomodated automatically.

A molecule description is scanned to determine if all mnemonics used are defined in the directory and if the valence requirements as designated in the directory are met by the topology. Two classes of atoms are specified by a group. The origin atom is at the end of the bond connecting the group to other groups and the internal atoms which do not lead to other atoms but are connected to the origin atom. This definition leads to the following scheme for atom numbering which determines the order of atomic coordinates:

1) The origin atom of group 1 is number 1.
2) The first atom of group 1 (origin atom of group two) is number 2.
3) Internal atoms of a group are given consecutive numbers and are numbered after the consecutively numbered origin atoms of connected groups.
4) The numbering of the atoms of a group is carried out in the same order as the groups occur.

These rules lead to the desired result that the atomic coordinates to be transformed for a given rotation about a bond forms a contiguous subset of defined number as shown in Fig. 2. Rotation about the bond between atoms #2 and #7 requires transformation of the coordinates of atoms #12 through #14, a contiguous subset of three. This numbering scheme allows a list to be associated with each rotable bond which gives the first atom (First Atom) to be transformed and the number of contiguous atoms (How Many) to be transformed by rotation about that bond.

Two major assumptions underlie the generation of coordinates. The first is that each group type has a standard geometry in terms of the orientations of the bonds between the

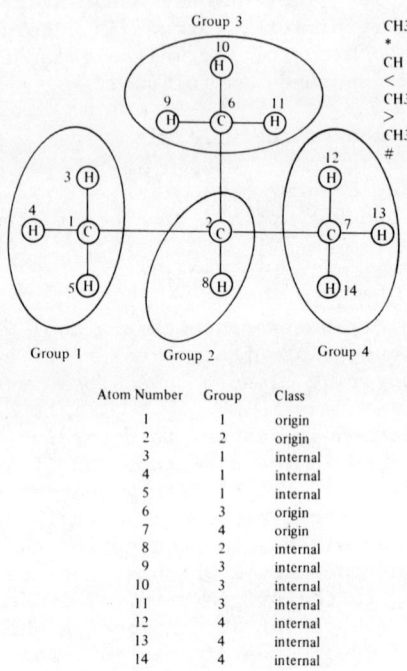

Fig. 2. Example of atom and group numbers and atom classifications.

origin and the internal atoms of the group. The second is that the bond lengths of the internal atoms are treated as a constant for that group while the bond lengths to that group from the proceeding group are determined by the respective two groups. While the geometry of most organic compounds is fairly consistent with these assumptions, exceptions do exist. This situation can be accomodated by definition of a new group, by overlay of the generated coordinates with crystal structure data utilizing TRICS (5), or by correction of the generated coordinates utilizing geometrical subroutines which allow for modification of bond lengths and bond angles.

It is convenient to use spherical polar angles to define the geometry of a group category. Rectangular coordinates are then computed for a local frame beginning with the last group. As one computes successive groups, the coordinates of the previous groups are transformed into those of the current local frame utilizing the First Atom and How Many lists mentioned earlier. This allows us to discard the transformation matrices once they are used. Branching of the structure does not present any problems as the application of the transformations is determined by the First Atom and How Many list which circumvents this difficulty.

Besides the atomic coordinates and the First Atom and How Many list, three other tables are generated. The atom type table consists of assigned type numbers which represent commonly occuring atoms. This is useful for display and labeling of certain atom types for identification as well as for potential energy calculations. The connectivity table lists the atom pairs which are convalently bonded in the molecule. The final table generated is a list of the atoms which have been tagged by letter attributes. This is useful for designating ring closure bonds, atoms which may participate in hydrogen bonding, etc. It has been found useful to have a final stage of the program which collects, compacts, and writes to tape at specific locations the data tables previously generated. This allows various configurations of the data structure to be utilized as molecule descriptions. This compact data structure is available for display and manipulation with the subprogram, MOLGRAPH. Upon loading, the program requests an address on tape where the desired molecule description can be found. The description most recently generated by CHEMGEN may be requested from a fixed location on tape or a molecule previously generated, manipulated and stored may be recalled. Manipulation of the structure is controlled manually either through the keyboard or through **potentiometer** knobs which are an integral part of the machine. A list of the primitive operators is given in Table 1. Automatic control by file program is through utilization of the manual operators as program subroutines.

One essential feature of the partial rotations used to change the conformation of a molecule should be emphasized. The traditional approach is that of Eyring (6) in which a local frame transformation matrix must be stored for each branch point or node. To transform coordinates of a given substructure requires the successive application of all the transformation matrices separating the substructure from the origin in the global frame. For a small computer where core space is small and especially for complex calculations where computation speed is a limiting factor, an alternative approach is preferred. The application of a single matrix which we call the T matrix (3), derived originally by Gibbs (7), to all the points specified in the First Atom and How Many list is sufficient. The equation which must be solved for each point is:
$\bar{X}' = T (\bar{X} - \bar{X}o) + \bar{X}o$ where $\bar{X}$ and $\bar{X}'$ are the vector before and after transformation and $\bar{X}o$ is any vector whose endpoint lies on the axis of rotation (in practice, the atoms at either

TABLE 1.

Primitive Keyboard Operators of CHEMAST

Cursor Operation
    Forward - Move selected bond forward one
    Back - Move selected bond back one
    Show n - Expand cursor to n bonds
    Delete - Remove bond selected by cursor
    Normal - Resore deleted bond

Global Rotation
    X-Axis - Rotate molecule about x-axis
    Y-Axis - Rotate molecule about y-axis
    Z-Axis - Rotate molecule about z-axis
    Bond - Rotate molecule about axis specified by
        selected bond

Partial Rotation
    Set-up - Prepare to rotate partial structure
        following bond about axis specified
        by selected bond
    Single Increment - Rotate by increment
    Continuous Increment - Rotate by increasing
        increments
    Freeze - Overlay displayed coordinates on
        reference set
    Restore - Overlay reference coordinates on
        display set

Parameter Change
    Increment - Change increment for rotations
    Scale - Change size of display
    Line - Change number of points displayed per line
    Stereo - Change amount of stereo transformation
    Bond - Sets cursor
    Perspective - Change amount of perspective correction
    Atom Bump - Determine whether program checks for first
        Van der Waals violations or all

Measure
    Length - Determines distance between 2 selected atoms
    Bond - Transfer control to geometric routines which
        allow bond angle and bond length measurement
        modification

Table 1 (Cont.)
I/O Control
  Tape Read - Reads molecule description from specified
              location
  Tape Write - Writes molecule description to specified
               location
  LIBCALL - Transfers control to programs on file
  RETURN - Transfers control to editor for preparation
           of molecule manuscript

---

end of the bond being rotated). T is a 3x3 rotation matrix in which $\underline{a}$, $\underline{b}$ and $\underline{c}$ are the direction cosines of the axis of rotation and τ is the amount of rotation as follows:

$$\begin{array}{lll} \underline{a}^2+(1-\underline{a}^2)\cos\tau & \underline{ab}(1-\cos\tau)-\underline{c}\sin\tau & \underline{ab}(1-\cos\tau)+\underline{b}\sin\tau \\ \underline{ab}(1-\cos\tau)+\underline{c}\sin\tau & \underline{b}^2+(1-\underline{b}^2)\cos\tau & \underline{bc}(1-\cos\tau)-\underline{a}\sin\tau \\ \underline{ac}(1-\cos\tau)-\underline{b}\sin\tau & \underline{bc}(1-\cos\tau)+\underline{a}\sin\tau & \underline{c}^2+(1-\underline{c}^2)\cos\tau \end{array}$$

Because of the problem of accumulated error using 12-bit arithemetic, coordinates are updated from a standard list to a display list by a single transformation where possible, i.e., continuous rotation uses an increase in rotation increment rather than successive transformations.

Checking for steric interaction consists of a pairwise comparison of distances between atoms against a list of minimum contact distances for the types of atom pairs. Only those atoms whose position in space is changed by the current rotation (Set B) are checked against those atoms whose position are not changed (Set A). This dynamic check is implemented through the use of the First Atom and How Many list. Set B is comprised of those atoms in this list, for these are exactly the atoms whose positions in space are being changed. Real-time additions to the connectivity list with a code for dotted rather than continuous line form the basis for the display of atoms whose position in space violate the minimum contact distances allowed by their Van der Waals radii (Fig. 3).

Because of a lack of line drawing hardware, a software version of the hardware binary-rate multiplier technique used in some displays has been implemented (3). The use of three dimensional data in the algorithm allows the application of an efficient stereo approximation to each point comprising the line. Simply adding the value of the Z component scaled right by three positions (divide by 8) to the horizontal coordinate for the right eye display and subtracting the same value from the horizontal coordinate for the left eye display allows the generation of convincing stereo pairs. As the display becomes

more complicated, the numbers of points per line can be reduced
to minimize the flicker without sacrificing the stereo display
as each point has its own registered stereo pair.

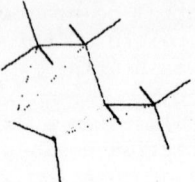

SINGLE INCREMENT

Fig. 3. Conformation with Van der Waals contacts indicated.

A geometrical package (8) allows measurement and modification of bond lengths and bond angles. This allows a model to be generated in the staggered configuration with CHEMGEN and then modified to fit a particular configuration as determined by crystallography or other physical techniques. Alternatively, a particular conformation selected by a file program or crystal data which has been imputed with TRICS may be measured and the bond lengths and angles recorded.

3. MMS (Macromolecular Modeling System) - A SYNOPSIS

Based on the experience and insight gained during the development of the CHEMAST system, a more ambitious effort to develop a system capable of similar display and manipulation of large structures such as proteins only awaited the availability of suitable hardware. Our efforts were extremely fortunate to be complemented by the development of restructurable computer components, macromodules, by the Computer Systems Laboratory (9). Designing with these components is somewhat analagous to assembly language programming while the user does not have to concern himself with engineering questions such as circuit loading or propagation delay normally associated with hardware design of a computer system. The system (10) used for modeling large molecular structures (primarily proteins) consists of a collection of hardware subroutines assembled from macromodules, a hardware matrix multiplier and line drawing scope;

and a small stored-program computer (the µ LINC 300) as shown in Fig. 4.

Two memory sections retain the data structure; one K within the LINC, comprising the molecule description, and a set of macromodular core memories which can also be accessed by the LINC. The molecule description within the LINC includes (1) a table of key parameters and addresses, (2) a table of structural features common to proteins, i.e., description of the twenty-four types of amino acid residues, (3) tables specifying the sequence of the protein model in terms of the standard residue table above, (4) tables specifying added or missing atoms from the regular structure, (5) tables specifying any non-peptide substructure(s) (6) tables for dynamic editing of the point-to-point (atom-to-atom) line connections and for incorporating small appended structures, and (7) storage for the presently selected model display options. This information is stored within the general-purpose computer to provide direct access from model input routines, user-interaction routines and special function routines.

The macromodular memory serves as storage for the coordinates and other large tables as well as parameters requiring rapid access by the macromodular hardware. As in the CHEMAST system, there are two coordinate work areas (12K of 24-bit memory each). One is for a reference coordinate set and the other for a display set. A connectivity table consist of 3K of 12-bit numbers for normal line display and 1K of 12-bit numbers for a blinking display (off-on pulsing at half-second intervals). Contour coordinate data for displaying the electron density contours comprises 20 K of 12-bit numbers with the connectivity encoded into the two least significant bits of the X-coordinate. Two 4K tables (12-bit) contain the First Atom and How Many List which utilize the tree-structure of the data to indicate the contiguous sets of coordinates to be transformed.

The macromodular section consists of a hardware version of subroutines rather than as a stored program computer, although this latter configuration was initially tried (11). Four major hardware functions are accessed by a short instruction set from the LINC. These are: Display molecule (DISM), Display contours (DISC), Update (UPD) and Bump Check (BUMP). From the point of view of programming the LINC, these complex functions as shown in Fig. 5. are reduced to the level of a machine language instruction.

The macromodules are connected with and control the display hardware which consists of approximately half of the LDS-1 system manufactured by Evans and Sutherland to interact with a PDP-10. The hardware matrix multiplier and line generator have

Fig. 4. Current version of the Macromolecular Modelling System. The components, from left to right, are (a) auxiliary memories (4K of 12-bit words to each box within the stacks, except for the lower two boxes which are a power supply and a controller), (b) macromodular processor, (c) (below) LINC-to-macromodule interface, (d) Evans and Sutherland LDS-1 Matrix Multiplier, (e) (foreground) LINC scope and keyboard, (f) Evans and Sutherland LDS-1 Line Drawing Scope and (g) micro-LINC 300.

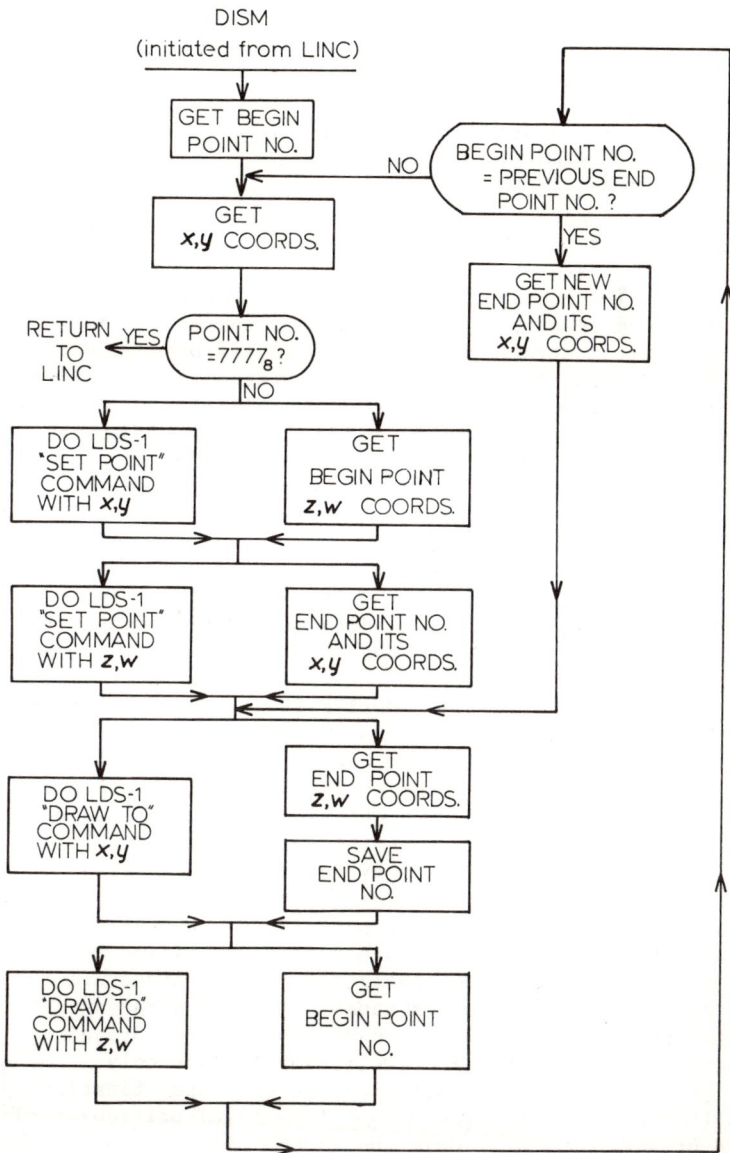

Fig. 5. Control sequence for the DISM macromodular hardware subroutine.

been interfaced to be compatible with macromodules and receive their appropriate commands in LDS order code as well as data from 24-bit macromodular registers. The matrix multiplier and line generator operate asynchronously in a pipeline fashion with a line being drawn while the next coordinates are being transformed. If the transformation changes the conformation of the molecule, the transformed coordinates are usually returned to memory for storage. The matrix multiplier was selected because of the digital nature of its design which allows its use in calculations as well as for display.

As this system has primarily evolved in the milieu of protein crystallography, it is not unusual that the software reflects concern with structural comparison of the over twenty protein crystal structures available to the user on tape (See Fig. 6) and model fitting of experimental electron density maps. Interaction with the system is primarily through question and answer displays presented on the LINC display scope and through potentiometer controls over such variables as position, size, orientation etc. A potentiometer controling position of a cursor which can be used to identify either a bond or an atom by intensification or blinking has been used extensively. A second potentiometer controling the span of consecutive connectivity table entries to be intensified has also found use in specifying electron density data to be deleted from the display in order to simplify the interpretion during model fitting.

Input to the system can derive from CHEMGEN or other CHEMAST input sources as well as through coordinate lists determined by x-ray crystallography, especially of proteins. Most of the data tables necessary for manipulation and display are generated on-line by routines which operate as macro-expanders based on the regular nature of the protein data and the molecular description of the particular protein being studied. In order for the generated connectivity, First Atom, How Many and Atom Type tables to correspond with the coordinate data, a rigid format for coordinate data must be specified and maintained. Fortunately, the divergence of data structure utilized by protein crystallographers appears to be decreasing and the initial task of conversion upon receiving a new protein structure for inclusion in the library is once only. The on-line generation of data tables allows easy specification by the user (through the question-answer format) of particular displays of interest, e.g. only the carbon-alpha backbone with aliphatic, hydrophobic residues (Leu, Val, Ile, Met,) shown and charged residues (Glu, Asp, His, Lys) blinking.

Electron density contours for a specified intensity and volume are generated on-line from a three dimensional array of

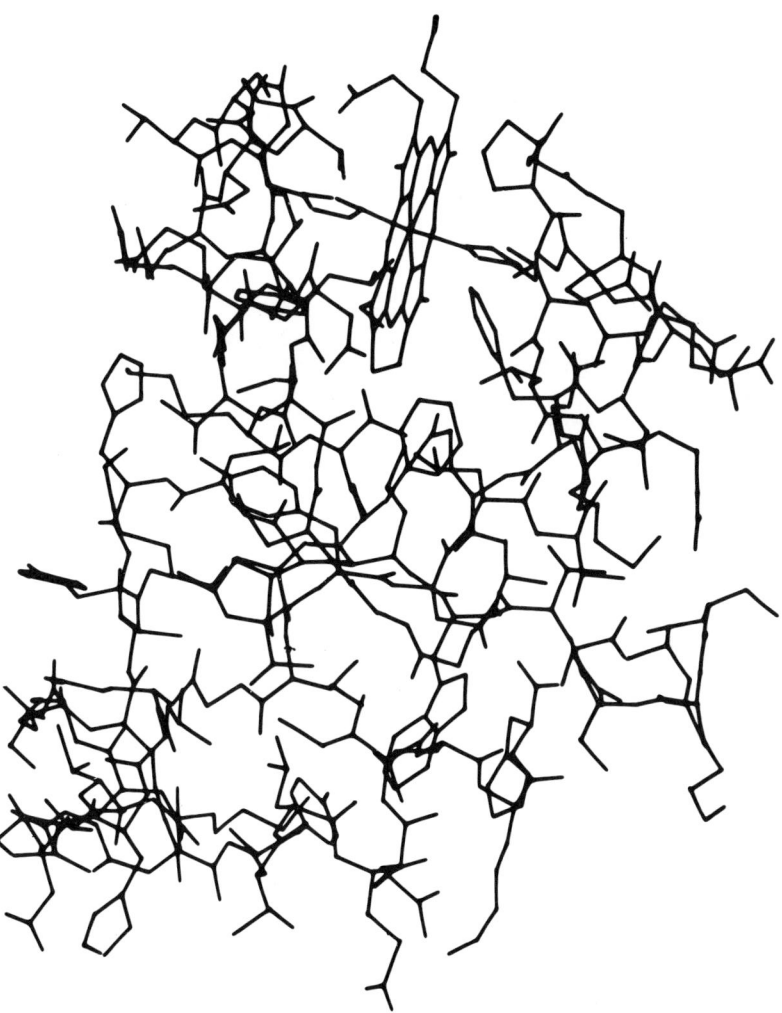

Fig. 6. Model of the protein Cytochrome b_5 as displayed by MMS. At the top-middle, the iron-bearing heme group appears, with the central iron atom in octahedral coordination (convergence of six lines). The electron-transport function of this protein resides in its iron atom. This molecule requires one-fourth of the current MMS capacity.

intensities stored on tape. The current system allows for
storage of two intensity levels of contours with selection by
switch of display of either level or both simultaneously.
Interactive editing of the contours allows simplification of the
display by eliminating noise and extraneous contours from the
section of the model currently being fitted.

4. THE TABLES

The tables, which compare the computer-based molecular
structure modeling systems for which we have printed information,
represent our attempt to characterize these systems. As with any
set of characterizations, we are concerned that many systems
have been slighted. Nevertheless, we feel that the utility of
this sort of comparison outweighs this potential difficulty.
There are four tables: Equipment, Molecule Input Forms, Display
& Manipulation Software, and Implementation and Programming.
Each entry is either a value for a parameter, a plus (+) for
inclusion, a minus (-) to indicate a feature the system does not
have, or a question mark (?) for unknown. Although we have
tried to verify as much of this data as possible, some entries
represent a best estimate.

Equipment

a. Central processor This column lists the computer
systems which are used for the majority of the programs. They
range from second generation machines such as the IBM 7094 and
Digital Equipment Corp. PDP-7 to modern high-performance machines
(IBM 360/91) and low-cost minicomputers (PDP-12, Nova, PDP-11,
etc.).

b. Graphics terminal. We use this designation
although, in several cases, the graphics equipment is not
strictly a terminal (the PDP-12 scope is part of the main
computer). The range in equipment is almost unbelievable --
from homemade, point-plotting scopes, color TV sets and modest
line-drawing devices to super terminals (Adage AGT 50, Evans
and Sutherland LDS-1) with extensive processing capacity and
costs of hundreds of thousands of dollars.

c. Core memory requirements. This category is
divided into two subcategories: CPU and terminal although many
times the graphics equipment does not have any separate memory.
In general, the smaller figures associated with the mini - and
midi- computers represent the total memory available which is
the same as the amount used by the system. For the larger

Table II
Equipment

System	Central Processor	Graphics Terminal	Memory CPU	Memory Terminal	Cycle Time	Word Length	Usable Lines	I/O Devices	Stereo	Graphics Hardware
Project Mac (MIT, 1965)	IBM 7094	PDP-7, DEC-340	32K	8K	2.0	36	<400	Tracker Ball		--
CHEMAST (WUSL, 1969)	LINC, PDP 12	CRT (pt.plot)	8K	--	1.6	12	30	potentiometer	lateral	--
BRAD (Brookhaven,	Sigma 7	BRAD	18K	--	0.7	32	limited on-resolution	Tracker Ball	red-green	--
OCSS (Harvard, 1969)	PDP-1	DEC-340		--	5	18	200	Tablet	--	--
CHEMGRAF (Columbia, 1970)	IBM 360/91	ADAGE AGT/50 Multiplexed with high speed link	2M bytes	16K	360/91 54ns AGT/50 1.5	32 30	5000	potentiometer joystick tablet	lateral	analog-translation, rotation, scale

Table II
(cont.)

System	Central Processor	Graphics Terminal	Memory CPU	Memory Terminal	Cycle Time	Word Length	Usuable Lines	I/O Devices	Stereo	Graphics Hardware
CHEMTEST (MIT, 1970)	PDP-7	DEC-340	8K	--	1.75	18	?	--	--	--
Molecular Biophysics (Oxford, 1971)	Ferranti Argus 500	Ferranti-30	12K	--	2	24	6000	Tracker Ball	Ortony	--
MMS (WUSL, 1971)	Spear µLINC	Macromodules LDS-0.5	8K	72K	1	12 / 24	8000	potentiometer	Ortony	digital-translation, rotation scale
Wiberg (Yale, 1970)	PDP-8	CRT (pt.plot)	4K	--	1.5	12	50	--	--	--
Bison (Argonne, 1970)	IBM 360/75	IBM 2250	?	?	0.75	32	--	--	--	--

Table II
(cont.)

System	Central Processor	Graphics Terminal	Memory CPU	Memory Terminal	Cycle Time	Word Length	Usuable Lines	I/O Devices	Stereo	Graphics Hardware
3-Dimensional (Syntex, 1970)	NOVA 4000	Conrac Color TV	4K+ 128K DISU	--	0.80	16	limited only by resolution	Tracker Ball	Red-Green	--
GRIP (North Carolina, 1971)	IBM 360/50	IBM 2250	110K Bytes +21 Bytes/Atm.	--	2	32	?	light pen	--	--
Mill Hill (London, 1971)	Honeywell DDP-16	CRT	8K	--	0.96	16	~100	potentiometer	lateral, Red-Green	--
Computer Graphics Lab (Princeton, 1972)	PDP-10	E&S LDS-1	64K	--	1	36	4000	3-D tablet potentiometer joystick animation	Time sequential	digital translation, rotation, scaling, clipping, perspective

Table II (cont.)

System	Central Processor	Graphics Terminal	Memory CPU / Terminal	Cycle Time	Word Length	Usuable Lines	I/O Devices	Stereo	Graphics Hardware
Steinrauf (Indiana, 1972)	PDP 15/30	VP-15B CRT	16K / --	0.80	18	~120	--	--	--
MMS (AWARE, 1972)	Varian 620 f	Color TV	16K+ 750K DISU / --	0.75	16	limited only resolution	joystick	--	--
DCRT/CIS (NIH, 1972)	PDP-10	ADAGE AGT/30, DEC 340	55K / ?	1	36	4000	--	--	analog-translation, rotation, scale
Prophet (BB&N, ?)	PDP-10	Computek 400	32K / --	1	36	storage	tablet	--	--
Crysnet (Texas A&M, ?)	PDP-11/40	Vector General	16K / --	1	16	6000	potentiometer	lateral	analog-translation, rotation, scale

Graphics Equipment   221

machines, the figures generally represent the core available only
and does not necessarily mean that the molecular modeling system
uses all of it. The cases where we have more accurate data are
noted. Note, that in almost all cases, the total amount of
programs far exceeds the available core space and the system
relies extensively on program overlay from mass storage devices
such as tapes and/or discs.

       d. Cycle time. This is the basic memory cycle time
of the CPU. While they are all near 1 and 2 microseconds, we
have included this for completeness.

       e. Word length. The important thing to note about this
category is that it does not make any significant difference;
molecular modeling systems can be implemented on systems with
almost any word length, although the smaller word lengths require
close attention to programming details in order to preserve
numerical accuracy.

       f. Number of usable lines. This is a very subjective
measure; what may be an acceptable degree of image flicker to
one viewer may be totally objectionable to another. This value
also depends on the persistance of the CRT phosphor and the
length of lines, and sometimes is limited by the memory size
and not by the display equipment. In general we have used the
numbers quoted by the system developers as indicative of the
number of lines that their displays typically contain. There are
two types of exceptions: (1) The TV-raster displays will display
as much data as is presented and are limited by the inherent low
resolution of the device and (2) direct-view storage tubes which
do not require image refreshing.

       g. I/O devices. Under this entry, we have indicated
devices specialized to computer graphics: potentiometers, data
tablets, joysticks, tracker balls, etc. Once again, note that
it is possible to implement systems without any of these devices,
although they certainly may be important to ease the use of the
system.

       h. Stereo. We have indicated the type of capability,
if any, for the system to present stereo images to the viewers.
Lateral denotes two non-overlapping images and generally requires
some sort of viewing device. Red/green refers to superimposed
two-color images generated by a color CRT and viewed through
color filtered glasses. Time-segmented involves displaying the
two images separated in time and using a device (such as the
Evans & Sutherland lorngette) to block the scope from first one

eye and then the other. Ortony denotes a form of vertical images superimposed and distinguished by polarization developed by A. Ortony (12) which greatly simplifies the required optics.

i. Special graphics hardware. This column indicates the use of special-purpose hardware for rotation, translation, scaling, and clipping of the image. The use of hardware for these functions permits real-time manipulations of large structures. All displays (except as noted) are assumed to have hardware for generating line segments on the CRT.

Molecule Input Forms

This table describes the forms in which the molecular structure is entered into the system:

a. Coordinate data. In this form of input, numerical tables of the coordinates for each atom in the structure are required. Length and angles means that a structure may be "built" from the entry of bond lengths and angles (generally more available than x,y,z coordinates by a program which generates coordinates for the atoms. FCC indicates the ability to enter data in fractional cell coordinates and having a program generate rectangular coordinates from these using the unit cell parameters. This capability is indicated only if it is provided on-line. Rectangular coordinates is an obvious method of entry, but it is surprising that not all systems have implemented it.

b. Character string. This form of input uses a description by a linear string of characters and generates a meaningful three-dimensional structure utilizing tables of standard bond lengths and angles. The methods of entering and/or generating these tables are an important aspect which we have not covered. WLN provides the entry of structures in the Wiswesser Line Notation and has generally been provided by groups working in the related field of chemical information retrieval or for compatibility with such systems. Defined groups permits the user to enter his structure by typing characters which represent commonly occuring chemical entitles (i.e., C, H, OH, CH2, etc.) and by using punctuation such as commas, parentheses, etc. to represent branching and ring closure. Other typically refers to the ability to generate structures from previously generated fragments. Typical of this is a directory of the common amino acid residues which are then referred to by a short, mnemonic name.

Table III

Molecule Input Forms

System	Coordinate Data			Character String			Graphical	
	Length & Angles	FCC	Rect.	WLN	Defined Group	Other	2-D	3-D
Project Mac (MIT)	−	−	−	−	−	−	−	−
CHEMAST (WUSL)	−	+	+	−	+	+	−	−
BRAD (Brookhaven)	−	+	+	−	+	+	−	−
OCSS (Harvard)	−	−	−	−	−	−	+	−
CHEMGRAF (Columbia)	−	−	+	+	−	+	+	−
CHEMTEST (MIT)	−	−	−	−	+	−	−	−
Wiberg (Yale)	+	−	−	−	−	−	−	−
Bison (Argonne)	−	−	−	−	−	+	−	−
3-Dimensional (Syntex)	−	+	−	−	+	+	−	−
Molecular Biophysics (Oxford)	−	+	+	−	−	+	−	−
MMS (WUSL)	−	+	+	−	+	+	−	−
GRIP (North Carolina)	−	−	+	−	−	−	−	−
Mill Hill (London)	−	−	+	−	−	+	−	−
Computer Graphics (Princeton)	−	−	+	−	−	−	+	+
Steinrauf (Indiana)	−	+	+	+	−	−	−	−
MMS (Aware)	−	−	+	−	−	+	+	−
DRCT/CIS (NIH)	−	−	−	−	−	−	−	−
Prophet (BB&N)	−	−	−	−	−	+	+	−
Crysnet (Texas A&M)	−	+	+	−	−	−	−	−

c. Graphical. While this is perhaps the input form most desired by the average chemist, it has seldom been implemented due to the attendent difficulties. 2-D is the use of a data tablet or light pen to sketch a two-dimensional representation of the structure. This technique is characterized by the necessity of generating a sterically valid structure from the sketch utilizing some form of energy minimization or are characterized by applications not requiring a sterically valid model (CHEMTEST). 3-D is the use of a three-dimensional data tablet (yes, they do exist) to sketch or trace an existing mechanical model. This capability is characterized by the general lack of availability of the requisite devices.

Display and Manipulation Software

a. Rotation and translation. This category describes the ability to rotate and translate the displayed structure. Without exception, all systems provide some form of global coordinate transformation to the entire structure. Only slightly less universal is the capability of transforming coordinates for part of the structure. Without this function, the system can provide little more than study of existing structures.

b. Bond length and angle. It is surprising to us how few systems provide this capability. With the additon of these transformations, a complete set of molecular structure manipulations is available.

c. Van der Waals check. Some systems provide a check for steric hindrance in additon to any energy calculations as a fast check of structure validity and indicate the overlapping atoms visually on the display. Also, some systems have provided a similar indication by displaying circles at each atom position which are equivalent to the Van der Waals radius. The ambiguities which result from differences in depth can be resolved by rotating the display.

d. Energy calculations. Of the systems which provide some form of energy calculation, relatively few provide for full energy minimization attesting to the difficulty of implementing this function. Other systems provide energy calculations which retain a single value for the energy of a particular conformation.

e. Electron density fitting. This capability generally requires the simultaneous display of electron density contour and molecular structural model which is then "fitted" to the density in a sort of computerized "Richards box" (13). Only

Table IV

Display & Manipulation Software

System	Rot.& Trans. Global	Trans. Partial	Bond Length-Angle	VdW Check	Energy Conformer	Energy Minimize	Electron Density Fit	Animation	Interaction KBD	MENU	Q&A	Scale Clipping
Project Mac	+	+	–	+	+	+	–	+	+	–	–	S
CHEMAST	+	+	+	+	+	+	–	+	+	–	–	S
BRAD	+	+	–	circles	–	–	–	–	+	–	–	S
OCSS	+	?	–	–	–	–	–	–	+	+	–	?
CHEMGRAF	+	+	–	+	+	+	+	+	–	–	–	+
CHEMTEST	–	–	–	–	+	+	–	–	–	–	–	–
Wiberg	+	–	–	–	–	–	–	–	–	+	+	+
Bison	–	–	–	–	–	+	–	+	–	–	–	?
3-Dimensional	+	+	+	circles	–	–	–	–	+	–	–	+
Molecular Biophyscis	+	+	–	+	+	–	+	+	–	–	–	S
MMS (WUSL)	+	+	+	–	–	–	+	–	+	+	+	+
GRIP	+	+	–	–	+	+	–	+	–	+	–	S
Computer Graphics	+	+	+	–	+	+	–	+	–	–	–	+
Steinrauf	+	+	–	+	+	–	–	+	–	–	–	–
MMS (Aware)	+	+	–	circles	–	–	–	–	–	?	–	S
DCRT/CIS	+	+	–	–	+	–	–	–	–	–	+	+
Prophet	+	+	+	+	?	–	–	–	–	–	–	S
Crysnet	+	+	–	+	–	–	+	–	–	+	–	+

the high-performance systems provide adequate display capability.

g. Animation. While it is possible to generate motion picture films by simply pointing a camera at the display scope, the lack of synchronization between the display refresh rate and the camera frame rate generally makes the results unsatisfactory. Systems with animation facility have, at the least, some form of computer-controlled motion picture camera synchronization. Some of these systems also have extensive software which permits the generation of sequences on-line for later filming.

h. On-line interaction. Systems which provide for on-line control must provide some form of input and selection of options for display and manipulation. Keyboard refers to the use of a keyboard to type commands to the system. Menu is the ability to point to descriptions of options on the scope with a light pen or data tablet. Q & A is the provision of a set of displayed option descriptions to which the user responds by a key stroke. The latter two provide some measure of self-documentation of the system.

i. Scaling and clipping. Many systems provide software (one uses hardware) to permit the user to zoom in and display a small portion of the structure in detail and exclude other areas. Typically, the user can specify a spherical or cubical volume about an atom in which he wants to see the parts of the structure which pass through that volume. Less sophisticated versions of this feature merely provide the ability to center and increase the scale of the structure with the display of parts off-scale prevented.

Implementation

a. User added features. Some systems provide facilities for users to add operations to the system. Most frequently, this is merely the ability for the user to write a program which calls on a set of subroutines which represent fairly powerful operations related to molecular structures. A few systems (GRIP and Prophet, in particular) provide for this extension as part of the system itself.

b. Language. It is interesting to note the variety of languages which have been used to do the basic implementation of the systems and the user additions. We see no trends, but do note the extensive use of FORTRAN which is generally not

Table V

Implementation Languages

System	User Added Features	System Language	User Language
Project Mac	–	MAD	–
CHEMAST	+	Assembly	Assembly & SubR.
BRAD	–	Fortran IV	–
OCSS	?	?	?
CHEMGRAF	+	Fortran IV	Fortran
CHEMTEST	–	Fortran II	–
Wiberg	–	Assembly	–
Bison	–	?	–
3-Dimensional	–	Assembly	–
Molecular Biophysics	–	Assembly	–
MMS (WUSL)	+	Assembly	Assembly & SubR.
GRIP	+	PL/I	PL/I + Special
Computer Graphics	+	Fortran	Fortran, LISP, SNOBOL, MACRO
Steinrauf	–	Fortran	–
MMS (Aware)	–	Assembly	–
DCRT/CIS	–	?	–
Prophet	+	Special Interpreter	PL/I
Crysnet	+	Assembly	Basic, Fortran

227

considered to be an appropriate language for computer graphics.
Even the FORTRAN implementations probably have fairly extensive
machine subroutines. It does not seem appropriate for the user
to do assembly language programming although we have been
amazed at what an appropriately motivated researcher can do using
this medium.

5. THE SYSTEMS

Project MAC (MIT; 1965)

This was the prototype system and served to demonstrate the
usefulness of computer molecular modeling. The system utilized
the Project MAC experimental time-sharing system and a satellite
graphics unit consisting of a vector drawing CRT controlled by a
small (for that time) computer. The system was used for studies
in protein folding, energy minimization, and molecular structure
(14).

CHEMAST (Washington University; 1969)

CHEMAST was the first system which provided general-purpose
molecular modeling with display and manipulation on a stand-alone
small computer. The system has been used for determining
sterically-allowed conformations of small molecules, energy
calculations, and molecular structure studies. The system also
served as a vehicle for development of techniques used in a
later, more extensive system and to whet the appetites of
potential users and maintain their interest (2-4).

BRAD (Brookhaven; 1969)

This system represents the first use of TV-raster scan
graphics and superimposed red/green images for stereo viewing
of molecular graphics. The system was the first to accept
crystal structures from a common repository or data bank.
Emphasis has been placed on interpretation of crystal structures
determined by direct methods and evaluation of the applicability
of this form of display technology which allows complex
presentation at relatively low cost. The system has been used
for small molecule and protein crystallography (15-16).

OCSS (Harvard; 1969)

Although the primary emphasis of OCSS was computer-aided
organic chemical synthesis, a graphics capability was provided.

The system was distinguished by the generation of sterically valid molecular structures from two dimensional sketches entered on a data tablet (1).

CHEMTEST (MIT; 1970)

CHEMTEST was developed as an aid to chemical education and used as an adjunct to a freshman course in chemistry. As such, the emphasis was on having the computer aid the student in constructing valid, two-dimensional models of molecules paying particular attention to electronic structure and bonding (17).

CHEMGRAF (Columbia University; 1970)

CHEMGRAF was implemented by the developers of the earlier MIT system. It was the first system to use specialized hardware for the translation and rotation of CRT displayed molecular models. Refinements of the previous work has led to a system with tremendous computation and display power. The system has been used for molecular structure modeling including monitoring direct methods in determining the crystal structure of dinucleotides. The system has also been used for three-dimensional reconstruction of biological structures from serial section photography and other applications in the area of image processing (18).

Wiberg (Yale; 1970)

This system was developed primarily as a teaching aid and emphasized computations related to experiments and associated instrumentation. The display and manipulation performance, while modest, nevertheless represents a useful and useable capability (19).

Bison (Argonne; 1970)

This system has been developed primarily to perform ab initio molecular orbital calculations, but is cited here for its use of interactive displays in the presentation of results (10).

Three Dimensional Display (Syntex, 1970)

This is a commercial version based on the Brookhaven system. It was designed to operate as a laboratory tool for the x-ray crystallographer. It makes efficient use of a small computer with disk mass storage (21).

Molecular Biophysics (Oxford, 1971)

This system developed capabilities approaching those of the high-performance and highly expensive systems using computation and display equipment of moderate performance and cost. The system has been used to fit molecular models of substrates and inhibitors of lysozyme to electron density data and to search for structures whose calculated NMR spectra correlated with experimentally observed spectra (22-23).

MMS (Washington University; 1971)

The use of reconfigurable digital computer building blocks called macromodules to provide high-performance, graphical-data-structure manipulation and specialized numerical calculations characterize this system. The actual graphics performance is achieved through the use of part of an LDS-1 system. An extensive library of protein structures has been assembled for use in comparative structure study. The system has also been used for fitting molecular models to electron density data, specialized calculations for the closure of small rings, and production of motion pictures to illustrate structural relationships and proposed mechanisms of catalytic action of proteins. Display of models of neuroanatomical data and cell fine-structure reconstruction has also been implemented (10, 24).

GRIP (University of North Carolina; 1971)

GRIP was developed to study the means for providing capabilities for extension and modification of the basic system as a reaction to specialized-user requirements. This system was implemented as a research effort in Computer Science and demonstrated the feasibility of this approach (25).

Mill Hill (London, 1971)

This system explored the use of a small on-site computer for interactive graphics in biomedical research. A stereoscopic display of crystal structures was generated which allowed interactive orientation of the molecule. The software allowed for a title display as well as captions for the atoms. The complexity of the display was limited to molecules on the order of vitamin B_{12} (26).

Computer Graphics Laboratory (Princeton, 1972)

This system is distinguished by use of the full Evans and

Sutherland LDS-1 graphics system which is capable of extremely high performance graphics. This system has produced a widely applicable, general-purpose set of FORTRAN-called graphics routines (GIGL). Considerable emphasis has been placed on the production of quality color and black-and-white motion pictures. The system is also characterized by the use of a three-dimensional graphics input tablet for sketching or tracing molecular models. Primary use has been for computer-aided organic synthesis and molecular structure studies of protein and polynucleotides (27).

Steinrauf (Indiana, 1972)

This system is designed to provide useful computing services (both on-line and off-line) for an x-ray crystallography laboratory. As such, less emphasis has been placed on the display and manipulation aspects although the resulting system has a reasonable capability in this area (28).

MMS (Aware Systems and Stanford; 1972)

This system is notable in its use of low-cost hardware to provide specialized capability in the study of semiconductor and superconductor substances (29).

DCRT/CIS Modeling System (NIH, 1972)

This system provides display on terminals with different capabilities: An Adage AGT 30 with hardware rotation and a DEC 340 which can only generate vectors. The system has been used for examination of protein structures and for preparation of movies presenting crystallographic results. This system has been developed rapidly due to its location in an environment oriented to the needs of a large community of users (30).

Prophet (Bolt, Beranek, & Newman; under development)

Prophet has been developed primarily concentrating on the organization and sharing of experimental data in pharmacological research. The system is characterized by the use of storage-tube graphics. Molecular-structure display and manipulation has had less emphasis in this system, but an effort to provide additional capability has begun. The system also provides extensive capabilities for user-added computation (31).

Crysnet (Texas A&M and Brookhaven; under development)

This system is distinguished by its use of moderate-cost, commercially-available equipment and by the interconnection of several systems over a computer network. This provides for the sharing of molecular structure by the formation of a common data base (32).

6. Applications

A. X-ray Crystallography

The most obvious application of interactive graphics is the area of model building once the phase problem has been solved and the electron density map determined. Although the development by Richards (13) of optical superposition of stacks of contours and Kendrew skeletal models has vastly improved this difficult process, there are still decided advantages in a computer modeling approach. Limitations on the scale of the physical model are imposed by the necessity for manual manipulation. This means that large, complex molecules such as t-RNA or multimeric proteins will require enormous facilities for model building and superposition. A second advantage is the elimination of the effort required to output the contour data onto transparent sheets for stacking. Although this can be automated, the increased scale of molecules under investigation imposes increased difficulties. Finally, once the model is constructed, it must reduced to a set of coordinates which again presents difficulties not present in a computerized version.

On the other hand, developing the software for a system which allows the crystallographer sufficient ease of interaction to be competitive with optical superposition for small protein molecules is a complex task. Most experience in this area has been in the fitting of small molecules, either substrates or inhibitors seen with difference maps in lysozyme (22) or as an adjunct to direct methods on dinucleotides (18). Fitting of protein structures is an active area of investigation at Washington University. Refinement of structures whose coordinates were intially determined using optical superposition has been investigated with cytochrome b_5 by the group of F. Scott Mathews (33) and with insulin using the 1.9Å resolution map by John and Sue Cutfield of Prof. Hodgkins' group (34). The model building of malate dehydrogenase in being pursued through simultaneous use of MMS and optical superposition in an attempt to assay the strengths and weaknesses of the current software and to evolve a system which is clearly superior for crystallographic use. An example of the display is shown in Fig. 7. The use of both stereo display (the Ortony Method) and real-time rotation would appear essential in resolving

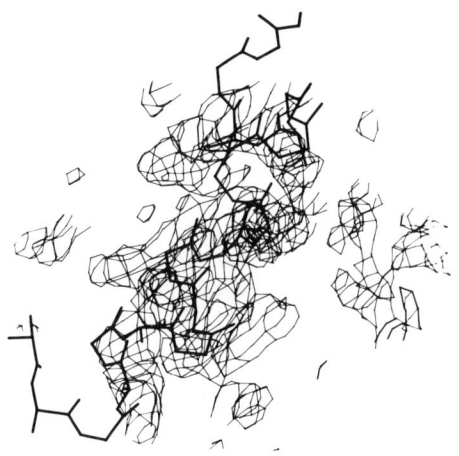

Fig. 7. Helical Segment from MDH (Courtesy of L. Webb).

questions of fit in a convenient manner. Other aspects under development include real-time indication of Van der Waals interactions and computer-assisted fitting in which guide points for the model are indicated by the crystallographer and the computer calculates alternative models which are displayed for selection. This feature appears highly desirable due to the complex (many simultaneous variables) nature of the fitting problem.

Another area which appears very productive is the use of computer animation to illustrate the results of crystallographic studies as well as mechanisms which may be proposed based on structural and other mechanistic studies. An Arriflex 16mm camera has been interfaced so that it is macromodular compatible (35). This has allowed movies to be made under computer control with prior editing and viewing with the MMS display. Movies illustrating the structure of insulin (10), cytochrome b_5 (36) and lactate dehydrogenase (37) have been prepared and shown at appropriate scientific gatherings to convey those features which are not immdiately apparent on examination of 2-dimensional diagrams or through photographs of a model.

B. Conformational Analysis.

Numerous physical techniques such as nuclear magnetic resonance, circular dichroism, and infrared spectroscopy provide information which is dependent upon the conformation, or set of quickly interchanging conformations, of a molecule. Some of the phenomena have a firm theoretical basis which allows prediction of the spectra based on the three-dimensional conformation of the molecule. Consistency between the observed spectra and that predicted is a necessary, but not sufficient condition for the existence of the proposed conformation.

The computer offers the spectroscopist a valuable adjunct in that one can systematically explore conformational space for those conformations which are consistant with physical observations. In any but the smallest molecules, the number of rotational degrees of freedom are too large to allow systematic exploration with physical models and investigators often settle for the first conformation found which is consistent with observations.

This systematic search of conformational space in order to determine those families of conformation whose properties are consistent with some observed parameter was first conceived at Washington University and the appropriate program, BURLESK, was developed there as an adjunct to the CHEMAST system (38). The detailed strategy and implementation of such an approach is, unfortunately, outside the scope of this review.

A prime example of the use of the computer is this area is the work of Barry et al. (23,29) using lanthanide shift reagents to determine the solution conformation of nucleotides. By use of a variety of lanthanide ions, it was shown that some of the ions complexed with the nucleotides and caused only chemical shifts of the NMR signals which were a function of the vector distance between the ion and the proton concerned and the angle between this vector and the principal symmetry axis of the metal ion. The application of the BURLESK approach led to family of conformations (contiguous in conformation space) whose predicted proton spectra was consistent with that observed.

C. Drug Design

The role of conformation in determining the pharmacological properties of a compound is implicit in the stereospecificity of biological receptors. One plausible explanation of similar pharmacological effects for different types of compounds is that

the critical three dimensional arrangement of electron density of
the different molecules is identical in the "active" conformations. An approach (40) to this problem is that of "active
analogs" in which the conformational space available to active
compounds is determined by the BURLESK approach using only
steric interactions to eliminate possible conformations. Once
this is accomplished, the conformational space available to the
two types of compounds can be examined to see if similar
three-dimensional arrangements of functional groups thought to
be essential are possible.

A similar approach has been used in order to gain insight
into the conformation assumed by the hormone, angiotensin II,
when bound to the biological receptor (41-42). Analogs with
restricted conformational freedom as determined by calculations
with BURLESK were synthesized which retained high levels of
biological activity. It is of particular interest that the
conformational restraints on the receptor-bound conformation
do not agree with the NMR observation on the conformation in
aqueous solution (43-44) implying that a conformational change
had occured in binding to the receptor.

While this area is still exploratory and full of logical
pitfalls, its worth in the design of pharmacologically
interesting molecules and in furthering our understanding of the
mechanism of drug action appears promising.

7. Acknowledgements

The authors have enjoyed the collaboration and support of
a number of colleagues during the development of the CHEMAST
and MMS systems. These efforts would not have become a reality
without the software support of C. David Barry, Sue Graesser,
John M. Fritsch, Janis Beitch and Thomas H. Jacobi, and the
general development of macromodular hardware by the Computer
Systems Laboratory. Especially critical to our needs were the
efforts of Charles Molnar and Gerald C. Johns. Of course, the
support of the National Institutes of Health, (RR-00396,
HE-14509), the American Heart Association (70-111, 73-754), the
European Molecular Biology Organization and Advanced Research
Projects Agency of the Department of Defense (Contract SD-302)
were essential and must be recognized.

References

1. E.J. Corey and W.T. Wipke, Science, 178 (1969).
2. C.D. Barry, R.A. Ellis, S.M. Graesser, and G.R. Marshall,
 Information Processing 71, North-Holland Publ. Co.,
 Amsterdam, 1972, p. 1552.

3. C.D. Barry, R.A. Ellis, S.M. Graesser, and G.R. Marshall, Pertinent Concepts in Computer Graphics, M. Faiman and J. Nievergelt, eds., University of Illinois Press, Chicago, 1969, p. 104.
4. C. Dickson, C.D. Barry, R.A. Ellis, J.M. Fritsch, and G.R. Marshall, A User's Guide to CHEMAST, Technical Memorandum #135, Computer Systems Laboratory, Washington University, St. Louis, 1972.
5. R.A. Ellis, "Appendix L: Using Crystallographic Coordinate Data as Input to MOLGRAPH (TRICS)", see Ref. 4.
6. H. Eyring, Phys. Rev., 39, 746 (1932).
7. J.W. Gibbs, Vector Analysis, Yale University Press, New Haven, 1901.
8. J.M. Fritsch, Rapid, Facile, Three Dimensional Manipulation of Vector Direction Relative to an Arbitrary Fixed Substructure, Technical Memorandum #205, Computer Systems Laboratory, Washington University, St. Louis, 1973.
9. W.A. Clark and C.E. Molnar, "Macromodular Computer Systems", Computers Biomed. Res., 4, Academic Press, N.Y. (in press).
10. G.R. Marshall, J. Beitch, R.A. Ellis, and J.M. Fritsch, Diabetes 21, Suppl. 2, 506 (1972).
11. R.A. Ellis, J.M. Fritsch, and C.B.W. Dodds, Molecular Modeling System-1 (MMS-1), Technical Memorandum #120, Computer Systems Laboratory, Washington University, St. Louis, 1971.
12. A. Ortony, Computer. J., 14, 140 (1971).
13. F.M. Richards, J. Mol. Biol., 37, 225 (1968).
14. C. Levinthal, Sci. Amer., 214, 42 (1966).
15. E.F. Meyers, Jr., J. Appl. Cryst., 3, 392 (1970).
16. E.F. Meyers, Jr., Nature, 232, 255 (1971).
17. J. de Rosnay and A. Lawee, CHEMTEST: An Interactive Graphics Display for Teaching Elementary Organic Chemistry, Educational Research Center, M.I.T., 1970.
18. L. Katz and C. Levinthal, Ann. Rev. Biophys. BioEng., 1, 465 (1972).
19. K.B. Wiberg, J. Chem. Ed., 47, 113 (1970).
20. A.C. Wahl, Industrial Res., 46 (1970).
21. Syntex Analytical Instruments, 10040 Bubb Rd., Cupertino, Calif. 95014.
22. C.D. Barry and A.C.T. North, Cold Spring Harbor Symp. Quat. Biol., XXXVI, 577 (1971).
23. C.D. Barry, A.C.T. North, J.A. Glasel, R.J.P. Williams, and A.V. Xavier, Nature, 232, 236 (1971).
24. J. Beitch, M.L. Dierker, R.A. Ellis, B. Mitchell, D.F. Wann, and T.A. Woolsey, Neuron Modeling System (NMS), manuscript in preparation.
25. W.V. Wright, An Interactive Computer Graphic System for

Molecular Studies, Dissertation, U. North Carolina, Chapel Hill, N.C., 1972.
26. W.J. Perkins, E.A. Piper, F.G. Tattam, and J.G. White, Computers Biomed. Res., 4, 249 (1971).
27. P.J. Bond, SIGGRAPH-ACM, 6, 13 (1972).
28. L.K. Steinrauf, Decus Proc. Spring '72, 49 (1972).
29. AWARE Systems, 630 Yosemite Ave., Mountain View, Calif., 94040.
30. R.J. Feldmann, S.R. Heller, and C.R.T. Bacon, J. Chem. Doc., 12, 234 (1972).
31. The Prophet System, Bolt Beranek and Newman Inc. and Div. of Research Resources, NIH.
32. E.F. Meyers, Jr., Personal Communication.
33. F.S. Mathews, P. Argos, and M. Levine, Cold Spring Harbor Symp. Quant. Biol., XXXVI, 387 (1971).
34. T.L. Blundell, J.F. Cutfield, S.M. Cutfield, E.J. Dodson, G.G. Dodson, D.C. Hodgkin, D.A. Mercola, and M. Vijayon, Abstr. 9th Int. Cong. Crystallography, III-4, (1972).
35. G.C. Johns, manuscript in preparation.
36. F.S. Mathews, P. Argos, and G. Brodsky, Abst. 9th Int. Cong. Biochem., Stockholm, 93 (1973).
37. A. Liljas and C.D. Barry, presented at Stockholm Symposium on The Structure of Biological Molecules, July, 1973.
38. H.E. Bosshard, C.D. Barry, J.M. Fritsch, R.A. Ellis, and G.R. Marshall, Proc. 1972 Summer Simulation Conf., San Diego, 581 (1972).
39. C.D. Barry, A.C.T. North, J.A. Glasel, R.J.P. Williams, and A.V. Xavier, Biochem. Biophys. Acta, 262, 101 (1972).
40. G.R. Marshall, in Peptides: Chemistry and Biochemistry, B. Weinstein and S. Lande, eds., M. Dekker, N.Y., 1970.
41. G.R. Marshall and H.E. Bosshard, Circulation Res. 31 (Suppl. 2), 143 (1972).
42. G.R. Marshall, H.E. Bosshard, N. Eilers, and P. Needleman, in Chemistry and Biology of Peptides, J. Meienhofer, ed., Ann Arbor Science, Ann Arbor, 1972, p. 571.
43. J.D. Glickson, W. Cunningham, and G.R. Marshall, Biochemistry 12, 3684 (1973).
44. J.D. Glickson, J. Dadok, and G.R. Marshall, Biochemistry, in press.

DARC SYSTEM IN CHEMISTRY

Jacques-Emile Dubois
Professor at Paris VII University

1. INTRODUCTION

The DARC System (1-5) provides an integrated information handling system through its major functions : Description, Acquisition, Retrieval, Correlation :

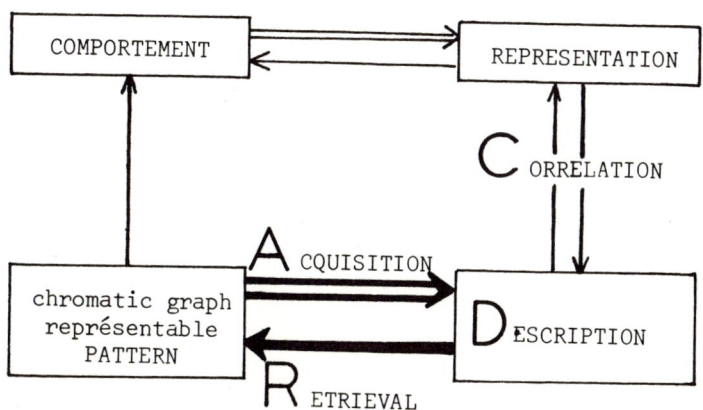

The broad scope of its basic principles and the consistency of its logic give the DARC all the features of an "open system", that is, one whose evolution proceeds through coherent extensions which do not modify the initial options.

It can handle any chromatic, graph-representable data, that is, a graph whose nodes and edges are symbolically differentiated by various colors. Chromatic graphs may be used to represent very diverse entities, such as electric network, patterns, syntactic graphs. In the case of chemical compounds, their skeletons are represented by black graphs and the various structure parameters are specified by chromatism, both primary chromatism (bond and atom nature) and secondary chromatism (charge, abnormal mass or valence).

This lecture on "the DARC system in chemistry" will be centered on the concepts of generation and of <u>ordered concentric limited environment</u> (ELCO) and will show in particular how these concepts facilitate consistent ordering of the familiar chemical notions of groups, molecules, families and suggest new concepts such as "ordered structure", "real or dummy ordered substructure", "hyperstructure", which meet the requirements of computer-based modern chemistry.

More specifically, the above concepts and the resulting methods provide a solution to the following problems :

- location of a site with respect to all the sites of an entity,
- dynamic approach to either a part of or an entire entity,
- location of an entity as an element of a generic set.

2. GENERATION AND ELCO

MOTIVATIONS. On the one hand, the structural diagram usually associated with a chemical structure is an extremely rich concept. Indeed, it fully translates the topology of a molecule and induces a preordering of the structure, that is, a set of neighborhood relations between its constituents. It is almost paradoxical that, on the other hand, both on the level of language and of conceptualization, the chemist's tools are the result of a STATIC FRAGMENTATION of a molecule which leads to a non-ordered understanding of the compound.

For instance, the systematic nomenclature does not allow for the localization of a site with respect to the whole molecule. In the case of labelled molecules -e.g. C_2H_5OD-, one is obliged to write down the entire internal structure of the OH group, replacing H by D in order to make the reference to C_2H_5OD(Ethanol-OD) quite clear.

A similar situation appears when trying to grasp an entity together with its implied comportment. The various systematics which have been proposed (6) (7) (8) (9) use an incremental process based on some groups and fragments and then correct the deviations resulting from the static nature of the fragmentation. The corrective terms are not coherent with the basic ones and generally become more important than the latter.

Further, both in nomenclature and systematics a group is perceived globally. Its various structural elements (its topology,-characterised by the black graph and its various chromatic elements,- atoms and bonds) are not distinguished. Thus, this static perception is both too incomplete and too global, and substantially limits its use as an aid in search of active, underlying, structural fragments.

In fact, the needs of the chemist should be expressed in terms of dynamic perception, and the problem is really one of pattern recognition. Indeed, when a chemist encounters a molecule, according to his preoccupations he may consider,

(α) a <u>localized site</u> in a molecule (for instance an atom at a specific location defined with respect to a reactional center)

(β) one or more parts (mass spectrum)

(γ) the whole compound seen from various angles.

Those needs require the definition of a complete ordering so as to be able to localize any site (case α), and moreover to translate concretely the thinking process of the chemist in its dynamic perception of the whole and the part (case β and γ).

GENERATION.

<u>Definition</u>. Grasping a pattern by means of generation consists in creating the pattern representation through an ordered process which reflects the sequential steps of the pattern building operation.

In the particular case of a chemical entity, this process involves the following steps :

- selecting an origin or focus (FO)
- building the environment $\mathcal{E}$ of the focus through gradual and ordered substitution of the hydrogen atoms (transparent atoms as opposed to "heavy" atoms).

The generation of a target compound proceeds in such a way that when voluntarily frozen at a given step :

- the corresponding site is located in the generation sequence. Thus each site is successively defined and the structure is totally ordered,
- an ordered subset of the target compound is defined,
- a specific compound, ancestor of the target compound in the generation, is identified.

Thus the entire family of compounds developed in the generation of the target compound is totally ordered.

<u>Generation automata and generation-description automata.</u>
The generation is implemented by means of an automata called generation automata, which changes a chromatic graph G_X into an ordered chromatic graph G_{X0}

$$G_X \xrightarrow{\tau_{G \to 0}} G_{X0}$$

In the framework of chemical implementation, the input of the automata $\tau_{G \to 0}$ may be a connectivity matrix or a code (CAS code, Wiswesser notation).

The composition of the automata with a description procedure Π_D leads to the Limited Environment Descriptor (DEL) of the ordered chromatic graph :

$$\tau_{G \to D} = \Pi_D \circ \tau_{G \to 0}$$

$\tau_{G \to D}$ is the generation-description automata :

$$G_X \xrightarrow{\tau_{G \to D}} \text{DEL}(G_{X0})$$

ORDERED CONCENTRIC LIMITED ENVIRONMENT (ELCO).
<u>Definition.</u>An ordered concentric limited environment is an environment centered on a focus (FO) and organized along two concentric layers (A and B layers), each one bearing atoms whose distance from the focus is respectively 1 and 2, and in such a way that each site is located unambiguously by means of a topological coordinate (A_i or B_{ij}) which expresses the introduction of the site into the ELCO. (fig. 2)

When $\tau_{G \to 0}$ is implemented, two procedures Π_{FO} and Π_{OC} allow for focalization and concentric organization.

Ordered Concentric Limited Environment   243

Figure 2

Ordered Concentric Limited Environment
(ELCO)

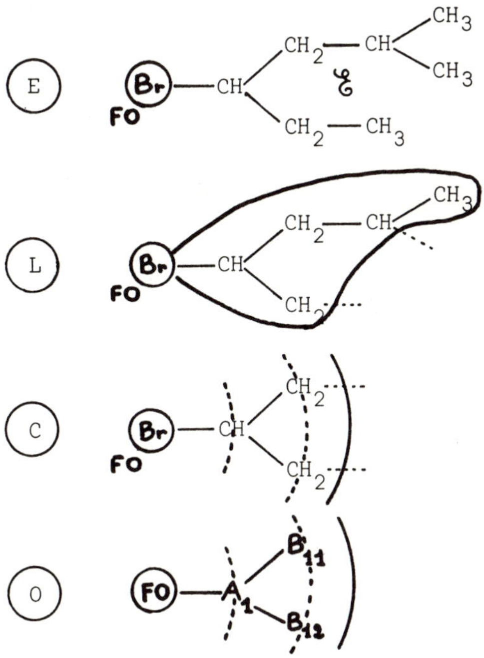

ELCO and propagation. Since ELCO enables us to grasp a limited environment with two layers, a continuous propagation of ELCO permits us to grasp an infinite environment. Thus, once the nth limited environment, which is centered on the FO^n focus, is generated, the symbolic expression :

$$(FO)^{n+1} = (FO)^n + E_B^n$$

defines the focus of E_B^{n+1} and the process is iterated.
This propagation is carried out by means of the Π_{PEL} procedure of the $\tau_{G \to 0}$ automata.

Figure 3

Continuous propagation of ELCO

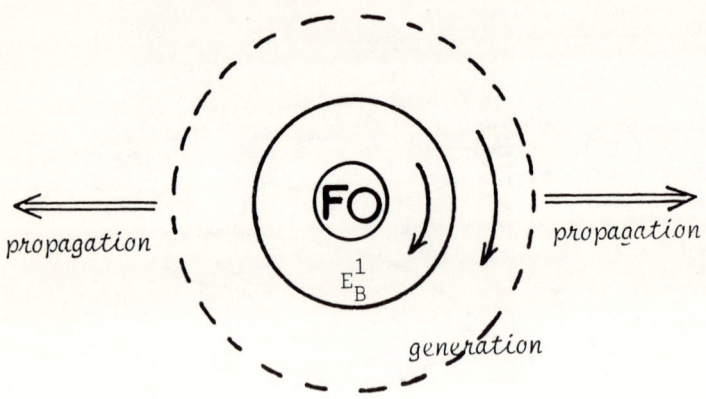

ELCO and order. Through the ELCO concept and the generation automata, a complete order is progressively introduced onto a chromatic graph, that is, in a chemical structure : the initial chromatic graph exhibits a pre-ordering. The focalization (Π_{FO}) and concentric organization (Π_{OC}) procedures bring partial order since a site is unambiguously located in the organization with respect to those of the lower and upper layers. The ELCO propagation procedure (Π_D) leads to a complete order, since each site located with respect to the other sites of its layer is unambiguously located on the unique generation pathway. (fig. 4).

Furthermore, in the course of the generation of a target compound, each site of the generation pathway is associated with a specific compound. All these compounds together constitute a completely ordered generation series.

Figure 4

Generation pathway and total ordering on structure

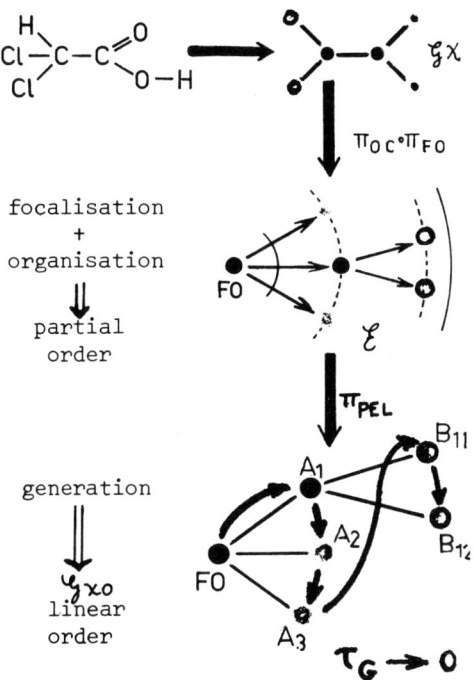

ELCO and ordering. To define the generation order of the sites, the Π_{PEL} procedure of the $\tau_{G \rightarrow D}$ generation automata applies an ordering function $\mathcal{F}$ which is divided into elementary ordering functions corresponding to basic criteria :

- topology ($\mathcal{E}$) or existence (EX) : $f\mathcal{E}$
- chromatism : bonds (LI) or atom nature (NA) : f_χ

When an elementary ordering function does not at once permit us to rank two sites of the same layer, the ordering function $\mathcal{F}$ applies the elementary functions in a specific sequence on certain sites of the following layers until the ambiguity is resolved.

The DARC canonical ordering function applied in the machine encoding is of a modular type : it is gradually implemented on each environment segment e_B^* and within each e_B. $f_\mathscr{E}$ and f_χ composition is carried out at the level of each type of position : A, B or development origin OD** and provides three priority rules :

$$P_A = f_\chi \circ f_\mathscr{E}$$
$$P_B = f_\chi$$
$$P_O = f_\mathscr{E}$$

$$\mathscr{F}(\mathscr{E}, \chi/e_B) = \prod_{e_B \in \mathscr{E}} (P_O \circ P_B \circ P_A) e_B$$

The ordering function is a parameter of the generation automata and depending on the type of application (computer-aided design in particular), both the sequence of implementation of the elementary ordering functions and their range of application on the environment may be differently modulated.

<u>ELCO and description</u>. Starting from an ordered chromatic graph, the Π_D procedure allows the limited environment descriptor DEL to be established.

---

* connected components of a limited environment E_B
** roots of the connected components of the limited environment

Figure 5

Building and DARC code

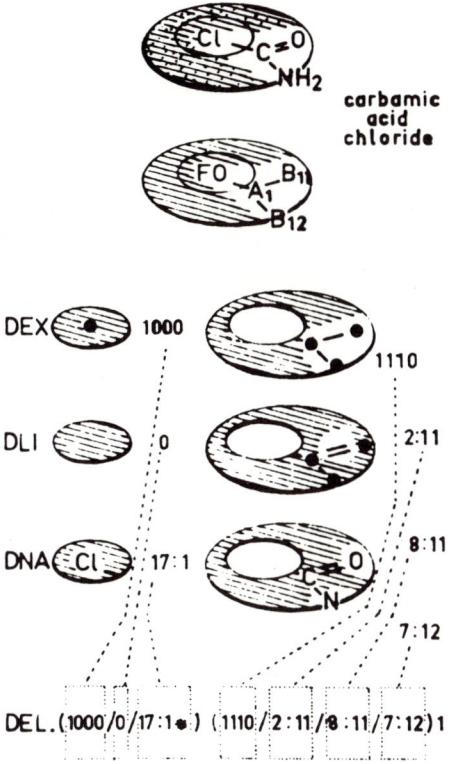

The DARC code results from the topological linking of modules, each of them consisting of three parts which describe respectively : the topology (DEX), the bond multiplicity (DLI), and the atom nature (DNA).

In the above example, there are two modules : the focus (chlorine atom) and the environment. The focus is described in the first three boxes, the environment in the following ones : 1000 (1st box) is the topological descriptor of the focus, 0 (2nd box) means no bond in the focus, 17 (3rd box) is the atomic number of chlorine, 1110 (4th box) is the topological descriptor of the environment, 2 (5th box) indicates a double bond in the environment, 8 and 7 (6th and 7th boxes) are the atomic numbers of the oxygen and nitrogen atoms of the environment.

Slashes and parenthesis are separators. Numbers which follow the colons and the closing parenthesis are topological coordinates. The star allows for module linking.

3. DARC SYSTEM IN CHEMISTRY : AN ORDERED AND COHERENT GRASP OF STRUCTURES, SUBSTRUCTURES AND HYPERSTRUCTURES

The second part of this presentation will show how, starting with the generation and the ELCO concept, one is able to order and therefore to grasp with a unified logic, the structures (S), the substructures (SS), and the hyperstructures (HS).

STRUCTURES (S).
<u>Polyvision</u>. By generation and propagation of an ELCO it is possible to order a structure starting from various origins or focuses. This approach answers one of the essential needs of the chemist who must be able to perceive a structure from various angles, each perception being linked to a specific concern (for instance : NMR, conformation study, acidity analysis).

Figure 6

ELCO and structure polyvision

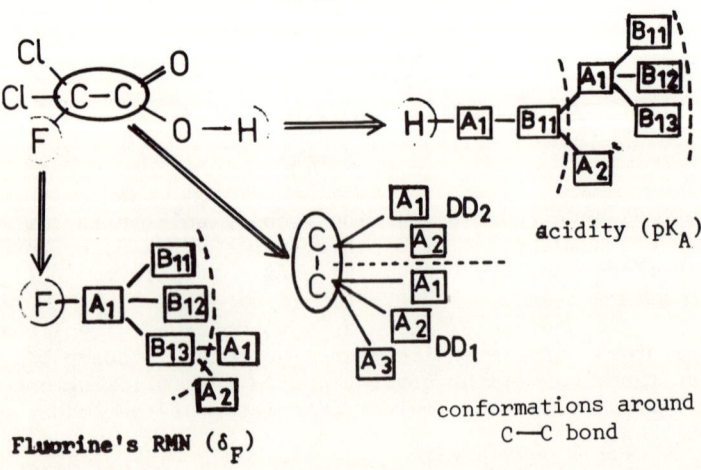

Changes of perception are achieved automatically by changes of focus. The corresponding procedure Π_{CFO} allows us to generate, from a given chromatic ordered graph G_{XO}, a new chromatic ordered graph G'_{XO} which will be centered on a different focus.

$$G_{XO} \xrightarrow{\Pi_{CFO}} G'_{XO}$$
$$(FO) \qquad\qquad (FO')$$

<u>Primary and secondary chromatism</u>. Primary chromatism includes bond nature (LI) and atom nature (NA). It allows for a one to one description of the vast majority of covalent compounds. The Limited Environment Descriptor (DEL) groups, for each segment, an existence descriptor (DEX), a bond (or link) descriptor (DLI) and a nature descriptor (DNA). A global ring descriptor further defines the location of the ring closure bonds and thereby the number of fundamental rings.

Other information is necessary to take into account the complexity of certain structures and to achieve exhaustivity. Secondary chromatism includes all the information related to unusual valence and atomic masses or to electric charges. This extension allows the DEL to encode ions, free radicals, radical ions, and isotopes related to all the elements including the specific case of hydrogen as well as salts and organic hydrates.

Secondary chromatism follows slightly different imperatives from those of primary chromatism. The specific features of a compound generally stem from a local change in a basic structure. In order to facilitate the automatic search of the modified compound and of the initial structure (for instance : labelled compound and non-labelled compound), the ordering of the part affected by the secondary chromatism must disturb the ordering of the rest of the molecule as little as possible. To fulfill this requirement the ordered chromatic graph is first established according to the topology and the primary chromatism (LI, NA). The secondary chromatism is only taken into account if the generation order of 2 nodes remains ambiguous after propagation of the ordering using primary topology and chromatism on all the environment.

<u>Orientation</u>. The ELCO concept allows an orientation to be induced at the level of certain specific sites of a molecule and, thus the stereoisomerism can be specified. The orientation procedure Π_{ORI} is based on :

- the generation of an ordered limited environment focused on the asymmetrical center, the ordering rule following the real

topology of the molecule and complying with the canonical ordering. The consistent ordering facilitates automatic handling.
- the observation of the relative arrangement of the sites from the lowest priority (highest index) A position.

By means of a general application of this procedure, any case of stereoisomerism may be included (10) (11). A stereochemistry descriptor (DST) is included for each segment and specifies the orientation of the asymmetrical centers inside the segment.

Figure 7

carbon asymmetric specification

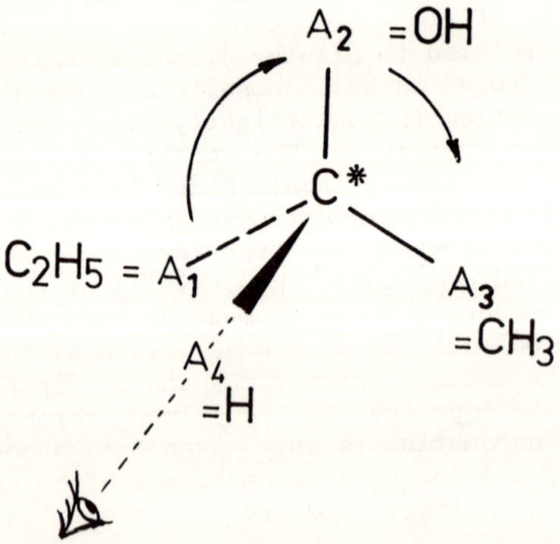

Hydrogen. In some instances, it is necessary to locate and describe hydrogen atoms (e.g., NMR). These are then included in the ordered chromatic graph, whereas ordinarily they are transparent and the carbon atoms are implicit in the DEL.

The ordering of the chromatic graph $G_x(H)$ does not take the hydrogen atoms into account. The ordered chromatic graph thus obtained is then completed by the sites of the hydrogen atoms.

In the DEL(H) no atom is transparent, and it is the nature of the hydrogen atom which becomes implicit. The DEL(H) descriptor may be automatically generated starting from the DEL.

Figure 8

DEL(H) of a compound

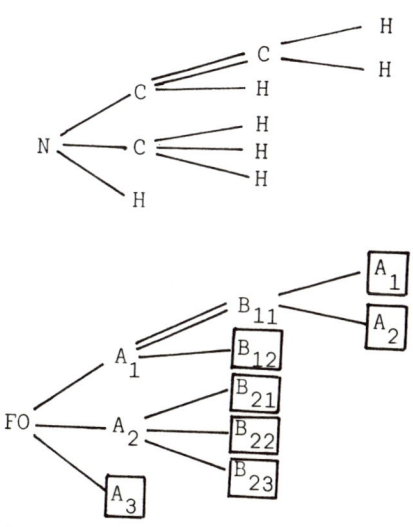

DEL.(1000/0/7*)(2100/2:11)1

DEL(H)-(1000/0/7*)(3221/2:11/6:1, 2,11*)1(2000)11

Thus the grasp of a chemical structure leads to a non-ambiguous, adjustable and exhaustive description of a chemical entity. In particular, starting from the DEL and a standard data base, it is possible to generate the 2-D and 3-D representations of a chemical pattern.

Table 1

Ordered grasp of a structure
(DEL)

DESCRIPTION			
	Potential	Polyvision	Possibility of grasping a given entity starting from various focuses
	Exhaustivity	Primary chromatism (LI, NA)	Cyclic and acyclic covalent compounds
		Secondary chromatism	Ions, radicals, isotopes,...
		Orientation	Stereoisomers
		Hydrogen	Complete set of sites (transparent and heavy) of an entity
		Metric (standard or real)	Chemical pattern

SUBSTRUCTURES. This question is related to the general problem of pattern recognition : starting from a whole, a part must be perceived and recognized. To solve this problem, one possibility would be to draw up an inventory of all parts which may have to be studied. This amounts to a static fragmentation of the pattern and a recording of all the fragments in a dictionary.

In chemistry, this is indeed complex, since drawing up an inventory of all fragments likely to interest chemists is an infinite combinatorial problem. However, any approach involving a static fragmentation leads to a closed system which reflects previous needs without fulfilling the requirements of innovation and conception.

The generation concept provides a dynamic and selective fragmentation which will be exemplified by the Limited Environment Fragment (FREL). The ELCO concept allows for grasping real or dummy substructures within a structure, while preserving the logic involved in grasping the entire structure.

Figure 9

Real and dummy substructures

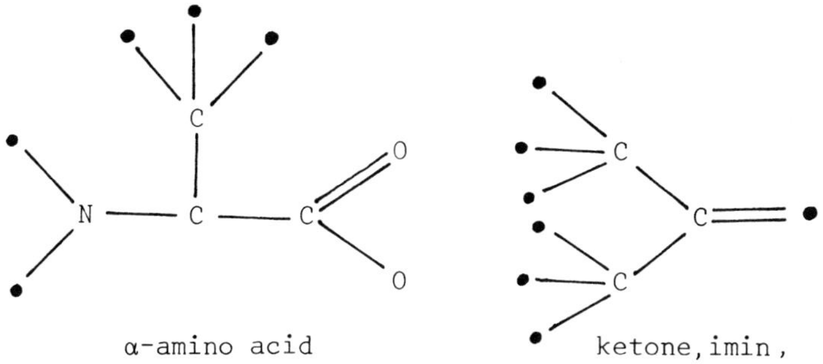

α-amino acid   ketone, imin, olefin

The resulting substructures, called Limited Environment Fragments (FREL), are obtained by means of ELCO generation around each dense focus of the structure, that is, each node with connectivity > 2. (fig. 10). The $FREL_S$ are real formal substructures as opposed to real chemical substructures.

Figure 10

ELCO and substructure

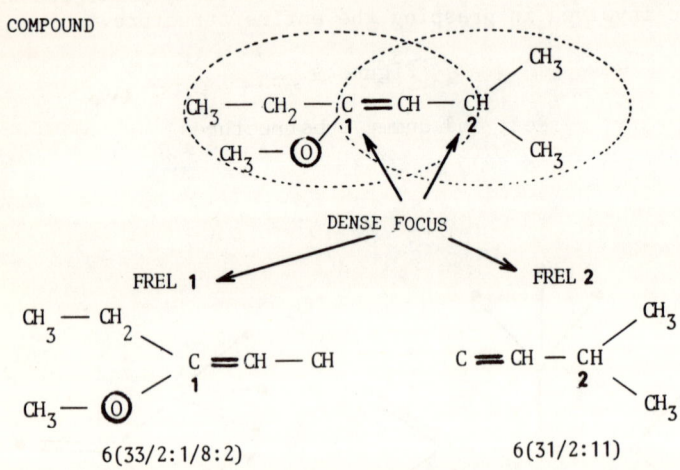

From the $FREL_S$ corresponding to real substructures, one can deduce dummy $FREL_S$, that is, those with partially specified chromatism (fig. 11). Furthermore, we have been able to show that the dummy $FREL_S$ implicitly cover the ring concept. The fact is that on a set of dummy $FREL_S$ corresponding to 10,000 compounds, it was possible to isolate skeletons of real $FREL_S$ or black dummy $FREL_S$ which only occur in cyclic compounds. Those $FREL_S$ consequently eliminate the need for topological analysis or frozen fragmentation of the corpus structures which would otherwise have been necessary to bring out their cyclic nature.

The dynamic nature and strong discriminating ability of the $FREL_S$ make them an important factor in machine documentation, and they are therefore integrated in the DARC Topological Screen System (TSS-DARC).

The possibility of analyzing a population by means of the black graph allows for anticipating very accurate parallels between compounds through the search for real or dummy $FREL_S$ which induce or determine a specific activity or behaviour.

Substructures

Figure 11

ELCO and dummy substructures

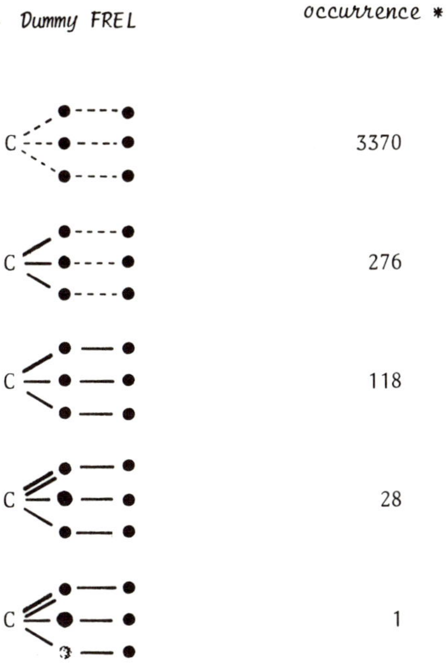

Dummy FREL	occurrence *
(structure 1)	3370
(structure 2)	276
(structure 3)	118
(structure 4)	28
(structure 5)	1

* *File of 10 000 structures from the CBAC - CAS*

HYPERSTRUCTURES. Chemists are very often led to handle diversified sets of structures or substructures. These sets are characterized by the structural relationships existing between their elements ; these relationships can be of various kinds : isomerism, homology, reactional filiation, common substructures, etc,... Although apparently diversified, the methods used to grasp such sets are very often identical in their approach : such is the case of combinatorial methods which aim at counting, listing and should the occasion arise, organizing such sets.

We propose the general concept of hyperstructure (HS) which within the framework of chemistry transcends in particular the notions of functional and reactional families.

Definition. A hyperstructure is a finite or infinite ordered set of discrete entities (structures or substructures).
The strength of the hyperstructure is determined by :
- the nature of the order defined between the entities (pre-order, partial order, total i.e. linear order)
- the consistency of this order with that defined between inner components of each entity.

Isomerism hyperstructures. More or less strong hyperstructures were conceived in order to grasp the problems of counting and listing isomers :

1- permutation combinatorics are used to present the "polytopal" rearrangements of penta- and hexa-coordinated complexes (12-18) of ionic transpositions (19) (20) and of sigmatropic transpositions (21). On usually very limited sets, those combinatorics induce a pre-order which is linked to the local structure of the isomers but which is not always automatically deducible.
2- More complex combinatorics allow for counting (22-25) and listing (26) isomers of larger families. Listing a large number of entities makes it necessary to automatically deduce a total order (listing order) from the structure of the entities. However, this order can be inconsistent with the structure : it is, for example, impossible to obtain a family of isomer alcohols without finding the ethers as well (27).

Substitution hyperstructures. Compared to the large number of publications on isomerism, few authors have built substitution hyperstructures :

1- Simple substitutions on several pre-determined sites lead to filiation-structured sets, which are therefore ordered through partial order (28) (29).
2- Gradual substitutions, which aroused interest as early as the XIXth century (A. Laurent and Ch. Gerhardt), had received no practical applications, save for the concept of linear homology where the consistency of the total order with the structure is commonplace.

ELCO and hyperstructure : anteriology. As an example, we will show how the concept of anteriology derived from ELCO allows for progressively inducing a partial order and a total order in any family.
A structure S is an anteriolog of a structure S' if S' can be generated from S.

Hyperstructures   257

As we emphasized in the first part of this lecture, the dynamics of a target compound generation allows for generating at each step a specific compound which belongs to the generation series of the target compound.

Figure 12

ELCO and hyperstructure
The canonical generation series

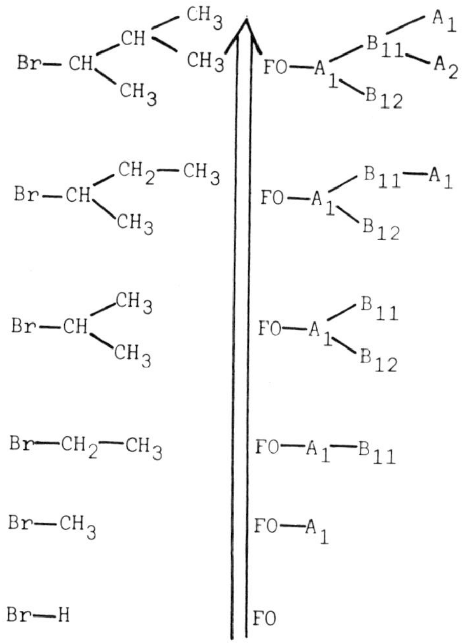

$$
\begin{array}{ll}
Br-CH\!\!\begin{array}{c}CH\!\!\begin{array}{c}-CH_3\\ CH_3\end{array}\\ CH_3\end{array} & FO-A_1\!\!\begin{array}{c}B_{11}\!\!\begin{array}{c}-A_1\\ -A_2\end{array}\\ B_{12}\end{array}\\[2em]
Br-CH\!\!\begin{array}{c}CH_2-CH_3\\ CH_3\end{array} & FO-A_1\!\!\begin{array}{c}B_{11}-A_1\\ B_{12}\end{array}\\[2em]
Br-CH\!\!\begin{array}{c}CH_3\\ CH_3\end{array} & FO-A_1\!\!\begin{array}{c}B_{11}\\ B_{12}\end{array}\\[2em]
Br-CH_2-CH_3 & FO-A_1-B_{11}\\[1em]
Br-CH_3 & FO-A_1\\[1em]
Br-H & FO
\end{array}
$$

The generation series is a specific case of the more general concept of anteriologous series, the series being such that each compound is an anteriolog of the following one.

In the most general case, if we consider a target compound, there are several possible anteriologous series (fig. 13). The canonical pathway corresponds to the generation series and to the implementation of the automata.

Figure 13

ELCO and hyperstructure

Two examples of anteriologous series
for a same target compound

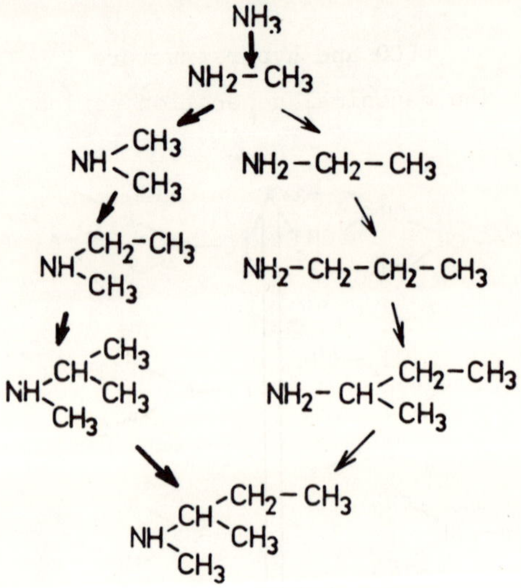

$$
\begin{array}{c}
NH_3 \\
\downarrow \\
NH_2-CH_3 \\
\swarrow \quad \searrow \\
NH{<}^{CH_3}_{CH_3} \quad NH_2-CH_2-CH_3 \\
\downarrow \quad \downarrow \\
NH{<}^{CH_2-CH_3}_{CH_3} \quad NH_2-CH_2-CH_2-CH_3 \\
\downarrow \quad \downarrow \\
NH{<}^{CH{<}^{CH_3}_{CH_3}}_{CH_3} \quad NH_2-CH{<}^{CH_2-CH_3}_{CH_3} \\
\searrow \quad \swarrow \\
NH{<}^{CH{<}^{CH_2-CH_3}_{CH_3}}_{CH_3}
\end{array}
$$

The set of anteriologous series associated with a given target compound defines an anteriology network, and thus confers on the set of anteriologs of a target compound the character of a strong hyperstructure (partial order) in which a compound may be situated with reference to its immediate ascendants and descendants.

Hyperstructure and retrieval. Starting from a substructure or a logical combination of substructures, it is possible to define the theoretically infinite hyperstructure of structures complying with these constraints.

Projecting this infinite hyperstructure ($H_S \infty$) on a real and finite collection (file in information system) results in a real and finite hyperstructure.

Thus, searching for the substructure amounts to generating the hyperstructure which, considering the procedure used, qualifies by its relevance to the question.

This generation may be carried out :
- either directly, that is, by a homomorphism search between the substructure and each structure of the real population
- or indirectly :
1- by splitting the substructure into pre-determined standard fragments. Since all substructure search questions cannot be formulated with a system of rigid fragments, it is necessary to change the question into a related one. This, however, involves a risk of very low recall or precision with respect to the initial question.
2- by assimilating the substructure to a set of elementary substructures (FREL) specific to each substructure, taking into account the structural sharpness of the FREL (real or dummy). Question formulation is then unlimited, recall equals 1 and precision is close to 1.

This method has been tested on a population of 10,000 structures from CBAC tapes of the Chemical Abstracts Service.
The set of FREL (about 5,000) related to this population has been generated (automatically from the DEL_S) and a first statistical analysis of the FREL occurrence brought out a number of noteworthy points for the substructure search.

Figure 14

FREL and retrieval

Retrieval of ortho-substituted nitrobenzenes
(Statistical analysis of a 10,000 compounds file from CBAC)

	FREL	OCCURRENCE
I 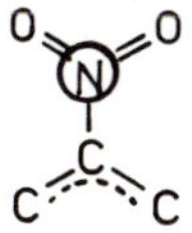	[structure]	319
II	[structure]	207
		COOCCURRENCE
	(I) et (II)	207

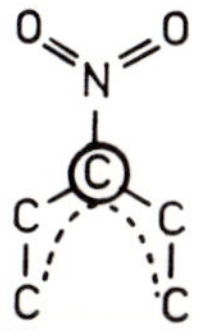

319 - 207 = 112 ortho-substituted

Thus figure 14 shows that a question which is simply formulated and quickly handled, such as :

(I) AND NOT (II)

provides with excellent precision all the answers to the question : "Which structures of the population are ortho-substituted nitrobenzenes ?".

Figure 15

FREL and retrieval

FREL		OCCURRENCE
I	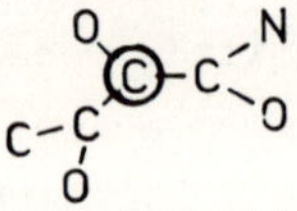 ![structure I]	510
II	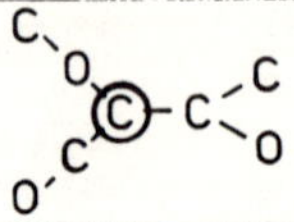 ![structure II]	384
III	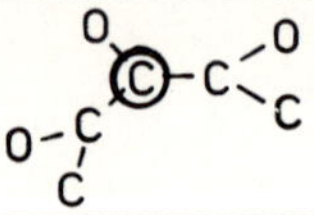 ![structure III]	203
IV	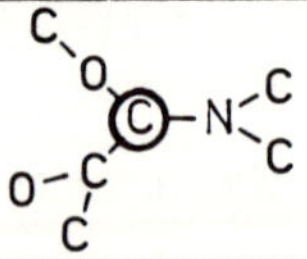 ![structure IV]	210
		COOCCURRENCE
(I) U (II) U (III) U (IV)		183

The figure 15 shows that the cooccurrence index of the 4 FREL

$$(I_C = \frac{\text{cooccurrence}}{\text{Min (occurrence)}})$$

is high (87 %). Probability rules for FREL overlapping allow us to predict with high probability that cooccurrence is due to the following substructure :

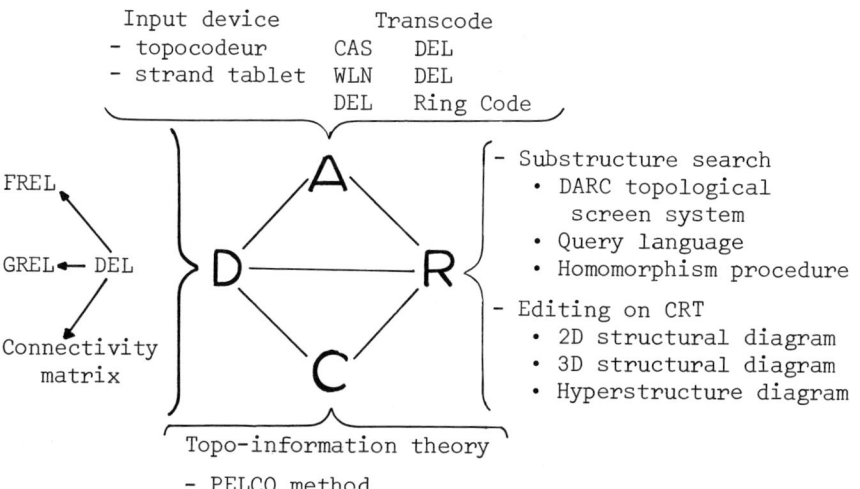

This substructure happens to be characteristic of nucleosides and nucleotides. The question which is simple (I) and quickly handled (I) AND (II) AND (III) AND (IV) allows all the nucleosides and nucleotides to be retrieved from the 10,000 structures population, with no need for a homomorphism procedure.

The statistical criteria which predicted high precision are corroborated, since in fact precision equals 1.

4. CONCLUSION

By way of conclusion, all the concrete realizations covered by the DARC system to date are mentioned in figure 16.

Figure 16

DARC present development

The generality of its basic principles, its coherent logic and its exhaustive nature have found expression in a software which supplies the chemist with a powerful aid for information and conception, one which he can adapt according to his needs and his means. The DARC System's implementation imposes no particular constraints on its user.

The automatic acquisition techniques and transcoding procedures free the user from learning the code. None the less, in case of manual coding, this effort can be made with no great difficulty, thanks to the code's logic and clarity which require only a very few rules, all coherent among themselves.

The user can extract, from a corpus transparent to him, all those structures containing a given sub-structure, even an unknown, unusual or complex one, according to his intuition and his needs. This end is achieved primarily by the Topological Query Language (TQL/DARC), easily assimilated by chemists, and by a system of performing screens (TSS/DARC) which optimize description with an eye to retrieval. Restitution is completed by the automatic edition of the 2D and 3D developed formulas on C.R.T. display.

Finally then, the DARC System comprises a coherent corpus of tried and tested methods whose implementation opens the way to considerable progress in the field of computer aided conception, of optimization of reaction pathways, of structure identification and correlation research.

References

1. J.E. Dubois, D. Laurent and H. Viellard, C.R. Acad. Sc. Paris, 263, série C, 764, (1966) ; ibid, 264, série C, 348, 1019, (1967).
2. J.E. Dubois, Entropie, 27, 1, (1969).
3. J.E. Dubois and H. Viellard, Bull. Soc. Chim. France, 900, 905, 913, (1968) ; ibid, 839, (1971).
4. J.E. Dubois, J.P. Anselmini, M. Chastrette and F. Hennequin, Bull. Soc. Chim. France, 2439, (1969).
5. J.E. Dubois, J. Chem. Doc., 13, (1), 8, (1973).
6. S.W. Benson, F.R. Cruickank, D.M. Golden, G.R. Hangen, H.E. O'Neol, A.S. Rodgers, R. Sham and R Walsh, Chem. Rev., (1969), 69, 279.
7. H.A. Skinner, J.Chem. Soc., 4396, (1962).
8. G.R. Somayajulu and B.J. Zwolinski, Trans. Farad. Soc., 62, 2327, (1966) ; ibid, J. Chem. Soc. Farad. Trans II, 68, (11), 1971, (1972).

9. J.E. Leffler and E. Grundwald, "Rates and equilibria of organic reactions", Ed. J. Wiley & Sons, N.Y., (1963).
10. J.E. Dubois, M.J. Alliot and H. Viellard, C.R. Acad. Sc. Paris, 271, série C, 14/2, (1970).
11. J.E. Dubois, M.J. Alliot and A. Panaye, C.R. Acad. Sc. Paris, 273, série C, 224, (1971).
12. A.T. Balaban, D. Farcasill and R. Banica, Rev. Roum. Chim., 11, 1205, (1966).
13. J.D. Dunitz and V. Prelog, Angew. Chem. Internat. Ed., 7, 725, (1968).
14. E.L. Muetterties, J. Amer. Chem. Soc., 90, 5097, (1968) ; ibid, 91, 1636, 4115, (1969) ; Rec. Chem. Prog., 31, 51, (1970).
15. P.C. Lauterbur and F. Ramirez, J. Amer. Chem. Soc., 90, 4929, (1968).
16. M. Gielen, Meded. Vlaam. Chem. Ver., 31, 185, 201, (1969).
17. K. Mislow, Accounts Chem. Res., 3, 321, (1970).
18. W.G. Klemperer, J. Amer. Chem. Soc., 94, 8360, (1972).
19. A.T. Balaban, D. Farcasill and R. Banica, Rev. Roum. Chim., 11, 1205, (1966).
20. H.W. Whitlock Jr and M.W. Siefken, J. Amer. Chem. Soc., 90, 4929, (1968).
21. R.B. Woodward and R. Hoffmann, Angew. Chem. Internat. Ed., 8, 781, (1969).
22. A. Cayley, Philog. Mag., 67, 444, (1874).
23. H.R. Henze and C.M. Blair, J. Am. Chem. Soc., 53, 3077, (1931).
24. G. Polya, Acta Math., 68, 145, (1937).
25. A.T. Balaban, Rev. Roum. Chim., 11, 1097, (1966).
26. J. Lederberg, G.L. Sutherland, B.G. Buchanan, E.A. Feigenbaum, A.V. Robertson, A.M. Duffield and C. Djerassi, J. Amer. Chem. Soc., 91, 2973, (1969).
27. G. Scharall, A.M. Duffield, C. Djerassi, B.C. Buchanan, G.L. Sutherland, E.A. Feigenbaum and J. Lederberg, J. Amer. Chem. Soc., 91, (26), 7440, (1969).
28. J.B. Hendrickson, J. Amer. Chem. Soc., 93, 6847, 6854, (1971).
29. J.E. Dubois and A. Panaye, Tetrahedron Letters, 1501, 3275, (1969).

Glossary

DEL	: Descriptor by propagation of an Environment Limited in B.
FO	: Focus.
	: Environment.
E_B	: Environment limited in B.
e_B	: segment of an environment E_B.
DEX	: Descriptor of EXistence.
DLI	: Descriptor of LInk.
DNA	: Descriptor of NAture of atoms.
DCY	: Descriptor of CYcles.
DST	: Descriptor of STereochemistry.
DVA	: Descriptor of abnormal VAlence.
DCH	: Descriptor of CHarge.
DMA	: Descriptor of non-usual MAss.
DPO	: Descriptor of POlymers.
FREL	: Fragment Restricted to an Environment Limited in B.
E/lco or ELCO	: Environment : limited, concentric, ordered.
PE/lco or PELCO	: Perturbation of an E/lco.

CHEMICAL DATA INTERPRETATION USING
PATTERN RECOGNITION TECHNIQUES

Peter C. Jurs
Department of Chemistry, The Pennsylvania
State University, University Park, Pennsylvania 16802

1. INTRODUCTION

Modern analytical instrumentation produces data at a prodigious rate. This has led to burgeoning interest in computer assisted methods for the accumulation, handling, and interpretation of chemical data. A relatively recent development is the application of pattern recognition methods to the interpretation of chemical data. The most thoroughly studied pattern recognition area in chemistry is that of learning machines, also known as adaptive binary pattern classifiers (BPC's) or threshold logic units (TLU's). Here the basic theory of learning machines will be discussed, and the application of this approach to the interpretation of one type of chemical data will be presented as an example of the capabilities of the technique. The specific task chosen as an example is that of developing the low resolution mass spectrum of a hydrocarbon directly from its molecular structure.

Pattern recognition comprises the detection, perception, and recognition of invariant properties among sets of measurements of objects or events. The purpose of pattern recognition is generally to categorize a sample of observed data as a member of the class to which it belongs. This general approach has been applied to problems from a great number of diverse fields. Several excellent reviews of the pattern recognition literature have appeared which dramatize the enormous breadth of pattern recognition applications (1-5). There is a growing literature addressed to the applications of pattern recognition to chemical data interpretation. Several reviews and more recent contributions are listed (6-27).

Types of data which have been analyzed by pattern recognition methods naturally fall into two categories—well-defined coded structures and pictorial representations.

Well-defined coded structures are exemplified by printed and handwritten letters and numerals, fingerprints, and other types of data that are (ideally) binary quantized. Pictorial representations refer to photographs and video data which must be encoded with levels of gray. Some data do not naturally fall into either category. Chemical data which have been studied using pattern recognition methods fall in the well-defined coded structure class, e.g. spectroscopic data or coded chemical structures.

BASIC PATTERN RECOGNITION SYSTEM. A general pattern recognition system must be capable of observing a sample of data, preprocessing and transforming the data, and classifying the data correctly. A schematic representation of this basic system is shown in Figure 1. It consists of three interrelated subunits: a transducer, a feature extractor (or preprocessor), and a classifier. The transducer translates information from the real world into the pattern space of the pattern recognition system, i.e., renders the raw data into computer compatible form. Normally, this computer compatible form is a string of scalars comprising a pattern vector with each dimension representing a physically measurable quantity. The feature extractor accepts the pattern vector to be classified and transforms or preprocesses it to make the classification task easier. To do this, the proprocessor attempts to pursue the following two goals simultaneously: (a) To reduce or eliminate the fraction of information contained in the raw data that is irrelevant or even confusing; and (b) To preserve sufficient information to allow discrimination among the pattern classes. The classifier operates on the transformed pattern vector to produce a classification decision. The dashed line indicates that the pattern recognition system may use the results of its classification to develop a superior feature extraction approach. The entire pattern recognition system is generally implemented with computer software.

Figure 1. Basic Pattern Recognition System

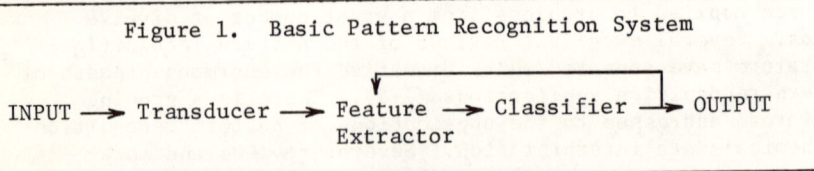

CLASSIFIERS. Methods of classification fall naturally into two categories: parametric and nonparametric methods. Parametric training methods consist of estimating the statistical parameters of the samples forming the training set and then using these statistical parameters for the specification of the discriminant function.

The most common parametric discriminant function is the Bayes rule because it is optimum for a well-defined class of problems. Classifications are performed using the Bayes rules as follows:

If $P_1 L_1 F_1(X) > P_2 L_2 F_2(X)$, classify X in category 1

If not, then classify X in category 2,

in which P_1 is the *a priori* probability of occurrence of a category 1 pattern, $P_2 = 1-P_1$, L_1 and L_2 are the losses associated with misclassifying a member of category 1 or category 2, and $F_1(X)$ and $F_2(X)$ are the probability density functions of category 1 and 2. On the assumption that the pattern vectors come from Gaussian distributions, and that the mean vectors and covariance matrices are truly representative of their classes, then the Bayes rule classification is optimum.

However, if the patterns of the training set do not warrant the above assumptions, then a nonparametric discriminant function such as a TLU must be used. Nonparametric discriminant functions are developed directly from a sample of the data themselves.

2. LEARNING MACHINES

Data to be used in pattern recognition studies are represented as vectors, $X \equiv (x_1, x_2, \ldots, x_d)$, where each x_j represents one piece of measurable data. For low resolution mass spectra each x_j could represent the suitably encoded intensity of the peak at m/e = j. In this way the mass spectrum of a C_6H_{14} compound with a molecular ion peak at m/e = 84 could be coded in a pattern vector with 84 components. An infrared spectrum recorded digitized every 0.1 µm from 2.0 to 15.0 µm could be represented by a 131-component vector. For reasons of computational convenience, one extra component is added to each pattern vector; this extra component is usually given a value of 1. The pattern vector then becomes $X \equiv (x_1, x_2, \ldots, x_d, 1)$.

These pattern vectors can be equivalently thought of as points in high-dimensional space (hyperspace). If one had a set of data coded as pattern vectors and placed them in a hyperspace, one might expect points which correspond to mass spectra of compounds with similar features to cluster in limited regions of the space. For example, mass spectra of alkanes might yield a cluster of points in one region of the space while mass spectra of ketones might yield a cluster of points in some other region of the hyperspace. With real data this expectation is met.

When spectra belonging to two chemical classes of components cluster in this manner, then it is possible to construct decision surfaces separating the clusters from each other. The simplest such surface in a d-dimensional hyperspace is a hyperplane which is analogous to an ordinary 3-dimensional plane in 3-space. As with all planes (in spaces of any number of dimensions) the hyperplane decision surface has a normal vector at the origin, $W = (w_1, w_2, \ldots, w_d, w_{d+1})$, which is orthogonal to the decision surface. Therefore, specification of the components of a weight vector is equivalent to complete specification of the position of a hyperplane decision surface.

Any pattern point in a d-dimensional space can be classified with respect to a hyperplane decision surface by taking the dot product between that pattern vector and the normal vector, called the weight vector: (1)

$$s = W \cdot X = w_1 x_1 + w_2 x_2 + \ldots + w_d x_d + w_{d+1} = |W||X| \cos \theta$$

in which θ is the angle between the two vectors. Since $|W|$ and $|X|$ are always positive, then the value of θ determines the size of the dot product:

For $-90° < \theta < 90°$, $\cos \theta > 0$ and $s > 0$.

For $90° < \theta < 270°$, $\cos \theta < 0$ and $s < 0$.

Therefore, for patterns for which $\theta < 90°$ (and thereby are on one side of the plane) the dot product is always positive, and for patterns for which $\theta > 90°$ the dot product is always negative. The dot product is normally computed from the summation of pairwise products of the components of the two vectors for convenience. The correspondence between category 1 and category 2 and the two sides of the hyperplane is arbitrary.

A schematic representation of the logical operation described above is given in Figure 2. The TLU accepts the pattern vector to be classified, calculates the dot product between the pattern vector and the weight vectors, compares the result against zero and classifies the pattern according to the sign of the dot product.

Figure 2. Threshold Logic Unit

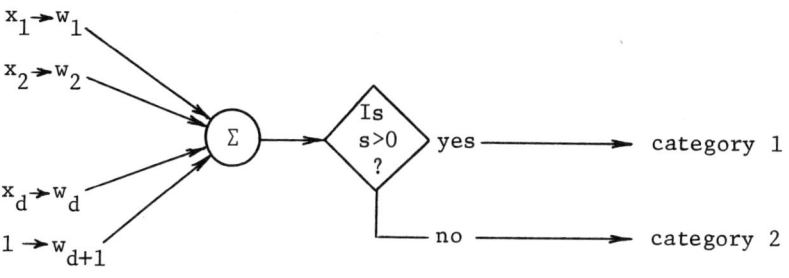

A parameter can be added to the basic TLU of Figure 2 to give a more general binary pattern classifier. In Figure 3 the basic TLU has been modified by addition of a deadzone, Z. This can be thought of as giving the decision surface thickness. A pattern is classified into one of the two categories only if the point lies outside the volume occupied by the decision surface. If it falls inside the decision surface, then no classification is made.

Figure 3. Threshold Logic Unit With Deadzone

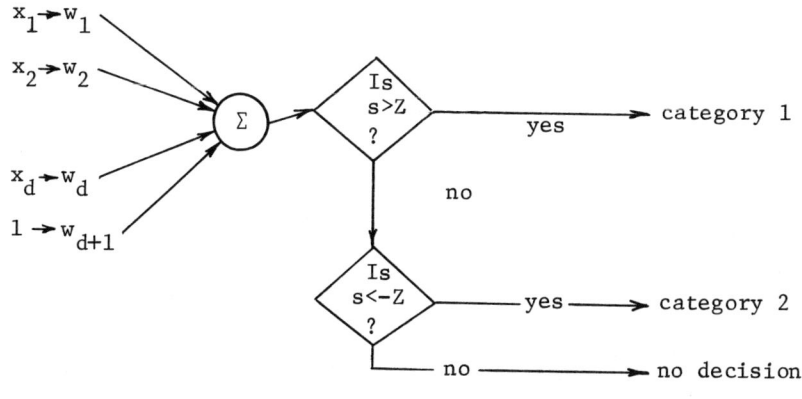

The discussion above refers to a single TLU. A slight generalization involves using two levels of TLU's as shown in Figure 4. In this approach the pattern to be classified is presented simultaneously to three (or five or seven, etc.)

TLU's which each operate in the normal manner. However, the outputs of the first layer of TLU's go to a second layer TLU which executes a majority rule decision. Thus, the committee of classifiers sends its output to a vote-taker TLU which classifies the pattern into the category agreed upon by the majority of the committee.

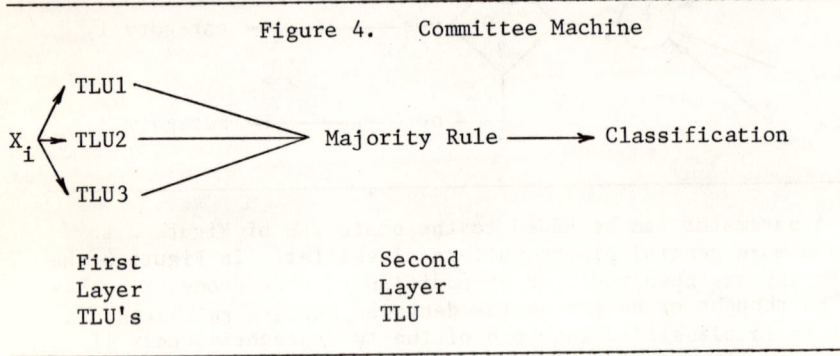

Figure 4. Committee Machine

DISCRIMINANT FUNCTION DEVELOPMENT. Given the system discussed above for performing classifications, the outstanding problem in the development of useful pattern classifiers becomes that of finding useful decision surfaces. This is done, for the non-parametric systems of interest, by a method called training. A training set of pattern whose correct classifications are known is used to develop an effective decision surface.

Single TLU. The members of the training set of spectra are presented to the TLU being trained one at a time. The weight vector being trained is initialized arbitrarily. When a correct classification is made, no corrective action is taken. Whenever an incorrect classification is made, the weight vector is altered. The alteration is performed to insure that the new improved weight vector will correctly classify the pattern. This process continues until all the patterns of the training set are correctly classified. If the procedure does not find a weight vector capable of correctly classifying all the members of the training set, then the routine is terminated in order to conserve computer time.

The actual feedback is performed in the following way. Consider the case where pattern i of the training set is misclassified, that is,

$$W \cdot X_i = s \tag{2}$$

where s has the incorrect sign for classifying X_i. It is desired to calculate an improved weight vector, W', such that

$$W' \cdot X_i = s' \tag{3}$$

where the sign of the scalar result, s', is opposite to what it was previously. The new weight vector, W', is calculated from the old one, W, by adding an appropriate multiple of X_i to it:

$$W' = W + cX_i \tag{4}$$

Combining equations (3) and (4) gives

$$s' = W' \cdot X_i = (W + cX_i) X_i \tag{5}$$

This can be rearranged for c to give

$$c = \frac{s' - s}{X_i \cdot X_i} \tag{6}$$

An effective way to perform feedbacks has been found to be to let $s' = -s$. This moves the decision surface along the perpendicular axis between the misclassified point and the surface so that after the correction the point is the same distance on the correct side of the decision surface as it was previously on the incorrect side. If $s' = -s$ is put into equation (6) then

$$c = \frac{-2s}{X_i \cdot X_i} \tag{7}$$

and the improved weight vector can be directly calculated using equations (7) and (4).

If a TLU with a nonzero threshold, Z, is being trained, the training procedure is as before, with the only change being the calculations of the correction increment:

$$c = \frac{2 (\pm Z - s)}{X_i \cdot X_i} \tag{8}$$

The sign is determined by the sense of the error being corrected.

Committee Machine Training.

An effective and simple training method is to make only the minimum necessary error correction feedback at each step in the training process. Thus, when an incorrect classification is made during training, then the weights of the TLU's that missed being correct by the smallest amount are altered using the feedback correction equations described above. Only enough TLU's are changed to ensure correct classification after the feedback.

LEARNING MACHINE ATTRIBUTES. The capabilities and performance of learning machines can be described in terms of four principal attributes: recognition, convergence rate, reliability, and prediction. Each of these is discussed in the following paragraphs.

Recognition is the ability of the trained binary pattern classifier to correctly classify the members of its training set. Recognition is 100% for a TLU whose decision surface is in the region between two separated clusters. That is, after training is complete for such a case, the TLU can correctly categorize any of the members of the training set with respect to the particular binary question for which the TLU was trained.

Convergence rate refers to the rate at which a TLU approaches 100% recognition. Since computer time is an expensive commodity, it is of interest to minimize training time. The training procedures used to find useful TLU's are commonly altered so as to force rapid learning.

Reliability refers to the ability of a trained TLU to correctly classify the members of its training set when they have been altered. Since real spectral data such as low resolution mass spectra will not be identical when repeated runs are made, it is of interest to use appropriate methods to make the TLU's as insensitive to spectral deformations as possible. The reliability of a TLU can be tested after training is complete by altering the members of the training set and classifying them.

Prediction refers to the ability of a TLU to correctly classify unknowns which were not members of the training set. Prediction is the most interesting and potentially useful of the attributes of learning machines for at least two reasons: high predictive ability demonstrates that the TLU has been able to learn something about how to discriminate between the two classes being trained for, and the ability to correctly classify unknown spectra into useful chemical categories is one drive behind all automation of chemical data interpretation. Predictive ability is normally tested by splitting the available data set into two parts--a training set and a predictive set. After training is complete, and without performing any further adjustment of the weight vector, the members of the predictive set are classified. The percentage correct is taken as the predictive ability.

DATA USED. The specific application of pattern recognition techniques to chemical data interpretation presented here is that of generating the mass spectra of hydrocarbons

directly from a description of their molecular structures. A
set of 377 hydrocarbons with molecular formulas in the range of
$C_{3-10}H_{2-22}$ were used. In order to proceed with the development
of the programs, two sets of data must be generated:
(1) Molecular structure descriptions in the required vector
format; and (2) A set of answers, i.e., the mass spectra
corresponding to the structures.

To be input to the learning machine programs, the molecular structure descriptions must be in the vector format previously discussed. Of the multitude of ways to do this, a combination of two popular approaches has been chosen: fragment codes and substructural codes. The technique of fragmentation coding, which has been reported previously (20, 26) consists of representing a compound as a composite of its predominant structural fragments and their relationships. These features are then assigned numerical descriptors. Table 1 lists the fragments used in the present molecular structure descriptions. They are mostly self-explanatory; the remainder are defined as follows. Largest cycle refers to the largest number of atoms that can be traversed to complete a cycle (ring), but going through each atom only once, e.g., napthalene has a largest cycle of 10. The smallest cycle is the least number of atoms that can be traversed in a cycle, e.g., napthalene has a smallest cycle of 6. Only compounds with at least two rings have nonzero values for the largest cycle and smallest cycle descriptors. One benzene ring only refers to monocyclic molecules. For purposes of classification a benzene ring is defined to have three double bonds. The branch point carbon number is the number of carbon atoms in the compound which are bonded directly to at least three other carbons. Methyl, ethyl, n-propyl, and n-butyl numbers are the numbers of each group that could be produced by a single bond rupture. There are twenty-nine fragment descriptors.

The descriptors are of two types--binary and numeric--and are labelled in Table 1. The binary descriptors can have only two values corresponding to yes and no. In a pattern vector a 1 corresponds to the presence of a fragment and a 0 corresponds to its absence in the structure being coded. Numeric descriptors can have values of up to 142 (the molecular weight of $C_{10}H_{22}$). Because of the wide variation in the ranges of the descriptors' values, it is necessary to normalize the values of the descriptors. The normalization constants are chosen to decrease the spread in the range of the descriptors over the data set. For example, the normalization constant for hydrogen number is 0.5, making its range 0 to 11. All the binary descriptors are normalized by a constant of value five.

Table 1.

Fragment Descriptors

1.	Molecular weight	N	
2.	Largest cycle	N	-not monocyclics
3.	Carbon number	N	
4.	Hydrogen number	N	
5.	Number of rings & double bonds	N	
6.	Vinyl end group	B	
7.	Aromatic	B	
8.	Benzene ring presence	B	
9.	One benzene ring only	B	
10.	Number of C=C	N	
11.	Number of C≡C	N	
12.	Acyclic	B	
13.	Branch point carbon number	N	
14.	Number of n-butyl groups	N	
15.	Number of methyl groups	N	
16.	Number of ethyl groups	N	
17.	Number of n-propyl groups	N	
18.	H = 2C+2	B	
19.	H = 2C	B	
20.	H = 2C-2	B	
21.	H = 2C-6	B	
22.	H = 2C-4	B	
23.	Number of contiguous methylenes	N	
24.	Methyl beta to C=C; C=C-C-CH$_3$	B	
25.	Isopropyl presence	B	
26.	Number of rings	N	
27.	Size of monocyclic	N	
28.	Smallest cycle	N	
29.	Fused rings	B	

The remainder of the descriptors are the twenty-six substructure descriptors listed in Table 2. They are all binary descriptors. The entire data set thus consists of 377 hydrocarbons with their structures coded into 55-dimensional pattern vectors.

The set of mass spectra used was taken from a collection of data on magnetic tape available from the Mass Spectrometry Data Centre, Atomic Weapons Research Establishment, United Kingdom Atomic Energy Authority. The 377 hydrocarbon spectra

Table 2.

Substructure Descriptors

30 $CH_2=CH-CH_2-$

31 $CH_2=CH-CH_2-CH_2-$

32 $CH_3-\underset{\underset{CH_3}{|}}{C}=CH-$

33 $CH_2=\underset{\underset{CH_3}{|}}{C}-CH_2-$

34 $CH_2=CH-\underset{\underset{CH_3}{|}}{CH}-$

35 $CH_3-CH=\underset{\underset{CH_3}{|}}{C}-$

36 $CH_3-CH=CH-CH_2-$

37 $CH_3-\underset{\underset{CH_3}{|}}{\overset{\overset{CH_3}{|}}{C}}-$

38 $CH_3-CH_2-\underset{\overset{\overset{CH_3}{|}}{}}{CH}-$

39 $CH_3-CH_3-CH_3-CH_3-$

40 $CH_3-\underset{\overset{\overset{CH_3}{|}}{}}{CH}-CH_2-$

41 $CH_3-\underset{\underset{CH_3}{|}}{CH}-\underset{\underset{CH_3}{|}}{CH}-$

42 $CH_3-\underset{\underset{CH_3}{|}}{\overset{\overset{CH_3}{|}}{C}}-CH_2-$

43 $\begin{matrix} CH_3-CH_2 \\ CH_3-CH_2 \end{matrix} CH-$

44 $CH_3-CH_2-\underset{\underset{CH_3}{|}}{\overset{\overset{CH_3}{|}}{C}}-$

45 $-\underset{\underset{CH_3}{|}}{\overset{\overset{CH_3}{|}}{C}}-$

46 $-\underset{}{\overset{\overset{CH_3}{|}}{CH}}-\underset{}{\overset{\overset{CH_3}{|}}{CH}}-$

Table 2.
-continued-

47
```
    CH₃ CH₃
     |   |
    -CH-C-
         |
         CH₃
```

48
```
    CH₃      CH₃
     |        |
    -CH-CH₂-CH-
```

49
```
         CH₃
          |
    CH₃ CH₂
     |   |
    -CH-CH-
```

50
```
    CH₃
     |
    -C-
     |
    CH₂
     |
    CH₃
```

51
```
         CH₃
          |
    -CH₂-C-CH₂-
          |
         CH₃
```

52
```
        CH₃ CH₃
         |   |
    -CH₂-CH-CH
```

53
```
    CH₃            CH₃
     |              |
    -CH-CH₂-CH₂-CH-
```

54
```
    CH₃    CH₂
     |      |
    -C-CH₂-CH-
     |
    CH₃
```

55
```
    -CH-CH-CH-
     |   |   |
    CH₃ CH₃ CH₃
```

used were taken from the part of the tape containing 2261 spectra from the American Petroleum Institute Research Project 44. The digitized intensities range from 0.01% to 100.00% in each spectrum. The intensity of each peak is transformed into a logarithmic scale by the following equation:

$$I' = 10 \log (10000 I)$$

in which I is the relative intensity of the peak as a percentage of the total ion current and I' is the transformed intensity. The transformed intensities have values of 0 or are on the range of 10 to 60. On the logarithmic scale 30 corresponds to 0.1% of the total ion current, 37 corresponds to 0.5%, and 40 corresponds to 1.0%.

A single training session for an individual TLU proceeds as follows. The overall data set of 377 structures coded in 55-dimensional vectors randomly divided into two subsets: a training set of 200 and a prediction set of 177. Then each subset has the structures removed for which the molecular weight is less than the m/e position being trained for. A set of correct responses is developed. For example, the TLU may be trained to determine if compounds have a mass spectral peak at m/e = 57 of magnitude greater than some cutoff intensity, say 35. Then the TLU will be trained using the 200 training set members so that it will give a positive result for those molecules having such a peak and a negative result for those lacking such a peak. After training is complete, the TLU is allowed to classify the (unknown) members of the prediction set. The percentage correctly predicted is reported as the predictive ability. In order to develop the ability to make decisions regarding the size of mass spectral peaks, a number of TLU's must be trained with different intensity cutoff values.

RESULTS AND DISCUSSION. Table 3 shows the results of training TLU's for several different intensity cutoffs for each of 25 mass positions. The left column lists the mass positions for which TLU's were trained. For each mass position, three TLU's were trained with intensity cutoffs that divided the training set into 1:3, 1:1, and 3:1 populations. For each TLU three data are reported: (1) the intensity cutoff used; (2) the identity of the training set used; and (3) the predictive ability. Three different, randomly chosen training sets labelled A, B, and C were used. During training with any one of these training sets, if convergence was not obtained in 2500 feedbacks (an economic limitation) then the five members of the training set which were most often missed were discarded and training was reattempted. The cycle could be repeated a second time if necessary. Thus, the designation B-10 for the first TLU for mass position 29 means that the discarding cycle eliminated 10 structures from training set B, whereupon convergence occurred.

The predictive abilities obtained for all 73 TLU's ranged between 70% and 97% with an average of 87.2%. The average predictive ability for the 1:3, 1:1, and 3:1 TLU's are given at the bottom of Table 3. Random guessing would yield 50% predictive abilities for all the TLU's. Prediction based on the known probabilities of the two classes 1:3 and 3:1 would yield

Table 3.

Results of Training TLU's

m/e	1:3 cutoff	1:3 training set	1:3 predictive ability	1:1 cutoff	1:1 training set	1:1 predictive ability	3:1 cutoff	3:1 training set	3:1 predictive ability
29	41	B-10	94.9	45	B-10	83.6	47	A-10	91.5
41	47	C-5	93.8	49	A-10	69.5	50	B-10	84.8
42	38	C-10	89.3	41	A-10	76.0	44	A-10	81.1
43	35	B-10	93.2	43	A-10	87.4	47	C	96.6
54	31	C	95.4	36	B-10	93.1	40	C-10	84.0
55	40	B-5	91.4	46	A-5	90.3	50	A-5	82.3
56	33	B-5	92.5	42	C-10	86.1	48	A-10	80.8
57	29	B-5	86.8	37	C-5	89.0	46	A	95.4
66	25	A	92.9	31	A-5	82.8	34	B-5	93.5
67	31	C-5	90.5	37	B-10	89.4	42	B	97.1
68	25	B-10	89.4	33	B-10	94.7	39	B-10	88.2
69	31	C-5	90.5	40	A-5	88.8	46	A	84.0
70	28	C-5	95.0	39	B-10	82.9	45	B-10	81.1
71	19	B-10	84.2	31	B-5	82.9	38	B-5	89.6
80	19	B-10	90.6	25	C-10	86.4	30	B	91.3
81	22	A-5	90.1	29	A	92.1	38	B-5	96.3
82	18	C-10	85.0	27	B-5	91.3	36	C-10	83.7
83	24	B-5	85.6	32	A-10	77.3	41	B-10	87.5
84	21	C-10	86.4	30	C-10	81.6	41	C-10	78.9
85	21	B-5	80.4	27	C-10	72.8	35	A-10	83.9
95	1	B-5	85.1	19	A-5	93.0	31	B-5	87.2
97	19	B-10	79.4	26	B-10	75.9	34	A-10	85.9

Table 3.
-continued-

m/e	1:3			1:1			3:1		
	cutoff	training set	predictive ability	cutoff	training set	predictive ability	cutoff	training set	predictive ability
98	21	B-5	82.8	28	A-5	78.9	41	A-10	83.7
105				1	B-5	90.8	31	B	92.7
106				1	B-5	88.9	24	C-5	93.2

50% for the 1:1 class. The actual predictive abilities are far higher than this. Evidently the TLU's have been able to distill some generalizations directly from the molecular structures about what makes structures give rise to mass spectral peaks of certain relative intensities.

Table 4 shows the results of applying a feature selection routine to the data sets used in Table 3. The feature selection routine attempts to discover which molecular structure descriptors are important in answering a specific chemical question. The procedure is as follows: For the particular mass spectral peak and intensity cutoff being investigated, two weight vectors are independently trained starting from different initializations. The feature selection process then discards those descriptors that contribute little or nothing to the solution of the problem. This is done by comparing the signs of the components of the two weight vectors. Only those descriptors for which both weight vector components agree in sign are retained. Then the two weight vectors of reduced dimensionality are retained. Feature selection continues until no unimportant descriptors remain.

Table 4 shows the feature selection results obtained for four mass positions. An average of 34 descriptors are retained. The number of descriptors retained for each TLU is shown in column six, and the number of fragment and substructure descriptors remaining is shown in column seven. Comparison of columns four and eight shows that training generally occurred either as fast or faster with a reduced number of descriptors compared to the entire set of 55 descriptors. The predictive abilities listed in the last column are almost always higher-- the average predictive ability for all 12 questions is 1.1% higher with only six-tenths as many descriptors.

These results demonstrate that the information relevant to the chemical questions being asked reside in a fraction of the raw pattern vectors' components. By discarding the irrelevant descriptors, performance of the TLU's is enhanced.

Table 5 shows the results of training committee machines for three mass positions. The training sets used for each committee were identical with those used in the previous tables. Column four shows the deadzone that was employed during training of the committees. The individual predictive abilities attained are given in the final column. The average predictive ability for the nine committees is slightly higher than for those nine individual TLU's in Table 3. It should also be noted that committee machines are much less prone to make errors due to mistakes in input data than are individual TLU's.

Table 4.
Feature Selection Results

m/e	cutoff	training set	55 descriptors		Reduced Patterns			
			feedbacks	average percent prediction	descriptors retained	fragments/ substructures	feedbacks	average percent prediction
29	41	B-10	193/268	94.4	26	17/9	131/285	94.4
	45	B-10	-1-	71.5	42	23/19	-1-	78.8
	47	A-10	1946/1981	90.4	38	20.18	18P8/2285	91.0
43	35	B-10	95/98	92.0	25	20/5	56/60	92.1
	43	A-10	1101/1048	87.1	39	21/18	1290/787	86.3
	47	C	2297/2276	95.8	38	22/16	2492/2501	95.8
67	31	C-5	2197/2504	91.1	42	23/19	2500/2505	91.6
	37	B-10	2005/1783	90.9	46	26/20	1857/1823	91.8
	42	C	2467/1464	92.0	27	22/5	867/384	93.2
68	25	B-10	346/570	90.8	27	18/9	349/323	92.0
	33	B-10	787/731	94.0	33	20.13	689/590	95.0
	39	B-10	309/229	90.5	23	18/5	161/169	91.4

Table 5.

Committee Machine Results

m/e	cutoff	training set	deadzone	complete training?	predictive ability
43	35	B-10	50	yes	91.5
	43	A-10	25	yes	89.1
	47	C	50	yes	96.1
67	31	C-5	25	yes	92.3
	37	B-10	50	no	88.8
	42	B	50	yes	95.9
68	25	B-10	50	yes	92.9
	33	B-10	50	yes	94.7
	39	B-10	50	yes	91.1

CONCLUSIONS. The formalisms of the pattern recognition technique have been discussed, and the method has been applied to an example set of data. It has been shown that the method can be used to predict some features of low resolution mass spectra directly from molecular structures. Predictive abilities on unknown molecules for some mass position--intensity cutoff values are as high as 97% with an average of 87.2% for 73 TLU's. Subjection of the data set to a feature selection routine has shown that the information relevant to answering the questions being posed reside in a fraction of the pattern vectors' components. Superior performance can be obtained using pattern vectors with a reduced number of components. Several example mass position-intensity cutoff values were chosen and committees machines were trained; slightly superior performance was obtained compared to single TLU's.

Finally, it should be emphasized that the pattern recognition techniques is applicable to a variety of chemical data interpretation tasks. Already the method has been applied to the interpretation of mass spectra, infrared spectra, gamma-ray spectra, mixtures of data from diverse sources, electrochemical data, and the generation of simulated mass spectra from molecular structures. It is felt that the approach will continue to make useful contributions to chemical data interpretation in the future.

ACKNOWLEDGMENT. Financial support from the National Science Foundation is gratefully acknowledged.

References

1. Minsky, Marvin, "Steps Toward Artificial Intelligence," Proc. IEEE, 49, 8 (1961).

2. Solomonoff, R. J., "Some Recent Work in Artificial Intelligence," Proc. IEEE, 54, 1687 (1966).

3. Rosen, C. A., "Pattern Classification by Adaptive Machines," Science, 156, 38 (1967).

4. Nagy, George, "State of the Art in Pattern Recognition," Proc. IEEE, 56, 836 (1968).

5. Levine, M. D., "Feature Extraction: A Survey," Proc. IEEE, 57, 1391 (1969).

6. Computerized Learning Machines Applied to Chemical Problems. Optimization of a Linear Pattern Classifier by the Addition of a "Width" Parameter. L. E. Wangen, N. M. Frew, T. L. Isenhour, Analytical Chemistry, 43, 845 (1971).

7. Machine Intelligence Applied to Chemical Systems: A Graph Theoretical and Learning Machine Study of Second-Order Effects in Low Resolution Mass Spectra. P. C. Jurs, Applied Spectroscopy, 25, 483-488 (1971).

8. Some Chemical Applications of Machine Intelligence. T. L. Isenhour and P. C. Jurs, Analytical Chemistry, 43 (10), (1971).

9. The application of a Piecewise-Linear Multicategory Pattern Classifier with Self-Evolving Capabilities to the Interpretation of Mass Spectra. N. M. Frew, L. W. Wangen, T. L. Isenhour, Pattern Recognition, 3, 281, (1971).

10. An Investigation of the Fourier Transform Representation of Mass Spectra for Analysis by Computerized Learning Machine. P. C. Jurs, Analytical Chemistry, 43, 1812-1815 (1971).

11. On Machine Intelligence Applied to Chemical Problems, T. L. Isenhour and P. C. Jurs, in The Application of Computer Techniques in Chemical Research, Peter Hepple, Ed., Institute of Petroleum, London, 1972.

12. The K-Nearest Neighbor Classification Rule (Pattern Recognition) Applied to Nuclear Magnetic Resonance Spectral Interpretation. B. R. Kowalski and C. F. Bender, Analytical Chemistry, 44, 1405 (1972).

13. Pattern Recognition. A Powerful Approach to Interpreting Chemical Data. B. R. Kowalski and C. F. Bender, JACS, 94, 5632 (1972).

14. Hamming Type Codes Applied to Learning Machine Determinations of Molecular Formulas. F. E. Lytle, Analytical Chemistry, 44, 1867 (1972).

15. Application of a Complex-Valued Nonlinear Discriminant Function to Low-Resolution Mass Spectra. J. B. Justice, Jr., D. N. Anderson, T. L. Isenhour, J. C. Marshall, Analytical Chemistry, 44, 2087 (1972).

16. Classification of Archaeological Artifacts by Applying Pattern Recognition to Trace Element Data. B. R. Kowalski, T. F. Schatzki, F. H. Stross, Analytical Chemistry, 44, 2176 (1972).

17. Computerized Pattern Classification of Strongly Overlapped Peaks in Stationary Electrode Polarography. L. B. Sybrandt and S. P. Perone, Analytical Chemistry, 44, 2331 (1972).

18. Iterative Least Squares Development of Discriminant Functions for Spectroscopic Data Analysis by Pattern Recognition. Lucio Pietrantonio and P. C. Jurs, Pattern Recognition, 4, 391 (1972).

19. Application of Pattern Separation Techniques to Mass Spectrometric Data. The Determination of Hydrocarbon Types and the Average Molecular Structure of Gasoline. D. D. Tunnicliff and P. A. Wadsworth, Analytical Chemistry, 45, 12 (1973).

20. Generation of Simulated Mass Spectra of Small Organic Molecules by Computerized Pattern Recognition Techniques. Joseph Schechter and P. C. Jurs, Applied Spectroscopy, 27, 30 (1973).

21. Pattern Recognition. II. Linear and Nonlinear Methods for Displaying Chemical Data. B. R. Kowalski and C. F. Bender, JACS, 95, 686 (1973).

References

22. Construction of Optimum Variables for Spectral Interpretation (Pattern Recognition). C. F. Bender and B. R. Kowalski, *Analytical Chemistry*, 45, 590 (1973).

23. Alternate Representation of Mass Spectra for the Spectral Identification Problem (Pattern Recognition). C. F. Bender, H. D. Shepard, B. R. Kowalski, *Analytical Chemistry*. 45, 617 (1973).

24. Learning Machines, T. L. Isenhour and P. C. Jurs, *Computers in Chemistry and Instrumentation*, 1, J. S. Mattson, H. B. Mark, Jr., and H. C. MacDonald, Jr., Eds., Marcel Dekker, Inc., New York, N. Y., (1973).

25. Multicategory Predictions Using Arrays of Binary Pattern Classifiers. W. L. Felty and P. C. Jurs, *Analytical Chemistry*, 45, 885 (1973).

26. Improved Discriminant Training and Feature Extraction for the Generation of Simulated Mass Spectra of Small Organic Molecules. J. Schechter and P. C. Jurs, *Applied Spectroscopy*, 27, (1973).

27. Applications of Artificial Intelligence: Relationships between Mass Spectra and Pharmacological Activity of Drugs. K.-L. H. Ting, R. C. T. Lee, G. W. A. Milne, M. Shapiro, A. M. Guarino, *Science*, 180, 417 (1973).

HEURISTIC DENDRAL: ANALYSIS OF MOLECULAR STRUCTURE

Dennis H. Smith, Larry M. Masinter and Natesa S. Sridharan
Departments of Chemistry and Computer Science
Stanford University, Stanford, California 94305

ABSTRACT. Generation, representation and manipulation of molecular structures in the context of the Heuristic DENDRAL algorithm are described. A summary of past activities and present efforts within the DENDRAL project is presented. Emphasis is placed on the recently completed cyclic structure generator.

1. INTRODUCTION

PURPOSES OF THE HEURISTIC DENDRAL PROJECT. The interdisciplinary effort behind the Heuristic DENDRAL project is aimed at fulfilling goals of interest to chemists, computer scientists and geneticists involved. The chemists are interested in the use of computers for automatic structure elucidation. A successful approach to this task involves systematization of knowledge about techniques for physical measurements and of the processes of chemical reasoning from data to inferences. This is a particularly valuable mechanism for promoting a deeper understanding of chemistry. The computer scientists are interested in modeling scientific reasoning in an area which is non-trivial and where successful performance of programs can benefit the practicing scientist. Geneticists are interested in potential applications of this approach to identification of chemical compounds isolated from bodily fluids; compounds which may be indicative of metabolic defects of genetic origin.

HISTORICAL BACKGROUND. Several years ago at Stanford University Professors Feigenbaum (Computer Science) and Lederberg (Genetics) initiated a study of the processes of scientific inference using the techniques of artificial intelligence (AI). Chemistry, and specifically that branch of chemistry which deals with molecular structure elucidation, was chosen as the task area for study. This choice was made for reasons of feasibility and utility. The limited nature of the task domain, the existence of a formal body of knowledge, availability of experts in the task area and the genuine usefulness of a powerful performance program were factors contributing to the choice. Collaboration with Professor Carl Djerassi and the experts in mass spectrometry has been fruitful in building and monitoring the development of the computer programs.

STRATEGY. The heuristic search paradigm[1] was chosen as the computer based model with which to study the inference processes connected with structure elucidation. The heuristic search paradigm treats the collection of all possible solutions as a "space". We attempt to find the correct solution by searching this space employing systematic methods for consideration of classes of solutions. In this case the space to be searched is the space of molecular structures (isomers) which represents possible solutions to a given problem (an empirical formula). The term "heuristics" refers to the judgmental rules which are used to guide the search, hopefully to a single, correct solution.

This approach to automated structure elucidation requires the ability to represent and manipulate several kinds of chemical information in a computer program. The ability to generate and represent the space of isomers according to the rules of topology and chemistry is required. There are several instances where one builds on existing structures or degrades structures into their composite partial structures. Spectroscopic or other physical data on an unknown compound must be transformed into information useful to the program, under the control of knowledge about the characteristics of the measurement technique. The subsequent sections discuss how these types of chemical information are represented and utilized in Heuristic DENDRAL.

ORGANIZATION OF DISCUSSION. The subsequent discussion is divided into four major sections (2-5). Section 2 discusses the importance of the structure generator and how a successful method was developed. Section 3 discusses how the generator is utilized in the Heuristic DENDRAL program to solve problems of structure elucidation. Section 4 briefly summarizes facilities for structure manipulation which are available to the program. Section 5 indicates areas presently receiving most attention in our research and some future directions.

2. STRUCTURE GENERATION

At the heart of the Heuristic DENDRAL program lies the structure generator, which is capable of listing all isomers of a specified empirical formula. Empirical formulae for unknown compounds are readily provided by various techniques, usually high resolution mass spectrometry. The two primary requirements for a generator are completeness and prospective avoidance of redundancy. The latter requirement affords economy of effort and the former guarantees thoroughness.

THE ACYCLIC GENERATOR. We are approaching the 100th anniversary of the first in a series of attempts to delineate the scope and diversity of chemical structure. Cayley[2] was the first to attempt an enumeration of alkane isomers.[3-5] Enumeration of simple ring systems has been attempted. The problem of arriving at the number of isomers is different in nature from the problem of explicitly defining each isomer. The isomer generation problem was solved for acyclic molecules in 1965 and the general structure generation problem was not solved until 1973.

The fundamental logic which underlies molecular structure, though simple, has not been generally apparent to chemists. This has prevented chemists from approaching structure elucidation via systematic specification of possible solutions. An effect of this is manifested in the teaching of chemistry, where problems of isomer generation are given to students, without a methodology for solution.

DENDRAL Notation. Efficient computer storage and manipulation of structural formulae can benefit from a linear notational system. Such systems, which specify the topology of the molecule in a linear string of symbols, also facilitate computer input of structural information. Connection tables, mentioned in subsequent sections, represent an alternative notation. Several linear notational systems have been proposed and utilized. Among them are the Hayward notation,[6] the International Union of Pure and Applied Chemistry (IUPAC) notation[7] and Wiswesser Line Notation (WLN).[8] Advantages and disadvantages of these systems have been reviewed.[9] WLN has received widespread acceptance and forms the basis for many chemical information storage, retrieval and substructure search systems. Other systems suited for specific problems have appeared, for example, the system proposed by Hendrickson[10] which expresses connectivity and functionality for use in computer-aided synthesis. Lederberg has proposed an alternative scheme[11-13] which has firm foundations in topological principles of molecular structure.

This scheme for unique linear representation of acyclic molecules uses few ad hoc rules, in contrast with other systems. Because connectivity alone is represented in structural formulae, molecular structures are subject to analysis by topological graph theory. In this case the graphs have nodes (atoms) connected to one another by edges (bonds). Graphs which are separable into two parts by cutting any single edge are called "tree graphs" and correspond to acyclic molecules. The tree graph of every acyclic molecule has a unique center, or centroid, which is a point that provides the most evenly balanced allocation of the nodes.[14] The centroid of a molecular graph provides the starting point for the mapping procedure which yields a unique specification of the structure.

The DENDRAL Acyclic Structure Generator. The concept of the topological centroid of a molecule provides a systematic way to consider acyclic structures. It also provides a mechanism for exhaustive, irredundant generation. This mechanism has been discussed previously[11-13] and some results indicating the diversity of acyclic isomers have been presented.[15] The generator works for a given composition by sequencing through all possible centroids and permuting pendant radicals in a systematic order. The generator will be exhaustive, since consideration of all centroids must include the tree graph for every isomer. Redundancy is avoided by the canons of precedence that order the constituent branches of every tree uniquely.[11-13]

THE DENDRAL CYCLIC STRUCTURE GENERATOR. It has been clear since the inception of the DENDRAL project that the use of heuristic search techniques for molecular structure determination would require generating all cyclic and acyclic structures for a specified composition. A reasonable solution to the problem of cyclic structure generation remained elusive for some time, however, because Lederberg's notational algorithm for acyclic structures could not be mapped easily into a generating algorithm for cyclic structures.[16] Prospective avoidance of duplicate structures is difficult for cyclic isomers, because cyclic structures can display complex symmetries.

The fundamental principles underlying cyclic structures have been derived from the topology of cyclic graphs.[17] As with tree graphs, these principles have not been utilized or even realized by most chemists, resulting in complex ad hoc rules for both nomenclature and linear notation. It is not our purpose to postulate new rules or systems. It is, however, useful to consider cyclic structures using these principles, for they provide the basis for their logical analysis and a means for generation of isomers.

Vertex-Graphs: The Foundations of Cyclic Structures. In discussing the topology of cyclic graphs, Lederberg classified ring systems according to their vertex-graphs.[12,17] Vertex-graphs do not contain acyclic chains or nodes of degree two (secondary nodes). (The terms degree of a node, and secondary, tertiary, ..., nodes have their usual chemical meaning, i.e., the number of (non-hydrogen) edges (bonds) to the node.) Vertex-graphs represent paths between the vertex-atoms in a cyclic structure, i.e., those atoms at which rings are fused in conventional descriptions. Thus vertex-graphs are cyclic structures from which nodes of degree two have been deleted. For most molecules, this corresponds to the set of trivalent cyclic graphs, the enumeration of which has been programmed, computed and described.[17] For the general case, some vertex-graphs possessing nodes of higher valence (e.g., one node of valence four for a spiro-fused ring system at a carbon atom) are required and can be computed.

Consider as an example the simplest, non-degenerate trivalent graph, 1, Scheme I. This graph possesses two tertiary nodes (all trivalent graphs possess an even number of nodes to satisfy the odd degree of each node).

SCHEME I

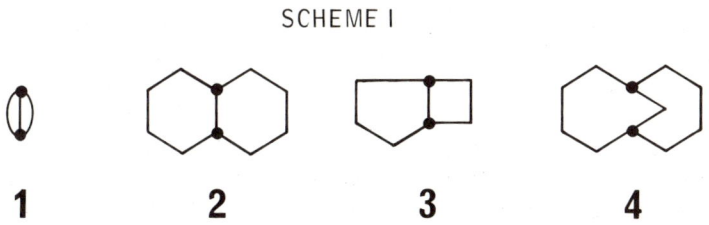

1   2   3   4

Chemical structures 2-4, Scheme I have 1 as their vertex-graph. The tertiary nodes are indicated in bold face to clarify the relationship of 2-4 to 1. A bit of thought should reveal that 1 is in fact the vertex-graph of all bicyclic ring systems independent of the number of secondary nodes on each edge, excluding spiro fusions.

As a second example, consider the basic steroid ring system 5, Scheme II. Ignoring secondary nodes, the trivalent nodes and their interconnections are indicated as 6, which is equivalent to 7. Graph 7

SCHEME II

```
    5            6        7          8
```

is one of the trivalent graphs of six nodes, and is the foundation for
many other ring systems besides the steroid skeleton, for example, the
perhydronaphthacene skeleton, 8, Scheme II.
    Regular trivalent graphs through order six (six nodes) and some
special cases including one quaternary node are indicated in Figure 1,
together with a structure based on each graph. Given the complete set
of vertex-graphs compatible with a given empirical formula, the
complete set of ring systems (and isomers) can be specified.[18]

    <u>Strategy</u>. Using the concept of vertex-graphs the procedure
for structure generation is as shown schematically in Figure 2. The steps
designated as "Partition" in Figure 2 decompose the given empirical
formula in a series of calculations specifying the set of vertex-graphs
necessary and sufficient to generate all isomers. The partitioning steps,
discussed in more detail below, are designed first to allocate the
atoms in all possible ways among ring systems and acyclic chains.
Additional partitioning steps specify the numbers and identities of nodes
and their distribution among edges and nodes of vertex-graphs. The
vertex-graphs depict only edges and nodes of degree three and higher.
These graphs must be expanded in a series of steps to final structures.
These steps all involve allocation of the results of the partitioning steps
(e.g., number of nodes of specified degree, number of bonds per node,
number of atoms of specified name) to the vertex-graphs. This procedure,
discussed below, involves "labelling" the graphs with the appropriate
information and provides the mechanism for avoiding duplicate structures.
    Our strategy is to partition the atoms in the empirical
formula in all unique ways into two separate pots, "superatompots" and
a "remaining pot". The atoms assigned to a superatompot will be
eventually incorporated into ring-superatoms based on the vertex-graphs
(Fig. 2). (A superatom is defined to be a structural sub-unit possessing

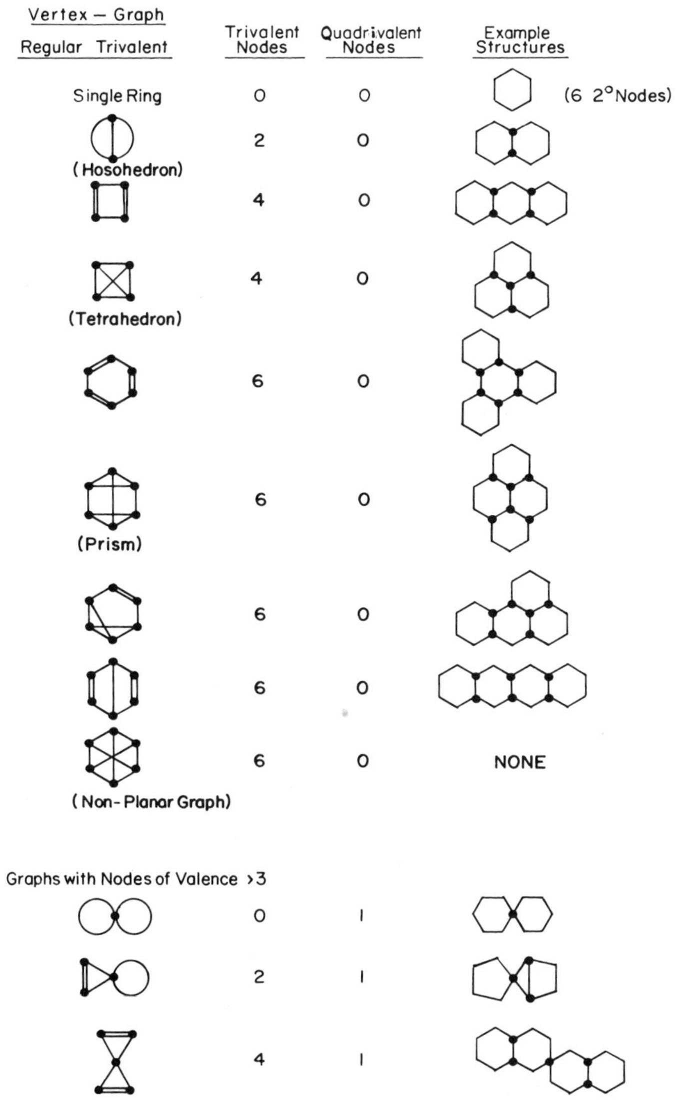

Strategy

Vertex – Graph Regular Trivalent	Trivalent Nodes	Quadrivalent Nodes	Example Structures
Single Ring	0	0	(6 2°Nodes)
(Hosohedron)	2	0	
	4	0	
(Tetrahedron)	4	0	
	6	0	
(Prism)	6	0	
	6	0	
	6	0	
(Non-Planar Graph)	6	0	NONE
Graphs with Nodes of Valence >3			
	0	1	
	2	1	
	4	1	

Figure 1. Some examples of vertex-graphs and a representative structure corresponding to each.

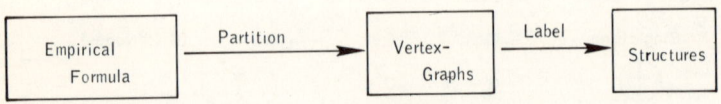

Figure 2. Strategy for structure generation.

at least one free valence. A free valence is a bond on an atom or superatom with an unspecified terminus. Ring-superatoms are two-connected structures; at least two edges must be broken to divide the graph into two parts.) There may be more than one superatompot in a single partition, resulting in more than one ring system in the final structures assembled from this partition. The remaining pot will form acyclic linkages and chains in the final structures.

The atoms assigned to a superatompot are used to construct ring-superatoms by further partitions, selection of vertex-graphs, and expansion of these graphs. The acyclic generator is used to connect the ring-superatoms with the acyclic chains from each original partition in all possible ways.

Isomerism. Isomers generated by the structure generator represent connectivity isomers in which atoms and their interconnections are specified. This category of isomerism takes no note of bond lengths, bond angles or any other geometrical consideration. The selection of a particular category of isomerism defines the set of allowed symmetry operations utilized in carrying out graph labelling. The implications of the selection of connectivity isomerism and other possible choices are elaborated in the subsequent section on graph labelling (also see Ugi, et al., reference 19, and references 21 and 22).

AN ALGORITHM FOR STRUCTURE GENERATION. A detailed description of the method for structure generation will appear separately.[20] The description below will be confined to presentation of selected parts of a single problem, generation of the isomers of $C_{10}H_{19}N_1$. This example serves to indicate some of the

An Algorithm for Structure Generation

basic principles and methods involved but does not indicate all aspects of the structure generator. The major steps in the algorithm are illustrated in Figure 3.

Partitioning. The empirical formula is expressed in terms of unsaturations (U.'s, rings plus double bonds) as hydrogen atoms are ignored by convention. Thus $C_{10}H_{19}N_1$ becomes $C_{10}N_1U_2$ (Fig. 3). Some of the flavor of the types of isomers which are generated from the superatom partitions may be determined from the examples presented in Figure 3. The first partition, $C_{10}N_1U_2$, will yield all structures in which all atoms and unsaturations are included in a single ring system, with no attached acyclic chains. The second partition, $C_9N_1U_2$, with C_1 alloted to remaining pot, will yield structures comprising $C_9N_1U_2$ in a single ring system, with C_1 (a methyl group) as an acyclic attachment. Similarly, the next partition, $C_8N_1U_2$ will yield the corresponding single ring system with C_2 (two methyl groups or an ethyl group) as acyclic parts. Another partition indicated in Figure 3, $C_{10}U_2(N_1)$, will yield single carbocyclic ring systems with one attached amino group. The final partition indicated, $C_5U_1/C_5N_1U_1$, will yield two ring systems, each containing C_5U_1 and one containing, in addition, a heterocyclic nitrogen. These ring systems will be linked only with a bond in all possible ways, as there are no atoms allocated to acyclic chains. Structure <u>9</u> is an example.

9

In this scheme of generation, double, triple, ... bonds are regarded as small ring systems. Chemists may feel uncomfortable with this concept. We have adopted it with hesitation, while still seeking alternate ways of considering aromatic structures. Thus the remaining pot in each partition will never contain an unsaturation as all unsaturations will be accounted for in the ring-superatoms.

Heuristic DENDRAL

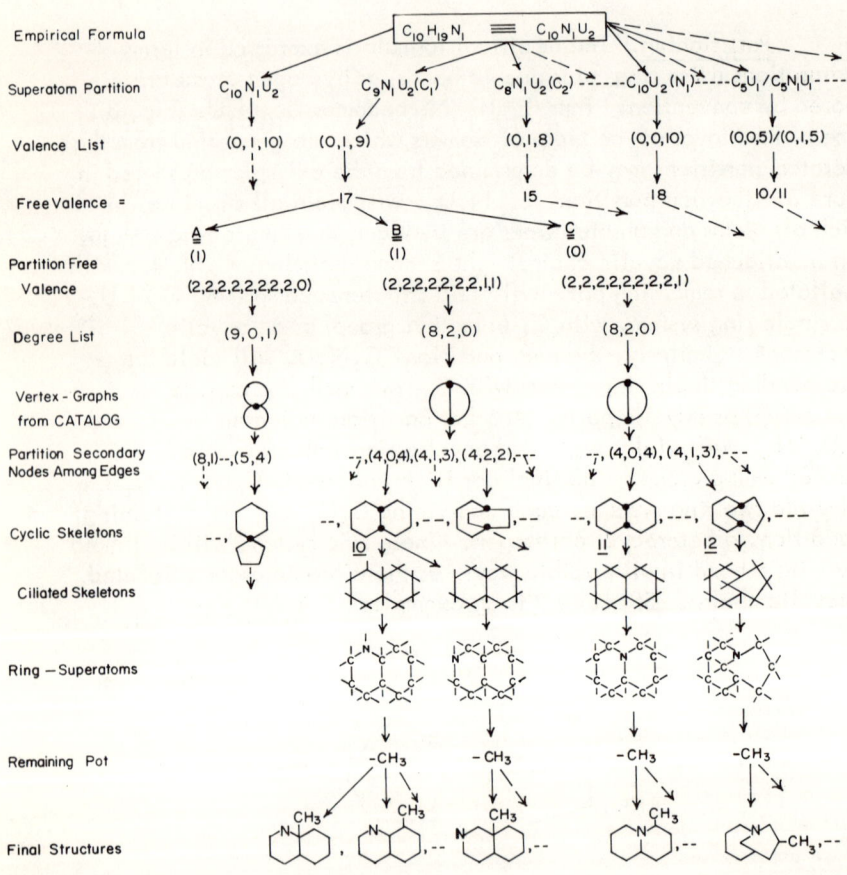

Figure 3. An outline of the operation of the structure generator for a portion of one superatom partition of the empirical formula $C_{10}H_{19}N_1$.

Partitioning

The next step in the structure building sequence (Fig. 3) is illustrated for only one of the many possible partitions. A valence list is assembled from each superatompot in a partition. The number of atoms of valence two, three, four and so forth are placed in order in this list independent of their respective atom names. (Univalent atoms can never be part of a ring-superatom. All such atoms (e.g., F, Cl, Br) are always placed in the remaining pot.) The superatompot $C_9N_1U_2$ contains zero bivalent atoms, one trivalent atom and nine tetravalent atoms, yielding the list (0,1,9). Other valence lists are indicated in Fig. 3 for other partitions.

The next step is calculation of the free valence of each valence list, using Equation 1. The free valence, defined previously, represents the number of bonds which remain unused after formation of the ring superatom. These bonds will be used to attach hydrogen

$$\text{Free Valence} = (2 + \sum_{i=3}^{n} (i-2) a_i) - 2U \qquad \text{Equation 1}$$

U = unsaturation of superatompot
i = valence
n = maximum valence in valence list
a_i = number of atoms with valence i

atoms and, where appropriate, other univalent atoms, acyclic chains or other ring superatoms to yield the final structures. Equation 1 applied to the valence list (0,1,9) gives seventeen free valences. The free valences (FV's) are then partitioned among the elements of the valence list subject only to valence constraints. Because ring-superatoms are two-connected structures two valences of every entry in the valence list must be reserved for connection of the entry to the ring-superatom. Bivalent entries can receive no FV's, trivalent entries can receive either zero or one FV's and tetravalent entries can receive from zero to two FV's. For the example illustrated in Figure 3, there are only three unique ways to partition seventeen free valences among the entries in the valence list (0,1,9). If the trivalent entry is allotted one free valence, there are two ways to partition the remaining sixteen among nine tetravalents. Either eight receive two FV's and one zero FV's, or seven receive two FV's and two receive one FV (partitions $\underline{A}$ and $\underline{B}$, Fig. 3, respectively). If the trivalent entry is allotted zero FV's, there is only one way to partition seventeen FV's among nine tetravalents (partition $\underline{C}$, Fig. 3).

It is now possible to predict some characteristics of the structures which will result from each of the three partitions. For example, partitions A and B, which allot one FV to a trivalent entry (we have only one, a nitrogen atom) will yield ring-superatoms containing a secondary nitrogen atom with one bond remaining for attachment to acyclic parts, for example, a hydrogen atom. These two partitions differ in that A will yield ring superatoms with a quaternary carbon atom (one tetravalent entry with no FV's) while B will yield ring superatoms with two tertiary carbon atoms. Partition C (Fig. 3) will yield ring-superatoms containing one tertiary nitrogen atom (zero FV's) and one tertiary carbon atom (one FV), the remaining being secondary.

As the preceding paragraph illustrates, the partition of free valences effectively specifies the degree of each node (eventually atoms) in the graphs which will represent the ring-superatoms. We speak then of the "degree list" of each partition. Allocation of FV's to entries in the valence list designates the degree of each entry in the degree list. Free valence partition A allots one FV to the trivalent entry, and two FV's to all but one tetravalent entry. This yields nine entries of degree two leaving one entry of degree four, or the degree list (9,0,1). In a similar fashion, FV partitions B and C yield the same degree list (8,2,0).

The degree lists are used to select appropriate vertex-graphs (Fig. 1) which are maintained in a CATALOG. Vertex-graphs do not contain secondary nodes, so that secondary entries in the degree lists are ignored. For each of the degree lists in the example there is only one possible vertex-graph, the "daisy" (Fig. 1) for the degree list (9,0,1), and the regular trivalent graph of two nodes for the degree lists (8,2,0), as shown in Figure 3. More complex problems involving more unsaturations require the introduction of the concept of "loops" for exhaustive generation.[20] Certain structures such as rings with multiple exocyclic double bonds are constructed utilizing loops.

The next step partitions the secondary nodes among the edges of the vertex-graphs. There are several unique partitions for each of the vertex-graphs, some of which are illustrated in Figure 3, each of which will result in a different ring system and a different set of final structures.

Graph Labelling. The next phase of structure generation involves expansion of the vertex-graphs in a series of steps to the final structures. All such steps involve the same problem and are solved by repeated application of a single algorithm.[21,22] Because a graph

structure is involved at each step, the procedure by which the possible
attachments of items (in the first instance, secondary nodes) to the graph
(in the first instance, the vertex-graphs) are specified may be viewed as
a "labelling" of the graph. The formal problem is that of association of
a set of m labels, not necessarily distinct, with a set of n objects, not
necessarily distinct, to yield a set of labelled objects without duplicates.
The graph labelling problem is solved by consideration of the symmetry
properties of the objects to be labelled. As was indicated previously,
methods for counting the number of solutions exist.[2-5] These counting
procedures have been generalized and extended to the counting of the
total number of isomers.[18b] These extended counting procedures have
been used to verify the program code for the graph labelling algorithm
and for the complete structure generator.

There are many possible definitions of symmetry and isomerism.[19]
In our case, we are generating connectivity isomers, as mentioned
previously. Thus, we are interested in the symmetry groups of connectivity isomers. For chemical graphs, every permutation of atoms and bonds
onto themselves is a symmetry transformation for connectivity symmetry
if each atom is mapped into another atom of like species, and the
connectivity of every pair of atoms is preserved in the mapping. The
most convenient means of representing our connectivity information for
computer manipulation is the connection table (see ref. 9a for a more
detailed exposition), which specifies every atom and its connections with
other atoms. We can define the connectivity symmetry group of a graph
as the set of transformations which yields identical connection tables.
For chemical structures, the connection tables contain atom name
designations, and these must also be preserved in the symmetry transformation. The labelling algorithm is, in principle, applicable to
any other type of isomerism, for example, optical isomerism, by
consideration of three dimensional symmetry operations. We have not
carried out these extensions.

The labelling procedures can be carried out recursively for
multiple labels of the same type and various numbers of labels of
different types.[21,22] The strategy is simple. Every labelling
reduces the symmetry of the graph structure or leaves it unchanged.
After each labelling, a new symmetry group is derived from the old group
in a simple manner[21] and additional labelling is carried out under the
new group. In practice, the symmetry groups of the vertex-graphs are
recorded with the graphs in the CATALOG.

Returning to the example of Figure 3, the first graph labelling
step is to label the edges of the vertex-graphs with the partitions of

secondary nodes. This labelling can be done manually by inspection for this example, as the loops of the daisy are equivalent, as are the three edges of the trivalent graph of two nodes. Thus each partition yields only one expansion of the vertex-graph in each case. The resulting graphs are indicated for a small number of the possible partitions. Note that spiro-fused ring systems result from the daisy, while bicyclic ring systems result from the trivalent graph of two nodes. A partition (not shown) which allots all secondary nodes to one edge of this trivalent graph will yield isomers containing a double bond within the ring, as illustrated in Scheme III. This is an example of the convention alluded to previously for viewing multiple bonds as small rings.

SCHEME III

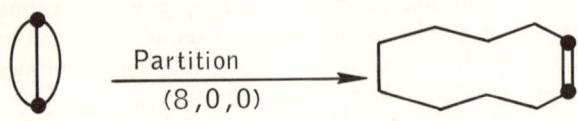

The next labelling step is to label the resulting graphs with partitions of free valence specified previously. Using the example of structure 10, Figure 3, together with the details of partition B, which state that one node must be secondary with one free valence (the single original trivalent node), seven nodes must be secondary with two free valences, and two nodes must be tertiary with one free valence, two possible labellings result, as illustrated. In a similar manner, graphs 11 and 12 are labelled with the free valence partition C, yielding in each case a single result.

The next step, labelling with atom names, is trivial in this example. The valence of each node is specified at this point and we have only one type of atom with a given valence. Thus, it is a simple matter to locate the single trivalent node in each of the illustrated structures and label it with a nitrogen atom, the rest being labelled with carbon atoms.

The acyclic generator is then utilized to generate all possible structures from the collection of ring-superatoms and the remaining pot. In the example, only a methyl radical can be constructed from a pot containing a single carbon atom. The operation of the acyclic

generator parallels the operation of the original acyclic generator.[11-13]
Differences are that the symmetries of the ring-superatoms must now be
considered, and that multiple bonds are now generated as ring-superatoms.

Performance. The numbers of isomers for some sample
compositions are presented in Table I. Particularly noteworthy from

Table I. Numbers of Isomers of Some Selected Organic Compounds.

Composition	Representative	Number of Isomers
C_6H_{14}	hexane	5
C_6H_{10}	cyclohexene	77
C_6H_6	benzene	217
$C_6H_{10}O$	cyclohexanone	747
C_6H_6O	phenol	2237

Table I is the great increase (approximately a factor of ten) in the
number of isomers when a single oxygen atom is added to the composition
lists C_6H_{10} and C_6H_6. For larger numbers of atoms the total number of
isomers may be only of academic interest. It was necessary, however,
to ensure that a complete list of isomers could in fact be generated. We
are reasonably confident of the completeness and irredundancy of the
generator and some limited tests to verify these features have been
carried out.[20] With the current state of technology, one cannot
assert that any large program, such as this, is free from errors.
Even though a formal proof of the algorithm exists[18a] we do not
guarantee the accuracy of the numbers of isomers in Table I because of
the possibility of program errors. Present work on the structure
generator is mentioned in Section 5.

3. STRUCTURE ELUCIDATION

The strategy for molecular structure elucidation is depicted in
Scheme IV. Spectroscopic, chemical and any other data are reviewed
at the Planning stage in attempts to infer the molecular formula,
compound class, functional groups and so forth. Information so
derived acts as constraints on the structure generator. Candidate
solutions from the generator are then tested with more detailed rules

SCHEME IV

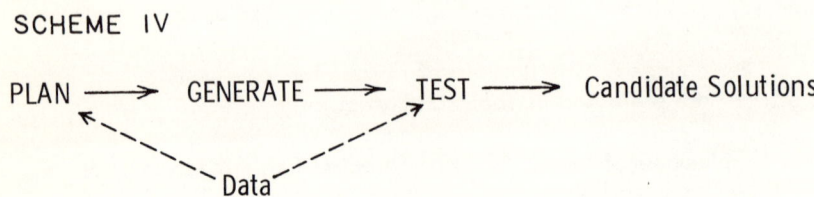

about spectrum/structure relationships for available spectral data, and solutions which meet specified criteria are ranked in order of plausibility and output. The strategy expressed in Scheme IV is completely general. In practice, however, primary emphasis has been placed on mass spectrometry as a source of structure-specific spectral information. This choice was motivated both by the specificity and sensitivity of the technique. We have attempted to maintain sufficient flexibility in our representation of structural information to permit use of a wide variety of additional data in this general scheme, and several instances are indicated in the subsequent sections.

SATURATED, ALIPHATIC, MONOFUNCTIONAL (SAM) COMPOUNDS. The strategy expressed in Scheme IV has been tested on a variety of saturated, aliphatic, monofunctional compounds, utilizing low resolution mass spectral data as the primary source of spectroscopic information. The following classes of compounds have been studied: ketones,[23] ethers[24] and amines.[25] The last study[25] also utilized some proton magnetic resonance data (PMR). A generalization of this approach including alcohols, thioethers and thiols has been presented.[26] This study[26] used a much more complex Planning section than previous work[23-25] as compound class was inferred directly from the mass spectrum. Thus the program knew at the outset only that the unknown compound belonged to the general class of SAM compounds.

Results achieved utilizing this computer based approach have been reviewed more recently.[13] Generally speaking, results were excellent and in all cases comparable to the performance of trained mass spectroscopists. It is not always possible to determine a unique solution, even with combined mass spectral and PMR data. This is best illustrated with the case of the amines[25] as different alkyl chain ends far

Saturated, Aliphatic, Monofunctional (SAM) Compounds

removed from the nitrogen atom are difficult or impossible to distinguish using these techniques. This particular problem has been solved recently through the use of C_{13} magnetic resonance data (CMR).[27, 28]

COMPLEX MOLECULES. Because structural studies on classes of complex molecules would be of greater benefit to ongoing research problems, the next class of compounds chosen for study was the class of estrogenic steroids. The performance of the program has been described in some detail.[29] High resolution mass spectrometry is utilized to specify the elemental composition of every ion in a mass spectrum to avoid the compositional ambiguities inherent in low resolution mass spectral data. Specification of the basic ring system for estrogens is required as input data. Also, all available mass spectral data are used during the Planning phase of the program (Scheme IV).

As originally conceived, Planning functions included only inference of compound class and molecular weight and formula. Predictions of the spectroscopic behavior (primarily mass spectrometric fragmentations) of candidate structures and matching predicted versus observed spectra were Test functions (Scheme IV) exercised on candidate structures from the generator.[23] This approach is efficient only if the number of candidate structures to be evaluated during Test is small. As the number becomes large, it appears that it is more efficient to incorporate some, if not all, of the spectroscopic rules during Planning rather than after structure generation. We have not attempted to quantify the difference in efficiency, but in view of the potentially huge numbers of isomers for relatively simple empirical formulae it seems clear that the generator should be constrained as severely as possible with as much structural information as can be obtained from the input data. In any case, the rules of chemical and spectroscopic behavior can in principle be used either during Planning or Testing.

A considerable amount of effort has been directed toward ensuring that the approach taken for structural analysis of complex molecules maintains the desired characteristics of flexibility and generality which have characterized earlier versions of Heuristic DENDRAL.

FLEXIBILITY AND GENERALITY. A useful program must be flexible so that the user is able to modify or extend the rules governing analysis. The program must also be general to avoid writing a new program for each new class of molecules. Flexibility and generality are maintained by requiring class specific information to be supplied as input data along with the mass spectrum. Thus, the input data consist of mass spectral data, the skeletal structure common to the class of molecules, fragmentation rules, and specific chemical rules. The program can utilize several types of mass spectral data including the high resolution mass spectrum in the form of a list of masses, elemental compositions and ion abundances, metastable ion (MI) data, low ionizing voltage (LV) data and results of isotopic exchange of labile hydrogens. MI and LV data are used to aid in determination of the molecular ion or ions. MI data are also used to establish definitive relationships between molecular and fragment ions. Isotopic exchange data yields a labile hydrogen count (-O-H,-N-H) for each molecular ion. The program carries out analysis of every molecular ion encountered and is capable of mixture analysis.[29, 30]

The molecular skeleton which is common to the class is input to the program in the form of a quasi-DENDRAL string with ring closures, if necessary, indicated as extra bonds.[29] The chemist may modify this skeleton if desired, using an extensive series of substitution functions in the form of (SUBST.....Node number) commands (see Section 4).

Fragmentation rules, which usually have been derived from empirical studies of a series of known compounds in the same class, are supplied to the program in a simple format.[29] These rules are used by the chemist to specify the structural manipulation to be performed by the program. Flexibility is important here as the chemist may wish to try different sets of fragmentation rules to optimize performance on known compounds. It is also possible to attach a weight ("break classification"[29]) to the importance of a particular fragmentation process.

Additional rules may be specified in the broad categories of chemical or natural rules. For example, a derivitization procedure may have been carried out which converts aromatic hydroxyl groups to methoxyl groups. The program will seek, if requested, structures with CH_3O- on an aromatic ring rather than HO-. This is a chemical rule. Natural rules may be based on the source of an unknown compound. Estrogenic steroids isolated from bodily fluids, for example, almost always have some oxygen functionality at C-3 and C-17. This type of rule may be used in Testing as a filter of candidate structures.[29]

The general scheme of analysis of mass spectra utilizing the above input data has been described in some detail.[29] The generality of the program has been tested and verified utilizing diverse classes of compounds such as steroids, steroidal sapogenins, alkaloids and amino acid derivatives. The features which allow this generality are described in the following section.

4. STRUCTURE MANIPULATION

One way to ensure the generality of a program, such as Heuristic DENDRAL, which requires manipulation of molecular structures is to express each type of manipulation in terms of one set of "primitive" functions. Class dependent functions are actually built up from a common set of primitives which work at the level of atoms, bonds, electrons and positive charges. Most of the primitives are completely general and would be useful, if not necessary, in other types of programs where structure manipulation is required. Similar functions have been utilized in a computer-aided synthesis program.[31]

Structure manipulation is required in every phase of Heuristic DENDRAL. For example, structures must be "built" from quasi-DENDRAL strings. Expansion of structures must be accomplished through the use of substitution functions. Fragmentation processes must be exercised at the atom/bond level along with appropriate electron bookkeeping. Descriptions of some of the primitives are presented in Tables II - IV.

SITUATION-ACTION RULES. It has proven extremely useful to place all structure manipulation procedures within a unified framework. The framework is that of situation-action rules (S-A Rules), which have been discussed in some detail[32] in the context of Meta-DENDRAL (see Section 5). Briefly, rules expressed in this form state that, "in a given situation perform the indicated action". The situation may be implicit in more general applications within this framework. For example, in analysis of the high resolution mass spectra of an estrogenic steroid, the implicit situation is the estrogen skeleton; the action is "perform fragmentations B, C, D, E and F on this skeleton".[29] At the level of primitive functions the situations and actions are usually stated explicitly. In this form they may be entered in a table of S-A rules which can be scanned by the program. Whenever a situation is true, the corresponding action is taken. If false, no action results.

Situations. Given a reasonable selection of functions for testing situations and performing actions, S-A rules of considerable complexity can be assembled and applied to structures. Some selected functions which can act as situations in the S-A formalism are presented in Table II, along with a brief description of each function.

Table II. Some Selected Functions, and Their Description, Which Act As Situations.

Function	Description
Adjacent [bond 1, bond 2]	Are bonds 1 and 2 adjacent?
Carbon [atom]	Is the atom a carbon atom?
Charged [atom]	Is the atom charged?
Double [bond]	Is the bond a double bond?
Heteroatom [atom]	Is the atom a heteroatom (N, O, ...)?
Isomorph [graph 1, graph 2]	Are graphs 1 and 2 isomorphic?
Juncture [bond]	Is the bond a ring juncture?
Poscharged [atom]	Is the atom positively charged?
Terminal [atom]	Is the atom on the terminal end of a chain?
Tertiary [atom]	Is the atom tertiary?
Vinyl [bond]	Is the bond vinylic?

There are many other functions available which determine various properties of structures. Some examples are presented in Table III, together with their descriptions. Combinations of these functions can also be used as situations in S-A rules by testing for various relationships involving these functions. For example, a true or false answer will result from the situation (Neighbors [atom 1] = Neighbors [atom 2]?).

Table III. Some Selected Functions Which Determine Properties of Structures.

Function	Description
Allbonds [atoms]	What bonds connect the atoms?
Bondorder [atom 1, atom 2]	What is the bond order between atom 1 and atom 2?
Chainlength [atoms]	What is the chainlength of the atoms?
Counthet [atoms]	How many heteroatoms among atoms?
Hydrogens [atom]	How many hydrogens on the atom?
Neighbors [atom]	What are the neighbors of the atom?
Type [atom]	What type of atom?
Weight [atoms]	What is the atomic weight of the atoms?

Actions. The functions comprising the actions in S-A rules allow modification of structures, either by fragmenting them into a number of smaller substructures, or expanding them by adding other atoms. The electron bookkeeping involved in these functions accounts only for valence electrons for much of chemistry, including mass spectrometry, does not involve inner shell electrons. Examples of selected actions are presented in Table IV.

Table IV. Actions: Structure Manipulation with Electron Bookkeeping.

Function	Description
Breakbond (atom 1, atom 2)	Remove the connection between atom 1 and atom 2, yielding two radical species.
Eliminateh (atom)	Remove a hydrogen from the atom, yielding a radical.
Losealpharad (atom)	Remove an alpha radical from an atom, yielding a radical.
Migrateh (atom 1, atom 2)	Migrate a hydrogen from atom 1 to atom 2, creating a new radical site and a new bond.
Subst (-BR, -OH, -CH$_3$, .. (atom))	Place the indicated substituent on the atom by removing a hydrogen radical and forming a new bond.

Applications. Using the above functions it is possible to carry out structure manipulations at a level sufficient to describe details of mass spectral fragmentation processes. This includes rearrangement processes, bond migrations, heterolytic and homolytic bond cleavages and charge and electron migration. Some descriptions of the use of the structure manipulation functions have been presented in the context of the Predictor[13,23] which, given a structure, predicts a mass spectrum. This prediction is carried out utilizing a suitable table of S-A rules alluded to previously in this section.

The situations in S-A rules may be of any required complexity. As an example, most available mass spectrometry rules for estrogens are used during Planning (see Section 3 and ref. 29). It is possible, however, that these rules are not strong enough to prevent several candidate solutions. It is possible in these cases to examine the candidates during Testing (Scheme IV, Section 3) with Predictor functions containing situation statements which include substituent-specific rules.

5. WORK IN PROGRESS

CONSTRAINTS ON THE CYCLIC STRUCTURE GENERATOR.
In problems of structure elucidation, one often possesses knowledge about the sample that can sharply limit the range of structures considered reasonable as inferences. This knowledge may include considerations of chemical stability, isolation or derivatization procedures, and details of molecular substructure inferred from spectroscopic techniques such as NMR and IR. The acyclic generator accepted constraints of this type in the form of GOODLIST (substructures known to be present) and BADLIST (substructures known to be absent).[15]

The principles of generation of cyclic structures have their roots in graph theory and do not parallel chemical knowledge. Thus the acyclic structure generator is less amenable to incorporation of GOODLIST and BADLIST. Presently, the generator can be constrained to produce only pure rings, or to produce only acyclic structures. There are other constraints which can be accomplished by altering the details of partitioning and labelling, and through interactive guidance. Considerable additional effort is required to exploit the analytical capabilities of the structure generator.

META-DENDRAL. The previous sections were concerned with use of rules, or heuristics, to guide DENDRAL from a set of data to plausible explanations of the data. Some of these rules are based on fundamental principles of chemistry, such as valence. Many of the rules, however, have been assembled from a long history of empirical studies of molecules. Some examples of rules in this category include our present ideas about chemical stability and reactivity. Rules concerning spectroscopic behavior of molecules have traditionally followed a pattern of empirical generalizations, perhaps eventually leading to theories which are capable of quite accurate prediction of this behavior. The Meta-DENDRAL effort is directed toward investigation of the processes by which such empirical rules and eventually theories are derived; in other words an investigation of the rule formation phase of scientific activity.[32]

Because a useful formalism for expression of rules has been developed in the form of situation-action (S/A) pairs (see Section 4), we have maintained this representation. Thus we seek to discover

conditional rules of the form S --→ A, where the situations and
actions can be described in terms of the primitive functions summarized
previously in Tables II-IV. A collection of rules in the conditional form
S--→A will be called a "theory" although this definition is oversimplified
for cases where the underlying rationale, or theory, which explains the
behavior of molecules is not explicit in the rule statements. The space
of possible theories which "explain" a set of data is the space of sets of
S--→A rules. Since this is a large space when considering the full
generality of possible situations and actions, we have, in our initial work
in the area of mass spectrometry, limited the situations and actions to be
a subset of those available. We believe that a great reduction in search
space with very little loss in generality is achieved by using situations
involving only subgraph or substituent location, and by limiting actions
to bond cleavage and hydrogen migration. It is our intention, as
further work develops, to investigate the expansion of this space.

The conceptual framework of the Meta-DENDRAL program is
illustrated in Scheme V. The actions may be regarded as the set of

Scheme V   DATA
              ↓
DATA INTERPRETATION: Generate Actions to explain data points
              ↓
       [Table of Plausible Actions]
              ↓
RULE FORMATION: Search for explanations for actions (situations)
              ↓
       [Table of Alternative Explanations]
              ↓
           THEORY FORMATION

processes which occur in an instrument ("effects"), in our case, the mass
spectrometer. The situations are descriptions of features of molecules
("causes"). We have initially focussed our attention on the techniques
of data interpretation, the first part of the overall strategy (Scheme V).
Preliminary results on rule formation have been presented.[32,34]

<u>Data Interpretation.</u> The observed data in a scientific
experiment represent the results of actions on objects. In this instance
our objects are molecules. Actions which generate the observed
spectroscopic data may range from absorption of light (e.g., UV/
visible spectrometry) to fragmentation of the molecule (mass spectrometry).

The set of actions in mass spectrometry is the set of fragmentation processes which act on a molecule.

It is, in fact, possible to generate the complete space of possible fragmentation processes (actions) and exercise the methodology of heuristic search to explore the space. The program, like the chemist, works with known molecular structures and their observed mass spectra. Because the rules of mass spectrometry are relatively class-specific, the usual approach is to examine sets of structures which are related in some way, usually by a number of structural features. Each molecule can be viewed as a different derivative of the basic "skeleton" which is comprised of these common features. A manual approach is to examine each structure/spectrum pair in turn attempting to relate observed ions in the spectrum with plausible fragmentations of the molecule. In addition to being tedious and time consuming when more than a few spectra are involved, considerable backtracking is required as each new structure/spectrum pair suggests a new mechanism which must then be "tested" on pairs examined previously. Needless to say, one quickly can become bogged down in trying to remember which molecule behaved in what way and whether or not this behavior is representative of the class.

This manual effort seemed to be ideally suited for modeling by computer techniques. We term the task, as performed by the computer program, "data interpretation". The program, in addition to searching the space of fragmentation processes for each structure/spectrum pair, performs a considerable amount of correlation and summary of the data. This provides a check on the occurrence and importance of a given fragmentation process across the entire set of molecules. The methods utilized by the program will be described in detail in a subsequent publication.[33] The three major steps of data interpretation are outlined in Scheme VI and discussed briefly below.

Scheme VI

1. Skeleton + Heuristics → ALLBREAKS/Process Generation: Space of actions (fragmentation processes).

2. Structure/Spectrum Pairs → Interpretation: Processes for which evidence can be found for each molecule.

3. Processes + Interpretation → Summary: Combined processes for all molecules.

ALLBREAKS and Process Generation. Given the basic skeleton common to the molecules under investigation, the function ALLBREAKS specifies all bonds which may be cleaved; a set of bond cleavages which results in a smaller, unique fragment is a fragmentation process. In addition to identifying fragmentations of the skeleton, fragmentations of substituents on the basic skeleton can be specified. As in the case of structure generation, there are many possibilities which are implausible. It is most efficient to remove these possibilities before or during generation of the space so that they will not be carried along in the processing only to be removed at the end. Thus a selection of heuristic limitations to the generation is provided[33] which can be used in any combination at the discretion of the chemist. Some examples include forbidding cleavage of multiple bonds or aromatic rings, cleavage of two carbon-carbon bonds to the same carbon atom and the number of hydrogen atoms which may be transferred in the fragmentation process. Like many heuristics these are judgmental rules which may not always hold true. But judgmental rules are used routinely in science and can be modified or discarded when a significant number of counter-examples are found.

Interpretation. With the space of possible processes defined, each spectrum/structure pair is examined in turn as the program seeks spectral evidence for each process. Each fragmentation process is performed on the known structure. The composition of the charged fragment is calculated and this fragment is searched for in the spectrum.

The elemental composition of an ion, as determined by high resolution mass spectrometry, does not specify the portion of the skeleton from which the fragment arose. The presence of substituents (at specific skeletal positions) which contain heteroatoms provide some clue, as many possible processes will be differentiated by the presence or absence of the substituent atoms in the observed ion. In general, however, there may be several processes which serve as explanations for an observed ion, resulting in considerable ambiguity.[33]

Summary. After all spectrum/structure pairs have been analyzed, the program performs a process-by-process summary.[33] For each process for which any evidence has been found, a list is provided indicating which of the compounds displayed evidence for the process. A complete summary of ambiguities is also provided which specifies alternative explanations for every ion. A brief manual review of this summary indicates which processes, if any, are general to the basic skeleton (evidence for the process exists in the spectrum of every compound).

Processes which are more dependent on particular substituents or their place of substitution on the skeleton are also easy to determine.

The summary quickly reveals where more work is necessary to elucidate the processes in more detail. It also provides rapid answers to the kinds of questions posed by mass spectroscopists when the spectra of several compounds are examined. Such questions have to do with how many compounds show a specified process, with or without hydrogen transfers, and to what extent; what are possible explanations for various intense peaks in a spectrum or several spectra, and so forth. The answers to any one of these questions might take many hours to determine manually with a large set of data. The computer can handle all these questions in a matter of minutes, making the data interpretation program, by itself, a useful adjunct to ongoing studies of the fragmentation of molecules.

EXTENSIONS TO THE PLANNER. We are presently extending the capabilities of the Heuristic DENDRAL program for complex molecules (the planner) in several areas. We are refining the techniques used for molecular ion determination to facilitate operation on the spectra of mixtures of compounds or of compounds which display no molecular ion. We are also extending the predictive capabilities of the planner. We can now, for example, examine candidate structures during Test (Scheme IV, above) and specify the minimum set of metastable ion determinations which would be required to differentiate among the candidates. This work is directed at "intelligent" design of experimental strategies when available data on a molecule are insufficient to determine uniquely its structure. We also plan to incorporate the cyclic structure generator into the present Heuristic DENDRAL program while making progress on implementing constraints (Section 5).

6. SUMMARY

We have described some of the philosophy of and ongoing activities within the DENDRAL project at Stanford University. We have indicated the various areas in our efforts where structure representation and manipulation are important. One of the most exciting of our recent results is the completion of the structure generator. This generator is essential for a wider application of Heuristic DENDRAL, not only including analysis of mass spectra but encompassing planning rules based on data from many different sources. This could represent the foundations for an analytical tool of broad scope.

7. ACKNOWLEDGEMENTS

The results reported here represent the fruits of a large interdisciplinary effort involving many persons in the Departments of Genetics, Computer Science and Chemistry under the leadership of Professors Lederberg, Feigenbaum and Djerassi. These people include B. G. Buchanan, R. S. Engelmore and W. C. White (Computer Science), A. M. Duffield (Genetics), and the supporting staff of Computer Science, Instrumentation Research Laboratory (Genetics) and the Mass Spectrometry Laboratory (Chemistry).

We are grateful for the generous financial assistance provided by the Advanced Research Projects Agency (SD-183) and the National Institutes of Health (RR 00612-03).

8. EXPERIMENTAL

The LISP programming language is used almost exclusively for the programs outlined in this work. This language is well-suited for our purposes because of its power and flexibility for manipulating symbolic data structures. It was initially chosen because the internal representation of acyclic structures exactly corresponds to branching graph-structures. The programs run on the Stanford University IBM 360/67. Some segments of the programs including the structure generator are available over the ARPA computer network.

REFERENCES

1) E. A. Feigenbaum, in "Information Processing 68", North Holland Publishing Co., Amsterdam, 1968.
2) A. Cayley, Ber., 8, 1056 (1875).
3) G. Polya, Helv. Chim. Acta, 19, 22 (1936).
4) T. L. Hill, J. Chem. Phys., 11, 294 (1943).
5) A. T. Balaban and F. Harary, Rev. Rumaine de Chimie, 12, 1511 (1967).
6) H. W. Hayward, Pat. Off. Res. Dev. Rep., No. 21, Patent Office, Washington, 1961.
7) G. M. Dyson, M. F. Lynch and H. L. Morgan, Inf. Stor. and Retrieval, 4, 27 (1968).
8) a) W. J. Wiswesser, "A Line-Formula Chemical Notation," T. Y. Crowell, New York, New York, 1954;

b)   E. G. Smith, "The Wiswesser Line-Formula Chemical Notation," McGraw-Hill, New York, New York, 1968.

9) a)   M. F. Lynch, Endeavour, 27, 68 (1968);
b)   W. J. Wiswesser, J. Chem. Doc., 8, 146 (1968).

10) J. B. Hendrickson, J. Amer. Chem. Soc., 93, 6847 (1971).

11) J. Lederberg, DENDRAL-64. Part I, NASA CR-57029, STAR No. N65-13158 (reprints available from Prof. J. Lederberg, Dept. of Genetics, Stanford University, Stanford, Ca. 94305).

12) J. Lederberg, "Topology of Molecules", in "The Mathematical Sciences," the MIT Press, Cambridge, Mass., 1969, p. 37.

13) B. G. Buchanan, A. M. Duffield, and A. V. Robertson, in "Mass Spectrometry: Techniques and Applications," G. W. A. Milne, ed., John Wiley and Sons, Inc., 1971, p. 121.

14) C. Jordan, Journal fur die reine und angewandte Mathematik, 70, 185 (1869).

15) J. Lederberg, G. L. Sutherland, B. G. Buchanan, E. A. Feigenbaum, A. V. Robertson, A. M. Duffield, and C. Djerassi, J. Amer. Chem. Soc., 91, 2973 (1969).

16) Y. M. Sheikh, A. Buchs, A. B. Delfino, G. Schroll, A. M. Duffield, C. Djerassi, B. G. Buchanan, G. L. Sutherland, E. A. Feigenbaum and J. Lederberg, Org. Mass Spectrom., 4, 493 (1970).

17) J. Lederberg, Am. Math. Monthly, 74, 522 (1965); J. Lederberg, DENDRAL-65, Part II, "Topology of Cyclic Graphs," NASA CR-68898, STAR No. N66-14074 (1965) (reprints available from Prof. J. Lederberg, Dept. of Genetics, Stanford University, Stanford, Ca., 94305).

18) a)   H. Brown and L. Masinter, submitted to Discrete Mathematics, 1973;
b)   L. Masinter, unpublished report, Computer Science Department, Stanford University.

19) I. Ugi, D. Marquarding, H. Klusacek, G. Gokel, and P. Gillespie, Angew.Chem. Internat. Edit., 9, 703 (1970).

20) L. Masinter, N. S. Sridharan, J. Lederberg, and D. H. Smith, J. Amer. Chem. Soc., submitted.

21) H. Brown, L. Masinter, and L. Hjelmeland, Discrete Mathematics, in press.

22) L. Masinter and N. S. Sridharan, J. Amer. Chem. Soc., submitted.

23) A. M. Duffield, A. V. Robertson, C. Djerassi, B. G. Buchanan, G. L. Sutherland, E. A. Feigenbaum, and J. Lederberg, J. Amer. Chem. Soc., 91, 2977 (1969).
24) G. Schroll, A. M. Duffield, C. Djerassi, B. G. Buchanan, G. L. Sutherland, E. A. Feigenbaum, and J. Lederberg, J. Amer. Chem. Soc., 91, 7440 (1969).
25) A. Buchs, A. M. Duffield, G. Schroll, C. Djerassi, A. B. Delfino, B. G. Buchanan, G. L. Sutherland, E. A. Feigenbaum, and J. Lederberg, J. Amer. Chem. Soc., 92, 6831 (1970).
26) A. Buchs, A. B. Delfino, A. M. Duffield, C. Djerassi, B. G. Buchanan, E. A. Feigenbaum, and J. Lederberg, Helv. Chim. Acta, 55, 1394 (1970).
27) H. Eggert and C. Djerassi, J. Amer. Chem. Soc., 95, 3710 (1973).
28) R. Carhart and C. Djerassi, submitted to J. Chem. Soc., (Perkin II).
29) D. H. Smith, B. G. Buchanan, R. S. Engelmore, A. M. Duffield, A. Yeo, E. A. Feigenbaum, and C. Djerassi, J. Amer. Chem. Soc., 94, 5962 (1972).
30) D. H. Smith, B. G. Buchanan, R. S. Engelmore, H. Adlercreutz and C. Djerassi, J. Amer. Chem. Soc., in press.
31) a) E. J. Corey and W. T. Wipke, Science, 166, 178 (1969).
    b) H. Gelernter, N. S. Sridharan, A. J. Hart, W. F. Fowler and H. J. Shue, Fortschr. Chem. Forsch., 1973, in press.
32) B. G. Buchanan, E. A. Feigenbaum and N. S. Sridharan, in "Machine Intelligence 7", Edinburgh University Press, 1972, p. 267.
33) D. H. Smith, B. G. Buchanan, W. C. White, E. A. Feigenbaum, J. Lederberg, and C. Djerassi, Tetrahedron, in press.
34) B. G. Buchanan and N. S. Sridharan, presented at the Third International Joint Conference on Artificial Intelligence, Stanford University, Stanford, California, Aug. 1973.

DETAILS OF GRAPHICS EQUIPMENT AND TRANS-ATLANTIC COMMUNICATIONS
USED IN DEMONSTRATION AT THE NATO-ASI IN HOLLAND

The NATO-ASI included a number of workshops and demonstrations associated with the projects described in this book. Many of the speakers have developed chemical information systems which are implemented on the computers in their respective institutions. Terminal equipment was borrowed from a number of manufacturers and a room was set aside at the ASI for the equipment and demonstrations (the gadgeteria). The purpose of the appendix is to give a description of the various pieces of equipment and how they were used.

Computer demonstrations can be given by connecting a terminal to a computer by means of dial-up telephone lines. When short distances are involved the telephone connection between the terminal and the computer presents no problem. E. Hyde and S. R. Heller communicated between Noordwijkerhout and Den Haag using both acoustic and conventional modems. If however the telephone lines go across national boundaries or across the Atlantic Ocean difficulties can be expected. A major difficulty lies in the differing standards which are used for data transmission. Each national telephone administration has different rules regarding the use of the modems which interface the terminal and the computer. The international standard for data communication (CCITT v21 - 300 baud full duplex) is different from the standard used in the United States. The mark-space frequencies are different, making it impossible to directly communicate to U.S. equipment using European couplers, yet U.S. couplers are not allowed in many parts of Europe. The organizers of the meeting invited two trans-Atlantic communications vendors to assist in the preparation of the communication equipment between the Netherlands and the United States, RCA-GLOBCOM and Western Union. Both installed modems in the demonstration area. RCA-GLOBCOM chose to use the American standard of data transmission for the entire route. Western Union chose to use the international standard of data transmission from the Netherlands to New York and the American standard from New York to the various computers in Maryland. New Jersey, Pennsylvania and California. Western Union's approach using the international standard in Europe and across the Atlantic seemed to achieve more consistent data transmission quality with very little noise or disconnection trouble. The Western Union Datel cables across the Atlantic were used. These lines have no echo suppression and are generally high grade lines. Normal direct dialed voice grade lines give trouble because echo suppressors cut off parts of transmission and one observes noise in the full duplex mode. A further advantage of the Western Union arrangement with back-to-back couplers in New York is that the signal level can be amplified by the repeater unit. This allows compensation for the loss over the trans-Atlantic cable, whereas a direct dialed line has no opportunity for amplification. The quality (cost) of the modems themselves is also an important determinant in the quality of data transmission. The trans-Atlantic communications were also affected by the density of traffic as a function of the time of day. Some sessions were without any data errors at all, while other sessions were plagued by many errors and/or line disconnections. In the graphics demonstrations the data errors turn up as vectors starting or stopping in unexpected places.

The cost of the trans-Atlantic telephone communications is on the order of \$240/hour, and is consequently a very strong deterrent to further use of chemical information systems by scientists on opposite sides of the Atlantic. It was in this respect that the advantages of computer networks were most apparent. The General Electric Computer network which was represented in the Netherlands by Honneywell-Bull makes it possible to use information systems without regard for the distance separating the user and the computer. There is however a 50-60% surcharge to use the GE system from Europe. One is currently limited to programs of no more than 16 K words by day and 32 K words by night on the GE system. S. R. Heller demonstrated the Aldermaston-NIH mass spectrum search and retrieval system by accessing the GE network in Den Haag. The program and data files reside in the GE computer center in Cleveland, Ohio. The representative of Zeta Research showed the graphic capabilities of a remote plotter by accessing the GE network in the same manner. The programs however which were used in this demonstration were in another GE computer center in Palo Alto, California. Networking has a strong evolutionary advantage over individual use of dial-up telephone lines. The network provides a mechanism for sharing the cost of data transmission over a population of users. Gradual expansion of networks in both the commercial and government sectors will make it possible for scientists to use chemical information systems without regard for physical distance.

Two types of terminals were available for demonstration--graphic and non-graphic. The non-graphic terminals supplied by Texas instruments (TI) and International Computers Limited (ICL) are capable of operating at 10 or 30 characters per second. E. Hyde used these terminals to communicate with an ICL computer located in Den Haag. The ICI reaction file and retrieval program was transferred from a Burroughs B3500 in Macclesfield, England. This was possible because the programs were coded in COBOL which is highly machine independent. P. Jurs used these terminals to communicate with an IBM 360/65 at State College,

Pennsylvania. Jurs demonstrated his mass spec analysis program.
    The graphics terminals consisted of a Tektronix T-4010 and a Digital Equipment Corp (DEC) GT-40. These graphics terminals were used to communicate with the Princeton and NIH PDP-10's. Although the graphics terminals are capable of utilizing data transmission rate of up to 960 characters per second, the trans-Atlantic telephone data transmission rate was limited to 30 characters per second. R. Feldmann used the T-4010 to demonstrate the interactive input of chemical structure queries, the search for structure classes and the display of search results as two and three dimensional structure diagrams. T. Wipke used the GT-40 with light pen to demonstrate the chemical synthesis program (SECS) which he and his group had developed. The light pen was used to input structures in two dimensions, to select control buttons and to select portions of the synthesis tree for further evaluation. Models were then built and displayed in three dimensions. Smooth rotation of the structures in three dimensions was achieved by transmitting successively rotated frames to the GT40 for local storage and then rapidly posting on the screen each frame in turn. Rotation is then rapid because one is only transmitting the posting command rather than the entire structure for each frame.
    The Digital Equipment Corp (DEC) made a PDP-12 computer available to G. Marshall for demonstration of the CHEMAST system. The PDP-12 is a stand-alone laboratory computer with a point plotting graphics capability. Marshall showed that the manipulation of small molecules by graphical techniques can be effectively accomplished without the help of a large computer. Also using a stand-alone equipment, W. Nubling demonstrated the search of a small reaction file using a simple card sorter.
    The longest distance demonstration was by D. Smith of the DENDRAL cyclic structure generator using an IBM 360/67 at SRI in Palo Alto, over the ARPA network through the node at MITRE Corporation via Bell Telephone to New York, and Western Union through London, and the Dutch PTT to Noordwijkerhout.
    We believe the considerable work expended to demonstrate programs rather than just describe them was worth the effort, for it convincingly illustrated the state of the art to the NATO ASI participants. A demonstration is to interactive computer applications in chemistry as an elemental analysis is to synthetic organic chemistry.

Index

13C NMR, 303
3-Bromocyclohexane, 19
AB initio chemical transform, 164
Abapmacro, 27, 28
Abbreviated mass spectrum, 177, 179
Accession number, 5
Acoustic tablet, three dimensional, 149, 152
Actual fragment overlap, 38
Acyalic structure generation, 288
Acyclic structure generator, 290
Addition, stereospecific 169
Additional data file, 28
Additions to multiple bonds, 137
Alchem, 165
Alchem statement evaluation, 167
Alcohols, mass spectra, 302
Aldrich Chemical Company files, 6
All breaks, 311
Amines, mass spectra, 302
Amino acid residues, 211, 222
Analysis of mass spectra, 304
Analysis, confirmational, 203
    conformational, 234
AND, 117
Angles, spherical polar, 206
Animation, 226
Anteriology, 256
Antithetic direction, 148
ARPA network, 313
Artificial intelligence, 287
ASCII data, 187
ASI, 145
Associative memory, 77
Asymmetric carbon atoms, perception of, 156
Atom centered fragment retrieval, 63
Atom centered fragments, 33
Atom connectivity, 7
Atom connectivity table, 3, 4, 8
Atom distances, 121
Atom groups, constitutionally equivalent, 135
Atom nature (DNA), 247
Atom nature (NA), 249
Atom sets, 157
Atom table, 154
Atom type, 214
Atom, first, 205, 206
Atom-by-atom search, 12
Atomic sequence idices (ASI), 135
Atoms, dummy, 115
  uniquely ordered, 135

Attribute list of atoms, 205
Augmented atoms, 33
Augmented pair types, 36
Automated structure elucidation, 288
Axial-equatorial relationships, 164

Badlist, 308
Badness indicators, 141
Bassmacro, 27, 28
Bayes rule, 267
Be-matrices, 131, 133, 134
  atomic sequential indexing of, 135
  block form, 131
  canonical indices, 132
  diagonal entries, 133
  example of sequential indexing, 136
  row/column permutation, 132
  row/column permutations, 131
  row/column sums, 131
  unacceptable, 138
Be-matrix, 145
  sequential indexing of, 136
Be-matrices, cross-sums, 131
Beson, 229
Binary data, 187
Binary matrix, 47
Binary pattern classifiers (BPC), 265
Binary vector, 48
Biological activity, 28
Biological tests, 16
Biology, 2
Bit fragment screen, 8
Bit strings, 117
Black graph, 240, 254
Bond angle, 224
Bond angles, 121, 152, 222
Bond centered fragments, 35
Bond classification, 23
Bond descriptor, 24
Bond energies, 141
Bond length, 224
Bond lengths, 152, 222
Bond multiplicity (DLI), 247
Bond nature (LI), 247
Bond sets, 158
Bond table, 155
Bond value, 113
Bond values, 116
Bonded atoms, 33
Bonding, hydrogen, 207
Bonds, breakable, 137
  made covalent, 132

320

INDEX 321

ring closure, 205
 types of, 113
Bong value, 113
Boolean and, 187
Bornylchloride, 137
BPC (Binary Pattern Classifier), 265
BRAD, 228
Browsing, 16
BUMP check, 211
By-products, 130
Byproduct, 19

Calcomp plotter, 185
Cambridge crystal file, 78
Candidate structures, 304
Canonical name, 160
Canonical renumbering, 69
Capabilities, list handling, 134
Cas structure registry file, 61
CBAC, 77, 259
CBAC (Chemical biological activities), 258
CCITT, 317
Coordinate transformation, 224
Cells, 187, 187, 189
Central processor, 216
Central search facility, 191
CG/MS, 175
Change the conformation of a molecule, 207
Character search data, 186
Character string, 222
Characteristic records of chemical informati, 31
Charge copled memory, 77
CHEMAST, 204, 211, 214, 228, 318
 keyboard operators of, 208
Chemgen, 204, 207, 214
Chemgraf, 229
Chemical abstracts service, 33, 61, 94
Chemical fragments, 204
Chemical ionization (CI), 180
Chemical profile terms, 50
Chemical reaction data base, 40
Chemical reaction documentation service, 100
Chemical reaction index, 18
Chemical reaction, coding of, 18
Chemical reactions, 130, 132
Chemical structure data bases, 33
Chemical structure representation, 3, 55
Chemical titles, 43
Chemical transform representation, 164
Chemical transformations, 92
Chemical typewriters, 106
Chemistry, closed shell, 133
 radical, 134
Chemlim, 145
Chemtest, 229
Chromatic graph (G(X)), 240
Chromatism, 240
CICLOPS, 145
 basic design, 139
 general features, 133
CICLOPS flowchart, 143
CIS (Chemical information system), 175
Classification, 192

Classification scheme, 23
Classifier in pattern recognition, 266
Classsify reactions, 17
Clinical history, 2
Cluster, 268
Cluster analysis, 176, 191, 192, 192, 193, 195, 199
Clusters, 197
CMR, 303
Coding, erroneous question, 120
 query, 115
 topological, 110
Collision, 187
Column vector, 120
COM (Computer output Microfiche), 185
Combined mass spec searchs, 182
Committee machine, 270, 271
Common data base, 33
Comparison of structure modeling systems, 216
Compound availability, 6
Compound file, 2
Compound information, 21
Compound oriented indexing methods, 91
Compound oriented reaction indexing methods, 94
Computer modeling, 203
Computer Output Microfiche (COM), 185
Computer-assisted synthetic analysis, 147
Concentric organization, 244
Configuration perception, 156
Conformation, 121
Conformation manipulation, 163
Conformational analysis, 203, 234
Conformational isomers, 162
Congestion, steric, 164
Connection table, 4, 9, 13, 27, 56, 113
 in SECS, 154
Connection table symbol dictionary, 29
Connection tables, 11, 22
Connectivity isomers, 299
Connectivity matrix, 111, 242
Connectivity table, 207
Constitutional isomers, 162
Constitutional synthesis, 148
Constitutional synthetic pathway, 130
Contours, display, 211
Convergence rate, 272
Coordinate data, 222
Coordinated atoms, 33
Coordinates, rectangular, 206
 transformation of, 205
Core memory requirements, 216
Cram's rule, 90
Crossbow, 4, 9, 21, 26
Crossbow connection table, 10
Crystal structure file, 78
Crystallography, 203, 214, 228
Crystallogrpahy, 232
Crystallogryahy, 231
Current abstracts of chemistry, 41
Cyclic structure generator, 287, 308
Cyclisations, 23
Cyclohexane, 19
Cystic strucutre generator, 290

322 INDEX

DARC, 239
Data correlation, 16
Data interpretation, 309
Data representation, 186
Data structure heirarchy, 154
Data structure, of synthesis tree, 169
Data structures, 134
Data, bibliographic, 21, 27
  biological, 5
  chemical, 5
  clinical, 5
  conditions, 27
  redundat, 118
  toxicology, 5
DCI (Bond Multiplicity), 247
DCRT/CIS, 59, 231
Deadzone (Z), 269
Dearch, of text, 27
DEC GT-40, 318
Decision surfaces, 268, 269
Defined groups, 222
DEL (Limited Environment Description), 242
DEL(H), 251
Dendral, 287
Dendral notation, 289
Dense clusters, 193
Description of reactions, 94
Design of fragmentation codes, 32
Detection in pattern recognition, 265
Detection of stereocenters, 161
DEX (Topology), 247
Dial-up telephone line, 317
Diasteriomers, 162
Differential description of characteristics, 31
Digital equipment GT40 graphics terminal, 150
Digram, 44
Dihedral angles, 152
Direct access storage device, 55
Direct substitution, 88
Discriminant function, 270
Disk block, 186
Disk head motion, 76
Disk latency, 76
Display, 13
Display contours, 211
Display molecule, 211
Display of double bonds, 171
Display of mass spectra, 185
Display, input phase of SECS, 150
  processing phase of SECS, 151
  synthetic tree of SECS, 151
Dissimilarity Index (DI), 184
Distribution of reaction types, 41
DNA (Atom Nature), 247
Double bond configuration, display, 171
Double bond, addition to, stereospecific, 169
  formation of, 169
Drectangular coordinates, 222
Drug design, 203, 234
Drug synthesis, 147
DST (Stereochemistry Descriptor), 250
DTABLE, connection, 113

Dummy atoms, 115
Dynamic reaction process, 84

E(Environment), 241
Economy of transmission, 31
Efficient reaction indexing, 90
EI mass spectra, 176
ELCO (Ordered Concentric Limited Environment), 240
Electron density, 235
Electron density contours, 214
Electron density fitting, 224
Electron pushing instruction, 132
Electrophilic attack, 93
Element, 117
Elimination, stereospecific, 169
EM, 145
Enantiomers, 162
End product, 86
Energy minimization, 224
Ensemble of starting material molecules EMA, 130
Environment of transform, 166
Epoxide opening, 166
Equivalence classes, 135
Error reducing, 115
Esterification reaction, 93
Ethers, mass spectra, 302
Evaluation criteria, 149
Evaluation of Be-matrices, 141
Evaluation of structures, 168
Evaluation of synthetic pathways, 141
Evans and Sutherland LDS-1 graphics system, 149
EXACH search, 66
EXACT substituent pattern, 66
Existing reaction indexing systems, 93
Experimental reaction conditions, 87
Eyring, 207

F(ordering function), 245
Feature extractor, 266
Feature selection, 280
Feedback, 271, 277
Field desorption (FD), 180
Field Ionization (FI), 180
FIEM, 130, 145
File generation flow, 72
File organisation, 26
File organization, 32, 68
Files, chemical structure, 2
  personalized, 2
  property data, 3
Final product, 86
Findmacro, 27, 28
First atom, 205, 206, 207, 214
Fixed length record, 6
FO (FOCUS), 240
FOCUS (FO), 241
Formula reader, photcell, 107
Formula reading machine, 108
Formula, line printed, 119
Fortran, 226, 228
Fragment code, 4
Fragment descriptors, 273, 274

INDEX 323

Fragment independence, 37
Fragment performance, 37
Fragment splitting, 168
Fragmentation, 305, 311
Fragmentation code, 83
Fragmentation codes, 3
Fragmentation coding, 273
Fragmentation rules, 304
Fragments, 25, 26, 27, 28
Fragments, chemical, 204
Free Valence (FV), 297
Frel (Limited Environment Fragment), 253
Functional group data structure, 160
Functional group numbering, 160
Functional group origin, 160
Functional group reactivities, 148
Functional group transformations, 23
Functions, of sets, 159
FV, 298
FV (Free Valence), 297
G(X) (Chromatic Graph), 242
G(XO) (Chromatic Graph), 242
Gas Chromatography/Mass Spectrometry (GS/MS), 175
GE Network, 192, 318
GE-635, 186
Generation automata, 242
Generation of stereo pairs, 209
Generation of structureal diagrams, 171
Geometry group, 205
Geometry of disk storage device, 47
GIBBS, 207
GIGL, 231
Goodlist, 308
Graph generator, 301
Graph labelling, 298
Graph theory, 193
Graphics terminal, 216
Graphics, molecular, 204
Graphs, 195, 290, 299
Gremas, 35, 95, 112, 113, 121
Gremas search program, 109
Gremas system, 108
Grid sheet, 114, 115, 120
Grignard reaction, 163
Grip, 230
Group, geometry, 205
GT-40, 185
GT40 graphics terminal, use with SECS, 149

Hansch data base, 6
Hardware matrix multiplier, 211
Hardware, graphics, 222
Hash coding, 187
Heterocyclic chemistry, 167
Heuristic dendral, 287
Heuristic search paradigm, 288
Hierarchical structure decomposition, 71
High resolution mass spectra, 176
Honeywell network, 192
Honeywell-Bull, 318
How many lists, 205, 206, 207, 214
HS (Hyperstructures), 248
Hydrogen bonding, 207
Hyperbolic distribution, 31

Hyperplane decision surface, 268
Hyperspace (High Dimesnional Space), 267
Hyperstructure, 258
Hyperstructures, 255, 256
Hyperstructures (HS), 247

IBM 360/91, 134
ICIFWADDT, 27
ICIFWPROD, 26
ICIFWREACTN, 26
ICL 1800, 318
IDC file, 106
Identical structures, recognizing, 162
Imbedded molecular formula search, 182
Imbedment search, 64
Implicit hydrogens, in stereochemistry, 155
Index chemicus, 41
Index chemicus registry system, 6
Indirect methods, 88
Information needs for synthesis, 154
Information theory, 31
Input device, 221
Input of structure for synthesis, 149
Input phase display, of SECS, 150
Input, topological, 205
Integerated structure-text searching, 51
Intensity compression, 177
Interactive formulation of structure queries, 60
Interactive graphics, 232
Interactive retrieval, 178
Interactive structure input, 56
Interactive structure search, 60
Interactive system, in synthesis, 149
International computer network, 192
Interpreter, alchem, 166
Inversion of stereocenter, 169
Invert command, 170
Ion series, 177
Irradiation, 87
Isomeric hyperstructures, 256
Isomerison, 299
Iterative path finding, 113
IUPAC, 57
IUPAC notation, 65

Kendal's coefficient, 37
Ketone reduction, steric effects, 164
Ketones, mass spectra, 302
Key set, 46
Key set size, 50
Keyboard operators of chemast, 208
Keys, 1

Labelling of graphs, 298, 299, 300
Laser storage technology, 77
Learning machine, 272, 318
Learning machines, 265, 267
Level of description, 38
Lhasa synthesis program, 148
LI (Bond Nature), 247
Library Lookup of molecules, 135
Library searching of mass spectra, 176
Light pen, 149
LILNE generator, 214

324   INDEX

Limitations of Interactive structure search, 75
Limited Environment Description (DEL), 242
Limited Environment Fragment (FREL), 253
Line generator, 211
Linear notation, 83
LISP, 313
List notation, for functional groups, 160
List notation, for rings, 159
Lists, how many, 206
Literature reference for reactions, 152
Local frame, 206
Logic centered approach, 148
Logic column, 117
Logical operators, 117
Low ionizing Voltage (LV), 304
Low resolution mass spectra, 265

Machine cost, 105
Macromodular memory, 211
Macromolecular modeling system, 210
Macromolecular modelling system, 212
Magnetic domain memory, 77
Magnetic tape storage, 55
Main matirx, 113
Main matrix, 112, 115, 120, 121
Majority rule, 270
Manipulation of stereochemistry, 169
Manipulation statement, 167
Manual file, 83
Manual reaction index, 23
Manual sub-file, 16
Manually assigned reaction descriptor, 23
Mapping of document identification, 47
Mapping transform, 166
Markush formulas, 105, 106, 109, 113, 115
Masks, 117
Mass SPEC Data Centre (MSDC), 192
Mass spectra, 302
Mass spectra of hydrocarbons, 272, 273
Mass spectrometry, 175, 310
Matching atom numbers, 111
Matrices, transformation, 207
Matrix multiplier, hardware, 211
Matrix multiplier, 214
Matrix output, 197
Matrix, connectivity, 111, 112
   T, 207
   upper triangular packed bond, 134
Memory, macromodular, 211
Menu, 226
Meta-Dendral, 308, 309
Metastable Ions (MI), 304
Microfiche, 185
Microstructure of records, 31
Mill hill, 230
Mini-computer, 189
Minimal spanning Tree (MST) clustering, 193
Minimum path, 195, 196
MMS, 230
MMS awaresystems and Stanford, 231
Model tracing, 153

Model, mathematical, 133
   sequence of the protein, 211
   three-dimensional, 152, 163
Molecular biophysics, 230
Molecular formula, 6, 9, 26, 27, 187
Molecular formula retrieval, 62
Molecular formula search, 182
Molecular fragments, 135
Molecular graphics, 204
Molecular model building, 152, 163
Molecular orbital, 203
Molecular orbital calculations, 203
Molecular property retrieval, 67
Molecular weight search, 180
Molecule weighting, 141
Molecule, display, 211
   sequentially ordered, 137
Molgraph, 204
Morgan algorithm, 59
Morgan name, 161
Morphine, 163
MSDC (Mass SPEC Data Centre), 191
MST Clustering, 193
Multi-levalsearch facilityx, 7
Multidisciplinary files, 2
Multiplicities, stereochemical, 170

N-bromo succinimide, 19
NA (Atom Nature), 247
Naming algorithm, stereochemically unique, 160
Neighbor weight vector (NWV), 135
Nested ring retrieval, 65
Nitration reaction, 92
NLM (Non-Linear Mapping), 193
NODES, 291, 292
Nomenclature file, 77
Non-Linear Mapping (NLM), 193
Non-Supervised Learning, 192, 193
Nonparametric discriminat functions, 267
Nonparametric methods, 266
NOT, 117
Novelty checking, 2
Nucleophilic substitution, 92
Numbering of atoms of a group, 205
Numeric key-value, 187, 189
Numeric search data, 186
NWV, 145

OCSS, 228
OCSS synthesis program, 148
Octuplets, 35
Omnigraph, 57
On-line evaluation, 17
On-line input, 106
On-line interaction, 226
On-line techniques, 1
Operators, logical, 117
OR, 117
Ordered Concentric Limited Environment (ELCO), 240
Ordered generation series, 244
Ordered-list notation for stereochemistry, 155
Ordering Function (F), 245

INDEX 325

Organic chemistry, 83
Organic synthesis design, 203
Organization of structure search, 72
Orientation (IN DARC), 249
Origin atom group, 205
Origin, of functional group, 160
Output device, 221
Overflow File, 6, 110

Packed matrix, 134
Pair Types, 35
Paradigm, 288
Parameters, ring, 113
Parametric discriminat functions, 267
Parametric methods, 266
Parities, stereochemical, 161
Partition, 298, 300
Partitioning of structure, 295
Patchouli alchol, sema numbering, 160
Path finding, iterative, 113
Pattern of hetero atoms, 65
Pattern of substituents, 65
Pattern recognition, 191
Pattern Recognition (PR), 265
Pattern vector, 267, 273
PDP-10, 56, 186, 318
PDP-10 computer, use by SECS, 152
PDP-12, 318
Peak SEARCH, 179
Pentagram, 44
Percept in pattern recognition, 265
Perception of stereochemistry, 155
Permuted index, 7
Personalised files, 2
Photocell formula reader, 107
Photocells, 106
Photothyristors, 108
Physical properties – Dato on yield, 21
Physical properties – Pressure, 21
Physical properties – Temperature, 21
Physical properties – Time, 21
Physical property, 2
PL/1, 134
PMR, 302
Pointer file, 186, 187, 189
Polyvision, 247
Portable terminals, 152
Potential energy calculations, 207
Potential fragment overlap, 38
PR (Pattern Recognition), 265
Pre-classification, 192
Precursor generation, 166
Precursor, synthetic, 133
Prediction, 272
Predictive set, 272
Preliminary screen, 7
Preprocessing data, 266
Presorting, 76
Primary chromatism, 240, 249
Priority rating of transform, 166
Probable ring size, 57
Processing phase display, SECS, 151
Product, 27
Products, 26
Profile logic, 50

Project mac, 228
Property data files, 5
Property, biological, 16
 chemical, 16
 medical, 16
 Phiysical, 16
 Toxicological, 16
Prophet, 231
Prostaglandins, 172
Proximity relationships, 163
Pseudo-element, 117
Pseudo-element symbols, 115
Pseuso-elemnt symbols, 116

Q-mode clustering, 193
Query coding, 115
Query Encoding, 36
Question encoding, 117
Question form, 117, 118
Question, sample, 116
Questions, involving acyclic units, 14
 involving rings, 14

R-matrices, 131, 133, 134, 139
 by addition, 132
 diagonal entries, 132
 example of, 132
 sum of, 132
R-MATRIX, 138, 145
 general types, 137
R-matrixes, off-diagonal entries, 132
RCA-Globcom, 317
Reacstion condition data, solvents, 21
Reactant, 18, 19, 22, 26, 27
 distinction between reagents, 18
Reactat, 21
Reaction analysis, 17
Reaction centers, 94
Reaction centre analysis, 25
Reaction centre coding, 25
Reaction centre descriptions, 22
Reaction code, 90, 96
Reaction condition data, Catlysts, 21
 physical properties, 21
 reagents, 21
Reaction conditions, 18, 87, 167
Reaction data base, 18
Reaction documentation, 83
Reaction file, 83, 318
Reaction index, 21, 22, 26
Reaction indexing, 90
Reaction matrix generation, 137
Reaction mechanisms, 3, 90
Reaction product, 96
Reaction products, 18
Reaction representation, 164
Reaction scheme, 41
Reaction sequences, 164
Reaction site analysis, 22
Reaction site classification, 23
Reaction type, 87
Reaction weight, 141
Reaction, condition data, 21
 multistage, 21
Reactive sites, 95

Reagent, 18, 21
  availability, 18
  cost, 18
Recognition, 272
Recognition in pattern recognition, 265
Record descriptions, 3
Rectangular coordinates, 206
Redundant data, 118
Reference file, 186, 189
Reference, literature, 152
Registry number, 62
Registry retrieval, 67
Regmaster, 33
Remote operation, of SECS by telephone, 152
Resonance structures, 135
Retrieval information on reactions, 83
Retrieval of chemical reactions, 40
Retrieval of specific compounds, 6
Retrospective search, 2
Richter-ordered molecular formula, 21
Ring analysis, 37
Ring centered fragments, 35
Ring classification, 23, 24
Ring closure bonds, 205, 207
Ring decomposition, 71
Ring nucleus, 65
Ring parameters, 113
Ring sets, 158
Ring system, 11, 24
Ring systems, 14
Ring value, 113
Ring, data structure, 159
Rotation, 224
Rotation about a bond, 205
Rotation and perspective hardware, 152
Roussel-UCLAF, 23
Rules for coding reaction, 19
Run length encoding, 50

S(Structures in Darc), 248
S-A Rules (Situation – Action Rules), 305
SA Rules, 306, 307, 309
SAM (Saturated, Aliphatic, Macrofunctional), 302
Sarett, Lewis, 147
Saturated Aliphatic Monsfunctional (SAM) COM, 302
Scalilng and clipping, 226
Screen generation, 36
Screen set evaluation, 37
Search algorithmn, 186
Search commands, 56
Search logic, 8, 9
Search strategy, 113
Search structure, 111
SEARCH, atom-by-atom, 9, 11, 12, 27, 28
  atom-by-atom example, 13
  bit fragment, 7
  example, 28
  example of, 13
  fragment, 11
  multi-leval, 12
  retrospective, 2
  string, 8, 14

  sub-structure, 1
  substructure, 7
  text, 21
  topological, 105
Searchable levels, 71
Searching methods, 55
Searching, structure driven, 167
Secondary chromatism, 240, 249
SECS, 230, 318
SECS synthesis program, 148
SECS, block diagram, 153
  example of synthesis generated, 172
  input phase display, 150
  organization, 152
  processing phase display, 151
  users view, 149
Selection of breakable bonds, 135
Selection rules, 137, 138
Selective reactions, 89
Selective reagent, 89
Selective transformations, 89
Selectivity, 89
SEMA, stereochemically extended morgan name, 161
Semiconductor storage technology, 78
Sequence of hetero atoms, 65
Sequence of numbering, 117
Sequence of the protein model, 211
Sequential accessability, 55
Sequential search, 177
Set functions, 159
Set reduction method, 113
Sets as a data structure, 157
Sets, atom, 157
  bond, 158
  example of use, 159
  ring, 158
  use in alchem, 168
Shortest Spanning Path (SSP), 195, 196
Similarity index, 177
Simple pairs, 36
Single step mechanistic alternatives, 133
Situation-Action (SA) Rules, 305
Spanning path, 195
Spatialization process, 59
Special graphics hardware, 222
Spectrum of search specificity, 64
Spectrum printout, 184
Sphere neighbor, 135
Spherical polar angles, 206
SS(Substructures in Darc), 247
SSP, 197, 199
SSP (Shortest Spanning Path), 195, 196
Stanford Research Institute, 56
Starting material library, 141
Starting material list, 130
Starting Materials, 18
Starting product, 86
Static fragmentation, 240
Statistical association, 37
Statistical Association between fragments, 32
Steinrauf, 231
Stereo capability, 221
Stereo information, 11

INDEX 327

Stereo pairs, generation of, 209
Stereobond, 157
Stereoceneter detection, 161
Stereocenter, inversion of, 169
Stereocenters, double bond, 155
Stereochemical descriptor, 161
Stereochemical multiplicities, 170
Stereochemical specification, 151
Stereochemical synthetic pathway, 130
Stereochemistry descripto (DST), 250
Stereochemistry, in synthesis, 148
Stereochemistry, representation, 155
Stereoisomers, 162
Steric environment, 148
Steric hindrance, 163, 224
Steric interaction, 209
Stirs, 177
Strategic bond, 162
String search, 8, 9, 11
Structural changes, 94
Structural diagram input, in SECS, 153
Structural diagram, generation of stereo-chem, 171
  output on teletype, 153
Structural diagrams, 29
Structural formula reconstruction, 120
Structural input, for synthesis, 149
Structural representation, connection table, 154
Structure block, 168
  relationships, 169
Structure decomposition, 71
Structure display, 7
Structure driven search, 167
Structure elucidation, 301
Structure encoding, 91
Structure evaluation, 168
Structure generation, 288
Structure generator, 294, 296
Structure indexing, 90
Structure input commands, 56
Structure manipulation, 2
Structure modeling systems comparison, 216
Structure output, 13
Structure query, 55
Structure registry file, 61
Structure retrieval, 55
Structure search systems, 55
Structure yield, 75
Structure, manipulation of, 207
Structure/activity relationships, 3
Strucutre manipulation, 305
Stucture display, 204
Substructure classification, 2
Substructure descriptors, 275, 276
Substructure search, 7, 27
  on product, 26
  on reactant, 26
Substructure searching, 90
Substructure, requirement of transform, 166
Sulfur classification, 199
Sulfur clusters, 197
Superatom, 292

Superatompots, 292
Superimposed bit screen, 109
Supertatom, 297
Supervised learning, 192
Suprafacial course, 170
Sussenguth, 113, 122
Symbolic configuration, 156
Symbolic stereochemistry, 169
Symbols, pseudo-element, 115
Symmetry, recognizing molecular, 162
Syncom, alchem compiler, 165
Syndthetic pathways, search for, 133
Syntex, 229
Synthesis, 130, 139
Synthesis tree, 140
Synthesis tree data structure, 169
Synthesis tree generation, 142
Synthesis tree structure, 142
Synthesis, decision processes in, 21
Synthetic analysis, conformation dependent, 163
  from secs, 172
  tree-dimensional, 147
Synthetic precursor evaluation, 152
Synthetic problems, classes of, 147
Synthetic tree display, 151
Synthetic tree, rerooting, 152
Synthsis, design of organic, 203
System design, 1

T matrix, 207
Tautomerism, 113
Tektronix 4010, 185
Tektronix T-4010, 317
Terminal, graphics, 216
Tetragram, 44
Texas instruments S-700, 318
Textual data bases, 43
Thermal printing terminal, 152
Thioethers, mass spectra, 302
Thiols, mass spectra, 302
Three dimensional graphics, 231
Three-dimensional drawing, 153
Threshold Logic Unit (TLU), 265
Time Limits, 133
Timesharing computer, 192
Timesharing computers, 186
TLU, 269, 270, 271, 272, 277
TLU (Threshold Logic Unit), 265, 267
Topoclogical superimposed Bit screen, 109
Topography preservation, 120
Topological coding, 83, 110
Topological comparison, 109
Topological connectivity matrix, 112
Topological encoding, 105
Topological input, 205
Topological Query Language (TQL), 262
Topological Screen System (TSS) of DARC, 254
Topological search, 105, 116, 121
  cost of, 108
Topology (DEX), 247
Toxicology, 2
TQL (Topological Query Language), 262
Tracking cross, 149

328   INDEX

Training, 271
Training committee machines, 280
Training set, 270
Trans-Atlantic, 317
Transacetalization reaction, 92, 95
Transducers in pattern recognition, 266
Transform driven search, 167
Transform library, 165
Transform selection, 166
Transform, chemical, 164
 contents of, 165
 example of, 166
Transformation matrices, 207
Transformation of the coordinates, 205
Transformation oriented indexing methods, 91
Transforming data, 266
Tree data structure, 169
Tree graph, 290
Trigram, 44
TSS, 262
TSS (Topological Screen system of darc), 254
Two-dimensional structure diagram, 13
Typewriters, Chemical, 106

Unambiguous Wedged/Hashed Representation, 156
Unique description, 5
Unique name, stereochemical algorithm, 160

Valence bond analysis, 138
Valence electrons, 131
Value, bond, 113

ring, 113, 113
Variety generator, 45
Variety generator methods, 51
Vector of atomic numbers, 134
Vector of unshared valence electron pairs, 134
Vertex graphs, 298, 299
Vertex-graph, 293
Vertex-graphs, 291, 292
Video display, 120

Wagner-Meerwein rearrangement, 137
Weight vector, 271, 272
Weight vectors, 268, 280
Western union, 317
Wiberg, 229
Wiswesser line notation, 4, 8, 21, 25, 60, 94, 204
Wiswesser Line Notation (WLN), 3
Wiswesser Notation Rules, 24
Wisswesswer Notation, 10
WLN, 3, 4, 7, 9, 11, 26, 27, 28, 30, 60, 204, 222, 289
Woodward-Hoffman rules, 90
Workshop, 317
Wort, 77
Write once read thereafter, 77

X-Ray structure, comparison with computed MO, 163

Zero elelements matrix, 120
Zeta plotter, 185
Zeta research, 317